10/

To John,

Thanks so much for your true Southern hospitality.

Best wishes,
Bob Shaiver

STRUCTURED METHODS THROUGH COBOL

STRUCTURED METHODS THROUGH COBOL

Robert T. Grauer, Ph.D.

University of Miami

Prentice-Hall, Inc.
Englewood Cliffs, New Jersey 07632

Library of Congress Cataloging in Publication Data

Grauer, Robert T. (date)
   Structured methods through COBOL.

   Bibliography: p.
   Includes index.
   1. COBOL (Computer program language)
2. Structured programming. I. Title.
QA76.73.C25G738 1983   001.64′24   82-13312
ISBN 0-13-854539-1

Editorial/production supervision
and interior design: **Kathryn Gollin Marshak**
Cover design: **Photo Plus Art**
Manufacturing buyer: **Gordon Osbourne**

© 1983 by Prentice-Hall, Inc., Englewood Cliffs, NJ 07632

All rights reserved. No part of this book
may be reproduced in any form or by any means
without permission in writing from the publisher.

Printed in the United States of America
10 9 8 7 6 5 4 3 2

ISBN 0-13-854539-1

Prentice-Hall International, Inc., *London*
Prentice-Hall of Australia Pty. Limited, *Sydney*
Editora Prentice-Hall do Brazil, LTDA, *Rio de Janeiro*
Prentice-Hall Canada Inc., *Toronto*
Prentice-Hall of India Private Limited, *New Delhi*
Prentice-Hall of Japan, Inc., *Tokyo*
Prentice-Hall of Southeast Asia Pte. Ltd., *Singapore*
Whitehall Books Limited, *Wellington, New Zealand*

To my loving wife

Contents

Preface — xv

1 STRUCTURED PROGRAMMING — 1

Overview — 1
Historical Perspective — 2
Definition — 2
Sufficiency of the Basic Structures — 4
Implementation in COBOL — 5
COBOL Case Study — 9
Advantages of Structured Programming — 10

    Extension of the Structured Theorem   13
        The GO TO Controversy   *13*

    Summary   15

    True/False   *15*

    Problems   *15*

    Projects   *18*

2 STRUCTURED DESIGN   21

    Overview   21

    Management Analogy   22

    Top Down Approach   26

    Documentation   28

    Underlying Theory   33

    The Structure Chart   35

    Coupling and Cohesion   37
        Levels of Cohesion   *37*
        Levels of Coupling   *39*

    Binding Time   42

    Span of Control   43

    Scope of Effect/Scope of Control   43

    Summary   47

    True/False   *48*

    Problems   *49*

    Projects   *50*

3 TOWARD COBOL PROFICIENCY   51

    Overview   51

    Table Processing   52
        Storage Organization   *52*
        Subscripts versus Indexes   *53*
        The SEARCH Verb   *55*
        Table Initialization   *58*

>> Two-Level Tables *60*
>> Three-Level Tables *63*
> **Calculations Involving Dates** 66
>> Converting a Julian Date to a Calendar Date *67*
> **Subprograms** 67
> **Sorting** 70
>> INPUT PROCEDURE/OUTPUT
>> PROCEDURE Option *72*
>> USING/GIVING Option *74*
> **COBOL Case Study** 74
> **Summary** 85
> *True/False* *85*
> *Problems* *86*
> *Projects* *88*

---

4 GUIDELINES, TECHNIQUES, AND PHILOSOPHIES   92

> **Overview** 92
> **Guidelines** 94
>> Indent *94*
>> Choose Meaningful Names *96*
>> Format the Data Division *97*
>> Space Attractively *98*
>> Avoid Commas *98*
>> Use Columns 73–80 *99*
>> Restrict Switches and Subscripts to a Single Use *99*
>> Avoid Constants *100*
>> Place Modules So They Can Be Found *102*
>> Use Appropriate Comments *102*
> **Techniques** 104
>> Perform Paragraphs, Not Sections *104*
>> Avoid MOVE CORRESPONDING *105*
>> Eliminate 77-Level Entries *106*
>> Use 88-Level Entries to Reduce Compound
>>   Conditions *107*
>> Use the COMPUTE Verb for Multiple
>>   Arithmetic Operators *108*
>> Avoid Literals *109*

Initialize Tables Dynamically *111*
Use READ INTO, WRITE FROM, and
 WS BEGINS HERE *111*
Pass a Single 01 Parameter to a Subprogram *113*
Consider Report Writer *114*

Philosophies   114

Keep It Simple *114*
Downplay Efficiency, but Choose the Algorithm
 Carefully *115*
Code Defensively *116*
Think First, Code Later *118*

Summary   119

True/False   *119*

Problems   *120*

Projects   *121*

---

5 TECHNIQUES OF STRUCTURED COMMUNICATION   122

Overview   122

The Traditional Flowchart   123

Pseudocode   124

Nassi-Shneiderman Charts   125

Comparison of Techniques   126

Decision Tables   129

Decision Trees   133

Structured Walkthroughs   133

Types of Walkthroughs *134*
The Walkthrough Procedure *135*
Suggestions for Successful Walkthroughs *135*

Summary   136

True/False   *137*

Problems   *138*

Projects   *138*

6 SEQUENTIAL FILE MAINTENANCE — 139

- Overview — 139
- Balance Line Algorithm — 140
- COBOL Case Study — 143
- Top Down Testing — 146
  - Stubs Program *147*
  - Completed Program *153*
- Program Maintenance — 158
- COBOL Extensions — 167
  - SELECT Statement *167*
  - I-O-CONTROL Paragraph *168*
  - FD Entry *169*
  - OPEN and CLOSE Statements *170*
- Summary — 171
- *True/False* — *172*
- *Problems* — *172*
- *Projects* — *173*

7 INDEXED FILES — 175

- Overview — 175
- Concepts of File Organization — 176
- COBOL Requirements — 180
  - Environment Division *181*
  - Procedure Division *182*
- Creating an Indexed File — 188
- COBOL Case Study—Nonsequential File Maintenance — 191
- IBM Differences (ISAM versus VSAM) — 202
- Summary — 203
- *True/False* — *203*
- *Problems* — *204*
- *Projects* — *204*

8 REPORT WRITER — 205

Overview — 205
Vocabulary — 206
Example 1—Two Control Breaks — 207
Data Division Requirements *208*
Procedure Division Requirements *213*

Example 2—Three Control Breaks — 213
Example 3—Finer Points of Report Writer — 218
How Report Writer Works — 223
Report Writer Syntax — 225
TYPE Clause *225*
RD (Report Description) *226*
Report Groups *227*

Summary — 229
True/False — *230*
Problems — *230*
Projects — *231*

9 SOURCE LEVEL DEBUGGING — 234

Overview — 234
Common Execution Errors — 235
Debugging Exercises — 239
Exercise 9.1—Control Breaks *240*
Exercise 9.2—Subprograms *244*
Exercise 9.3—Sequential File Maintenance *251*
Exercise 9.4—Report Writer *257*

Solutions — 261
Exercise 9.1 *261*
Exercise 9.2 *262*
Exercise 9.3 *263*
Exercise 9.4 *264*

Summary — 265

Appendix A THE NEXT COBOL STANDARD	266
Overview	266
Different Versions of the Standard	267
Highlights	267
Changes Not Affecting Existing Programs	267
Changes Potentially Affecting Existing Programs	270
Structured Programming Enhancements	274

   PERFORM   *274*
   EVALUATE   *275*
   IF   *276*

Public Reaction	277
Appendix B TEAM PROJECT	280
Acknowledgement	280
Overview	280
The Mugwump Fertilizer Problem	282

   Introduction   *283*
   The Open-Order File   *283*
   Format of Input to the Program   *286*
   Other Editing Requirements   *290*
   Output from the Program   *291*
   Extension   *291*

Appendix C ANSWERS	293
Bibliography	308
Index	311

Preface

Structured Methods Through COBOL is a pragmatic approach to aspects of structured methodology which are of interest to COBOL programmers. It does not focus on theory per se, as Yourdon and his colleagues have done a superb job in that area. It does concentrate on the *application* of these techniques from the viewpoint of the "person in the trenches," i.e., the COBOL programmer.

The main objective of *Structured Methods Through COBOL* is to illustrate aspects of the structured methodology in a manner which can readily be understood and applied by the COBOL programmer. A secondary aim is to cover *advanced* elements of the language, and consequently *the book is suitable for two courses in DPMA's Model Curriculum.* These are CIS-3, the advanced COBOL course, and CIS-7, the capstone course on software development.

A major strength of this book is the *large* number of COBOL programs to illustrate the salient points of each chapter. There are three complete programs associated with Report Writer, two dealing with indexed files and DECLARATIVES, four on debugging, three on sequential file maintenance, and one or more for table processing, subprograms, and sorting. The chapter summaries are as follows:

Chapter 1 succinctly defines structured programming, and moves immediately to a COBOL case study illustrating its application. The philosophy throughout the book is to *use* the structured techniques, and consequently theoretical discussions are kept as brief as possible.

Chapter 2 progresses from structured programming to structured design. A poorly conceived program, structured or otherwise, is difficult to follow and maintain. This chapter introduces the hierarchy chart as the primary design tool, and also covers various evaluation criteria. It, too, contains a COBOL case study to amplify the discussion.

Chapter 3 develops proficiency in advanced features of the language, including subprograms, indexing, sorting, and multilevel table processing. These techniques are illustrated in the case study at the end of this chapter, and in subsequent chapters as well.

Chapter 4 addresses the need for standards, and presents a set of guidelines and philosophies for COBOL coding.

Chapter 5 covers techniques of structured communication, contrasting the traditional flowchart with pseudocode and Nassi-Shneiderman charts. It also looks at decision tables and decision trees, as means of unambiguous problem specification. It discusses the structured walkthrough, suggests guidelines for its implementation, and indicates when walkthroughs should be held.

Chapter 6 presents the balance line algorithm, a general approach to file maintenance. It illustrates the top down approach to program testing and the use of program stubs. The chapter discusses *maintenance* of existing programs through a case study and suggested project. Of greater import, it *applies* much of the earlier theory of structured design to a COBOL setting.

Chapter 7 is primarily a "COBOL" chapter focusing on indexed files. It presents all elements of the ANS 74 standard dealing with this type of file organization, including use of DECLARATIVES and the FILE STATUS bytes. It, too, contains a COBOL case study with emphasis on nonsequential file maintenance.

Chapter 8 presents Report Writer, an extremely powerful COBOL feature which can be used to good advantage in structured (as well as nonstructured) environments. The chapter contains *three* illustrative programs and discusses virtually all major aspects of Report Writer.

Chapter 9 provides realistic debugging exercises over a wide range of programming projects. Although use of structured techniques can reduce the number of program errors, the author believes that logic errors will remain with us for the foreseeable future, and consequently some debugging experience is essential. The chapter contains modified versions of COBOL programs from Chapters 1 through 8, in which the reader is asked to find and correct the bugs.

Appendix A, *The Next COBOL Standard*, highlights anticipated changes in the new ANS standard. As practitioners are undoubtedly aware, the subject has been surrounded by controversy and even a threatened lawsuit. The author voices his opinion and provides an indication of what to expect.

Appendix B contains a *complex* project to be done throughout the semester. The intent of this "super project" is to provide students with the experience of working as team members on a detailed system. In addition, it requires students to integrate material from many chapters and serves as an ideal review.

Appendix C contains answers to selected exercises. One of the major strengths of the book are the many problems which appear at the end of each chapter. No peeking, however, until you have made an honest attempt at your own solution.

Acknowledgements

Several people have helped bring this book to fruition. First and foremost, the author acknowledges the contributions of students and seminar attendees for their many suggestions and perceptions. He is especially indebted to Professor George Goldstein of Miami Dade Community College for his reference to the balance line algorithm, and to his colleague Dr. Joel Stutz at the University of Miami for his always available ear. He thanks his reviewers, Professor Mel Franz of Central Missouri State University and Professor N. D. Brammer of Colorado State University, for their incisive comments.

The people at Prentice-Hall are truly fantastic. Jim Fegen is the editor responsible for the project and an unending source of encouragement. Kathryn Marshak, production editor, is a true professional and a delight to work with. Herb Daehnke, the artist, is to be thanked for his patience and attention to detail. The author commends his students, Ms. Jackie Clark and Mr. Mark Paris, for their thoroughness as proofreaders. Last, but certainly not least, he appreciates the efforts of his typist, Ms. Sheila Grossman, who always managed to decipher his near illegible notes on yellow pads.

The following information is reprinted from COBOL Edition 1965, published by the Conference on Data Systems Languages (CODASYL), and printed by the U.S. Government Printing Office:

> Any organization interested in reproducing the COBOL report and specifications in whole or part, using ideas taken from this report as the basis for an instructional manual or for any other purpose is free to do so. However, all such organizations are requested to reproduce this section as part of the introduction to the document. Those using a short passage, as in a book review, are requested to mention "COBOL" in acknowledgment of the source, but need not quote this entire section.
>
> COBOL is an industry language and is not the property of any company or group of companies, or of any organization or group of organizations.

No warranty, expressed or implied, is made by any contributor or by the COBOL Committee as to the accuracy and functioning of the programming system and language. Moreover, no responsibility is assumed by any contributor, or by the committee, in connection therewith.

Procedures have been established for the maintenance of COBOL. Inquiries concerning the procedures for proposing changes should be directed to the Executive Committee of the Conference on Data Systems languages.

The authors and copyright holders of the copyrighted material used herein:

FLOWMATIC (Trade mark of the Sperry Rand Corporation), Programming for the Univac (R) I and II, Data Automation Systems copyrighted 1958, 1959, by Sperry Rand Corporation; IBM Commercial Translator Form No. F28-8013, copyrighted 1959 by IBM; FACT, DSI 27A5260-2760, copyrighted 1960 by Minneapolis-Honeywell

have specifically authorized the use of this material in whole or in part, in the COBOL specifications. Such authorization extends to the reproduction and use of COBOL specifications in programming manuals for similar publications.

STRUCTURED METHODS THROUGH COBOL

1 Structured Programming

Overview

Structured programming means many things to many people; indeed, success of the methodology has led to a proliferation of things that are "structured." We have, for example, structured programming, structured design, structured analysis, structured testing, structured walkthroughs, and so on. The primary objective of this chapter is to establish a *concise* definition of the term *structured programming*. (Later chapters discuss other aspects of the structured methodology.)

We begin with a brief historical perspective, then offer a short definition of structured programming. We cover implementation in COBOL, illustrating the discussion with a complete program. We show that a structured program has the essential attributes of a "good" program; namely, it works and is easily modified.

Historical Perspective

Today's common acceptance of structured programming belies a rather shaky beginning. The original presentation of the structured theorem occurred at an International Colloquium in 1964, in Israel. The authors, Bohm and Jacopini, presented their work in Italian and were essentially ignored in the United States. The English translation of their paper,[1] published in 1966 in *Communications of the ACM*, did not gain a great deal of attention either, due to its theoretical nature.

It was only after a 1968 letter to the editor,[2] by Edsger W. Dijkstra of the Netherlands, that the American data processing community began to take notice. In his letter, entitled "GO TO Statement Considered Harmful," Dijkstra wrote "that the quality of programmers is a decreasing function of the density of GO TO statements in the programs they produce." He further suggested that "the GO TO statement should be abolished from all higher level programming languages . . . it is an invitation to make a mess of one's program."

The first large-scale commercial application was the information retrieval system for the New York Times by IBM. The project was large (83,000 lines of source code), practical (a real customer paid real money), successful (programmer productivity was four to six times normal), and relatively "bug free" (4 errors per 10,000 lines of code).[3]

Structured programming projects began to appear with greater frequency in the mid and late 1970s. Today it is safe to say that most practitioners at least acknowledge merits of the discipline. The acceptance is evidenced by many facts, not the least of which is the DPMA model curriculum for the 1980s.

Definition

Structured programming is defined by the now-classical Bohm and Jacopini paper which proved that any problem can be solved using the three logic structures of Figure 1.1: sequence, selection, and iteration. Note well that each of these structures has *exactly one entry point and one exit point.* A structured program is a program *made up exclusively of these kinds of building blocks.*

The *sequence structure* is the simplest of the three, and formally

---

[1] Bohm and Jacopini, "Flow Diagrams, Turing Machines and Languages with Only Two Formation Rules," *Communications of the ACM* (May 1966).

[2] E. W. Dijkstra, "GO TO Statement Considered Harmful," *Communications of the ACM* (March 1968).

[3] F. T. Baker, "Chief Programmer Team Management of Production Programming," *IBM Systems Journal* (January 1972), pp. 56–73.

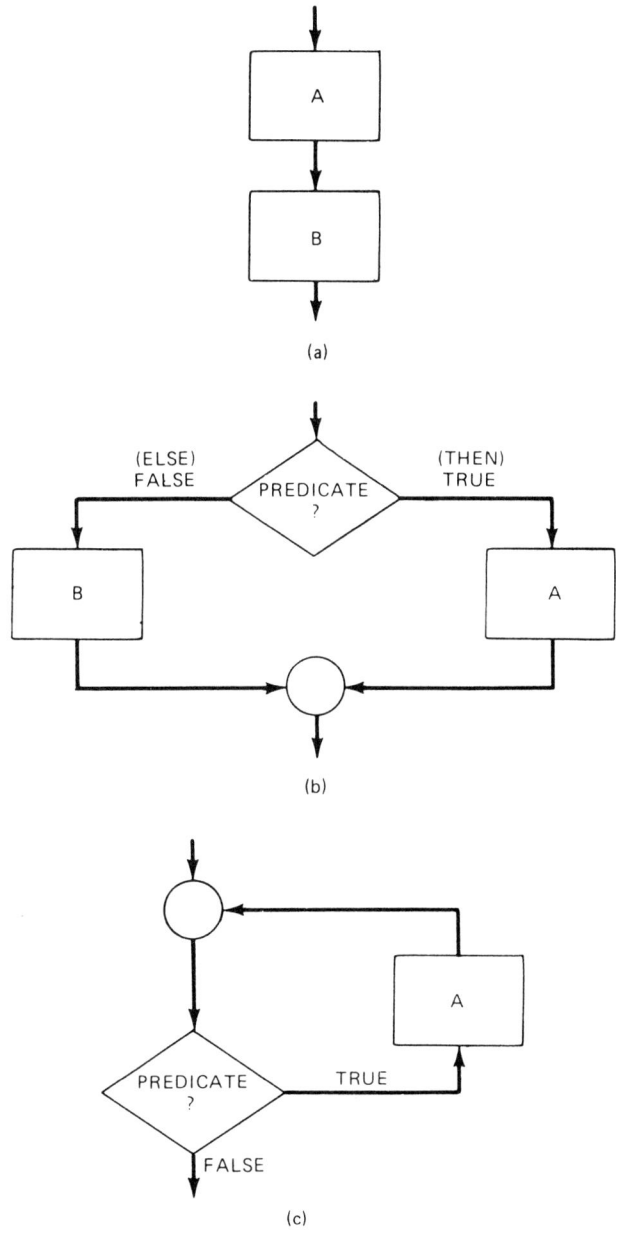

FIGURE 1.1 The building blocks of structured programming. (a) Sequence; (b) selection; (c) iteration.

specifies that statements are executed sequentially, in the order in which they appear. The two blocks, A and B, may denote anything from single statements to complete programs.

Selection (also known as IF/THEN/ELSE) is the choice between two actions. A condition (known as a predicate) is tested. If the predicate is true, block A is executed; if it is false, block B is executed. The predicate is a *single entry* point to the structure, and both paths meet in a *single exit* point.

Iteration (also known as DO/WHILE) calls for *repeated* execution of a block of code while a condition holds true. The condition is tested. If true, block A is executed; if false, the structure relinquishes control to the next sequential statement. Again, there is exactly *one entry* point and *one exit* point from the structure.

Sufficiency of the Basic Structures

Although the preceding definition may seem somewhat limited, it is sufficient to produce any required logic. This is possible because an entire structure may be substituted anywhere block A or B appears. Figures 1.2 and 1.3 contain combinations of the basic structures.

The entry point to Figure 1.2 is a selection structure to evaluate predicate$_1$. If predicate$_1$ is true, an iteration structure is entered. If predicate$_1$ is false, a sequence structure is executed instead. Both the iteration and sequence structures meet at a single point, which in turn becomes the exit point for the initial selection structure.

In Figure 1.3 the entry point is again a selection structure. If predicate$_1$ is true, a second selection structure for predicate$_2$ is entered. If this is

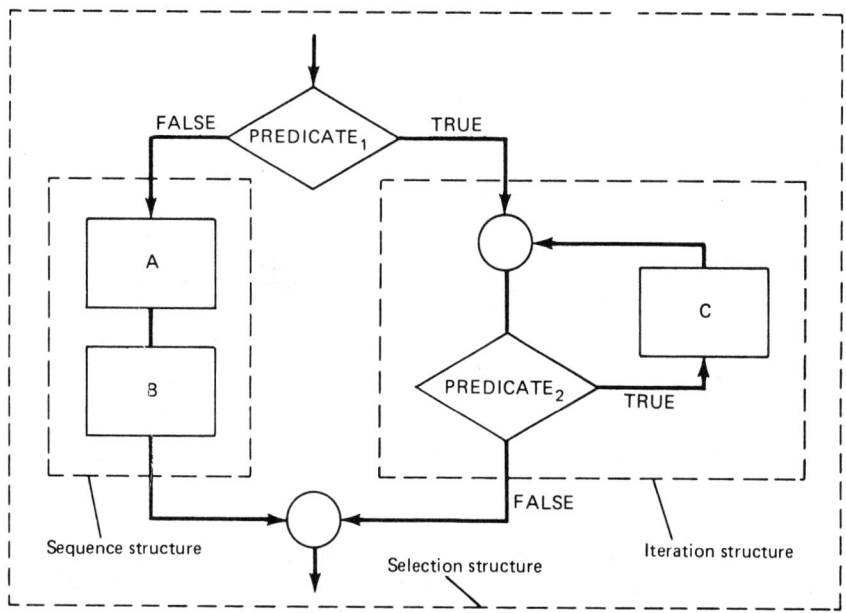

FIGURE 1.2 Combinations of logic structures.

Chapter 1—Structured Programming

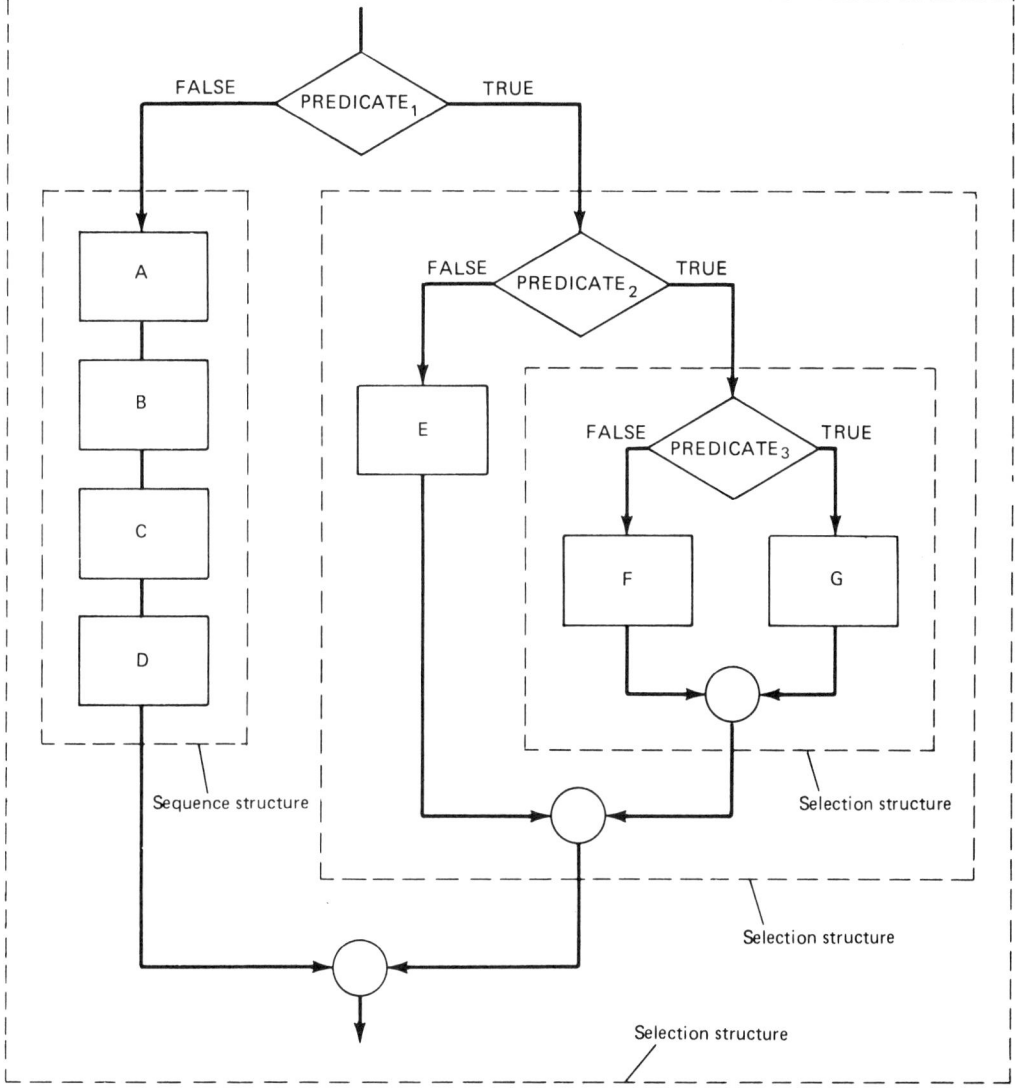

FIGURE 1.3 Additional combinations of logic structures.

also true, a third selection structure for predicate₃ is entered. Note that the alternate paths for each selection structure always meet in a single exit point for that structure. Note also that the entire logic structure of Figure 1.3 has a single entry, and also a single exit point.

Implementation in COBOL

Thus far nothing has been said about implementation in a specific language. This is perfectly fitting, for the theory of structured programming is *lan-*

guage independent. Since this book is about COBOL however, we must pause to consider the structured discipline within the context of the language.

The *sequence* structure is implemented by coding statements sequentially. *Selection* is accomplished through an IF/ELSE statement and is also straightforward. *Iteration* is implemented by PERFORM/UNTIL and may pose difficulties for the uninitiated, particularly in reading a file. Consider Figure 1.4, which shows correct and incorrect ways for processing a file of transactions.

Figure 1.4a, the *incorrect* implementation, causes *the last record of INPUT-FILE to be processed twice.* To understand better how this happens, consider a file with only two records, A and B. Recall that the perform statement evaluates the UNTIL condition *prior* to branching, and further,

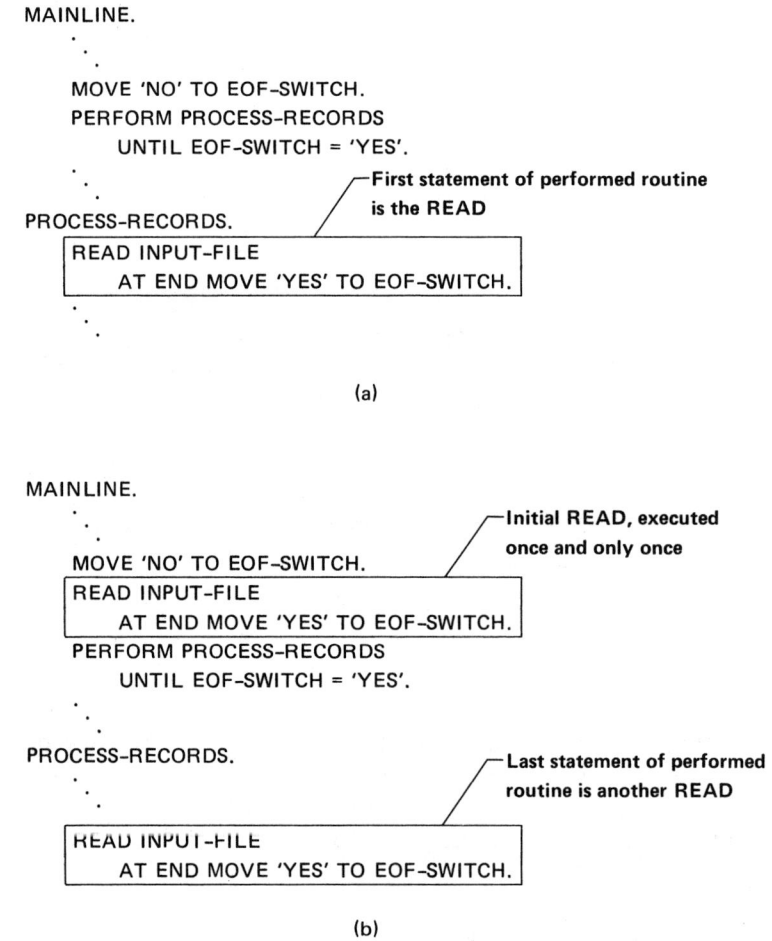

FIGURE 1.4 (a) Incorrect implementation of iteration structure. (b) Correct implementation of iteration structure.

that a file with *two* records is read *three* times; once for each record and once to sense the end of the file.

Record A is read the first time PROCESS-RECORDS is performed. Execution continues through the remainder of the PROCESS-RECORDS paragraph for record A. When the end of the paragraph is reached, EOF-SWITCH is still set to 'NO.' Hence, PROCESS-RECORDS is executed a second time, during which it reads and processes record B. EOF-SWITCH remains set at 'NO,' causing PROCESS-RECORDS to be executed a third time. The end of file condition is sensed immediately, but in the *middle* of the paragraph. Execution continues to the end of the paragraph, with the last record read processed a second time.

The alternative, and *correct*, structure of Figure 1.4b has an *initial* (or priming) read which is executed *only once*. It reads the first record and performs PROCESS-RECORDS for record A. The *last* statement of PROCESS-RECORDS is a second read statement. Since record B, (rather than the end of file) is read, PROCESS-RECORDS is executed a second time, this time with record B. Again the last statement of the performed routine is a read, but this time it senses the end of file, and the perform statement is terminated. (Note that the paragraph PROCESS-RECORDS was executed twice, once for each record.)

Undoubtedly, there are those who object to the presence of two read statements for the same file. This is easily handled by putting the read statement into a one statement paragraph, and performing the paragraph (albeit from *two* places in the program). To summarize, Figure 1.4b is the most common way of implementing the iteration structure. It consists of an initial read which is coded in line or performed, as well as a second read as the *last* statement of the performed routine.

Figure 1.5 contains an *alternative* way of correctly implementing the iteration structure. The reader should be convinced that the code is logically correct, and further that it conforms to the structured theorem. Neverthe-

```
MAINLINE.
    .
    .
    MOVE 'NO' TO EOF-SWITCH.
    PERFORM PROCESS-RECORDS
        UNTIL EOF-SWITCH = 'YES'.
    .
    .
PROCESS-RECORDS.
    READ INPUT-FILE
        AT END MOVE 'YES' TO EOF-SWITCH.
    IF EOF-SWITCH NOT EQUAL TO 'YES'
        PERFORM REST-OF-PROCESSING.
REST-OF-PROCESSING.
    .
    .
```

FIGURE 1.5 Alternative correct implementation of iteration structure.

```
00001              IDENTIFICATION DIVISION.
00002              PROGRAM-ID.   MERGEFL.
00003              AUTHOR.    R.GRAUER.
00004
00005              ENVIRONMENT DIVISION.
00006              CONFIGURATION SECTION.
00007              SOURCE-COMPUTER.   IBM-4341.
00008              OBJECT-COMPUTER.   IBM-4341.
00009              INPUT-OUTPUT SECTION.
00010              FILE-CONTROL.
00011                  SELECT INPUT-FILE-ONE ASSIGN TO UT-S-FILEONE.
00012                  SELECT INPUT-FILE-TWO ASSIGN TO UT-S-FILETWO.
00013                  SELECT MERGED-FILE ASSIGN TO UT-S-MERGED.
00014
00015              DATA DIVISION.
00016              FILE SECTION.
00017              FD   INPUT-FILE-ONE
00018                   LABEL RECORDS ARE STANDARD
00019                   BLOCK CONTAINS 0 RECORDS
00020                   RECORD CONTAINS 80 CHARACTERS
00021                   DATA RECORD IS INPUT-RECORD-ONE.
00022              01   INPUT-RECORD-ONE                 PIC X(80).
00023
00024              FD   INPUT-FILE-TWO
00025                   LABEL RECORDS ARE STANDARD
00026                   BLOCK CONTAINS 0 RECORDS
00027                   RECORD CONTAINS 80 CHARACTERS
00028                   DATA RECORD IS INPUT-RECORD-TWO.
00029              01   INPUT-RECORD-TWO                 PIC X(80).
00030
00031              FD   MERGED-FILE
00032                   LABEL RECORDS ARE STANDARD
00033                   RECORD CONTAINS 80 CHARACTERS
00034                   DATA RECORD IS MERGED-RECORD.
00035              01   MERGED-RECORD                    PIC X(80).
00036
00037              WORKING-STORAGE SECTION.
00038              01   WS-RECORD-ONE.
00039                   05   WS-REC-ONE-ID               PIC X(9).
00040                   05   WS-REC-ONE-NAME             PIC X(20).
00041                   05   WS-REC-ONE-SALARY           PIC 9(6).
00042                   05   WS-REC-ONE-DEPARTMENT       PIC 9(4).
00043                   05   WS-REC-ONE-LOCATION         PIC X(10).
00044                   05   FILLER                      PIC X(31).
00045
00046              01   WS-RECORD-TWO.
00047                   05   WS-REC-TWO-ID               PIC X(9).
00048                   05   WS-REC-TWO-NAME             PIC X(20).
00049                   05   WS-REC-TWO-SALARY           PIC 9(6).
00050                   05   WS-REC-TWO-DEPARTMENT       PIC 9(4).
00051                   05   WS-REC-TWO-LOCATION         PIC X(10).
00052                   05   FILLER                      PIC X(31).
00053
00054              PROCEDURE DIVISION.
00055              005-MAINLINE.
00056                   OPEN INPUT INPUT-FILE-ONE
00057                              INPUT-FILE-TWO
00058                        OUTPUT MERGED-FILE.
00059                   PERFORM 020-READ-FIRST-FILE.         ⎤── Initial reads
00060                   PERFORM 030-READ-SECOND-FILE.        ⎦
00061                   PERFORM 010-PROCESS-FILES
00062                       UNTIL WS-REC-ONE-ID = HIGH-VALUES
00063                         AND WS-REC-TWO-ID = HIGH-VALUES.
00064                   CLOSE INPUT-FILE-ONE
00065                         INPUT-FILE-TWO
00066                         MERGED-FILE.
00067                   STOP RUN.
```

FIGURE 1.6 Merge program.

```
00068
00069            010-PROCESS-FILES.                              Nested IF
00070
00071            IF WS-REC-ONE-ID LESS THAN WS-REC-TWO-ID
00072                WRITE MERGED-RECORD FROM INPUT-RECORD-ONE
00073                PERFORM 020-READ-FIRST-FILE
00074            ELSE
00075                IF WS-REC-TWO-ID LESS THAN WS-REC-ONE-ID
00076                    WRITE MERGED-RECORD FROM INPUT-RECORD-TWO
00077                    PERFORM 030-READ-SECOND-FILE
00078                ELSE
00079                    DISPLAY 'DUPLICATE IDS ' WS-REC-ONE-ID
00080                    PERFORM 020-READ-FIRST-FILE
00081                    PERFORM 030-READ-SECOND-FILE.
00082
00083            020-READ-FIRST-FILE.
00084                READ INPUT-FILE-ONE INTO WS-RECORD-ONE
00085                    AT END MOVE HIGH-VALUES TO WS-REC-ONE-ID.
00086
00087            030-READ-SECOND-FILE.
00088                READ INPUT-FILE-TWO INTO WS-RECORD-TWO
00089                    AT END MOVE HIGH-VALUES TO WS-REC-TWO-ID.
```

FIGURE 1.6 *continued*

less, most practitioners, the author included, use the technique of Figure 1.4b rather than Figure 1.5. This is because Figure 1.5 introduces an extra level of perform which tends to obscure program flow. Regardless of the technique you adopt, realize the validity of both Figure 1.4b and 1.5, as well as the flaw of Figure 1.4a.

COBOL Case Study

The author's overall objective is to discuss structured methodology within the context of COBOL, and what better way is there to accomplish this goal than to present complete COBOL programs? To that end we move to our first case study; a two-file merge. Two input files, both in sequential order, are to be merged into a third; i.e., an output file. However, if the same ID number appears on both input files, an error message is required, and neither record is to be written to the merged file.

Figure 1.6 contains a structured COBOL program to accomplish these objectives. The Identification, Environment, and Data Divisions are straightforward and should present no difficulty. (The Environment Division uses IBM OS SELECT statements. The BLOCK CONTAINS 0 RECORDS entry of lines 19 and 26 is unique to IBM OS systems. It means that the block size will be entered at execution time through the JCL and consequently yields a more flexible program. The remainder of Figure 1.6 adheres fully to the ANS 74 standard, and should run on any conforming compiler.)

The MAINLINE paragraph opens all three files, then does an *initial* read for each input file by performing single statement paragraphs. (An alternative technique would have been to code the reads inline.) The paragraph PROCESS-FILES is performed until both input files are out of data, after which the files are closed and the program terminated.

The program is driven by the nested IF of lines 71–81. If the current ID on the first file is less than the current ID on the second file, the merged record is written from the first file and another record is read from that file only. If, however, the current ID from the second file is less than the current ID from the first file, the merged record is written from the second file, and another record is read from the second file. Finally, if the IDs are equal, an error message is displayed, neither record is written to the merged file, and new records are read from both files.

Those who are not completely familiar with COBOL may question the use of HIGH-VALUES in the AT END clauses of each read statement (lines 85 and 89). HIGH-VALUES is a COBOL reserved word, with a value larger than any other, and it is a convenient way to handle end of file processing. Assume, for example, that INPUT-FILE-ONE is the first file to hit the end of file condition. The AT END clause of line 85 causes WS-REC-ONE-ID to have an artificially large value. When the nested IF of lines 71–81 is next executed the remaining record IDs in INPUT-FILE-TWO are all less than the current record of INPUT-FILE-ONE. Hence, the remaining records in INPUT-FILE-TWO will be correctly written to the end of the merged file. Analogous reasoning holds if INPUT-FILE-TWO is the first file to reach the end of file condition. Realize also that the perform statement of lines 61–63 will be correctly terminated if both files become empty simultaneously.

Advantages of Structured Programming

The two most important criteria for any program are: (1) that the program work, and work under all conditions, and (2) that the program be easily read and maintained by someone other than the original author. This is not to imply that all nonstructured programs do not work and/or that nonstructured code cannot be maintained. The author does believe, however, that a structured program is more apt to meet these criteria.

Consider the first requirement—program correctness. Programs with multiple file inputs are frequently error-prone on end of file or unusual conditions. What happens, for example, in a sequential update when the first transaction comes before the first record on the old master; when the last transaction occurs after the last old master record, and so on?

The program of Figure 1.6 was tested with the three distinct sets of test data in Figure 1.7, and produced correct output in each instance. (Figure 1.6 happens to be the first, and only, version of the program; i.e., the author managed to write a correct program the first time, and did not require two or three cycles to "get the bugs out.") As to the second statement—program modification—despite the best intentions of users, supervisors, and so on, program specifications are forever changing. In commercial situations it is the maintenance programmer who bears the brunt of this task, and he or she is often justifiably in dire fear of playing with someone else's program. One

Set 1: Records are interspersed among the two files

Input File 1	Input File 2	Merged File
100000000	111111111	100000000
200000000	222222222	111111111
300000000	333333333	200000000
400000000	444444444	222222222
500000000	555555555	300000000
		333333333
		400000000
		444444444
		500000000
		555555555

Set 2: All records in file 1 precede all records in file 2

Input File 1	Input File 2	Merged File
100000000	600000000	100000000
200000000	700000000	200000000
300000000	800000000	300000000
400000000	900000000	400000000
500000000		500000000
		600000000
		700000000
		800000000
		900000000

Set 3: File 2 is empty

Input File 1	Input File 2	Merged File
100000000		100000000
200000000		200000000
300000000	Empty	300000000
400000000		400000000
500000000		500000000

FIGURE 1.7 Test data for the merge program.

of the strongest arguments for structured programming is that it simplifies program maintenance.

Assume, for example, that the original specification on duplicate IDs is altered. Under the new specs, if duplicate IDs are detected (i.e., the same ID number appears in both input files), the record with the *higher* salary is to be written to the merged file. If, however, both records have the same salary, then neither record is to be written and the error message is to be printed.

Advantages of Structured Programming

As Figure 1.6 now stands, COBOL line 79 accommodates duplicate IDs. To affect the modification, this line can be replaced by the statement, PERFORM 015-PROCESS-DUPLICATES. The maintenance programmer then develops his or her own routine, 015-PROCESS-DUPLICATES, to handle the change. The suggested code is shown in Figure 1.8.

```
015-PROCESS-DUPLICATES.
    IF WS-REC-ONE-SALARY > WS-REC-TWO-SALARY
        WRITE MERGED-RECORD FROM WS-RECORD-ONE
    ELSE
        IF WS-REC-TWO-SALARY > WS-REC-ONE-SALARY
            WRITE MERGED-RECORD FROM WS-RECORD-TWO
        ELSE
            DISPLAY 'DUPLICATE IDS' WS-REC-ONE-ID.
```

FIGURE 1.8 Modification for duplicate IDs.

As a second example, consider a change which requires that the input files be checked to ensure that records are in ascending sequence, and further that duplicate IDs are not present in the same file. Incorporation of this nontrivial change is accomplished by modifying the performed read routine for each file. The paragraph 020-READ-FIRST-FILE is expanded to include an IF statement for the sequence check, as shown in Figure 1.9.

```
020-READ-FIRST-FILE.
    READ INPUT-FILE-ONE INTO WS-RECORD-ONE
        AT END MOVE HIGH-VALUES TO WS-REC-ONE-ID.
    IF WS-REC-ONE-ID < PREVIOUS-REC-ONE-ID
        DISPLAY 'FILE ONE OUT OF SEQUENCE'
        MOVE HIGH-VALUES TO WS-REC-ONE-ID, WS-REC-TWO-ID
    ELSE
        IF WS-REC-ONE-ID = PREVIOUS-REC-ONE-ID
            DISPLAY 'FILE ONE HAS DUPLICATE IDS'
            MOVE HIGH-VALUES TO WS-REC-ONE-ID, WS-REC-TWO-ID
        ELSE
            MOVE WS-REC-ONE-ID TO PREVIOUS-REC-ONE-ID.
```

FIGURE 1.9 Modification for sequence checking.

As can be seen from the additional code, HIGH-VALUES are moved to each ID if a record is out of sequence or if duplicate IDs are present. This will cause the next test of the PERFORM UNTIL statement of lines 61–63 to be met and thereby terminate processing. (This approach is followed because a program should end from its mainline routine; hence, STOP RUN never appears in a performed procedure.)

Parallel code would be added to the read routine for the second file. The modification also requires that two data names, PREVIOUS-REC-ONE-ID and PREVIOUS-REC-TWO-ID, be established in Working-Storage; both data names should be initialized to LOW-VALUES.

Extension of the Structured Theorem

Although any program can be developed as a function of the three basic structures, the *case* structure is often included as a fourth permissible logic form. This structure conveniently expresses a multibranch situation and is shown in Figure 1.10. As with the three fundamental structures of Figure 1.1, there is one entry and one exit point.

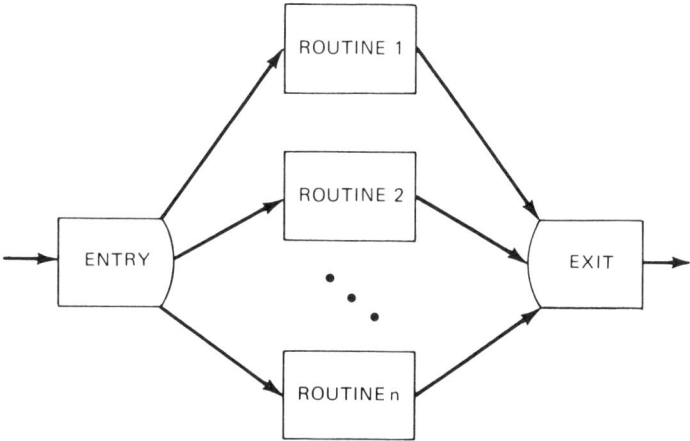

FIGURE 1.10 The case structure.

Implementation in COBOL is through the GO TO DEPENDING statement and is illustrated in Figure 1.11. The GO TO DEPENDING statement tests the value of a code, in this instance INCOMING-YEAR-CODE. If it is equal to 1, control passes to the first paragraph specified, i.e., FRESHMAN. If INCOMING-YEAR-CODE is equal to 2, control passes to the second paragraph, i.e., SOPHOMORE, etc. If the code has any value other than 1, 2, 3, 4, or 5 (since five paragraphs were specified), control passes to the next statement immediately following the GO TO DEPENDING, which should be an error routine. Indentation in the GO TO DEPENDING is strictly for legibility; it is not required by COBOL.

The GO TO Controversy

Figure 1.11 contains five "villainous" GO TO statements, but their use in this instance is completely acceptable (to the author, if not to the most rigid advocate of structured programming). The case structure expresses a multibranch situation; the criticism, if any, lies in the COBOL implementation. The alternative to Figure 1.11 is a five-level nested IF which may spurn even stronger objections. (Happily, however, the new COBOL standard introduces an EVALUATE statement to implement the case structure more easily—see Appendix A.)

```
        YEAR-IN-COLLEGE.
            GO TO
                FRESHMAN
                SOPHOMORE
                JUNIOR
                SENIOR
                GRAD-SCHOOL
            DEPENDING ON INCOMING-YEAR-CODE.
            ...process error...
            GO TO YEAR-IN-COLLEGE-EXIT.
        FRESHMAN.
            ...process...
            GO TO YEAR-IN-COLLEGE-EXIT.
        SOPHOMORE.
            ...process...
            GO TO YEAR-IN-COLLEGE-EXIT.
        JUNIOR.
            ...process...
            GO TO YEAR-IN-COLLEGE-EXIT.
        SENIOR.
            ...process...
            GO TO YEAR-IN-COLLEGE-EXIT.
        GRAD-SCHOOL.
            ...process...
        YEAR-IN-COLLEGE-EXIT.
            EXIT.
```

FIGURE 1.11 COBOL implementation of the case structure.

Returning to the use of GO TO in a structured COBOL program, realize that *the goal of structured programming is to produce working programs which are easily read and maintained, not necessarily to eliminate the GO TO statement.* There are certain *limited* situations where use of a GO TO statement can add to, rather than detract from program clarity. Implementation of the case structure is one example, use of the INPUT PROCEDURE option of the SORT verb is another (see Figure 3.18).

If the GO TO statement is used, it must branch *forward* (i.e., down the page) to an EXIT paragraph. The branch must occur *within* the range of a performed routine or *within* the INPUT or OUTPUT procedures of the SORT verb. (A common technique is to PERFORM PARAGRAPH-A THRU PARAGRAPH-A-EXIT, then GO TO PARAGRAPH-A-EXIT.) One may *never* branch out of a performed routine nor branch backward in a program. (The latter implies a loop and loops are implemented via the iteration; i.e., PERFORM/UNTIL construct.)

Although a *forward* GO TO statement can be justified under certain conditions as described above, one must still be extremely prudent in its use. Think twice before using it, then think again. Failure to do so will quickly bring about a return to nonmaintainable code.

Summary

The chapter began with a pragmatic definition of structured programming; namely, a program comprised solely of three logic structures—sequence, selection, and iteration. These basic building blocks can be combined in endless variety to produce any required logic. The goal of the methodology is to produce working programs which are easily maintained.

The implementation of structured programming in COBOL was discussed, with particular attention to the iteration structure. A COBOL program to merge two files was developed and shown to be correct. The program also proved easy to maintain.

The structured theorem was extended to include the case structure for multibranch situations. It is implemented in COBOL by the GO TO DEPENDING statement; hence, a *forward* GO TO statement is acceptable in a structured COBOL program in certain *limited* circumstances.

True/False

1. A structured program is guaranteed not to contain logic errors.
2. Structured programming can be implemented in a variety of languages.
3. The ANS 74 compiler will reject nonstructured code.
4. The COBOL PERFORM UNTIL corresponds exactly to the DO WHILE construct of structured programming.
5. The logic of any program can be expressed as a combination of only three types of logic structures.
6. The "one entry/one exit" philosophy is essential to structured programming.
7. Structured programming began in the United States.
8. Adoption of structured programming eliminates the need for coding standards.
9. A structured program should *never* contain a GO TO statement.
10. COBOL is an ideal language in which to implement structured programming theory.
11. The new COBOL standard will contain several structured programming enhancements.
12. The case construct is one of the basic logic structures.
13. A COBOL program may contain two READ statements for the same file.
14. COBOL requires that every IF have a corresponding ELSE.

Problems

1. Figure 1.12 represents different implementations of the iteration structure. Explain the difference between DO WHILE (Figure 1.12a), and DO UNTIL (Figure 1.12b).

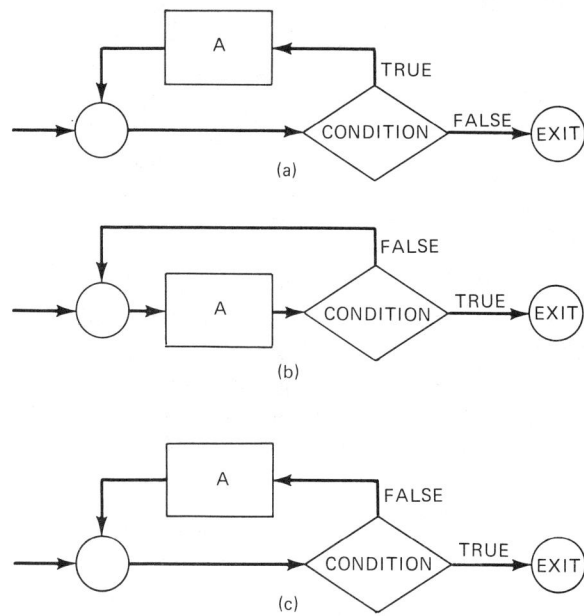

FIGURE 1.12 (a) DO WHILE. (b) DO UNTIL. (c) COBOL PERFORM UNTIL.

What is the *minimum* number of times block A is executed in each structure? Which structure does the COBOL PERFORM UNTIL (Figure 1.12c) more closely resemble?

2. Do you have a strong preference as to how the case structure should be implemented in COBOL? Do you think a multilevel nested IF is preferable to GO TO DEPENDING?

3. Modify Figure 1.6 to count the number of times duplicate IDs occur. Terminate processing, with the message "EXCESSIVE NUMBER OF ERRORS", if 10 or more errors occur.

4. How many times would PARAGRAPH-A be executed as a consequence of each of the following PERFORM statements?

   (a) PERFORM PARAGRAPH-A
         VARYING SUBSCRIPT FROM 1 BY 1
         UNTIL SUBSCRIPT > 5.
   (b) PERFORM PARAGRAPH-A
         VARYING SUBSCRIPT FROM 1 BY 1
         UNTIL SUBSCRIPT = 5.
   (c) PERFORM PARAGRAPH-A
         VARYING SUBSCRIPT FROM 1 BY 1
         UNTIL SUBSCRIPT < 5.

5. Given Figure 1.11, illustrating the use of GO TO DEPENDING:

   (a) What would happen if all the GO TO statements were removed and INCOMING-YEAR-CODE were equal to 1?
   (b) What would happen if INCOMING-YEAR-CODE were equal to 6?
   (c) Suppose that the codes of interest were 10, 20, 30, 40, and 50 rather than 1, 2, 3, 4, or 5. Explain how the GO TO DEPENDING construct could still be used.

(d) Assume that the codes of importance were 11, 17, 23, 46, and 65, which would preclude use of GO TO DEPENDING. Develop alternative code (i.e., a nested IF) to accommodate the logic of Figure 1.11.

6. Given the flowchart of Figure 1.13:

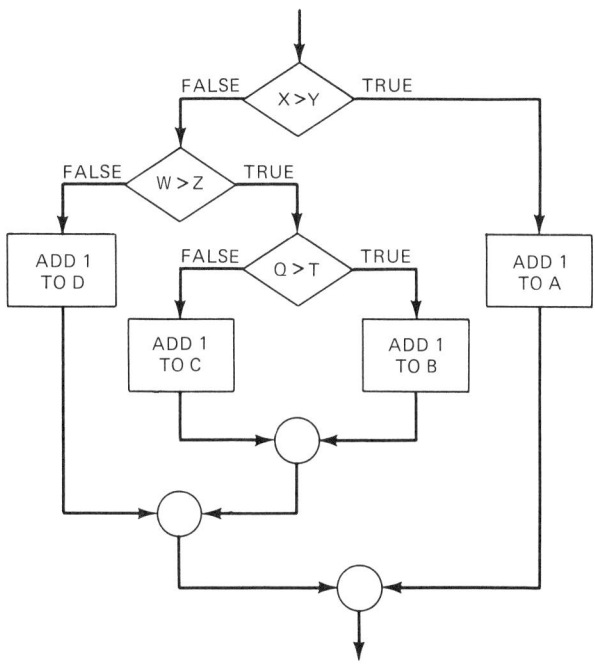

FIGURE 1.13 Flowchart for Problem 6.

(a) Write a COBOL IF statement to accomplish this logic.
(b) Respond true or false to the following based on the flowchart.

   i. If $X > Y$ and $W > Z$, then *always* add 1 to B.
   ii. If $X < Y$, then *always* add 1 to D.
   iii. If $Q > T$, then *always* add 1 to B.
   iv. If $X < Y$ and $W < Z$, then *always* add 1 to D.
   v. There are no conditions under which 1 is added to A and B simultaneously.
   vi. If $W > Z$ and $Q < T$, then *always* add 1 to C.

7. Draw a flowchart corresponding to the following COBOL statements:

(a) IF A > B
        IF C > D
            MOVE E TO F
            MOVE G TO H
        ELSE
            ADD I TO J
    ELSE
        ADD K TO L
        ADD M TO N.

Problems 17

(b) IF A > B
    IF C > D
        IF E > F
            MOVE 1 TO G
        ELSE
            ADD 1 TO H.

8. The chapter made no mention of coding standards. Nevertheless, the author follows certain conventions to make his code easier to follow. Comment on the practices implicit in the program of Figure 1.6 which you found to be most helpful.

9. Do you agree with the author that *structured* COBOL programs can, under certain circumstances, contain GO TO statements? Why or why not?

Projects

1. *Two-file merge*—Write a program to merge two sequential files (EMPLOYEE-FILE and EEO-FILE) to produce MERGED-FILE. As can be seen from the record descrip-

```
    FD  EEO-FILE
        LABEL RECORDS ARE OMITTED
        RECORD CONTAINS 80 CHARACTERS
        DATA RECORD IS EEO-RECORD.
    01  EEO-RECORD.
        05  EEO-SOC-SEC-NUMBER            PIC X(9).
        05  EEO-SEX                       PIC X.
        05  EEO-ETHNIC-BACKGROUND         PIC X.
        05  FILLER                        PIC X(69).
                            (a)
    FD  EMPLOYEE-FILE
        LABEL RECORDS ARE OMITTED
        RECORD CONTAINS 80 CHARACTERS
        DATA RECORD IS EMPLOYEE-RECORD.
    01  EMPLOYEE-RECORD.
        05  EMP-SOC-SEC-NUMBER            PIC X(9).
        05  EMP-NAME-AND-INITIALS         PIC X(15).
        05  EMP-DATE-OF-BIRTH.
            10  EMP-BIRTH-MONTH           PIC 99.
            10  EMP-BIRTH-YEAR            PIC 99.
        05  EMP-DATE-OF-HIRE.
            10  EMP-HIRE-MONTH            PIC 99.
            10  EMP-HIRE-YEAR             PIC 99.
        05  EMP-LOCATION-CODE             PIC 99.
        05  EMP-EDUCATION-CODE            PIC 9.
        05  EMP-TITLE-DATA.
            10  EMP-TITLE-CODE            PIC 9(3).
            10  EMP-TITLE-DATE            PIC 9(4).
            10  EMP-PERFORMANCE           PIC 9.
        05  EMP-SALARY-DATA OCCURS 3 TIMES
                        INDEXED BY SAL-INDEX.
            10  EMP-SALARY                PIC 9(5).
            10  EMP-SALARY-TYPE           PIC X.
            10  EMP-SALARY-DATE.
                15  EMP-SALARY-MONTH      PIC 99.
                15  EMP-SALARY-YEAR       PIC 99.
            10  EMP-SALARY-GRADE          PIC 9.
        05  FILLER                        PIC X(4).
                            (b)
```

FIGURE 1.14 (a) EEO-FILE. (b) EMPLOYEE-FILE. (c) MERGED-FILE.

```
    FD  MERGED-FILE
        LABEL RECORDS ARE OMITTED
        RECORD CONTAINS 80 CHARACTERS
        DATA RECORD IS MERGED-EMPLOYEE-RECORD.
    01  MERGED-EMPLOYEE-RECORD.
        05  MGD-SOC-SEC-NUMBER              PIC X(9).
        05  MGD-NAME-AND-INITIALS            PIC X(15).
        05  MGD-DATE-OF-BIRTH.
            10  MGD-BIRTH-MONTH             PIC 99.
            10  MGD-BIRTH-YEAR              PIC 99.
        05  MGD-DATE-OF-HIRE.
            10  MGD-HIRE-MONTH              PIC 99.
            10  MGD-HIRE-YEAR               PIC 99.
        05  MGD-LOCATION-CODE               PIC 99.
        05  MGD-EDUCATION-CODE              PIC 9.
        05  MGD-TITLE-DATA.
            10  MGD-TITLE-CODE              PIC 9(3).
            10  MGD-TITLE-DATE              PIC 9(4).
            10  MGD-PERFORMANCE             PIC 9.
        05  MGD-SALARY-DATA OCCURS 3 TIMES
                        INDEXED BY SAL-INDEX.
            10  MGD-SALARY                  PIC 9(5).
            10  MGD-SALARY-TYPE             PIC X.
            10  MGD-SALARY-DATE.
                15  MGD-SALARY-MONTH        PIC 99.
                15  MGD-SALARY-YEAR         PIC 99.    EEO fields appear in
            10  MGD-SALARY-GRADE            PIC 9.     merged file, but not in
        05  MGD-SEX                         PIC X.     EMPLOYEE-FILE
        05  MGD-ETHNIC-BACKGROUND           PIC X.
        05  FILLER                          PIC X(2).
```

(c)

FIGURE 1.14 *continued*

```
                            No matching record in EEO file
100000000DOE        J  1244117730315511772230000M1178521500H1177500000
200000000WILCOX     P  1048117730314511772190000M1178517500H1177400000
300000000SMITH      J  1155077640414507762150000M0778514000M0777513200H01775
400000000LEVINE     S  0150087630414508762190000H08765000000      00000
500000000CRAWFORD   M  0346017240416011772280000M0876726500M0575725000M05746
600000000SUPERPROG  S  0457107740514510771390000H1077800000       00000
700000000LEE        B  1053027630614502771200000P0578510000H0277400000
800000000PERSNICKETY P  0851037840314503781090000H0378600000       00000
900000000MILGROM    MB 1155097730614509772100000M0578409000H0977400000
                                                            Original master file does not have any EEO data

200000000M1
300000000M1
333333333F2
400000000F5     Social security number appears in both files
500000000F1
600000000M2
700000000M1
888888888M2    No matching record in employee file
900000000F3
```

(a)

FIGURE 1.15 Test data and intended output. (a) Input files; (b) merged file; (c) error messages.

```
200000000WILCOX      P  10481177303145117721900OM1178517500H1177400000       M1
300000000SMITH       J  11550776404145077621500OM0778514000M0777513200H01775M1
400000000LEVINE      S  015008763041450376219000H0876500000       00000      F5
500000000CRAWFORD    M  034601724041601177228000M0876726500M0575725000M05746 F1
600000000SUPERPROG   S  045710774051451077739000H1077800000       00000      M2
700000000LEE         B  105302763061450277120000P0578510000H0277400000       M1
900000000MILGROM     MB 115509773061450977210000M0578409000H0977400000       F3
```

EEO information obtained from EEO file

(b)

```
NO EEO RECORD FOR:    100000000
NO MASTER RECORD FOR: 333333333
NO EEO RECORD FOR:    800000000
NO MASTER RECORD FOR: 888888888
```

(c)

FIGURE 1.15 *continued*

tions in Figure 1.14, all three files have different record formats. (The merged file is a combination of the two input files.)

Test data and intended output are shown in Figure 1.15. Note that both input files must contain the same social security number to produce a merged record. An appropriate error message is to be written if a record is missing from either file.

2. *Three-file merge*—Write a COBOL program to merge *three* input files, all with identical record formats. A unique identification number is in record positions 1-9, and the remaining positions can be assumed to contain filler entries.

   Duplicate ID numbers are not permitted, hence, if the same ID appears on more than one input file, an error message is to appear and neither record is to be written to the merged file.

   Each of the three input files can be assumed to be in sequence. However, it is possible that duplicate ID numbers appear on the same file; e.g., file one contains two occurrences of record 888-88-8888. If this happens, the first occurrence is to be written to the merged file (unless, of course, the ID in question also occurs on another file).

   The reader is to make up his or her test data, as an integral part of this project is construction of sufficient test data to test the program adequately.

2 Structured Design

Overview

Unfortunately, adherence to the structured programming guidelines of Chapter 1 does not guarantee a "good" program. There are countless examples of structured programs which fail to work, and are impossible to follow. Even an advocate as enthusiastic as Ed Yourdon has talked about the failure of the first structured revolution. The fault, however, does not lie in structured programming per se. No discipline, structured or otherwise, can successfully implement systems of poor design or no design (as is often the case). Clearly something else is required prior to the implementation (or coding) phase.

Structured design can be defined as a series of techniques that produce a *hierarchical* solution with the same components and relationships as the problem it is intended to solve. Structured design is *not* structured programming, modular programming, top down design, or a guarantee of success.

It is a discipline based largely on the work of Larry Constantine and his associates, who first used the term in 1974.[1]

The objective of this chapter is to present sufficient material, *of a practical nature*, so that the methodology can be used productively by the COBOL programmer. The author stresses *application* at the expense of theory. Individuals seeking a rigorous theoretical treatment are referred to the classic book by Yourdon and Constantine.[2] The reader is also referred to a book by Wayne Stevens (a co-author of the original article on structured design) for a well-balanced mixture of theory and application.[3]

The present chapter introduces the subject by considering a management analogy to structured design; namely, that a company's organization chart corresponds to a program's hierarchy chart. Various principles of management are shown to apply equally well to organizations *and* programs. We demonstrate that a program's hierarchy chart is useful as both a design aid and a documentation technique. We include a COBOL program for processing multiple control breaks, and show the associated hierarchy chart to be the most effective way of communicating program function. We consider the associated, albeit different, topic of top down design and demonstrate that the hierarchy chart is a key element in program testing. We present the Yourdon Structure Chart as a variation of the basic hierarchy chart. Finally, we consider several heuristics for the evaluation and refinement of hierarchy charts.

Management Analogy

Many structured design concepts are easily introduced through a corporate management analogy. Consider the organization chart of the Hatfield family business shown in Figure 2.1. The president, A. Hatfield, has been complaining of falling profits since he brought his sons, B. and C. Hatfield, into the company.

It doesn't take an extensive management background to realize that the company is top heavy. A. Hatfield does nothing other than manage B. Hatfield, who in turn controls C. Hatfield, whose role in life is to manage I. R. Milgrom. I. R. Milgrom, on the other hand, is overloaded in that he has 40 people reporting to him. The problems are related to *span of control;* i.e., the number of subordinates reporting directly to a manager. I. R. Milgrom has too many, whereas each member of the Hatfield family has too few.

A better structure is exhibited by the McCoy family in Figure 2.2.

---

[1] W. G. Stevens, G. J. Myers, and L. L. Constantine, "Structured Design," *IBM Systems Journal*, vol. 13, no. 2 (May 1974).

[2] E. Yourdon, and L. Constantine, *Structured Design* (Englewood Cliffs, N.J.: Prentice-Hall, 1979).

[3] W. Stevens, *Using Structured Design* (New York: John Wiley, 1981).

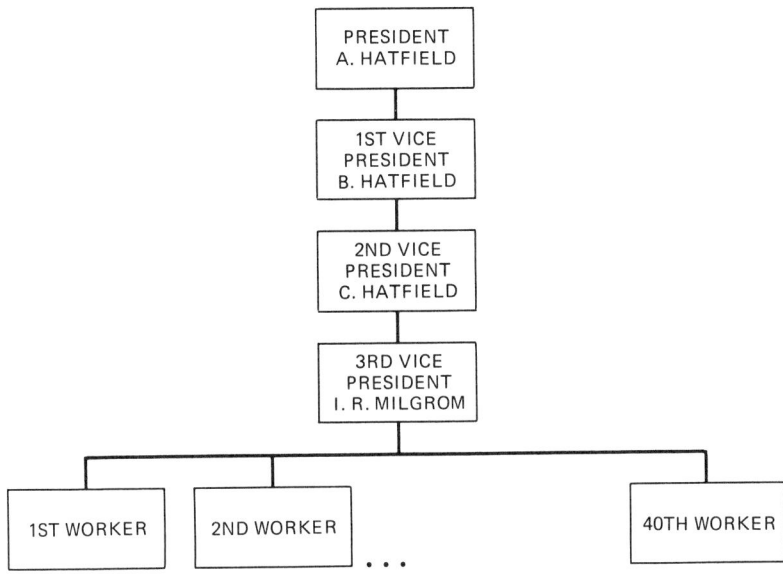

FIGURE 2.1 Hatfield organization chart.

Here, the president manages three vice presidents, who in turn each manage seven subordinates. Profits have continued to rise, even after the introduction of the McCoy offspring, and the company appears to be well run. This does not imply that every organization must have exactly three vice presidents, nor must every vice president have exactly seven subordinates. The McCoys are simply better organized than the Hatfields due to a more effective *span of control*. The McCoys may of course have other problems which cannot be perceived from Figure 2.2. We do know, however, that the Hatfields exhibit structural problems not evidenced by the McCoys.

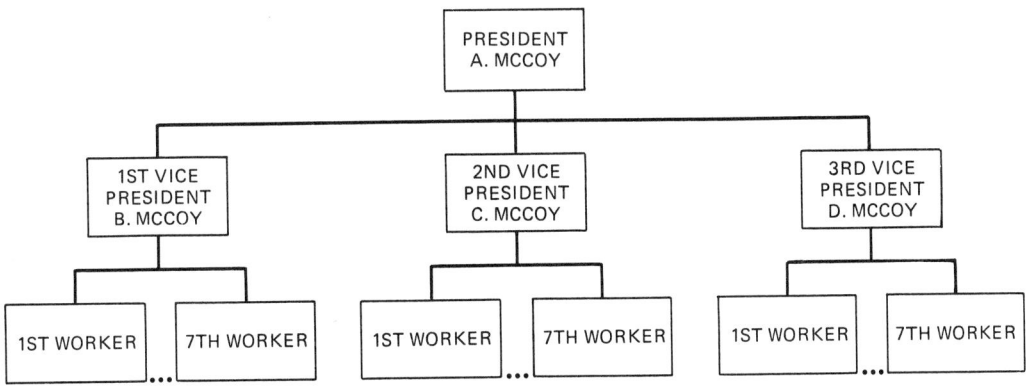

FIGURE 2.2 McCoy organization chart.

Management Analogy

A *hierarchy* (or *structure*) chart is an organization chart of a COBOL program or information system. It is the major tool of structured design. A hierarchy chart shows the relationship of *paragraphs* within a program (or programs within a system), just as an organization chart shows the relationship of people within a company.

Figure 2.3 is a hierarchy chart for a payroll program. *Each box in the hierarchy chart represents a paragraph in the program.* The box at the top, PREPARE-PAYROLL, is the "boss" of the program. It in turn has three subordinates on the second level of the chart. One of these, PROCESS-PAY-RECORDS, calls three lower level modules, which in turn call still lower level routines.

The higher up a person appears on a company's organization chart, the more responsible the position, and the more money he or she makes. In much the same way, paragraphs appearing toward the top of a hierarchy chart generally contain more complex logic than those near the bottom. The latter usually contain detailed, but trivial, logic and are least important in terms of the overall program flow.

A company's organization chart clearly expresses manager-subordinate relationships. A program's hierarchy chart indicates the relationships between called and calling routines. Each line in the hierarchy chart of a

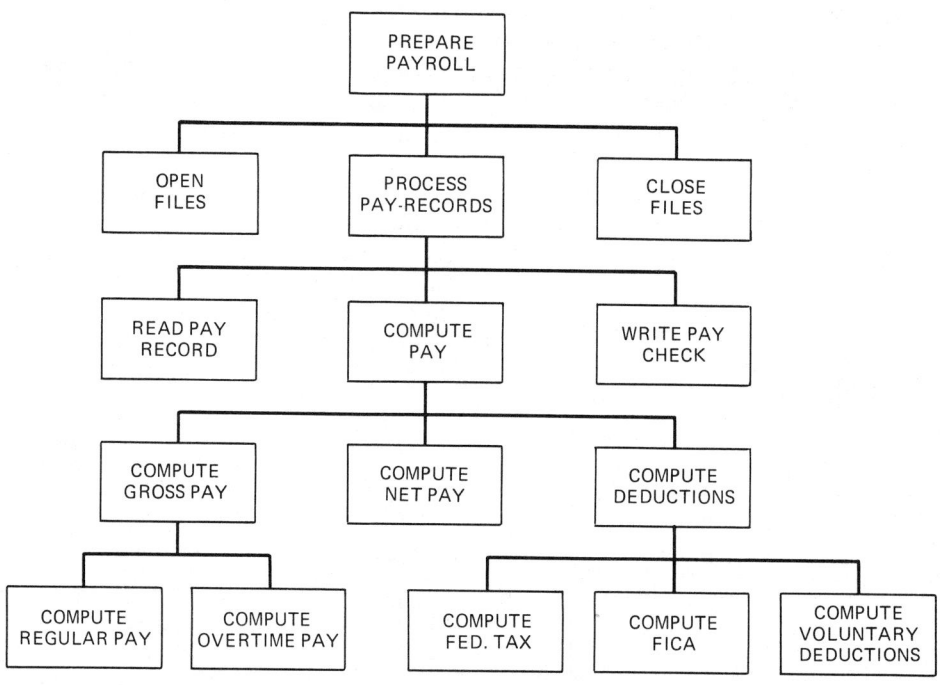

FIGURE 2.3 Hierarchy chart of a payroll program.

COBOL program corresponds to a perform statement. PREPARE-PAY-ROLL, for example, will contain three perform statements, one for each subordinate routine. PROCESS-PAY-RECORDS will perform COMPUTE-PAY and COMPUTE-PAY in turn performs COMPUTE-GROSS-PAY (as well as COMPUTE-NET-PAY and COMPUTE-DEDUCTIONS). Finally, COMPUTE-GROSS-PAY performs COMPUTE-REGULAR-PAY and COMPUTE-OVERTIME-PAY.

An organization chart indicates the various *functions* inherent in running a company, just as a hierarchy chart establishes the functions necessary within a program. The overall function of a COBOL module can be implied from the module name, just as a person's role can be deduced from his or her title, e.g., READ-PAY-RECORD, COMPUTE-VOLUNTARY-DEDUCTIONS, etc. The exact nature of a person's job is fully described by a detailed job description. The logic within a module can be specified by pseudocode, flowchart, or Nassi-Shneiderman chart (see Chapter 5).

Additional principles of structured design can yet be drawn from the management analogy. An individual in a company is not happy if others constantly interfere with his or her job performance; i.e., an accountant does not want to hear from a purchasing agent how to do his job, and vice versa. Nor should the action of a purchasing agent have a direct effect on how the accountant balances the books. What we are saying is that people in a company (or paragraphs in a program) should be as *independent* as possible. Structured design attempts to develop modules which are *loosely coupled;* i.e., modules which are independent of one another. The beneficial effect of this strategy is that a change in one module (during maintenance) will *not* affect the inner workings of another module.

An additional design principle has to do with the *function* of the individual. Every organization has at least one person who tries to do too much; i.e., he or she voluntarily or otherwise does too many jobs at once. That individual is a strong candidate for burnout, and depending on his value, the organization may or may not develop serious problems when he leaves. In analogous fashion, a COBOL paragraph which performs too many functions is also a cause for concern. Ideally, a paragraph should perform a *single* function. When every statement within a module is related to a common task, the module is said to be *highly cohesive.*

Subsequent portions of the chapter will further discuss the structured design concepts of span of control, coupling, and cohesion. In addition, we will consider evaluation criteria which enable the designer to select one chart over another. For the time being, however, we will concentrate on two *applications* of the hierarchy chart for the COBOL programmer. These are in top down design and documentation.

The author hopes that by initially concentrating on concrete applications of the hierarchy chart, he can instill in the reader an overall appreciation for structured design. Once this has been accomplished, we will return to additional design considerations.

Top Down Approach

The top down approach is often confused with structured design, but the subjects are quite different. The term *top down* simply refers to the *order* in which a system is tested and/or implemented. It has been practiced intuitively by some programmers for years, and certainly prior to the formal introduction of structured design in 1974. However, merely implementing a system in top down fashion does not guarantee a good design, as truly horrible systems have been implemented from the top down. Structured design, on the other hand, is concerned with the *quality* of a design. It provides guidelines for establishing a good hierarchy chart which can then be implemented in top down fashion.

Intuitive understanding of the top down methodology can also be drawn from a corporate analogy. When an individual is sufficiently motivated to start a new company, he or she proceeds from the top of the organization down. More than likely, the entrepreneur installs himself as president, then hires vice presidents for the various corporate functions of engineering, finance and so on. Eventually, *when the top of the organization is in place*, assembly line workers, salespeople, etc. are hired at the bottom of the organization to make and sell the product. Since this approach works rather well in the corporate world, it makes intuitive sense to try to develop systems and programs in the same way.

The top down philosophy leads naturally to top down testing, in which one implements a program from the top of its hierarchy chart (just as a new company originates with the president and not the janitor). The underlying premise is that the modules at or near the top of the chart are the most important (just as the people near the top of an organization chart have the biggest and most complex jobs).

Top down testing suggests *that a program be tested even before it is completely coded.* This is accomplished by initially coding lower level modules as program *stubs;* e.g., single sentence routines consisting of a DISPLAY statement to indicate only that the module has been called. This approach results in several "working" versions of a program as more and more modules progress from mere stubs to completed code.

The major advantage of testing a program in this fashion is that bugs are detected earlier and more easily than with conventional testing. It ensures that the higher level modules which typically contain the most complex logic are tested more frequently than lower level routines. It allows testing and coding to become parallel activities which provides early feedback to the programmer.

Let us apply this approach to the hierarchy chart of Figure 2.3, which depicted a payroll program. Version 1 can be made ready almost immediately. It pays everyone exactly $150 for regular pay and either nothing or $100 for overtime. It computes federal tax as a flat 15% of gross pay, deducts $10 for FICA, does not allow any voluntary deductions, and displays but doesn't format data for a paycheck. Obviously, the program isn't finished, but it is *complete* in the sense that every module exists, if only as a stub.

No user will accept version 1 as currently written. Nevertheless, it does accomplish significant testing in that it verifies the *interfaces* between modules. Data are correctly passed back and forth between modules, and further, the programmer can verify that the modules are being called in correct sequence.

Version 2 of the program computes regular pay correctly, but still hedges on overtime. It calculates federal tax correctly but still deducts only $10 for FICA. It allows only one of three voluntary deductions, and formats the paycheck, but not the stub. Versions 3 and 4 may further refine the system until version 5 finally becomes the finished product. (The reader should appreciate the role of the hierarchy chart in establishing a testing plan. He or she should be able to indicate which modules function as stubs in versions 1 and 2.)

What, if anything, is to be gained by this approach? First and foremost, realize that top down implementation does not guarantee a happy ending. Systems can still be late and over budget. However, the top down approach generally leaves one in a stronger position in that the user is presented with several versions of a *working* system. True, the intermediate products are not complete, but they do produce *demonstrable* output. The user is at least given something. This is in contrast to the 95% syndrome—i.e., "the program is 95% complete and will be finished next week . . . " (of course it isn't; and the program usually remains 95% completed forever). Moreover, the term 95% completeness is essentially meaningless—how does one know that 95% of the code has been written, debugged, etc., until one has completed the entire program?

A second advantage is that testing begins sooner, with the happy consequence that bugs are found earlier and thus are easier to correct. Later versions can still contain errors, but in the *lower* level modules where fixing them is easier. The more difficult problems arise in the interfaces between modules and these problems have already been resolved in the initial tests.

Last, and certainly *not* least, programmer morale is improved. Testing and coding become parallel activities making the programmer's life much more enjoyable. Consider Figure 2.4, which contrasts testing patterns. Figure 2.4a depicts the traditional panic mode. No testing is done for the first 11 months of the project, until the weekend before the system goes live. Last minute panic sets in with abundant overtime and chaos. By contrast, Figure 2.4b indicates a more uniform pattern of testing, which begins almost immediately and continues throughout the project's duration.

The top down approach relies heavily on the hierarchy chart produced by the design phase. The end result is only as good as the design itself; consequently, considerable effort must be expended in evaluating alternate

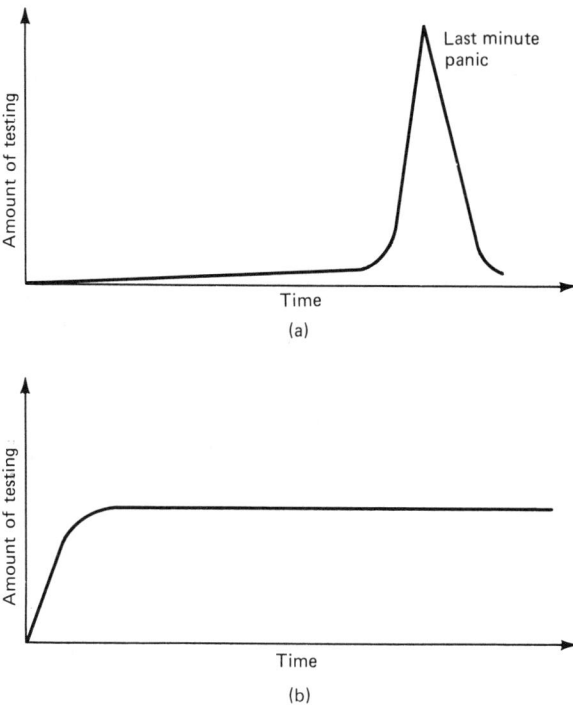

FIGURE 2.4 Testing patterns. (a) Traditional mode; (b) Top down mode.

designs. That is the subject of the latter half of this chapter. Before addressing that subject, however, we will demonstrate the utility of a hierarchy chart in providing documentation.

Documentation

When the author mentions the word documentation in classes and/or seminars, the usual response is, "I document all my programs because our release procedures require a flowchart be submitted with every production program." The author's next question is, "When do you draw a flowchart?" to which three out of four respond, "After I finish the program."

The value of such flowcharts is dubious to say the least. They reflect *what the programmer thinks the program is doing, rather than what is actually happening.* They are seldom, if ever, maintained and do not reflect the program's overall structure. Fred Brooks indicated very strong feelings when he said, "The detailed blow by blow flowchart is an obsolete nuisance, suitable only for initiating beginners into algorithmic thinking."[4]

The hierarchy chart describes overall program structure. It does not

[4] F. Brooks, "The Flow Chart Curse," *The Mythical Man-Month* (Reading, Mass.: Addison-Wesley, 1975).

replace the flowchart as it does something very different. A hierarchy chart depicts *function* whereas a flowchart indicates sequence and decision making logic. A hierarchy chart shows what has to be done, rather than when. It lists all the paragraphs in a program in a way which indicates their relative importance.

The utility of the hierarchy chart as a documentation aid is best demonstrated by example. Figure 2.5 contains a COBOL program to process two control breaks, on salesman and location. The object of the program is to obtain totals for each individual salesman, each location, and the company

```
00001              IDENTIFICATION DIVISION.
00002              PROGRAM-ID.    CBREAK.
00003              AUTHOR.        R. GRAUER.
00004
00005              ENVIRONMENT DIVISION.
00006              CONFIGURATION SECTION.
00007              SOURCE-COMPUTER.    IBM-4341.
00008              OBJECT-COMPUTER.    IBM-4341.
00009
00010              INPUT-OUTPUT SECTION.
00011              FILE-CONTROL.
00012                  SELECT SALES-FILE
00013                      ASSIGN TO UT-S-SYSIN.
00014                  SELECT PRINT-FILE
00015                      ASSIGN TO UT-S-PRINT.
00016
00017              DATA DIVISION.
00018              FILE SECTION.
00019              FD  SALES-FILE
00020                  LABEL RECORDS ARE STANDARD
00021                  BLOCK CONTAINS 0 RECORDS
00022                  RECORD CONTAINS 80 CHARACTERS
00023                  DATA RECORD IS SALES-RECORD.
00024              01  SALES-RECORD            PIC X(80).
00025
00026              FD  PRINT-FILE
00027                  LABEL RECORDS ARE STANDARD
00028                  RECORD CONTAINS 133 CHARACTERS
00029                  DATA RECORD IS PRINT-LINE.
00030              01  PRINT-LINE              PIC X(133).
00031
00032              WORKING-STORAGE SECTION.
00033              01  PROGRAM-SWITCHES.
00034                  05  WS-DATA-REMAINS-SW    PIC X(3)  VALUE 'YES'.
00035                  05  WS-PREVIOUS-SALESMAN  PIC X(15) VALUE SPACES.
00036                  05  WS-PREVIOUS-LOCATION  PIC X(15) VALUE SPACES.
00037
00038              01  CONTROL-BREAK-TOTALS.
00039                  05  THIS-SALESMAN-TOTAL   PIC S9(6)V99 VALUE ZEROS.
00040                  05  THIS-LOCATION-TOTAL   PIC S9(6)V99 VALUE ZEROS.
00041                  05  COMPANY-TOTAL         PIC S9(6)V99 VALUE ZEROS.
00042
00043              01  TRANSACTION-WORK-AREA.
00044                  05  TR-SALESMAN-NAME      PIC X(15).
00045                  05  TR-ACCOUNT-NUMBER     PIC 9(6).
00046                  05  TR-AMOUNT             PIC 9(4)V99.
00047                  05  TR-CODE               PIC X.
00048                      88  RETURNS      VALUE 'R'.
00049                      88  SALE         VALUE 'S'.
00050                  05  TR-LOCATION           PIC X(15).
00051                  05  FILLER                PIC X(37).
00052
```

FIGURE 2.5 Two level control break program.

```
00053          01  HDG-LINE-ONE.
00054              05  FILLER                PIC X(25)      VALUE SPACES.
00055              05  FILLER                PIC X(24)
00056                  VALUE 'SALES ACTIVITY REPORT - '.
00057              05  HDG-LOCATION          PIC X(15)      VALUE SPACES.
00058              05  FILLER                PIC X(69)      VALUE SPACES.
00059
00060          01  HDG-LINE-TWO.
00061              05  FILLER                PIC X(15)      VALUE SPACES.
00062              05  FILLER                PIC X(10)      VALUE 'SALESMAN: '.
00063              05  HDG-NAME              PIC X(15).
00064              05  FILLER                PIC X(25)      VALUE SPACES.
00065              05  FILLER                PIC X(78)      VALUE SPACES.
00066
00067          01  HDG-LINE-THREE.
00068              05  FILLER                PIC X(10)      VALUE SPACES.
00069              05  FILLER                PIC X(11)      VALUE 'ACCOUNT # '.
00070              05  FILLER                PIC X(15)      VALUE SPACES.
00071              05  FILLER                PIC X(7)       VALUE 'RETURNS'.
00072              05  FILLER                PIC X(15)      VALUE SPACES.
00073              05  FILLER                PIC X(5)       VALUE 'SALES'.
00074              05  FILLER                PIC X(70)      VALUE SPACES.
00075
00076          01  DETAIL-LINE.
00077              05  FILLER                PIC X(14)      VALUE SPACES.
00078              05  DET-ACCOUNT-NUMBER    PIC 9(6).
00079              05  FILLER                PIC X(14)      VALUE SPACES.
00080              05  DET-RETURNS           PIC $Z(3),ZZ9.99.
00081              05  FILLER                PIC X(11)      VALUE SPACES.
00082              05  DET-SALES             PIC $Z(3),ZZ9.99.
00083              05  FILLER                PIC X(70)      VALUE SPACES.
00084
00085          01  SALESMAN-TOTAL-LINE.
00086              05  FILLER                PIC X(25)      VALUE SPACES.
00087              05  FILLER                PIC X(21)
00088                  VALUE '*** SALESMAN TOTAL = '.
00089              05  PRT-SALESMAN-TOTAL    PIC $Z(3),ZZ9.99CR.
00090              05  FILLER                PIC X(74)      VALUE SPACES.
00091
00092          01  LOCATION-TOTAL-LINE.
00093              05  FILLER                PIC X(25)      VALUE SPACES.
00094              05  FILLER                PIC X(21)
00095                  VALUE '*** LOCATION TOTAL = '.
00096              05  PRT-LOCATION-TOTAL    PIC $Z(3),ZZ9.99CR.
00097              05  FILLER                PIC X(73)      VALUE SPACES.
00098
00099          01  COMPANY-TOTAL-LINE.
00100              05  FILLER                PIC X(25)      VALUE SPACES.
00101              05  FILLER                PIC X(21)
00102                  VALUE '*** COMPANY TOTAL = '.
00103              05  PRT-COMPANY-TOTAL     PIC $Z(3),ZZ9.99CR.
00104              05  FILLER                PIC X(74)      VALUE SPACES.
00105
00106          PROCEDURE DIVISION.
00107          010-CALCULATE-CONTROL-BREAKS.
00108              OPEN INPUT SALES-FILE
00109                   OUTPUT PRINT-FILE.
00110              READ SALES-FILE INTO TRANSACTION-WORK-AREA
00111                  AT END MOVE 'NO' TO WS-DATA-REMAINS-SW.
00112              PERFORM 015-PROCESS-ALL-LOCATIONS
00113                  UNTIL WS-DATA-REMAINS-SW = 'NO'.
00114              PERFORM 080-WRITE-COMPANY-TOTAL.
00115              CLOSE SALES-FILE
00116                    PRINT-FILE.
00117              STOP RUN.
00118
```

FIGURE 2.5 *continued*

```
00119        015-PROCESS-ALL-LOCATIONS.
00120            PERFORM 065-WRITE-LOCATION-HEADING.
00121            MOVE TR-LOCATION TO WS-PREVIOUS-LOCATION.
00122            MOVE ZEROS TO THIS-LOCATION-TOTAL.
00123            PERFORM 020-PROCESS-ALL-SALESMEN
00124                UNTIL TR-LOCATION NOT EQUAL WS-PREVIOUS-LOCATION
00125                OR WS-DATA-REMAINS-SW = 'NO'.
00126            PERFORM 075-WRITE-LOCATION-TOTAL.
00127
00128        020-PROCESS-ALL-SALESMEN.
00129            MOVE TR-SALESMAN-NAME TO WS-PREVIOUS-SALESMAN.
00130            MOVE ZEROS TO THIS-SALESMAN-TOTAL.
00131            PERFORM 060-WRITE-SALESMAN-HEADING.
00132            PERFORM 030-PROCESS-ONE-SALESMAN
00133                UNTIL TR-SALESMAN-NAME NOT EQUAL WS-PREVIOUS-SALESMAN
00134                OR TR-LOCATION NOT EQUAL WS-PREVIOUS-LOCATION
00135                OR WS-DATA-REMAINS-SW = 'NO'.
00136            PERFORM 070-WRITE-SALESMAN-TOTAL.
00137
00138        030-PROCESS-ONE-SALESMAN.
00139            MOVE SPACES TO DETAIL-LINE.
00140            MOVE TR-ACCOUNT-NUMBER TO DET-ACCOUNT-NUMBER.
00141
00142            IF SALE
00143                MOVE TR-AMOUNT TO DET-SALES
00144                ADD TR-AMOUNT TO THIS-SALESMAN-TOTAL
00145                ADD TR-AMOUNT TO THIS-LOCATION-TOTAL
00146                ADD TR-AMOUNT TO COMPANY-TOTAL
00147            ELSE
00148                MOVE TR-AMOUNT TO DET-RETURNS
00149                SUBTRACT TR-AMOUNT FROM THIS-SALESMAN-TOTAL
00150                SUBTRACT TR-AMOUNT FROM THIS-LOCATION-TOTAL
00151                SUBTRACT TR-AMOUNT FROM COMPANY-TOTAL.
00152
00153            WRITE PRINT-LINE FROM DETAIL-LINE
00154                AFTER ADVANCING 1 LINE.
00155            READ SALES-FILE INTO TRANSACTION-WORK-AREA
00156                AT END MOVE 'NO' TO WS-DATA-REMAINS-SW.
00157
00158        060-WRITE-SALESMAN-HEADING.
00159            MOVE TR-SALESMAN-NAME TO HDG-NAME.
00160            WRITE PRINT-LINE FROM HDG-LINE-TWO
00161                AFTER ADVANCING 2 LINES.
00162            WRITE PRINT-LINE FROM HDG-LINE-THREE
00163                AFTER ADVANCING 3 LINES.
00164
00165        065-WRITE-LOCATION-HEADING.
00166            MOVE TR-LOCATION TO HDG-LOCATION.
00167            WRITE PRINT-LINE FROM HDG-LINE-ONE
00168                AFTER ADVANCING PAGE.
00169
00170        070-WRITE-SALESMAN-TOTAL.
00171            MOVE THIS-SALESMAN-TOTAL TO PRT-SALESMAN-TOTAL.
00172            WRITE PRINT-LINE FROM SALESMAN-TOTAL-LINE
00173                AFTER ADVANCING 2 LINES.
00174
00175        075-WRITE-LOCATION-TOTAL.
00176            MOVE THIS-LOCATION-TOTAL TO PRT-LOCATION-TOTAL.
00177            WRITE PRINT-LINE FROM LOCATION-TOTAL-LINE
00178                AFTER ADVANCING 2 LINES.
00179
00180        080-WRITE-COMPANY-TOTAL.
00181            MOVE COMPANY-TOTAL TO PRT-COMPANY-TOTAL.
00182            WRITE PRINT-LINE FROM COMPANY-TOTAL-LINE
00183                AFTER ADVANCING 5 LINES.
```

FIGURE 2.5 *continued*

```
                   DATA FILE
    BAKER          444444010000RATLANTA
    BAKER          555555030000RATLANTA
    SMITH          100000030000SATLANTA  ── R indicates a "return", and causes the
    SMITH          400000070000RATLANTA      transaction amount to be subtracted
    SMITH          878787123456RBOSTON
    FORD           987654200000SBOSTON
    FORD           444333100000SBOSTON
    FORD           555666200000SBOSTON
                (a)
```

```
          SALES ACTIVITY REPORT - BOSTON

    SALESMAN: SMITH
                         ╱Salesman is the minor control break
    ACCOUNT #          RETURNS              SALES
     878787           $ 1,234.56

         *** SALESMAN TOTAL = $ 1,234.56CR

    SALESMAN: FORD

    ACCOUNT #          RETURNS              SALES
     987654                               $ 2,000.00
     444333                               $ 1,000.00
     555666                               $ 2,000.00

         *** SALESMAN TOTAL = $ 5,000.00

         *** LOCATION TOTAL = $ 3,765.44
                              ╲Location is the major control break

         *** COMPANY TOTAL = $ 2,965.44
```

```
          SALES ACTIVITY REPORT - ATLANTA

    SALESMAN: BAKER

    ACCOUNT #          RETURNS              SALES
     444444           $   100.00
     555555           $   300.00

         *** SALESMAN TOTAL = $   400.00CR

    SALESMAN: SMITH                        ── Transactions include
                                              $700 return and
    ACCOUNT #          RETURNS              SALES   $300 sale, producing
     100000                                              negative $400 total.
     400000           $   700.00          $   300.00

         *** SALESMAN TOTAL = $   400.00CR

         *** LOCATION TOTAL = $   800.00CR
```

                (b)

FIGURE 2.6 (a) Test data. (b) Report.

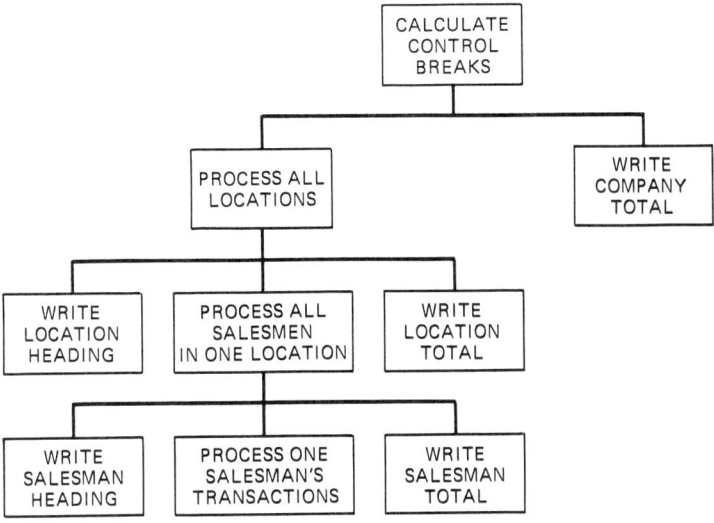

FIGURE 2.7 Hierarchy chart for two-level control break program.

as a whole. Figure 2.6 shows test data and sample output. (Note well that "returns" are decremented from all totals.)

The reader is left to his own devices to review the program; the author will provide no additional explanation other than the hierarchy chart of Figure 2.7. That, however, is precisely the point—a program's hierarchy chart provides more in the way of explanation than words, flowchart, pseudocode, or whatever else may be used in documentation.

IBM recognizes the importance of the hierarchy chart in its HIPO (Hierarchy plus Input/Output) methodology.[5] IBM uses the term VTOC, *V*isual *T*able *Of C*ontents, to refer to the hierarchy chart of a system. Indeed, every reference in the chapter to hierarchy chart could be replaced by VTOC with no loss of meaning.

Underlying Theory

Thus far, we have been exposed to the hierarchy chart as the principal tool of structured design. We have seen how this technique has intuitive appeal by drawing an analogy between a program and an organization. We have shown how the hierarchy chart can express paragraph relationships, how it facilitates top down implementation, and how it aids in the documentation of completed programs.

The remainder of the chapter is concerned with formalizing the discussion. We begin with coverage of *why* the theory *may* work. (Unfor-

[5] See the IBM publication, *HIPO—A Design Aid and Documentation Technique*, GC20-1851-1.

tunately, there is little in the way of documented research to prove that it does work.) We do know, however, that traditional methods tend not to work and result in unreliable and unmaintainable systems. Structured design does not guarantee successful systems, but the discipline is at least worth a try.

The underlying premise is very simple; *structured design attempts to reduce a program's complexity by dividing it into smaller, more manageable modules.* This assumes that a program of $2n$ statements is more than twice as complex as one of only n statements; i.e., a four page program is more than twice as involved as a two page program. Is this assumption reasonable?

Let us compare programs of one and two pages. The latter is twice as long and takes twice as much time to code. In addition, it requires *extra* time to establish *interfaces* between the two pages, and hence the extra complexity. Put another way, doubling the size of a program more than doubles the time required for implementation, or more generally, "program complexity increases exponentially with program size." This relationship is expressed in Figure 2.8.

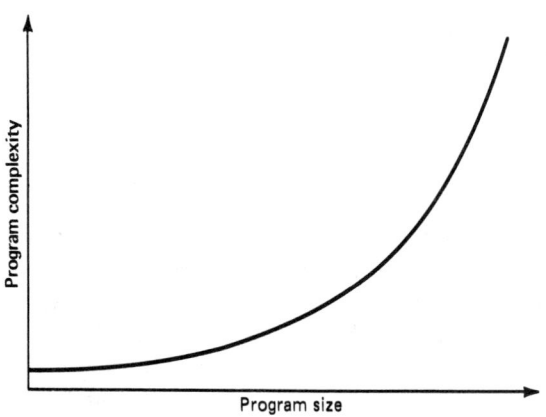

FIGURE 2.8 Program complexity versus program size.

Given that Figure 2.8 holds true, it is at least possible that developing a program as two or more *independent* modules reduces the overall effort associated with that program. There is a point of diminishing returns, however. The logical extension of the preceding argument is that the least effort results from a program consisting of a very large number of one-line modules, which is obviously not true. There exists, then, a hypothetical *optimal number of* modules, and *structured design is concerned with developing hierarchy charts consisting of the optimal number of modules, connected by proper relationships, to minimize overall development effort.*

Realize also that structured design implies considerably more than simply modular programming. Individuals have always divided complex programs into modules, but with little thought as to how many modules there should be, and/or the relationship between modules. (A typical procedure was to count the number of available programmers, and use that as the optimal number of modules.) Structured design, on the other hand, seeks to develop the proper number of modules with respect to the physical problem, as well as the proper relationship of modules to one another.

The ensuing sections develop structured design terminology and establish evaluation criteria for comparing alternative hierarchy charts. However, be aware that the so-called "rules" of structured design are more accurately "rules of thumb"; i.e., they are qualitative in nature and do not provide exact answers. Such procedures are termed *heuristics*, in that they often work but are not guaranteed, nor do they always provide unequivocal results.

The Structure Chart

Stevens, Myers, and Constantine formally introduced the *structure chart* in 1974 which expands considerably the hierarchy chart shown earlier. Figure 2.9 illustrates the additional notation.

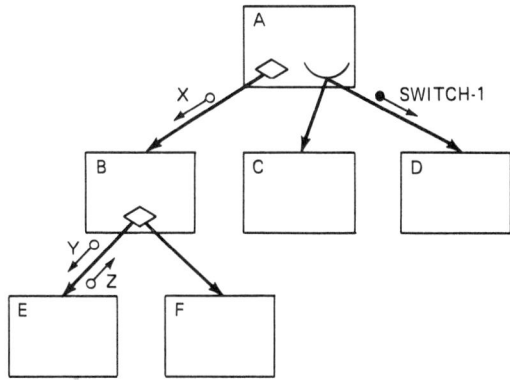

FIGURE 2.9 The structure chart.

A structure chart indicates major decisions and loops, indicated by diamonds and semicircles, respectively. Module A calls module B, for example, on the basis of a decision in module A; modules E and F are called from B, based on a decision made in B. Modules C and D are called repetitively from A, as implied from the semicircle notation. However a structure chart should indicate only the *major* decisions and loops to avoid unnecessary clutter.

A structure chart also contains the data and/or control information (i.e., switches) passed between modules. X is passed from A to B, Y from B to E, and Z from E to B. SWITCH-1 is passed from A to D. Names of the passed elements are written next to the arrow. A *data* element is indicated with an open circle on the end of the arrow. A *control* element, e.g., a switch or flag, is indicated by a darkened circle at the end of the arrow.

The modules in a structure chart are connected by arrows which point from the calling to the called module. (It is understood that control is always returned to the calling module.)

Yourdon has introduced several additional terms useful in discussing structure charts. *Morphology* refers to the overall shape of a system. Although shape, in and of itself, does not determine overall quality, well-designed systems tend to *fan-out at the top* and *fan-in at the bottom.*

The executive modules, near the top of a hierarchy chart, are generally decision-making modules with a higher number of subordinates than those near the bottom. Conversely, detailed worker modules which may be called from *several* places exist near the bottom, and exhibit high fan-in. Figure 2.10 contains a system with these characteristics.

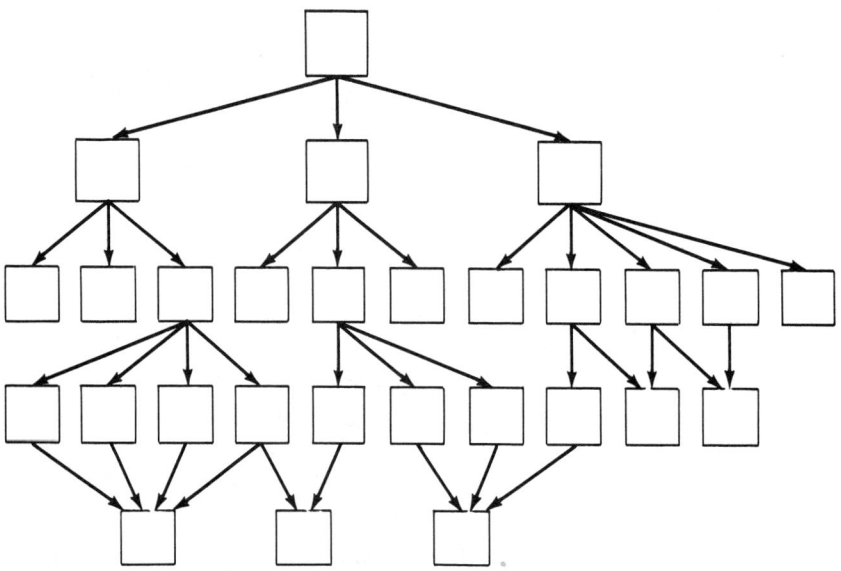

FIGURE 2.10 Fan-out and fan-in characteristic of well-designed systems.

Factoring refers to the separation of decision making and actual processing; i.e., computation or data manipulation. A well-factored system should have its decision making concentrated near the top of its hierarchy chart, with the bulk of its processing near the bottom. Again, the corporate analogy holds. Executives are paid to make decisions, and the higher one is in a company, the more decisions one ought to be making.

A formal definition of the word *module* itself is also in order. Yourdon and Constantine define a module as a "bounded contiguous group of statements having a single name by which it can be referred to as a unit." This definition can apply to a complete program, subprogram, paragraph, or section. A hierarchy chart, therefore, depicts the relationship of *either* paragraphs within a program, *or* programs within a system.

Good design requires that one be able to invoke a module without knowing specifically the instructions within it. One must know the input, output, and associated function or transformation, but one need not know how the transformation takes place. Such modules are termed *black boxes*. One knows what they do, but not how they work. The box is black, and one cannot see inside.

Viewing modules as black boxes is extremely useful in the design phase of a program. Initially, the designer merely determines which modules will be necessary, and postpones the details until absolutely necessary. Eventually, each module has to be designed and coded, but that should wait until implementation. In other words, one should "do no coding whatsoever in the design phase."

Coupling and Cohesion

Structured design can be viewed as an exercise in *dividing* a problem into pieces, and then properly *organizing* the pieces. The fundamental question is where and how shall one divide the problem? The answer is intuitive, yet very meaningful. The problem should be divided so that:

1. highly related parts of the problem should be put into related parts of the solution, and
2. unrelated parts of the problem belong with unrelated parts of the solution.

Structured design defines the terms *coupling* and *cohesion* to measure how well we succeed. *Coupling* refers to the relationship *between* modules. Good designs have *low coupling*, and unrelated or independent modules. *Cohesion* measures the strength *within* a module. Good designs have *high cohesion* where every statement in a module is related to a single function.

Coupling and cohesion can be viewed as opposite measures of the same phenomenon. All programs have elements of highly related code. The objective is to place the related elements in the same module to achieve cohesion, rather than scatter them in several modules to produce coupling.

Levels of Cohesion

A module in which all elements are dedicated to accomplishing one and only one task is said to be *functionally cohesive*. This property is highly desirable in that it facilitates subsequent maintenance. If a program consisting of functionally cohesive modules has to be changed, it is usually apparent where to make the change, and further, the modification should not affect any other module. The ability to identify where changes are to be implemented, and then being able to make the change without affecting other aspects of the progam is the ultimate goal of good design (just ask any maintenance programmer).

The original Stevens, Myers, and Constantine paper established seven different levels of cohesion, listed from high to low in Table 2.1. As previously stated, *functional cohesion* is the ideal objective.

TABLE 2.1 Levels of Cohesion

Functional	Best
Sequential	
Communicational	
Procedural	
Temporal	
Logical	
Coincidental	Worst

The seven points of Table 2.1 do not constitute a linear scale, nor are there exact numerical values which can be assigned to measure cohesion, and/or differentiate between adjacent levels. The distinction is qualitative. However, modules exhibiting functional, sequential, or communicational cohesion are usually acceptable, whereas temporal, logical, and/or coincidental cohesion generally suggest a poor design.

Yourdon and Constantine provide a thorough description of the levels of cohesion, and the earlier reference is suggested. The present discussion is limited to the extremes, functional and coincidental cohesion, to provide a clearer distinction between good and poor practice.

Coincidental cohesion results when elements in a module are put together for no reason other than "they had to go somewhere." This kind of design was prevalent in earlier systems when memory was at a premium. Different modules within a system invariably contained duplicate code. A coincidentally cohesive module would be formed by extracting redundant occurrences of common statements. The module would be called from several points in the program and the situation is depicted in Figure 2.11.

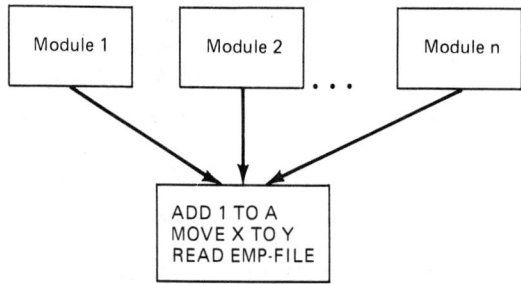

FIGURE 2.11 Coincidental cohesion.

The problem arises when there is a change in the specification of one of the calling modules; e.g., module 2 now requires that 1 be added to B rather than A. "No problem," says the designer. "Set a switch in module 2 and test for it in the common module. If the switch is on, add 1 to B, if it's off, add 1 to A." The solution sounds plausible until another specification changes, leading to another switch, and so on. Worse yet, consider what happens if module 2 fails to reset the switch properly, and module 1 subsequently calls the common module. *The results produced by module 1 will then be in error because of a mistake in module 2.* This is a cardinal violation of good design, because the results of one module should not affect the internal workings of another.

By contrast, every element in a *functionally* cohesive module is aimed at a *single* objective. The module elements, e.g., program statements, are deliberately placed in the module rather than appearing by coincidence. One way to decide whether a module is functionally cohesive is to examine its name. A well-chosen name *will not contain:*

1. More than one verb; e.g., READ-AND-WRITE;
2. More than one object; e.g., EDIT-NAME-AND-ACCOUNT-DATA;
3. Nondescriptive or time-related terms; e.g., HOUSEKEEPING, TERMINATION-ROUTINE, INITIALIZATION, MAINLINE, etc.

In other words, a module's function should be readily apparent from its name, which in turn should consist of a verb, adjective or two, and an object; e.g., READ-EMPLOYEE-RECORD, COMPUTE-SALES-TAX, etc. If a module cannot be named in this fashion, it may not be properly cohesive, and redesign of the individual module and/or the hierarchy chart should be considered.

Levels of Coupling

Coupling is a measure of the interdependence among modules. A highly coupled system has its modules interrelated to a high degree. Hence, a change in one module of a highly coupled system is likely to affect other modules. Coupling also affects the readability of both design and code. If coupling is minimized, then one can read and understand a given module, without having to look inside other modules to achieve complete understanding.

Myers[6] recognizes several different levels of coupling, listed in Table 2.2 from best to worst.

TABLE 2.2 Types of Coupling

Data	Best
Stamp	
Control	
Common	
Content	Worst

In the real world coupling cannot be eliminated entirely. There must be some connection between modules, else they would not be parts of the same system. However, coupling can and should be minimized, and some types of coupling are better or worse than others.

[6] G. J. Myers, *Composite Structured Design* (New York: Van Nostrand Reinhold, 1978).

Data coupling is the passing of data from one module to another. A program may calculate gross pay and pass that value to a subprogram which calculates federal withholding tax. Data coupling will *always* exist because a module must act upon data to be useful. However, one can minimize the amount of data coupling by paying strict attention to the complexity of the interfaces between modules.

One may reduce that complexity by passing few parameters rather than many. (See the guideline in Chapter 4 on passing only a *single* 01 parameter to a subprogram.) One should pass actual data rather than a pointer to the data. One should pass data only on a "need to know" basis, and avoid *stamp* coupling, the passing of an entire record when only a field is required. One should also eliminate the use of excess switches which leads to *control* coupling, i.e., switches or controls passed up and down a hierarchy chart because decisions are made in the wrong places.

In general, one should minimize coupling wherever possible. With respect to Table 2.2, data coupling is the least harmful form of interdependence and cannot be avoided. Stamp and/or control coupling are acceptable but *can be reduced* with forethought of design. Common and/or content coupling are at the bottom of the list and should be eliminated altogether.

Common coupling occurs when many modules have access to the same data. This is potentially dangerous in that one module can modify data necessary for the execution of another, without the latter module realizing that a modification has taken place. Since entries in the Data Division are accessible to all paragraphs in the Procedure Division, every COBOL program exhibits common coupling to some degree. Nevertheless, there are certain practices which increase (or decrease) the amount of common coupling present in a program. Consider Figure 2.12.

At one time, the total sales tax on an item purchased in New York City was 8%. Four percent went to the city, and 4% to the state. There is no doubt that the code of Figure 2.12 will work as intended.

Now consider what happens if the state percentage increases to five percent. Chances are that the maintenance programmer will look only in the CALCULATE-NY-STATE-TAX module, and change the VALUE clause

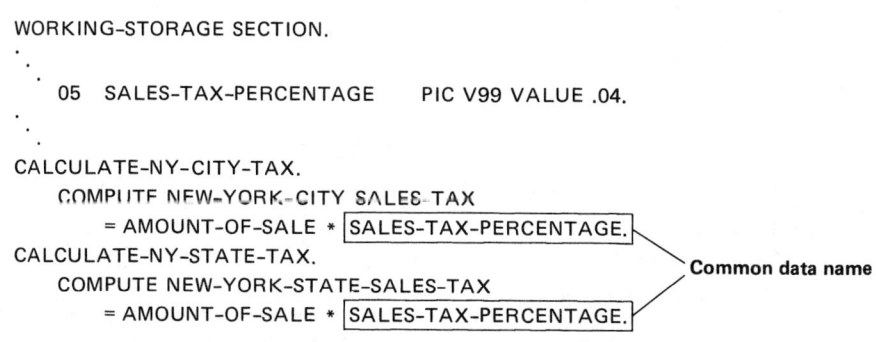

FIGURE 2.12 Common coupling.

for SALES-TAX-PERCENTAGE. This is a straightforward change to the maintenance programmer. Further, it works when tested; i.e., NEW-YORK-STATE-SALES-TAX will be correct.

However, NEW-YORK-CITY-SALES-TAX is no longer correct because SALES-TAX-PERCENTAGE appeared in *two* modules, and was used for *two* purposes. Although this particular example is somewhat trivial, it effectively illustrates the dangers associated with common coupling, namely, a change in one module causes changes in other apparently unrelated modules. Accordingly, one should take definite steps to minimize this kind of coupling. These include:

1. Restrict all data names to a single purpose; hence, the example of Figure 2.12 requires two distinct data names, NY-STATE-SALES-TAX-PERCENTAGE and NY-CITY-SALES-TAX-PERCENTAGE.
2. Define a separate subscript or index for *every* table in a program. In addition, if a given table is referenced in more than one module, consider multiple subscripts for that table. In that way, it is not possible to change a subscript in one module and have it affect another.
3. Restrict all indicators and switches to a *single* purpose. Hence, a given indicator reflects the answer to one and only one question.

Content coupling is the worst entry in Table 2.2, and occurs when one module references the inside of another, and/or when a module branches into the middle of another. Yourdon has coined the term "pathological connection" to refer to this kind of coupling, and deems it very sick indeed.

Although most practitioners recognize the dangers inherent in content coupling, one may fall into it quite innocently. IBM compilers, for example, provide an ENTRY statement as an extension to the ANS 74 standard. This makes it possible to enter a subprogram at more than one point and this is depicted in Figure 2.13.

The *normal* way of calling a subprogram is via the first CALL statement, CALL 'SUBRTN', where SUBRTN is the entry in the PROGRAM-ID paragraph of the called program. When the CALL is executed, control passes to the first executable statement in the subprogram; i.e., the statement immediately after its Procedure Division header. (See Chapter 3 for additional information on subprograms.)

The second CALL statement of Figure 2.13 references INMIDDLE, which was specified in an ENTRY statement in the subprogram. Control is now transferred to the first executable statement after ENTRY, rather than the first executable statement in the program. An individual reading the IBM manual might initially be impressed with this seemingly powerful capability. After some reflection, one should realize that program flow is greatly obscured, and that the one entry point/one exit point philosophy of structured programming is violated.

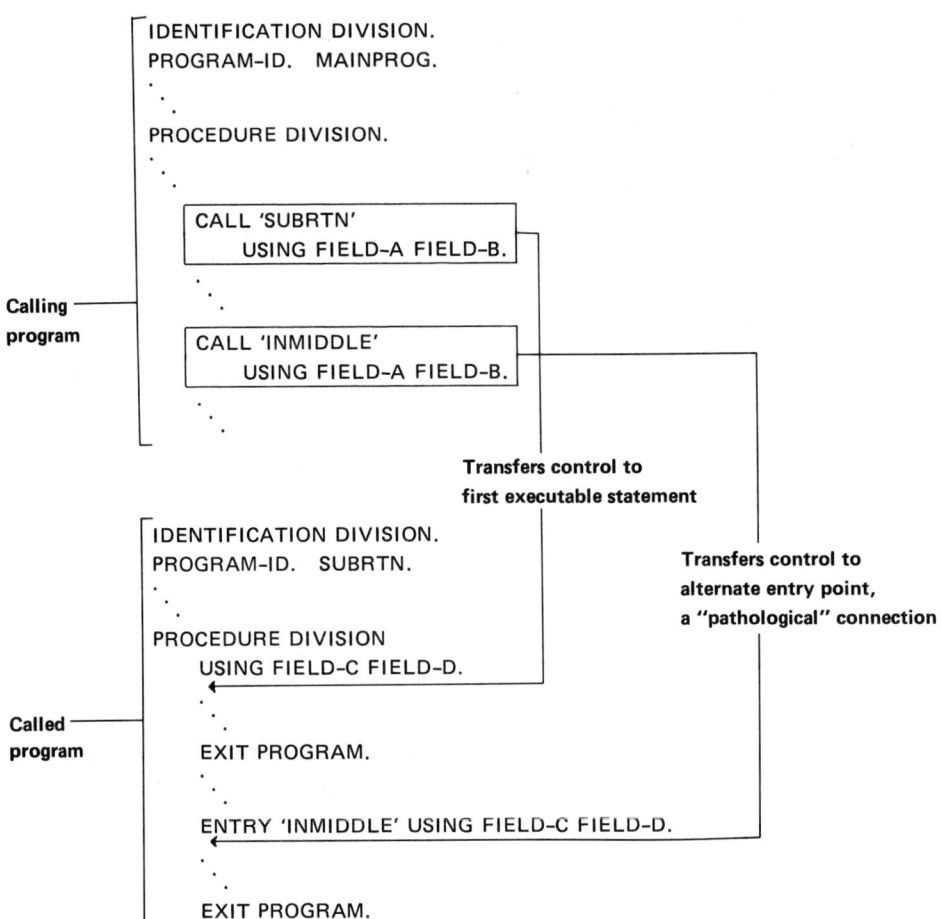

FIGURE 2.13 IBM's ENTRY statement (content coupling).

Binding Time

Binding refers to the assignment of a value to a piece of information. Binding can occur at several points; e.g., on the coding sheet via a VALUE clause, or at execution time. The *time* at which binding occurs is related to the interdependence, i.e., coupling, between modules. *The later binding does occur, the easier it is to modify the program.*

Assume, for example, that a program processes a table of 50 elements, and that the constant 50 is "hard coded" throughout. A change from 50 to 51 elements is indeed painful, requires numerous recompilations, and is highly error-prone. Even if the change is made globally using a text editor, errors are likely to occur because a "different 50" may be inadvertently changed.

It is preferable to code all references to 50 as a function of a data

42   Chapter 2—Structured Design

name; e.g., NUMBER-OF-TABLE-ELEMENTS, and define it with a VALUE clause. However, increasing the number of table elements still requires that the program be recompiled, retested, rereleased, and so on.

The best solution is for the number of table elements to be input as a parameter at execution time. Neither recompilation nor program modification would be required and the system could function indefinitely. (Prudent practice, however, would dictate defensive programming checks to ensure that the original table size was not exceeded—see guideline in Chapter 4 on initializing tables dynamically.)

Another common example of deferring the binding time is the IBM OS feature, BLOCK CONTAINS 0 RECORDS. This causes the blocking factor to be determined at *execution* time from the JCL, rather than at *compilation* time, and is a standard in most shops. The advantage is that a program may process files with different blocking factors without the need for recompilation. Another IBM OS feature is the use of device independent SELECT statements which determine the physical device; e.g., tape or disk, at execution time. (See Figure 6.9 for examples.)

Span of Control

The original management analogy indicated that there were problems in the Hatfield organization chart of Figure 2.1. These were related to span of control, i.e., the number of subordinates reporting to various individuals. It was shown that a span of 1 was too small whereas a span of 40 was too large. The concept holds regardless of whether the subordinates are people in an organization chart or COBOL paragraphs in a hierarchy chart. Can one infer anything about spans of 2 and 39, 3 and 38, and so on, from this example?

George Miller,[7] a psychologist, wrote that the human ability to process information is limited to 7 ± 2 entries; i.e., the average person can consider only 7 items simultaneously, after which there is a large increase in the number of errors. Accordingly, 9 may be established as the *maximum* desired value for span of control. This is not to say that a COBOL program is poorly designed if it contains spans outside the range from 5 to 9, because the nature of COBOL is such that lower spans are common, and acceptable. What we are saying is that span of control is an effective design criterion, and ideal spans will range from 2 or 3 to 9. When and if a span outside this range occurs, the designer should consider a modification.

Scope of Effect/Scope of Control

The *scope of control of a module* is defined as the module and all of its subordinates. The *scope of effect of a decision* is the set of modules de-

---

[7]G. A. Miller, "The Magical Number Seven, Plus or Minus Two: Some Limits on Our Capacity for Processing Information," *Psychological Review*, vol. 63 (1956), pp. 81-97.

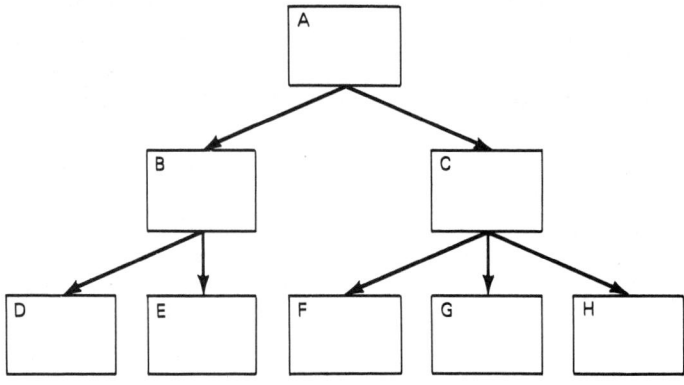

FIGURE 2.14 Scope of control.

pendent on that decision. These definitions are illustrated with the aid of Figure 2.14.

In Figure 2.14, the *scope of control* of module B is modules B, D, and E; the scope of control of module C is modules C, F, G, and H.

The *scope of effect* of a decision is not so readily apparent. Assume, for example, that a decision is made in module B, and that processing in module H is conditional upon that decision. Module H would then be in the scope of effect of the decision made in module B. (This is not a desirable situation, as will be shown.)

A guideline of structured design is that *the scope of effect of a decision should be a subset of the scope of control of the module in which the decision is located. In addition, the decision should be made as close as possible to the actual processing.* Bear in mind that this is a *heuristic;* i.e., a guideline which should generally be followed, but which may also have reasonable exceptions. Consider Figure 2.15.

Figure 2.15a illustrates a distinct violation of the guideline. A decision is made in C which affects processing in D, and module D is decidedly out of the scope of control of module C. (Note that violation of the guideline results in passing a switch up and down the hierarchy chart.)

Figure 2.15b remedies the violation by introducing a duplicate decision in B. However, duplicate decision making is also poor design strategy and should be avoided.

Figure 2.15c moves the decision up a level in the hierarchy to module A, and satisfies the heuristic. One might argue, however, that the decision is made too far from the actual processing.

Figure 2.15d moves module D directly under module C and appears to be an ideal solution in that the scope of effect modules are directly subordinate to the module where the decision is being made.

Figure 2.15e offers an alternative solution by combining modules. The decision remains in A, but module D has been compressed into module B, and module I into module C. This represents an improvement on Figure

44   Chapter 2—Structured Design

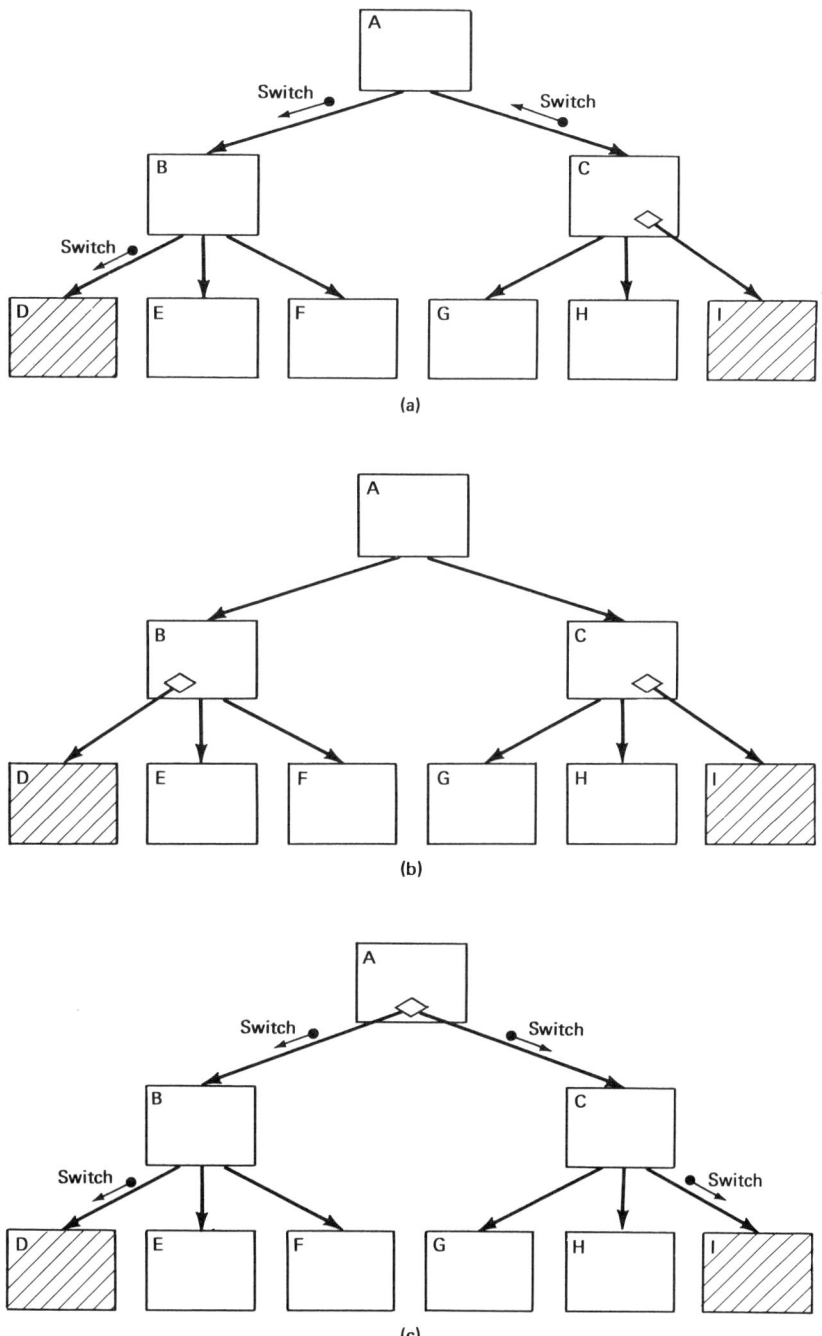

FIGURE 2.15 Variations in scope of control/scope of effect. (a) Violation. (b) Duplicate decision. (c) Moving the decision. (d) Moving the module. (e) Combining modules. Shaded areas indicate modules whose processing is dependent on the indicated decision.

Scope of Effect/Scope of Control 45

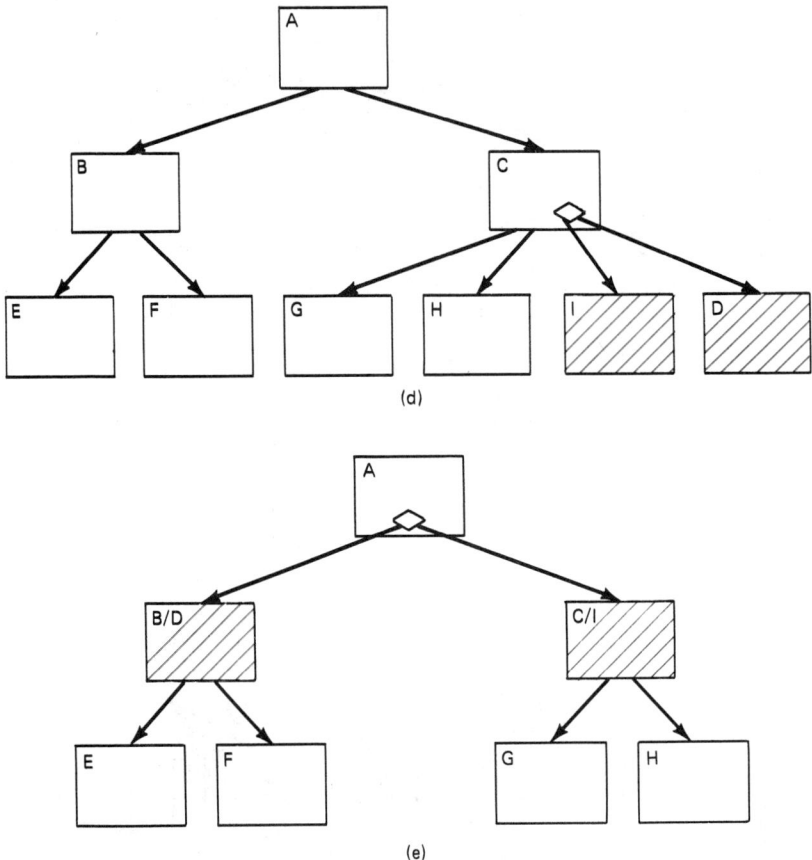

FIGURE 2.15 *continued*

2.15c in that processing now occurs immediately under the associated decision. This solution may not be desirable, however, if the expanded modules are no longer functionally cohesive.

Figure 2.15 highlights different options available to the designer when confronted with scope of effect/scope of control problems. These include:

1. Placing the decision in a higher level module as was done in Figure 2.15c,
2. Moving the module in which processing takes place (Figure 2.15d),
3. Combining modules (Figure 2.15e), or
4. Living with the situation, and its inherent problem of excessive switch passing.

Every situation is different and must be handled accordingly. Scope of effect/scope of control is an effective heuristic, but like all heuristics does not guarantee an unequivocal solution.

Summary

This chapter dealt with structured design, a discipline geared to produce a hierarchical solution with the same components and relationships as the problem it is intended to solve. Its proponents claim that it will eliminate the problems inherent in traditional systems: namely, that they are unmanageable, unsatisfying, unreliable, and unmaintainable.

Unfortunately, there is little in the way of documented research to substantiate these claims. We do know, however, that the "old ways" tend not to work. Programmers invariably quit after a year or less, and always in the critical stages of a project. Documentation is unreadable and inaccurate, making maintenance impossible. Systems are late and don't work, and so on. The author does not suggest, and certainly cannot prove, that structured design will instantly make your troubles disappear. He does believe that it is worth a try.

The first half of this chapter presented the hierarchy chart as the principal tool of structured design. The technique was shown to have considerable intuitive appeal through a management analogy. The hierarchy chart is also useful as a documentation aid, as was demonstrated with a COBOL program for processing control breaks.

The second half of the chapter concentrated on more theoretical aspects of structured design. The Yourdon structure chart was presented as an extension of the basic hierarchy chart. Several heuristics (guidelines) were postulated as aids in the evaluation of alternative structures. These are summarized here:

- Design by levels; begin at the top of the chart and work down. Be sure the chart is *complete*, and contains all functions necessary to solve the problem.
- Treat modules as *black boxes*. Understand a module's function completely; know its input, output and transformation, but do not be concerned with how the transformation is accomplished. Defer details and do *not* code in the design phase.
- Develop modules which are *functionally cohesive;* i.e., where all statements in the module relate to a single task. Choose a module's name so that it reflects the function; i.e., a verb, an adjective or two, and an object. Avoid modules of low cohesion, where the only reason for putting statements together is "they had to go somewhere."
- Develop *loosely coupled*, i.e., independent modules so that a change in one module is unlikely to affect the workings of another.
- Never branch into the middle of a module, as this constitutes a "pathological connection." Avoid the use of IBM's ENTRY statement, which allows this to happen; adhere to the one entry/one exit philosophy of structured programming.

- Keep the interfaces between modules as simple as possible. Pass data on a "need to know" basis. Do not pass an entire record if only a field is required. Pass data rather than a pointer to the data. Be aware of the *binding* time of connections; the later, the better.
- Use effective spans of control, generally between 2 and 7. Study the the overall morphology of a system. High fan-in is desirable at the bottom of a hierarchy chart, and implies the use of general purpose routines called from many places. High fan-out is acceptable at the top.
- Scope of control/scope of effect is important; make a decision as close as possible to the modules whose processing depends on that decision, and try to have the scope of effect *within* the scope of control. Concentrate decision making near the top of the hierarchy chart, and place detail processing near the bottom.

True/False

1. Top down design and structured design are synonymous.
2. Modules in a good design should be highly coupled.
3. Functional cohesion is less desirable than temporal cohesion.
4. A program must be completely coded before any testing can begin.
5. A hierarchy chart applies to systems only, and cannot be used for individual programs.
6. MAINLINE is a good module name.
7. READ-WRITE-AND-COMPUTE is a good module name.
8. A single COBOL paragraph should accomplish many functions for optimal efficiency.
9. Top down design guarantees a successful design.
10. Program testing should be concentrated in the last 25% of the development phase.
11. A span of control from 15 to 25 COBOL paragraphs is desirable for the highest level modules.
12. The rules of structured design provide exact and unequivocal answers for selecting one hierarchy chart over another.
13. Structured design and modular programming are synonymous.
14. A program's complexity is directly proportional to its length.
15. The optimal number of modules in a system is equal to the number of programmers available for coding.
16. Lower level modules should be coded and tested first.
17. Identical statements appearing in many modules should always be extracted into a single module.

18. Data coupling is inferior to content coupling.

19. The IBM extension, ENTRY, which provides multiple entry points to a called program, should be used as often as possible.

20. A module in a hierarchy chart can be called from another module on its own level.

21. A module in a hierarchy chart can be called from more than one module.

22. Decision making should generally occur in higher, rather than lower, level modules.

23. It is reasonable to restrict all COBOL paragraphs to a maximum of 50 lines of code.

24. A Yourdon structure chart and IBM's VTOC are synonymous.

25. Scope of effect should be a subset of scope of control.

Problems

1. (a) Redraw the hierarchy chart of Figure 2.3 as a Yourdon structure chart. Be sure to include:
      i. An indication of which modules are likely to contain loops and/or decisions.
      ii. Suitable names for data and control couples; indicate same on the structure chart.
   (b) Which diagram do you prefer: the hierarchy chart in the text or the expanded Yourdon chart?
   (c) What kind of information is included in the Yourdon chart that is not present on a plain hierarchy chart?

2. (a) Construct a flowchart for the program of Figure 2.5. Is it as easy to draw as a hierarchy chart? Is it worth the effort?
   (b) Pseudocode has come to replace the traditional flowchart and is discussed in Chapter 5. If you are already familiar with this technique, develop pseudocode corresponding to the program of Figure 2.5.
   (c) Assume that the incoming SALES-RECORD has been expanded to include region, and that three levels of control breaks are now required; region, location, and individual salesman. Indicate the necessary modifications on the hierarchy chart of Figure 2.7.
   (d) Assume that individual transactions are no longer to appear in the printed report. Which modules in the hierarchy chart should be deleted or changed?
   (e) Assume that location headings are no longer required in the printed report, and further that the location total line is to be modified to include the location name. Which modules are to be eliminated or changed? Does the ease and confidence with which parts (c), (d), and (e) were answered develop credibility for the hierarchy chart as a design aid and/or documentation technique?
   (f) Modify either the flowchart from part (a) or the pseudocode from part (b) to accommodate the control break on region. How long was this modification compared to the one in part (c)?

3. The chapter made no mention of a module's length. Do you think there is a quantitative guideline for the number of statements in a module? Could such a guideline be used as an indication of when a hierarchy chart is complete?

4. Do you think it is possible to develop a COBOL program, with 1000 statements in its Procedure Division, *correctly* on the first attempt? Is it possible to develop an error-free 40 line Procedure Division program on the first attempt? Could you code 25 such programs? How about 23 of 25? Do your answers provide an intuitive justification for the top down, iterative approach to program development?

Projects

1. This project and the next specifically avoid a business context. The author wished to select problems with which the reader was unfamiliar, and consequently for which he or she had no preexisting bias toward a solution. Accordingly, consider the following "non-data processing" problems.

   (a) Develop a hierarchy chart to allow a user to interactively play a series of Tic Tac Toe games against a computer. The following modules were used in the author's solution: PLAY-SERIES, PLAY-GAME, CLEAR-BOARD, GET-USER-MOVE, VALIDATE-USER-MOVE, CHECK-FOR-WINNER, UPDATE-BOARD, GET-COMPUTER-MOVE, DISPLAY-BOARD, DISPLAY-MESSAGE. (The last module, DISPLAY-MESSAGE, may be called from several places.) The module names should in and of themselves be indicative of the module functions.

   (b) View each module as a black box and list its associated input and output.

   (c) Expand your hierarchy chart to a Yourdon structure chart by including data elements and flags which are passed between modules. Indicate the major loops and decisions.

2. Develop a hierarchy chart for the game of blackjack (also known as "21"). Include sufficient modules to accommodate:

   (a) Doubling down—if the player's first two cards total 11, he may double his bet and receive one additional card.

   (b) Purchasing insurance—if the dealer's "up" card is an ace, the player may place an additional side bet. If the dealer has "blackjack," the player receives a payout of 2 to 1 on his side bet, but loses his initial bet. If the dealer does not have blackjack, the side bet is lost and play continues.

   (c) Splitting pairs—if the player has a pair he may double his bet and play two hands.

   The rules of blackjack state that the dealer must draw with 16 or less, and stand with 17 or more. Your hierarchy chart should contain the necessary module(s) to keep a running total of the player's winnings (or losses).

Toward COBOL Proficiency

3

Overview

This chapter might well have been taken from a basic book on COBOL, and indeed much of it was (Grauer and Crawford, *Structured COBOL: A Pragmatic Approach*, Prentice-Hall, 1981). It covers several elements of the language, none of which is unique to structured programming. It is included, however, to develop the necessary proficiency in COBOL per se.

The chapter begins with a thorough discussion of table processing. We include elementary coverage of the OCCURS clause, and proceed through indexing and multilevel tables. We cover various ways to initialize a table, as well as use of SEARCH, SET, and SEARCH ALL. We extend the discussion on tables through calculations involving dates, conversion from calendar to Julian dates, and use of the reserved words DAY and DATE.

Subprograms are discussed completely, along with the associated COBOL elements (CALL USING, PROCEDURE DIVISION USING, EXIT PROGRAM, and the LINKAGE SECTION). We conclude with material on sorting, covering the SORT, RELEASE, and RETURN verbs; the INPUT PROCEDURE/OUTPUT PROCEDURE and USING/GIVING options; and the COBOL SD. The chapter ends with a COBOL program illustrative of the major features.

Table Processing

Table processing is of paramount importance. This discussion includes material on several topics associated with tables; specifically: indexing, the SEARCH and SET verbs, variable-length tables, and multidimensional tables. It is dedicated to the practitioner who is expected to know anything and everything about tables, but who somehow may never have acquired complete understanding.

Establishment of a table (i.e., the allocation of space) requires an OCCURS clause in the Data Division, with the general format:

$$\underline{\text{OCCURS}} \begin{Bmatrix} \text{integer-1} \ \underline{\text{TO}} \ \text{integer-2 TIMES} & \underline{\text{DEPENDING}} \ \text{ON data-name-3} \\ \text{integer-2} & \text{TIMES} \end{Bmatrix}$$

$$\left[\begin{Bmatrix} \underline{\text{ASCENDING}} \\ \underline{\text{DESCENDING}} \end{Bmatrix} \ \text{KEY IS data-name-1} \ [\text{data-name-2}] \ldots \right]$$

$$[\underline{\text{INDEXED}} \ \text{BY index-name-1} \ [, \text{index-name-2}] \ldots]$$

As can be seen, there are several options within an OCCURS clause. The DEPENDING ON clause is used with variable-length tables and enjoys frequent application. INDEXED BY is required if either indexing or the SEARCH verb is to be used in processing the table. The ASCENDING (or DESCENDING) KEY clause is necessary if a binary search is to be implemented.

Storage Organization

The OCCURS clause can appear with either a group or an elementary item. Figure 3.1 shows the OCCURS clause with a group item and the associated storage layout.

A total of 150 bytes are set aside in storage for LOCATION-TABLE. The first three bytes contain LOC-CODE (1), and the next 12 contain LOC-NAME (1). Bytes 16–18 are for LOC-CODE (2), bytes 19–30 for LOC-NAME (2), and so on.

Figure 3.2 also defines a 150-byte table, LOCATION-TABLE, but uses two OCCURS clauses on the elementary level. Accordingly, the 30 bytes for the location codes are assigned contiguous locations and appear before the 120 bytes for the location names. Thus, bytes 1, 2, and 3 are for LOC-CODE (1); bytes 4, 5, and 6 for LOC-CODE (2); bytes 28, 29, and 30 for LOC-CODE (10); bytes 31–42 for LOC-NAME (1); and bytes 139–150 for LOC-NAME (10).

LOC-CODE (1) and LOC-NAME (1) are valid COBOL entries in both

```
          05  LOCATION-TABLE OCCURS 10 TIMES.
              10  LOC-CODE     PIC X(3).
              10  LOC-NAME     PIC X(12).
```

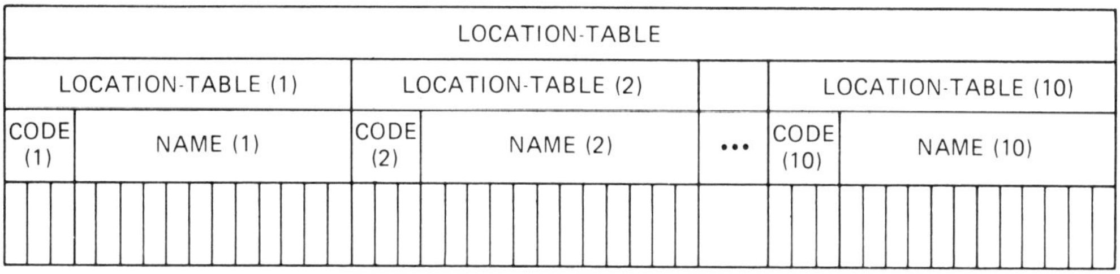

FIGURE 3.1 OCCURS clause with a group item.

Figures 3.1 and 3.2, denoting the code and name of the first location, respectively. Figure 3.1 also permits a reference to LOCATION-TABLE (1) to refer to the 15 bytes for code and name of the first location. The latter is *not* permitted in Figure 3.2.

```
          05  LOCATION-TABLE.
              10  LOC-CODE OCCURS 10 TIMES     PIC X(3).
              10  LOC-NAME OCCURS 10 TIMES     PIC X(12).
```

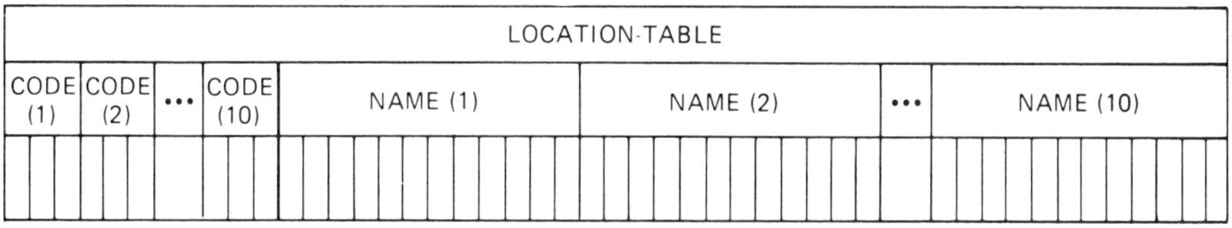

FIGURE 3.2 OCCURS clause with elementary item.

Subscripts versus Indexes

Subscripts and indexes are both used in table processing. Indexing results in more efficient object code and for that reason is preferred by many practitioners. In addition, indexing is *required* for the SEARCH statement, a powerful means of table processing, which is explained in a subsequent section.

A subscript and an index are *conceptually the same*, in that both reference an entry in a table. A subscript, however, represents an *occurrence*, whereas an index is a *displacement* within a table. Consider the following COBOL entries:

```
05  LOCATION-TABLE OCCURS 10 TIMES
                INDEXED BY LOCATION-INDEX.
    10  LOC-CODE        PIC X(3).
    10  LOC-NAME        PIC X(12).
```

The OCCURS clause establishes a table with 10 entries, LOCATION-TABLE, occupying a total of 150 bytes. Valid subscripts for LOC-CODE are 1, 2, 3, . . . , 10 (i.e., LOC-CODE can occur 10 times). Valid displacements for LOC-CODE are 0, 15, 30, . . . , 135. The first element in the table is referenced by a subscript of 1 or a displacement of 0; the second element by a subscript of 2 or a displacement of 15; the tenth element by a subscript of 10 or a displacement of 135.

In practice, the COBOL programmer is *not* concerned with the actual value of an index. Instead, one regards an index as a subscript and trusts in compiler-generated instructions to calculate the proper displacement. This is accomplished through the SET verb, whose only purpose is to manipulate indexes. The SET verb has two forms:

Format 1:

$$\underline{\text{SET}} \begin{Bmatrix} \text{index-name-1} & [\text{index-name-2}] \\ \text{identifier-1} & [\text{identifier-2}] \end{Bmatrix} \ldots \underline{\text{TO}} \begin{Bmatrix} \text{index-name-3} \\ \text{identifier-3} \\ \text{literal-1} \end{Bmatrix}$$

Format 2:

$$\underline{\text{SET}} \quad \text{index-name-1} \; [\text{index-name-2}] \; \ldots \begin{Bmatrix} \text{UP} \; \underline{\text{BY}} \\ \underline{\text{DOWN}} \; \text{BY} \end{Bmatrix} \begin{Bmatrix} \text{identifier-1} \\ \text{literal-1} \end{Bmatrix}$$

Figure 3.3 illustrates the use of a SET verb to initialize and increment an index. A variable-length table is established, whose length depends on the number of checks written. It varies from 11 to 1100 bytes (i.e., there are 11 bytes per entry and the number of entries ranges from 1 to 100). In the Procedure Division, the SET verb is used to both initialize and increment the index, CHECK-INDEX.

Note well that indexing is *not* required in COBOL; it is preferred because it generates more efficient object code. One could, for example, achieve the same results as Figure 3.3 through subscripting. It would be necessary to create a Working-Storage entry for CHECK-SUBSCRIPT, remove the INDEXED BY clause, substitute CHECK-SUBSCRIPT for CHECK-INDEX in the SUBTRACT statement, and change the two SET statements to MOVE 1 TO CHECK-SUBSCRIPT and ADD 1 TO CHECK-SUBSCRIPT, respectively. Such changes have no effect on the complexity of the source code. Indeed, their impact can only be measured by examining Procedure Division maps and generated object code.

Indexes do, however, offer one syntactical advantage over subscripts. *COBOL permits addition and/or subtraction of indexes, but not of sub-*

```
            DATA DIVISION.
                .
                .
                .
                05  CHECKS-PROCESSED
                    OCCURS 1 TO 100 TIMES DEPENDING ON NUMBER-OF-CHECKS
                    INDEXED BY CHECK-INDEX.
                    10   CHECK-NUMBER           PIC 9(4).
                    10   CHECK-AMOUNT           PIC 9(5)V99.
                .
                .
                .
            PROCEDURE DIVISION.
                SET CHECK-INDEX TO 1.
                PERFORM COMPUTE-CHECKBOOK-BALANCE NUMBER-OF-CHECKS TIMES.
                .
                .
                .
            COMPUTE-CHECKBOOK-BALANCE.
                SUBTRACT CHECK-AMOUNT (CHECK-INDEX) FROM INITIAL-BALANCE.
                SET CHECK-INDEX UP BY 1.
```

FIGURE 3.3 Illustration of SET verb with variable-length table.

scripts. Consider Figure 3.4, which illustrates the calculation of percent salary increase for several pairs of salaries.

Figure 3.4 defines a table of 5 salaries, and calculates the associated percent salary increases. SALARY (1) denotes the present salary, SALARY (2) the previous salary, SALARY (3) the second previous salary, and so on. PERCENT-INCREASE (1) is the increase from SALARY (2) to SALARY (1), PERCENT-INCREASE (2) the increase from SALARY (3) to SALARY (2), and so on. [PERCENT-INCREASE (5) has no meaning.]

In general, percent salary increase is computed by subtracting the old salary from the new salary, dividing by the old salary, and multiplying by 100. The code in Figure 3.4 is straightforward and should present no difficulty. (Note well the check to ensure that a previous salary exists to prevent division by zero.) The essential point is that SALARY-INDEX is incremented by 1 *within* the parentheses; i.e., *arithmetic is performed on an index.* If subscripts were used rather than indexes, then an extra statement, ADD 1 TO SUBSCRIPT GIVING DUMMY, is required prior to the COMPUTE statement. The computation would involve SALARY (SUBSCRIPT) and SALARY (DUMMY). This is certainly not a catastrophe, but one has to wonder why arithmetic is permitted with indexes and not subscripts.

The SEARCH Verb

Data are invariably stored in *coded* rather than expanded format, with the obvious advantage that less space is required in the storage medium. How-

```
                                    ┌─── An index is defined with the table to which it refers.
      05  SALARY-TABLE OCCURS 5 TIMES
          INDEXED BY SALARY-INDEX.
          10  SALARY              PIC 9(5).
          10  SALARY-DATE         PIC 9(4).
          10  PERCENT-INCREASE    PIC 9(3)V9.
      .
      .

      PERFORM CALCULATE-SALARY-INCREASES
          VARYING SALARY-INDEX FROM 1 BY 1
              UNTIL SALARY-INDEX > 4.

  CALCULATE-SALARY-INCREASES.
      IF SALARY (SALARY-INDEX + 1) > 0         ┌── Present salary
          COMPUTE PERCENT-INCREASE (SALARY-INDEX)        ┌── Previous salary
              = 100 * (SALARY (SALARY-INDEX))  -  SALARY (SALARY-INDEX + 1))
              / SALARY (SALARY-INDEX + 1)
      ELSE
          MOVE ZERO TO PERCENT-INCREASE (SALARY-INDEX).
```

FIGURE 3.4 Calculation of percent salary increase to illustrate arithmetic in indexes.

ever, since printed reports rarely contain coded information, a conversion from one form to the other has to take place. This can be accomplished by using a subscript or index to address the table directly. For example, if the value of an incoming location code is 99, then location (99) refers *directly* to the expanded element in the table. In many instances, however, this kind of direct access is not possible (e.g., nonnumeric codes), and conversion requires a table lookup or search routine.

A *linear search* examines entries in a table sequentially. A *binary search* begins in the *middle* of a table, and then with each successive search eliminates half the remaining entries. A linear search works regardless of how table elements are arranged; a binary search requires that table entries be in sequence, either ascending or descending.

To illustrate the difference, assume that one is to guess a number from 1 to 1000, and further that the number is 327. A linear search begins at 1 and progresses in sequential fashion. Next guess is 2, then 3, 4, 5, . . . , and finally, 327, a total of 327 guesses. The binary search starts at 500, then 250 (since the number is less than 500), then 375, 313, and so on, until the number is found. A *maximum of 10 tries* is required for a binary search, regardless of what number was chosen (2^{10} = 1024, which implies that any number up to 1023 can be found in 10 guesses). The linear (or sequential) search could require as many as 1000 guesses (if the number picked were 1000). Thus, a binary search is more efficient than a linear search for large tables; indeed, the larger the table, the greater the advantage.

The syntax for the COBOL SEARCH verb follows:

SEARCH Statement—Sequential Search

    SEARCH identifier-1   [VARYING $\begin{Bmatrix} \text{identifier-2} \\ \text{index-name-1} \end{Bmatrix}$]
      [AT END imperative-statement-1]
        WHEN condition-1 $\begin{Bmatrix} \text{imperative-statement-2} \\ \text{NEXT SENTENCE} \end{Bmatrix}$
      [WHEN condition-2 $\begin{Bmatrix} \text{imperative-statement-3} \\ \text{NEXT SENTENCE} \end{Bmatrix}$] ...

SEARCH ALL Statement—Binary Search

    SEARCH ALL identifier-1
      [AT END imperative-statement-1]
      WHEN $\begin{Bmatrix} \text{relation-condition-1} \\ \text{condition-name-1} \end{Bmatrix}$
        [AND $\begin{Bmatrix} \text{relation-condition-2} \\ \text{condition-name-2} \end{Bmatrix}$] ...
      $\begin{Bmatrix} \text{imperative-statement-2} \\ \text{NEXT SENTENCE} \end{Bmatrix}$

SEARCH ALL denotes a binary search; SEARCH by itself specifies a linear search. Identifier-1, in both formats, designates a table defined in the Data Division containing OCCURS and INDEXED BY clauses. If a binary search is specified (i.e., SEARCH ALL), identifier-1 must also contain an ASCENDING (DESCENDING) KEY clause.

The AT END clause is optional in both formats, *although prudent programmers will always supply it.* The WHEN clause specifies a condition and imperative sentence. Note that more than one of these clauses may be contained in a linear search (e.g., searching a table for one of two keys and the required action depends on which key is matched). A VARYING option is also possible with a linear search, but is not discussed here.

The capsule summary of Figure 3.5 illustrates the SEARCH verb. Definition of the table requires an INDEXED BY clause for either SEARCH or SEARCH ALL; however, the ASCENDING KEY clause is necessary only if a binary search is used. A SET statement is required prior to a linear search, to initiate where in the table the search is to begin (i.e., the search need not start at the first entry). The SET statement is *not* used in conjunction with a binary search, as the SEARCH ALL verb will always calculate its starting position.

Figure 3.5 also contains a statement to illustrate direct access to table entries, in which the incoming code points directly to the expanded value. This technique is faster than even a binary search because there are no comparisons at all. However, its use is limited to numeric codes and tables of moderate size.

Observe also the use of REDEFINES to initialize the DEPARTMENT-TABLE of Figure 3.5. COBOL does not permit the same entry to contain both OCCURS and VALUE clauses. (This makes intuitive sense when one

```
01  DEPARTMENT-VALUES.
    05  FILLER                          PIC X(15)   VALUE '001ACCOUNTING'.
    05  FILLER                          PIC X(15)   VALUE '002ADVERTISING'.
     .
     .
     .
    05  FILLER                          PIC X(15)   VALUE '100WAREHOUSE'.

01  DEPARTMENT-TABLE REDEFINES DEPARTMENT-VALUES.
    05  DEPARTMENT-ENTRIES OCCURS 100 TIMES
                ASCENDING KEY IS DEPARTMENT-CODE
                INDEXED BY DEPARTMENT-INDEX.
        10  DEPARTMENT-CODE         PIC 9(3).
        10  DEPARTMENT-EXPANSION    PIC X(12).

*LINEAR SEARCH                          SET statement is used with a sequential
    SET DEPARTMENT-INDEX TO 1.          SEARCH, but not a binary SEARCH
    SEARCH DEPARTMENT-ENTRIES
        AT END MOVE 'NO MATCH' TO OUTPUT-FIELD
        WHEN INCOMING-DEPARTMENT-CODE = DEPARTMENT-CODE (DEPARTMENT-INDEX)
            MOVE DEPARTMENT-EXPANSION (DEPARTMENT-INDEX) TO OUTPUT-FIELD.

*BINARY SEARCH
    SEARCH ALL DEPARTMENT-ENTRIES
        AT END MOVE 'NO MATCH' TO OUTPUT-FIELD
        WHEN DEPARTMENT-CODE (DEPARTMENT-INDEX) = INCOMING-DEPARTMENT-CODE
            MOVE DEPARTMENT-EXPANSION (DEPARTMENT-INDEX) TO OUTPUT-FIELD.

*DIRECT ACCESS TO DEPARTMENT ENTRIES
    MOVE DEPARTMENT-EXPANSION (INCOMING-DEPARTMENT-CODE) TO OUTPUT-FIELD.
```

FIGURE 3.5 Capsule summary for table lookups.

considers the function of these clauses. OCCURS defines a table with *multiple* entries. VALUE assigns an initial, i.e., *single*, value to a data name. The two clauses cannot be applied *simultaneously* because one should not assign a single value to multiple entries.)

The REDEFINES clause is a way out of this dilemma, as it assigns a new name to *previously* allocated space. Hence, in Figure 3.5, the multiple FILLER entries assign initial values to the 01 entry DEPARTMENT-VALUES. The latter is then given a new name via the REDEFINES clause, so that DEPARTMENT-TABLE references the *same* physical locations as DEPARTMENT-VALUES. Hence, DEPARTMENT-CODE (1) has a value of 001, DEPARTMENT-EXPANSION (1) a value of ACCOUNTING, and so on.

Table Initialization

Tables are generally initialized in one of two ways: through a REDEFINES clause (as was done in Figure 3.5), or by reading values from a file, as shown in Figure 3.6. The author views the latter technique as preferable because *table values can be changed without requiring recompilation of a program.* Moreover, if several programs utilize the same table, changes need be made in only one place (i.e., the input file).

Several features of Figure 3.6 bear mention. The variable-length table is defined with an INDEXED BY clause, presumably to accommodate a subsequent SEARCH statement. Note also that even though the table is defined with an index, *it may still be referenced with a subscript;* e.g., LOCATION-SUBSCRIPT. (It is equally correct, however, to substitute LOCATION-INDEX for LOCATION-SUBSCRIPT and eliminate the latter entirely. Realize also that the PERFORM statement can manipulate indexes directly, without having to resort to SET statements.)

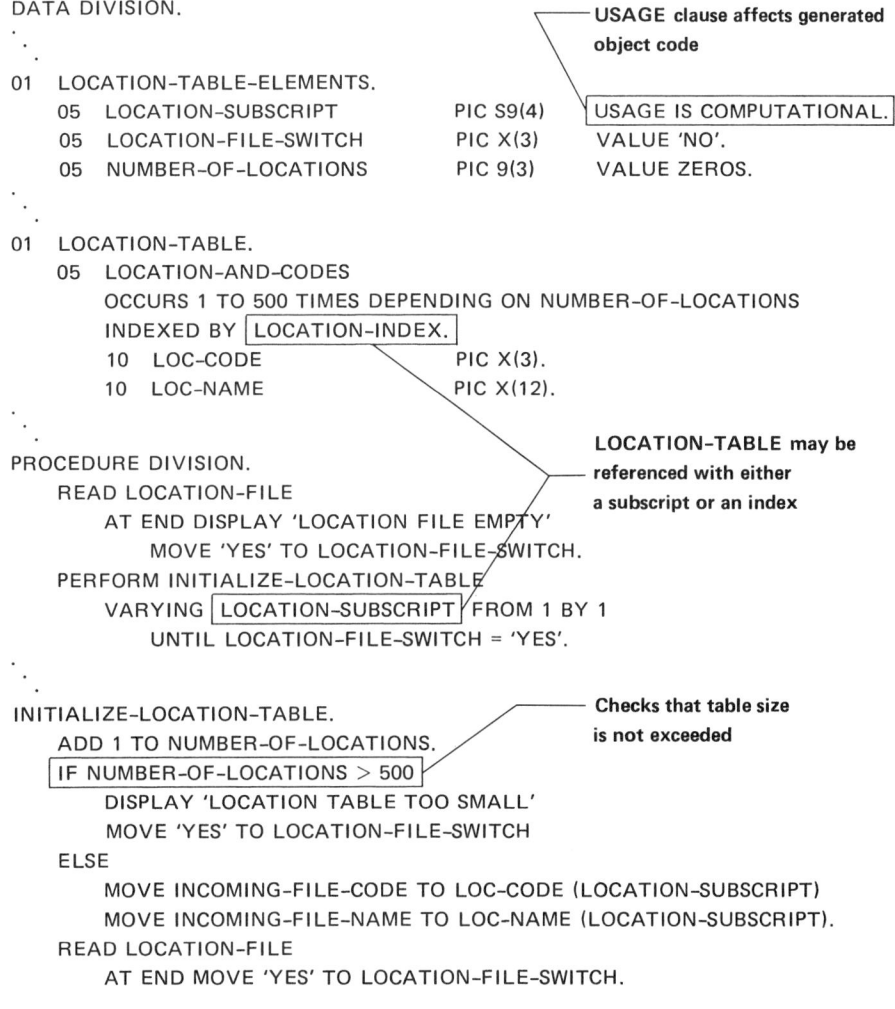

FIGURE 3.6 Initialization of a one-dimension table by reading from a file.

In Figure 3.6, LOCATION-SUBSCRIPT is defined as binary by the entry USAGE IS COMPUTATIONAL. The USAGE clause affects generated object code (and consequently machine efficiency), but not Procedure Division logic. In other words, a program will produce identical output with or without USAGE clauses; it is only the compiler generated instructions which vary. Hence, to truly appreciate the effects of a USAGE clause, one needs to know some Assembler. (See Chapter 14 of *Structured COBOL: A Pragmatic Approach*, Grauer and Crawford, Prentice-Hall, 1981.)

Figure 3.6 also contains two checks for potential errors. The initial read assures that the location file is not empty, while the IF statement verifies that the number of entries in the file does not exceed the allocated storage space. The latter is particularly important to prevent subscript (index) errors, which can cause a variety of perplexing errors and wasted programmer time.

Two-Level Tables

Figure 3.7 shows a two-dimensional table to determine entry-level salaries in Company X. The personnel department has established a policy that starting salary is a function of both responsibility level (values 1–10) and experience (values 1–5). For example, an employee with responsibility level of 4 and experience level of 1 receives $10,000. An employee with responsibility of 1 and experience of 4 would receive $9,000.

		Experience				
		1	2	3	4	5
	1	6,000	7,000	8,000	9,000	10,000
	2	7,000	8,000	9,000	10,000	11,000
	3	8,000	9,000	10,000	11,000	12,000
	4	10,000	12,000	14,000	16,000	18,000
Responsibility	5	12,000	14,000	16,000	18,000	20,000
	6	14,000	16,000	18,000	20,000	22,000
	7	16,000	19,000	22,000	25,000	28,000
	8	19,000	22,000	25,000	28,000	31,000
	9	22,000	25,000	28,000	31,000	34,000
	10	26,000	30,000	34,000	38,000	42,000

{ Responsibility level = 4
{ Experience level = 1

{ Responsibility level = 1
{ Experience level = 4

FIGURE 3.7 Entry-level salary (illustration of a two-dimension table).

Establishment of space for the table in Figure 3.7 requires Data Division entries as follows:

```
01  SALARY-TABLE.
    05  SALARY-RESPONSIBILITY OCCURS 10 TIMES.
        10  SALARY-EXPERIENCE OCCURS 5 TIMES     PIC 9(5).
```

COBOL provides additional flexibility to reference data at different hierarchical levels. Definition of the two-dimension table automatically allows reference to other one-dimension tables as well. However, the *order* of the subscripts and level of reference is absolutely critical. Some examples:

SALARY-TABLE: Refers to the entire table of 50 elements (250 bytes). SALARY-TABLE may *not* be used with any subscripts.

SALARY-RESPONSIBILITY (1): Refers collectively to the five experience levels associated with the first level of salary responsibility; SALARY-RESPONSIBILITY must always appear with a single subscript.

SALARY-EXPERIENCE (10, 5): Refers to salary responsibility level 10, experience level 5. SALARY-EXPERIENCE must always be referenced with two subscripts.

SALARY-EXPERIENCE (5, 10): Syntactically correct in that SALARY-EXPERIENCE has two subscripts. The entry will compile cleanly, but cause problems in execution because it refers to responsibility and experience levels of 5 and 10 respectively, which are inconsistent with the table definition.

The preceding entries cause a total of 250 consecutive storage positions to be allocated (10 × 5 × 5) as shown:

SALARY-TABLE											
SALARY-RESPONSIBILITY (1)					SALARY-RESPONSIBILITY (2)					
Exp 1	Exp 2	Exp 3	Exp 4	Exp 5	Exp 1	Exp 2	Exp 3	Exp 4	Exp 5	...

The first 25 bytes in storage refer to the five experience levels for the first responsibility level. Bytes 1-5 refer to experience level 1, responsibility level 1; bytes 6-10 refer to experience level 2, responsibility level 1; and so on. In similar fashion, bytes 26-50 refer to the experience levels for responsibility level 2; bytes 51-75 to the experience levels for responsibility level 3; and so on.

Figure 3.8 illustrates the use of REDEFINES to initialize the two-dimension table of Figure 3.7. This technique is made necessary because a COBOL entry which contains an OCCURS clause *cannot* also have a VALUE clause.

```
01    SALARY-TABLE.
      05    FILLER  PIC X(25)   VALUE '06000070000800009000010000'.
      05    FILLER  PIC X(25)   VALUE '07000080000900010000011000'.
      05    FILLER  PIC X(25)   VALUE '08000090001000011000012000'.
      05    FILLER  PIC X(25)   VALUE '10000120001400016000018000'.
      05    FILLER  PIC X(25)   VALUE '12000140001600018000020000'.
      05    FILLER  PIC X(25)   VALUE '14000160001800020000022000'.
      05    FILLER  PIC X(25)   VALUE '16000190002200025000028000'.
      05    FILLER  PIC X(25)   VALUE '19000220002500028000031000'.
      05    FILLER  PIC X(25)   VALUE '22000250002800031000034000'.
      05    FILLER  PIC X(25)   VALUE '26000300003400038000042000'.

01    SALARY-MIDPOINTS REDEFINES SALARY-TABLE.
      05    SALARY-RESPONSIBILITY OCCURS 10 TIMES.
            10    SALARY-EXPERIENCE OCCURS 5 TIMES    PIC 9(5).
```

FIGURE 3.8 Initialization of a two-dimension table via the REDEFINES and VALUE clauses.

The statement SALARY-MIDPOINTS REDEFINES SALARY-TABLE gives another name to SALARY-TABLE, and consequently places specified values in subscripted entries. The first VALUE clause fills the first 25 bytes in storage, the second VALUE clause fills bytes 26-50, and so on. The order of the VALUE clauses is critical and coincides with Figure 3.7.

Two-level tables are frequently processed with a PERFORM VARYING statement that manipulates two subscripts (indexes) simultaneously. (The reader would do well to review the use of PERFORM VARYING in one dimension, and the difference between an equal and greater than sign in the relational condition—see Problem 4 at the end of Chapter 1.) Consider:

```
PERFORM PROCESS-TABLE
    VARYING SUB-1
        FROM 1 BY 1 UNTIL SUB-1 > 3
    AFTER SUB-2
        FROM 1 BY 1 UNTIL SUB-2 > 2.
```

The preceding statement will execute the paragraph PROCESS-TABLE *six* times. It will simultaneously vary SUB-1 from 1 to 3 and SUB-2 from 1 to 2. The *bottom* subscript (SUB-2 in this case) is always manipulated first. Hence, the six pairs of SUB-1 and SUB-2 are:

SUB-1	SUB-2
1	1
1	2
2	1
2	2
3	1
3	2

Extending this discussion to the table of Figure 3.8 would result in a PERFORM VARYING statement as follows:

```
PERFORM PROCESS-SALARY-TABLE
    VARYING RESPONSIBILITY-SUB FROM 1 BY 1
        UNTIL RESPONSIBILITY-SUB > 10
    AFTER EXPERIENCE-SUB FROM 1 BY 1
        UNTIL EXPERIENCE-SUB > 5.
```

Three-Level Tables

Three-dimensional tables require three subscripts (indexes) to identify an elementary item. Consider a corporation with four sales regions, three states in each region, and five salesmen in each state. A three-dimensional table is defined as follows:

```
01  CORPORATION.
    05  REGION OCCURS 4 TIMES
            INDEXED BY REGION-INDEX.
        10  STATE OCCURS 3 TIMES
                INDEXED BY STATE-INDEX.
            15  SALESMAN OCCURS 5 TIMES
                    INDEXED BY SALESMAN-INDEX    PIC 9(5).
```

There are 60 (4 X 3 X 5) elements in the table. SALESMAN is the only elementary item, hence the only entry with a PICTURE clause. The value contained in each elementary item (i.e., the value in SALESMAN) might be an individual's sales to date. A total of 300 bytes (60 elements X 5 bytes per element) will be allocated, as shown in Figure 3.9. *The presence of three index clauses does nothing to affect the storage layouts, but speeds subsequent processing.*

As can be inferred from Figure 3.9, bytes 1–75 refer to the first region, bytes 76–150 to the second region, bytes 151–225 to the third region, and bytes 226–300 to the fourth region. Positions 1 to 25 refer to the first state in the first region and positions 1–5 to the first salesman in the first state in the first region.

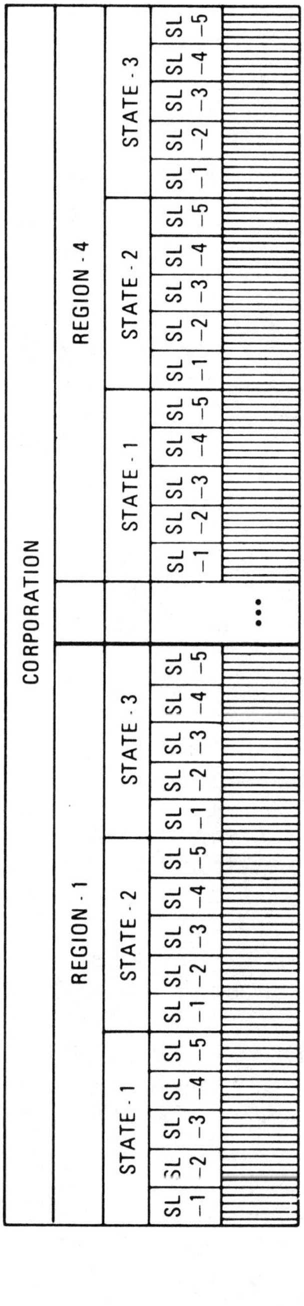

FIGURE 3.9 Storage allocation for a three-dimensional table.

64 Chapter 3—Toward COBOL Proficiency

Consider the following examples to illustrate the flexibility associated with references at different hierarchical levels, as previously discussed under two-dimensional tables. In particular:

SALESMAN (1, 2, 3): Refers to sales of the third salesman, in the second state, of the first region.

SALESMAN (3, 4, 5): Is incorrect, since there are only three states per region (not four) (i.e., STATE OCCURS 3 TIMES and hence the second subscript should not exceed 3). This entry will compile cleanly in that SALESMAN has the proper number of subscripts but will pose problems in execution.

CORPORATION: Refers to the entire table of 60 elements and may *not* be referenced with a subscript.

REGION (1): Refers collectively to the 15 entries in the first region.

STATE (1, 2): Refers collectively to the five entries (i.e., salesmen) in the second state of the first region.

It should be noted that the COBOL community is not unanimous in endorsing the use of three-level tables. Some installations maintain that three subscripts are too confusing and discourage their use. Others argue that if the situation fits, three subscripts will clarify program logic. The author is of the latter opinion but will not proselytize in this area.

The PERFORM VARYING statement is extended to three variables to accommodate three-level tables. Consider:

```
PERFORM PROCESS-TABLE
    VARYING SUB-1
        FROM 1 BY 1 UNTIL SUB-1 > 2
    AFTER SUB-2
        FROM 1 BY 1 UNTIL SUB-2 > 3
    AFTER SUB-3
        FROM 1 BY 1 UNTIL SUB-3 > 4.
```

The paragraph PROCESS-TABLE is executed a total of 24 (2 × 3 × 4) times. SUB-1 is varied from 1 to 2, SUB-2 from 1 to 3, and SUB-3 from 1 to 4. The *bottom* subscript (SUB-3 in this case) is varied first, and the 24 sets of SUB-1, SUB-2, and SUB-3 are shown in Table 3.1.

One can extend the discussion of PERFORM VARYING to the three-level CORPORATION table, defined in Figure 3.9. The following code calculates total corporate sales:

```
MOVE ZERO TO TOTAL-CORPORATE-SALES.
PERFORM CALCULATE-TOTAL-SALES
    VARYING REGION-INDEX
        FROM 1 BY 1 UNTIL REGION-INDEX > 4
```

```
        AFTER STATE-INDEX
            FROM 1 BY 1 UNTIL STATE-INDEX > 3
        AFTER SALESMAN-INDEX
            FROM 1 BY 1 UNTIL SALESMAN-INDEX > 5.
    .
    .
    CALCULATE-TOTAL-SALES.
        ADD SALESMAN (REGION-INDEX, STATE-INDEX, SALESMAN-INDEX)
            TO TOTAL-CORPORATE-SALES.
```

TABLE 3.1 Manipulation of Three Subscripts

SUB-1	SUB-2	SUB-3
1	1	1
1	1	2
1	1	3
1	1	4
1	2	1
1	2	2
1	2	3
1	2	4
1	3	1
1	3	2
1	3	3
1	3	4
2	1	1
2	1	2
2	1	3
2	1	4
2	2	1
2	2	2
2	2	3
2	2	4
2	3	1
2	3	2
2	3	3
2	3	4

Calculations Involving Dates

The ACCEPT verb is used to obtain the date or time of execution. Consider:

$$\underline{\text{ACCEPT}}\ \text{identifier-1}\ \underline{\text{FROM}}\ \left\{\begin{array}{l}\underline{\text{DATE}}\\ \underline{\text{DAY}}\\ \underline{\text{TIME}}\end{array}\right\}$$

In all cases, identifier-1 is a programmer-defined work area to hold the information being accepted. If DATE is specified, then identifier-1 will receive a six-digit numeric field in the form yymmdd. The first two digits contain the year, the next two the month, and the last two the day of the month, e.g., 790316, denoting March 16, 1979. If DAY, rather than DATE, is specified, a five-digit numeric field, corresponding to the Julian date, is returned to the work area. The first two digits represent year and the last three the day of the year, numbered from 1 to 366. March 16, 1979 would be represented as 79075, but March 16, 1980, as 80076 since 1980 is a leap year. (IBM compilers specify CURRENT-DATE to provide the date of execution in the form mm/dd/yy. However, CURRENT-DATE is a deviation from the ANS 74 standard and is not discussed further.)

TIME returns an eight-digit numeric field in a 24-hour system. It contains the number of elapsed hours, minutes, seconds, and hundredths of seconds after midnight, in that order, from left to right. 10:15 A.M. would return as 10150000; 10:15 PM, as 22150000.

Converting a Julian Date to a Calendar Date

A common requirement is to convert from Julian to calendar date, or vice versa. Figure 3.10 illustrates the first calculation.

The number of days in each month is established via a series of VALUE, OCCURS, and REDEFINES clauses. Observe, however, that no value is initially assigned to February because of leap year. The indication of a leap year is obtained by dividing the year by 4 and checking for a zero remainder; e.g., 1980 will be determined to be a leap year whereas 1981 will not. (Figure 3.10 has to be modified to account for the fact that the year 2000 is *not* a leap year, even though it is evenly divisible by 4, but that is omitted for simplicity.)

The paragraph COMPUTE-DAYS will be performed from zero to 11 times until the days remaining from the original Julian field do not exceed the days in the current month. The values of DDD and MONTH-SUB are then moved to the appropriate fields in CALENDAR-DATE. (Figure 3.10 also illustrates the use of a nonunique data name, YY, and the associated qualification in the Procedure Division.)

Subprograms

A sub (or called) program contains the four divisions of a regular program. In addition, it contains a LINKAGE SECTION in its Data Division that passes information to and from the main (or calling) program. The same program may call several subprograms, and a subprogram may in turn call another subprogram.

Consider Figure 3.11, which depicts skeletal code illustrating the linkage between a main and a subprogram. The main program contains a CALL statement somewhere in its Procedure Division. When the CALL is executed, control is transferred to the first statement in the Procedure

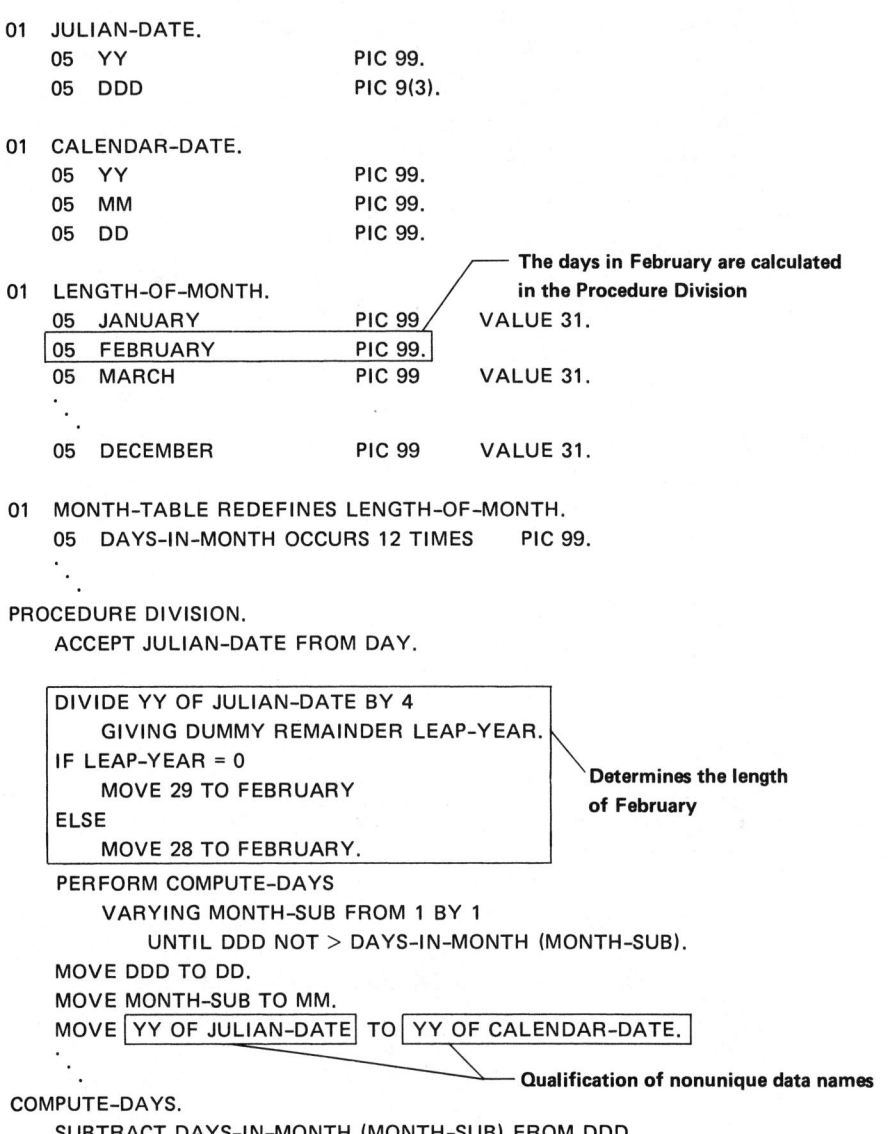

FIGURE 3.10 Converting a Julian date to a calendar date.

Division of the subprogram. The latter will continue executing until it encounters an EXIT PROGRAM statement, at which point control returns to the main program to the statement immediately following the initial CALL. *EXIT PROGRAM must be in a paragraph by itself.*

Data are passed between the main and subprogram via USING clauses, which appear in the CALL statement of the main program and in the Procedure Division header of the subprogram. Data names that are passed as arguments are defined in the Linkage Section of the subprogram. Any

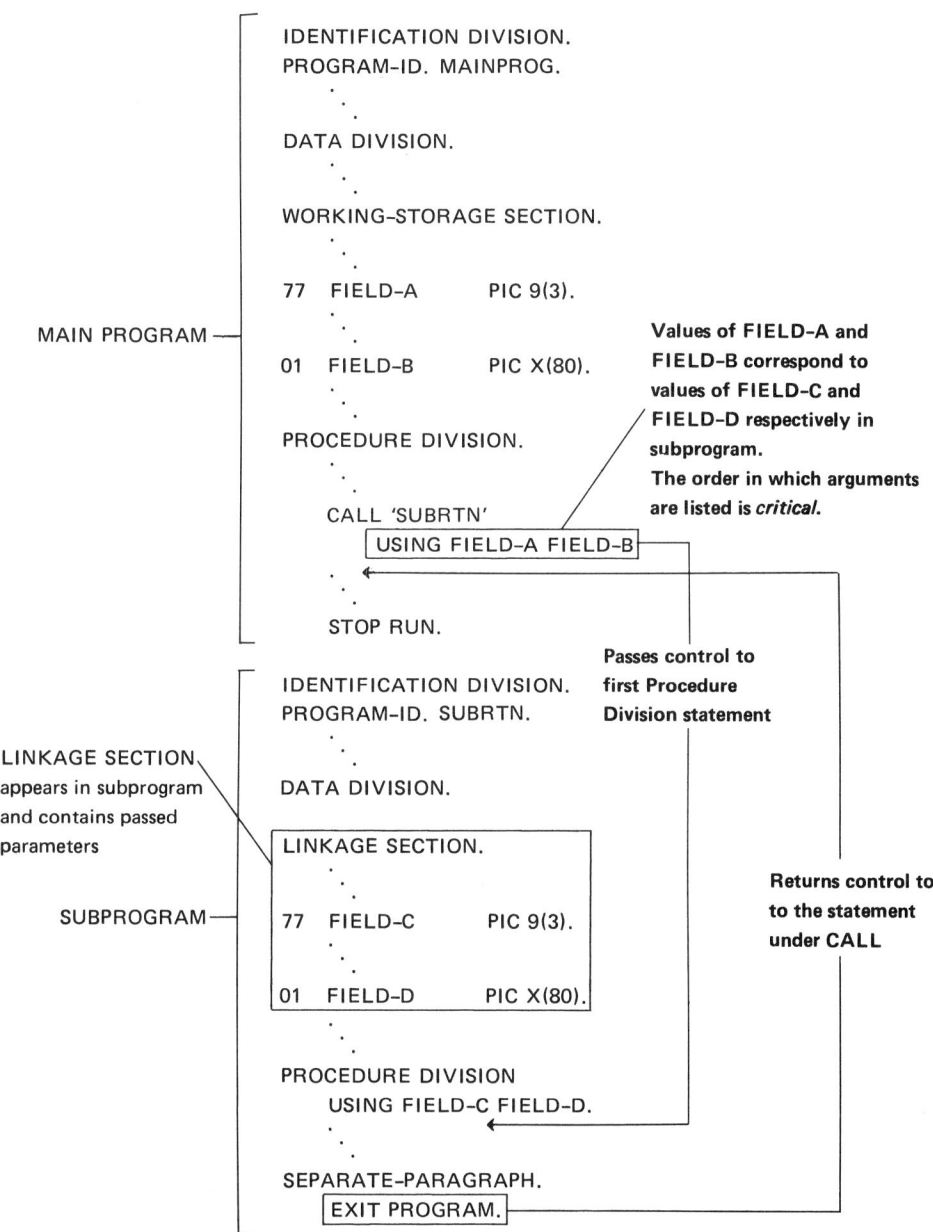

FIGURE 3.11 Skeletal code for calling a subprogram.

CALL statement in the main program contains a USING clause that specifies the data on which the subprogram is to operate; for example, CALL 'SUBRTN' USING FIELD-A FIELD-B. The subprogram in turn contains a USING clause in its Procedure Division header, for example, PROCEDURE DIVISION USING FIELD-C FIELD-D.

The data names in the main and subprogram USING clauses may be different, but the *order* of data names within these clauses is critical. The first item in the USING clause of the main program, FIELD-A, corresponds to the first item in the USING clause of the subprogram, FIELD-C. Both are defined as three-position numeric fields. In similar fashion, FIELD-B of the main program corresponds to FIELD-D of the subprogram. Note that as *either program changes the value of a passed parameter, the value changes in the other program as well*, because only a *single* storage location is assigned to *both* data names. This situation is illustrated in Figure 3.12.

As can be seen from Figure 3.12, FIELD-A in the main program and FIELD-C in the subprogram reference the *same* locations in memory. In similar fashion, FIELD-B and FIELD-D also reference a common area. The COBOL compiler allocates the same space for FIELD-A and FIELD-C, or FIELD-B and FIELD-D.

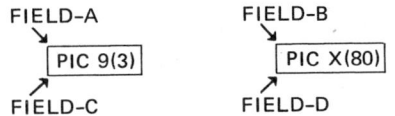

FIGURE 3.12 Storage allocation for passed parameters.

The parameters of the subprogram, FIELD-C and FIELD-D, are defined in the Linkage Section of the subprogram. In other words, any data name appearing in a Linkage Section already has had space allocated, i.e., by the program which called it. Hence, the space for FIELD-C and FIELD-D was previously assigned in the main program to FIELD-A and FIELD-B, respectively. The USING clauses in both programs establish the correspondence between the data names.

All passed parameters must be defined as either 01 or 77-level entries, and the order in which these arguments are listed is critical. Passing parameters in the wrong sequence is one of the most frequent problems in modular systems consisting of several programs.

Sorting

Sorting is usually accomplished in one of two ways; either by a "stand alone" sort in which a utility sort program is called explicitly, or in the program itself via the COBOL SORT verb. Both methods are equally acceptable. Both use the *same* sort program because the compiler generated code associated with the SORT verb transfers control to the utility program.

This section deals exclusively with a COBOL sort. The technique is the preference of many programmers because they already know the COBOL language, and are spared having to learn the utility program's parameters. Use of the SORT verb requires knowledge of the RELEASE, RETURN, and SD statements in addition to the verb itself. The latter has the format shown and is the basis for the following discussion.

```
SORT file-name-1
     ON  {ASCENDING / DESCENDING} KEY data-name-1 [data-name-2] ...

    [ON  {ASCENDING / DESCENDING} KEY data-name-3 [data-name-4] ...] ...

    [COLLATING SEQUENCE IS alphabet-name]

    { USING file-name-2 [file-name-3] ...
      INPUT PROCEDURE
         IS section-name-1 [{THROUGH / THRU} section-name-2]
      GIVING file-name-4
      OUTPUT PROCEDURE
         IS section-name-3 [{THROUGH / THRU} section-name-4] }
```

As can be seen, four combinations are possible. One can use INPUT PROCEDURE in combination with either GIVING or OUTPUT PROCEDURE. In similar fashion, USING may be used in conjunction with either GIVING or OUTPUT PROCEDURE. INPUT PROCEDURE is a more general technique than USING in that it permits one to sort on a calculated field, bypass records in an input file, combine matching records from two files into a single record for the sort, and so on.

Assume, for example, that an incoming record has both an employee's present and previous salary. USING permits a sort on *either* field, but *not* on percent salary increase because the latter is a *calculated* field (i.e., it is not contained in an incoming record per se but is calculated from two fields which are). The INPUT PROCEDURE option is required if sorting is on percent salary increase or, for that matter, on any other calculated field. Our discussion focuses on this option in conjunction with OUTPUT PROCEDURE.

When the SORT verb is encountered in a COBOL program, control passes to the *section* (or sections) specified as the INPUT PROCEDURE. The primary function of the INPUT PROCEDURE is to process incoming records and *release* them to the sort work file. When the INPUT PROCEDURE has concluded, a utility sort program takes control and sorts the file. After sorting, control is passed to the *section* (or sections) in the OUTPUT PROCEDURE, which *returns* records from the sorted file, prepares reports, and so on. At the conclusion of the OUTPUT PROCEDURE, control returns to the statement immediately under the SORT verb.

The syntax of the SORT verb shows that COLLATING SEQUENCE is an *optional* clause and may be associated with any of the four formats. Its inclusion, together with appropriate entries in the SPECIAL-NAMES paragraph, permits a choice of collating sequences; i.e., EBCDIC or ASCII. Omission of the clause defaults to the normal collating sequence of the machine; e.g., EBCDIC for IBM. (Collating sequence assumes importance only for alphanumeric keys. Letters come *before* numbers under EBCDIC, but *follow* numbers under ASCII.)

Within the SORT verb, multiple sort keys are listed in order of importance. (A maximum of 12 sort keys is permitted, but the user is kidding himself if he or she specifies more than three or four.) The statement

```
SORT EMPLOYEE-FILE
    ASCENDING KEY EMPLOYEE-LOCATION
    DESCENDING KEY EMPLOYEE-SERVICE
    ASCENDING EMPLOYEE-NAME...
```

has EMPLOYEE-LOCATION as the major (primary) key and EMPLOYEE-NAME as the minor (tertiary) key. The word KEY is an optional reserved word in the SORT statement and need not appear (e.g., ASCENDING EMPLOYEE-NAME). In this example, EMPLOYEE-FILE is the sort work file, and must be designated in an SD in the Data Division. An SD is analogous to an FD, and has the following syntax:

$$\text{SD file-name} \left[\text{DATA} \begin{Bmatrix} \underline{\text{RECORD}} \text{ IS} \\ \underline{\text{RECORDS}} \text{ ARE} \end{Bmatrix} \text{data-name-1 data-name-2} \right]$$

$$\left[\underline{\text{RECORD}} \text{ CONTAINS [integer-1 } \underline{\text{TO}}] \text{ integer-2 CHARACTERS} \right]$$

The RELEASE and RETURN verbs are required with the INPUT PROCEDURE/OUTPUT PROCEDURE format. The RELEASE verb appears in the INPUT PROCEDURE and has the format:

<u>RELEASE</u> record-name [<u>FROM</u> identifier]

The effect of the RELEASE verb is to *write* a record to the sort file. It provides the capability of passing only selected records to the sort program and/or to calculate new fields in selected records.

The RETURN statement appears in the OUTPUT PROCEDURE and has the form:

<u>RETURN</u> file-name [<u>INTO</u> identifier] AT <u>END</u> statement

The RETURN verb *reads* a record from the sorted file.

Use of the SORT verb and related statements is highlighted in the capsule summaries of Figures 3.13 and 3.14. Note well the following observations:

INPUT PROCEDURE/OUTPUT PROCEDURE Option

1. The INPUT PROCEDURE option is required to sort on a calculated field; it also permits the sort record to have a different record description than the incoming record. Further, only a *limited* number of designated records in the incoming file need to be passed to sort.

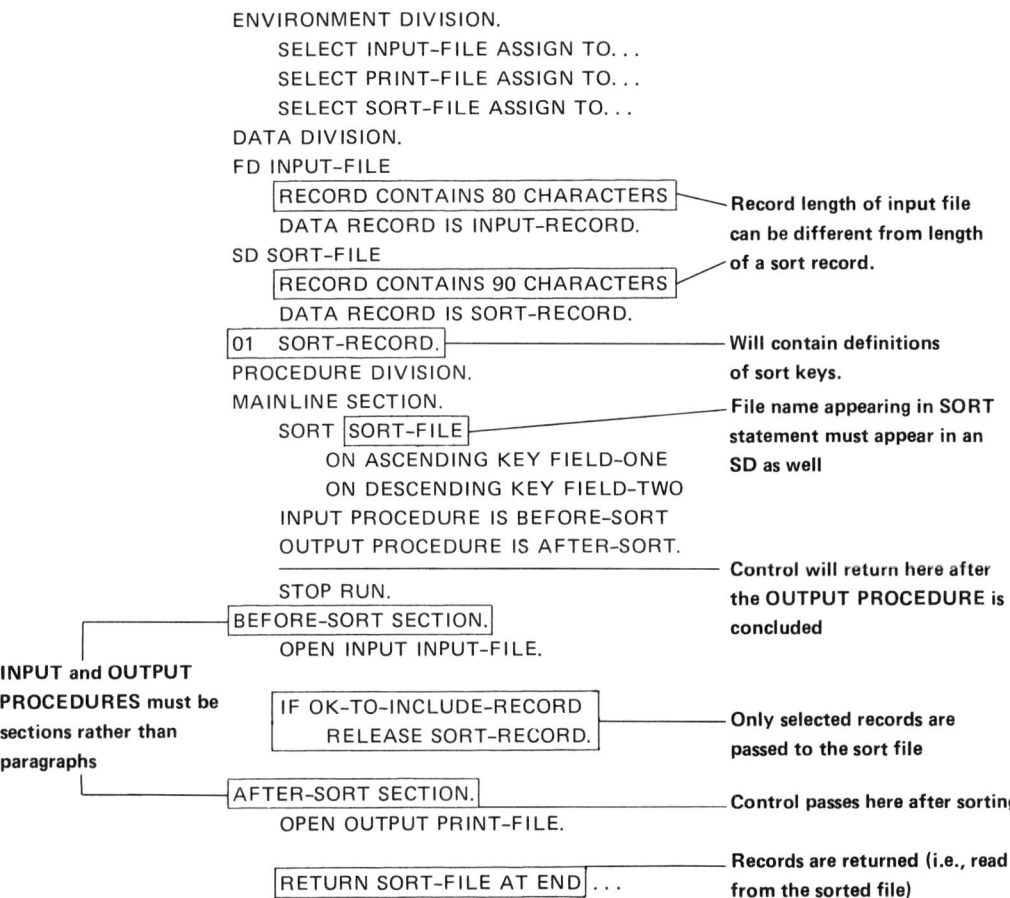

FIGURE 3.13 INPUT PROCEDURE/OUTPUT PROCEDURE option.

2. Both the INPUT and OUTPUT PROCEDURE *must* designate section names.

3. RELEASE is analogous to WRITE, and appears in the INPUT PROCEDURE to send a record to sort.

4. RETURN is analogous to READ, and appears in the OUTPUT PROCEDURE to read a record from the sorted file.

5. STOP RUN should appear in the "mainline" of the Procedure Division and must *not* appear in the OUTPUT PROCEDURE. When the SORT statement is executed, it transfers control to the INPUT PROCEDURE, after which control goes to the sort utility, and then to the OUPTUT PROCEDURE. When the latter is concluded, control returns to the statement under SORT. If STOP RUN is *wrongly* included in the OUTPUT PROCEDURE, control

```
ENVIRONMENT DIVISION.
    SELECT INPUT-FILE ASSIGN TO...
    SELECT SORT-FILE ASSIGN TO...          ── Extra file required to hold results from sort
    SELECT ORDERED-FILE ASSIGN TO...
DATA DIVISION.
FD INPUT-FILE
    RECORD CONTAINS 80 CHARACTERS
    DATA RECORD IS INPUT-RECORD.           ── All three files must have identical record layouts
FD ORDERED-FILE
    RECORD CONTAINS 80 CHARACTERS
    DATA RECORD IS ORDERED-RECORD.
SD SORT-FILE
    RECORD CONTAINS 80 CHARACTERS
    DATA RECORD IS SORT-RECORD.
01 SORT-RECORD.                            ── Will contain definitions of sort keys
PROCEDURE DIVISION.
    SORT SORT-FILE
        ON ASCENDING KEY FIELD-ONE
        ON DESCENDING KEY FIELD-TWO
    USING INPUT-FILE
    GIVING ORDERED-FILE.
```

FIGURE 3.14 USING/GIVING option.

will *still* be transferred to the statement under the SORT verb and the program will not terminate correctly.

USING/GIVING Option

1. The sort itself handles the I/O associated with the incoming file, and hence the RELEASE and RETURN verbs do *not* appear with the USING/GIVING option. The programmer must not open or close the incoming file.
2. The record descriptions for the input, sort-work, and ordered files must be identical; hence, the USING option *cannot* be used for a calculated field. Further, *every* record in the incoming file is automatically passed to sort.
3. Control passes directly to the sort utility which automatically reads records from the input file, and releases them to sort. When the sort is complete, control returns to the statement immediately under the SORT verb.
4. Sections are optional in the Procedure Division.

COBOL Case Study

This chapter discussed a number of diverse COBOL elements aimed at achieving proficiency in the language. The various statements, their syntax and capabilities, are best tied together by a complete example. Accordingly, we develop a program, and associated subprograms, to process a file of student records whose format is described in Figure 3.15:

```
01  STUDENT-RECORD.
    05  STU-SOC-SEC-NUMBER                      PIC X(9).
    05  STU-NAME-AND-INITIALS.
        10  STU-LAST-NAME                       PIC X(18).
        10  STU-INITIALS                        PIC XX.
    05  STU-DATE-OF-BIRTH.
        10  STU-BIRTH-MONTH                     PIC 99.
        10  STU-BIRTH-YEAR                      PIC 99.
    05  STU-SEX                                 PIC X.
    05  STU-MAJOR-CODE                          PIC X(3).
    05  STU-SCHOOL-CODE                         PIC 9.
    05  STU-CUMULATIVE-CREDITS                  PIC 9(3).
    05  STU-CUMULATIVE-POINTS                   PIC 9(3).
    05  STU-UNION-MEMBER-CODE                   PIC X.
    05  STU-SCHOLARSHIP                         PIC 9(3).
    05  STU-COURSES-THIS-SEMESTER OCCURS 6 TIMES.
        10  STU-COURSE-NUMBER                   PIC XXX.
        10  STU-COURSE-CREDITS                  PIC 9.
    05  FILLER                                  PIC X(8).
```

FIGURE 3.15 Student record description.

The required program is in essence a "glorified print program" in which incoming coded data are to be printed in a more readable format. STU-MAJOR-CODE and STU-SCHOOL-CODE are to be expanded in a subprogram using the techniques of a *sequential search* and *direct access* to table entries respectively. Individual course numbers for courses taken this semester are to be expanded in a *second* subprogram using a *binary search*. The table of course codes itself is to be initialized by reading values from a course file.

The input file has its records in sequence by social security number, while the printed report is to list students in decreasing order of grade point average. The latter is a calculated field, obtained by dividing STU-CUMULATIVE-CREDITS by STU-CUMULATIVE-POINTS. Moreover, only students with grade point averages of 3.00 or higher are to appear in the printed report.

Figures 3.16 and 3.17 present test data and associated output to further clarify the specifications. Figures 3.18, 3.19, and 3.20 contain the main and subprograms.

The Procedure Division of Figure 3.18 begins with the SORT statement of lines 169–172. SORT-FILE is a sort-work file and is defined in a SELECT statement (lines 16 and 17) and SD (lines 34–36). The sort key,

```
100000000ALBERT       A 0159MSTAL059118Y0151002200330044004501 3
200000000BROWN        B 0258FSTA1089275N0251002200330044004113 4443
233300000BAKER        B 0457FEEN3070275N02511134443
300000000CHARLES      C 0658MHIS2109286Y1005013503350435053506 3
```

Record is not selected because grade point average is too low (118/59)

FIGURE 3.16 Test data.

SRT-GRADE-POINT-AVERAGE, is defined *within* the record description of SORT-RECORD (line 56).

The SORT statement specifies an input and output procedure, both of which are *sections*. The input procedure does the necessary I/O for the sort work file. It reads records from STUDENT-FILE, calculates grade point average, and writes; i.e., *releases* a sort record.

The PERFORM verb of lines 180–181 is followed by a GO TO statement which may appear as a violation of structured programming. Recall, however, that the goal of structured programming is not the elimination of GO TO per se, but rather the development of easy-to-follow programs.

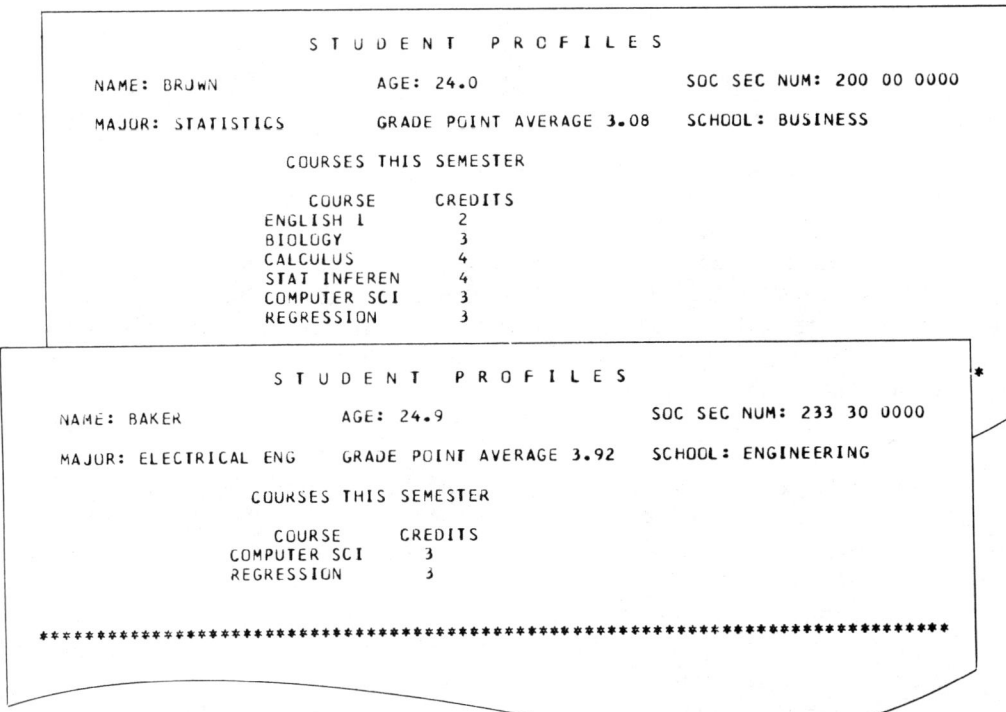

FIGURE 3.17 Sample output.

```
00001              IDENTIFICATION DIVISION.
00002              PROGRAM-ID.    MAINPROG.
00003              AUTHOR.        R. GRAUER.
00004
00005              ENVIRONMENT DIVISION.
00006              CONFIGURATION SECTION.
00007              SOURCE-COMPUTER.    IBM-4341.
00008              OBJECT-COMPUTER.    IBM-4341.
00009
00010              INPUT-OUTPUT SECTION.
00011              FILE-CONTROL.
00012                  SELECT STUDENT-FILE
00013                      ASSIGN TO UT-S-STUD.
00014                  SELECT PRINT-FILE                  Sort work file requires a SELECT statement
00015                      ASSIGN TO UT-S-PRINT.
00016                  SELECT SORT-FILE
00017                      ASSIGN TO UT-S-SORTWORK.
00018
00019              DATA DIVISION.
00020              FILE SECTION.
00021              FD  STUDENT-FILE
00022                  LABEL RECORDS ARE STANDARD
00023                  BLOCK CONTAINS 0 RECORDS
00024                  RECORD CONTAINS 80 CHARACTERS
00025                  DATA RECORD IS STUDENT-RECORD.
00026              01  STUDENT-RECORD              PIC X(80).
00027
00028              FD  PRINT-FILE
00029                  LABEL RECORDS ARE STANDARD
00030                  RECORD CONTAINS 133 CHARACTERS
00031                  DATA RECORD IS PRINT-LINE.
00032              01  PRINT-LINE                  PIC X(133).
00033
00034              SD  SORT-FILE                          Sort work file is defined in an SD
00035                  RECORD CONTAINS 80 CHARACTERS
00036                  DATA RECORD IS SORT-RECORD.
00037              01  SORT-RECORD.
00038                  05  SRT-SOC-SEC-NUMBER      PIC X(9).
00039                  05  SRT-NAME-AND-INITIALS.
00040                      10  SRT-LAST-NAME       PIC X(18).
00041                      10  SRT-INITIALS        PIC XX.
00042                  05  SRT-DATE-OF-BIRTH.
00043                      10  SRT-BIRTH-MONTH     PIC 99.
00044                      10  SRT-BIRTH-YEAR      PIC 99.
00045                  05  SRT-SEX                 PIC X.
00046                  05  SRT-MAJOR-CODE          PIC X(3).
00047                  05  SRT-SCHOOL-CODE         PIC 9.
00048                  05  SRT-CUMULATIVE-CREDITS  PIC 9(3).
00049                  05  SRT-CUMULATIVE-POINTS   PIC 9(3).
00050                  05  SRT-UNION-MEMBER        PIC X.
00051                  05  SRT-SCHOLARSHIP         PIC 999.
00052                  05  SRT-COURSES-THIS-SEMESTER
00053                      OCCURS 6 TIMES.
00054                      10  SRT-COURSE-NUMBER   PIC XXX.
                                                        Sort key is defined within sort record (see line 170)
00055                      10  SRT-COURSE-CREDITS  PIC 9.
00056                  05  SRT-GRADE-POINT-AVERAGE PIC 9V999.
00057                  05  FILLER                  PIC X(4).
00058
00059              WORKING-STORAGE SECTION.
00060              01  FILLER                      PIC X(27)
00061                  VALUE 'WS-MAIN PROGRAM BEGINS HERE'.
00062
00063              01  PROGRAM-SUBSCRIPTS.
00064                  05  WS-COURSE-SUB           PIC S9(4)  COMP.
00065
```

FIGURE 3.18 Main (calling) program.

```
00066           01  PROGRAM-SWITCHES.
00067               05  WS-DATA-REMAINS-SWITCH      PIC X(3) VALUE SPACES.
00068               05  WS-END-OF-SORT-FILE-SW      PIC X(3) VALUE SPACES.
00069
00070           01  WS-STUDENT-RECORD.
00071               05  STU-SOC-SEC-NUMBER          PIC X(9).
00072               05  STU-NAME-AND-INITIALS.
00073                   10  STU-LAST-NAME           PIC X(18).
00074                   10  STU-INITIALS            PIC XX.
00075               05  STU-DATE-OF-BIRTH.
00076                   10  STU-BIRTH-MONTH         PIC 99.
00077                   10  STU-BIRTH-YEAR          PIC 99.
00078               05  STU-SEX                     PIC X.
00079               05  STU-MAJOR-CODE              PIC X(3).
00080               05  STU-SCHOOL-CODE             PIC 9.
00081               05  STU-CUMULATIVE-CREDITS      PIC 9(3).
00082               05  STU-CUMULATIVE-POINTS       PIC 9(3).
00083               05  STU-UNION-MEMBER            PIC X.
00084               05  STU-SCHOLARSHIP             PIC 999.
00085               05  STU-COURSES-THIS-SEMESTER
00086                   OCCURS 6 TIMES.
00087                   10  STU-COURSE-NUMBER       PIC XXX.
00088                   10  STU-COURSE-CREDITS      PIC 9.
00089               05  FILLER                      PIC X(8).
00090
00091           01  WS-SUBROUTINE-PARAMETERS.
00092               05  WS-MAJOR-CODE               PIC X(3).
00093               05  WS-MAJOR-VALUE              PIC X(15).
00094               05  WS-SCHOOL-CODE              PIC 9.
00095               05  WS-SCHOOL-VALUE             PIC X(12).
00096
00097           01  WS-PASSED-COURSE-TABLE.
00098               05  CODE-AND-VALUE OCCURS 6 TIMES.
00099                   10  PASSED-COURSE-CODE      PIC X(3).
00100                   10  PASSED-COURSE-VALUE     PIC X(12).
00101
00102           01  WS-AGE                          PIC 99V9.
00103
00104           01  DATE-WORK-AREA.                           ─Holds date of execution
00105               05  TODAYS-YEAR                 PIC 99.    (see line 236)
00106               05  TODAYS-MONTH                PIC 99.
00107               05  TODAYS-DAY                  PIC 99.
00108
00109           01  PROFILE-LINE-ONE.
00110               05  FILLER                      PIC X    VALUE SPACES.
00111               05  FILLER                      PIC X(21) VALUE SPACES.
00112               05  FILLER                      PIC X(31)
00113                   VALUE 'S T U D E N T    P R O F I L E S'.
00114               05  FILLER                      PIC X(80) VALUE SPACES.
00115
00116           01  ASTERISK-LINE.
00117               05  FILLER                      PIC X    VALUE SPACES.
00118               05  FILLER                      PIC X(80) VALUE ALL '*'.
00119               05  FILLER                      PIC X(32) VALUE SPACES.
00120
00121           01  PROFILE-LINE-TWO.
00122               05  FILLER                      PIC X(3) VALUE SPACES.
00123               05  FILLER                      PIC X(6) VALUE 'NAME: '.
00124               05  PL2-NAME                    PIC X(18).
00125               05  FILLER                      PIC X    VALUE SPACES.
00126               05  FILLER                      PIC X(5) VALUE 'AGE: '.
00127               05  PL2-AGE                     PIC Z9.9.
00128               05  FILLER                      PIC X(18) VALUE SPACES.
00129               05  FILLER                      PIC X(13)
00130                   VALUE 'SOC SEC NUM: '.
00131               05  PL2-SOC-SEC-NUMBER          PIC 999B99B9999.
00132               05  FILLER                      PIC X(54) VALUE SPACES.
00133
00134           01  PROFILE-LINE-THREE.
```

FIGURE 3.18 *continued*

```
00135            05  FILLER                    PIC X(3)    VALUE SPACES.
00136            05  FILLER                    PIC X(7)    VALUE 'MAJOR: '.
00137            05  PL3-MAJOR                 PIC X(15)   VALUE SPACES.
00138            05  FILLER                    PIC X(3)    VALUE SPACES.
00139            05  FILLER                    PIC X(20)
00140                VALUE 'GRADE POINT AVERAGE '.
00141            05  PL3-GRADE-POINT-AVERAGE   PIC 9.99.
00142            05  FILLER                    PIC X(3)    VALUE SPACES.
00143            05  FILLER                    PIC X(8)    VALUE 'SCHOOL: '.
00144            05  PL3-SCHOOL                PIC X(12)   VALUE SPACES.
00145            05  FILLER                    PIC X(58)   VALUE SPACES.
00146
00147        01  PROFILE-LINE-FOUR.
00148            05  FILLER                    PIC X(20)   VALUE SPACES.
00149            05  FILLER                    PIC X(22)
00150                VALUE 'COURSES THIS SEMESTER'.
00151            05  FILLER                    PIC X(91)   VALUE SPACES.
00152
00153        01  PROFILE-LINE-FIVE.
00154            05  FILLER                    PIC X(22)   VALUE SPACES.
00155            05  FILLER                    PIC X(18)
00156                VALUE 'COURSE      CREDITS'.
00157            05  FILLER                    PIC X(93)   VALUE SPACES.
00158
00159        01  PROFILE-LINE-SIX.
00160            05  FILLER                    PIC X(18)   VALUE SPACES.
00161            05  PL6-COURSE                PIC X(12).
00162            05  FILLER                    PIC X(5)    VALUE SPACES.
00163            05  PL6-CREDITS               PIC 9.
00164            05  FILLER                    PIC X(97)   VALUE SPACES.
00165
00166    PROCEDURE DIVISION.
00167    SORTING SECTION.
00168    0000-MAINLINE.
00169         SORT SORT-FILE                                          ─── SORT statement
00170             DESCENDING KEY SRT-GRADE-POINT-AVERAGE
00171             INPUT PROCEDURE A-PROCESS-INPUT-FILE
00172             OUTPUT PROCEDURE B-PREPARE-REPORTS.
00173         STOP RUN.
00174                                                  ─── Input procedure is a section
00175    A-PROCESS-INPUT-FILE SECTION.
00176    A100-MAINLINE.
00177         OPEN INPUT STUDENT-FILE.
00178         READ STUDENT-FILE INTO WS-STUDENT-RECORD
00179             AT END MOVE 'NO' TO WS-DATA-REMAINS-SWITCH.
00180         PERFORM A200-READ-STUDENT-RECORDS
00181             UNTIL WS-DATA-REMAINS-SWITCH = 'NO'.
00182         CLOSE STUDENT-FILE.
00183         GO TO A300-EXIT.     ─── Forward GO TO to an EXIT paragraph
00184
00185    A200-READ-STUDENT-RECORDS.
00186         MOVE WS-STUDENT-RECORD TO SORT-RECORD.
00187         COMPUTE SRT-GRADE-POINT-AVERAGE
00188             = SRT-CUMULATIVE-POINTS / SRT-CUMULATIVE-CREDITS.
00189         RELEASE SORT-RECORD.   ─── Writes records to sort work file
00190         READ STUDENT-FILE INTO WS-STUDENT-RECORD
00191             AT END MOVE 'NO' TO WS-DATA-REMAINS-SWITCH.
00192
00193    A300-EXIT.   ─── Terminates input procedure
00194         EXIT.
00195                                          ─── Output procedure is a section
00196    B-PREPARE-REPORTS SECTION.
00197    B100-MAINLINE.                                    ─── Initial read
00198         OPEN OUTPUT PRINT-FILE.
00199         RETURN SORT-FILE
00200             AT END MOVE 'YES' TO WS-END-OF-SORT-FILE-SW.
00201         PERFORM B200-PROCESS-SORTED-RECORDS
00202             UNTIL WS-END-OF-SORT-FILE-SW = 'YES'.
```

FIGURE 3.18 *continued*

```
00203                CLOSE PRINT-FILE.
00204                GO TO B500-EXIT.
00205
00206          B200-PROCESS-SORTED-RECORDS.
00207                IF SRT-GRADE-POINT-AVERAGE > 3.00 OR = 3.00
00208                   PERFORM B300-EXPAND-CODES
00209                   PERFORM B400-PRINT-STUDENT-PROFILE.
00210                RETURN SORT-FILE
00211                   AT END MOVE 'YES' TO WS-END-OF-SORT-FILE-SW.
00212
00213          B300-EXPAND-CODES.
00214                MOVE SRT-MAJOR-CODE TO WS-MAJOR-CODE.
00215                MOVE SRT-SCHOOL-CODE TO WS-SCHOOL-CODE.
00216                CALL 'SUBRTN2'
00217                   USING WS-SUBROUTINE-PARAMETERS.
00218                MOVE SPACES TO WS-PASSED-COURSE-TABLE.
00219                PERFORM B350-BUILD-COURSE-TABLE
00220                   VARYING WS-COURSE-SUB FROM 1 BY 1
00221                      UNTIL WS-COURSE-SUB > 6
00222                         OR SRT-COURSE-NUMBER (WS-COURSE-SUB) = SPACES.
00223                CALL 'SUBRTN1'
00224                   USING WS-PASSED-COURSE-TABLE.
00225
00226          B350-BUILD-COURSE-TABLE.
00227                MOVE SRT-COURSE-NUMBER (WS-COURSE-SUB)
00228                   TO PASSED-COURSE-CODE (WS-COURSE-SUB).
00229
00230          B400-PRINT-STUDENT-PROFILE.
00231                WRITE PRINT-LINE FROM PROFILE-LINE-ONE
00232                   AFTER ADVANCING PAGE.
00233
00234                MOVE SRT-LAST-NAME TO PL2-NAME.
00235                MOVE SRT-SOC-SEC-NUMBER TO PL2-SOC-SEC-NUMBER.
00236                ACCEPT DATE-WORK-AREA FROM DATE.
00237                COMPUTE WS-AGE = TODAYS-YEAR - SRT-BIRTH-YEAR
00238                   + (TODAYS-MONTH - SRT-BIRTH-MONTH) / 12.
00239                MOVE WS-AGE TO PL2-AGE.
00240                WRITE PRINT-LINE FROM PROFILE-LINE-TWO
00241                   AFTER ADVANCING 2 LINES.
00242
00243                MOVE WS-MAJOR-VALUE TO PL3-MAJOR.
00244                MOVE SRT-GRADE-POINT-AVERAGE TO PL3-GRADE-POINT-AVERAGE.
00245                MOVE WS-SCHOOL-VALUE TO PL3-SCHOOL.
00246                WRITE PRINT-LINE FROM PROFILE-LINE-THREE
00247                   AFTER ADVANCING 2 LINES.
00248
00249                WRITE PRINT-LINE FROM PROFILE-LINE-FOUR
00250                   AFTER ADVANCING 2 LINES.
00251
00252                WRITE PRINT-LINE FROM PROFILE-LINE-FIVE
00253                   AFTER ADVANCING 2 LINES.
00254
00255                PERFORM B450-WRITE-COURSE-LINE
00256                   VARYING WS-COURSE-SUB FROM 1 BY 1
00257                      UNTIL WS-COURSE-SUB > 6
00258                         OR PASSED-COURSE-VALUE (WS-COURSE-SUB) = SPACES.
00259
00260                WRITE PRINT-LINE FROM ASTERISK-LINE
00261                   AFTER ADVANCING 3 LINES.
00262
00263          B450-WRITE-COURSE-LINE.
00264                MOVE PASSED-COURSE-VALUE (WS-COURSE-SUB) TO PL6-COURSE.
00265                MOVE SRT-COURSE-CREDITS (WS-COURSE-SUB) TO PL6-CREDITS.
00266                WRITE PRINT-LINE FROM PROFILE-LINE-SIX
00267                   AFTER ADVANCING 1 LINE.
00268
00269          B500-EXIT.
00270                EXIT.
```

FIGURE 3.18 *continued*

There are, in fact, some special situations where *there is no way of avoiding a GO TO statement*, and where its use may actually add to program clarity. *Such situations are extremely rare*, and must be restricted to a *forward* GO TO which transfers control to an EXIT paragraph.

In order to justify the presence of the GO TO statement, consider its removal from Figure 3.18. After the PERFORM statement of lines 180–181 terminates, STUDENT-FILE is closed, and the paragraph A200-READ-STUDENT-RECORDS would be reexecuted *after* the end of file had already been reached. Recall that the input procedure *must* be a section, and that it ends when the next section begins. Consequently, it is necessary to branch around the paragraph A200-READ-STUDENT-RECORDS, and hence the necessity of the GO TO statement. (The EXIT statement per se *does nothing;* it merely provides a destination for the forward GO TO. Realize also that the *ANS 74 standard* does not permit one to perform a section outside the input procedure. Given these restrictions, one *cannot avoid* a forward GO TO statement when using the input procedure. Its use, however, should certainly not be viewed as a catastrophe.)

After the input procedure concludes, control goes to the sort utility, then to the output procedure. The latter is also a section and begins on line 196. Its function is to prepare the desired report by reading (i.e., *returning*) records from the sort work file. Note the familiar structure of an initial "read" in line 199, followed by a PERFORM statement in which the *last* statement of the performed routine is a second read. PRINT-FILE is closed and a *forward* GO TO transfers control to the end of the output procedure. Execution continues with the STOP RUN statement of line 173; i.e., the statement immediately after the initial SORT verb of lines 169–172.

The logic in the output procedure is straightforward. Note well the two CALL statements for the *different* subprograms. Observe also that only a single 01 parameter is passed as an argument to each subprogram; hence, the need to build WS-SUBROUTINE-PARAMETERS and WS-PASSED-COURSE-TABLE prior to the respective CALL statements. The date of execution is obtained by the ACCEPT statement of line 236, after which WS-AGE is calculated. (The COMPUTE statement of lines 237 and 238 is best verified by "plugging in data," and playing computer.)

Figure 3.19 contains the subprogram to expand course codes to course descriptions. In addition, it contains logic necessary to initialize the course table by reading values from a file. The use of WS-ALREADY-EXECUTED-SWITCH in lines 56 and 57 ensures that the initialization is done only the first time the subprogram is called. The logic of 0080-INITIALIZE-COURSE-TABLE and 0090-READ-COURSE-FILE parallels that of Figure 3.6 and is not explained further.

The Linkage Section defines the subprogram's parameters, which are also referenced in the USING clause of the subprogram's Procedure Division header. The PERFORM statement of lines 60–63 executes a *maximum* of six times, once for each course. The SEARCH ALL statement of lines 69–73 implies a binary search and is executed for each entry in PASSED-COURSE-

```
00001              IDENTIFICATION DIVISION.
00002              PROGRAM-ID.    SUBRTN1.
00003              AUTHOR.        R. GRAUER.
00004
00005              ENVIRONMENT DIVISION.
00006              CONFIGURATION SECTION.
00007              SOURCE-COMPUTER.     IBM-4341.
00008              OBJECT-COMPUTER.     IBM-4341.
00009
00010              INPUT-OUTPUT SECTION.
00011              FILE-CONTROL.
00012                  SELECT COURSE-FILE
00013                      ASSIGN TO UT-S-COURSE.
00014
00015              DATA DIVISION.
00016              FILE SECTION.
00017              FD  COURSE-FILE
00018                  LABEL RECORDS ARE STANDARD
00019                  BLOCK CONTAINS 0 RECORDS
00020                  RECORD CONTAINS 80 CHARACTERS
00021                  DATA RECORD IS COURSE-RECORD.
00022              01  COURSE-RECORD.
00023                  05  IN-COURSE-CODE           PIC X(3).
00024                  05  IN-COURSE-VALUE          PIC X(15).
00025                  05  FILLER                   PIC X(62).
00026
00027              WORKING-STORAGE SECTION.
00028              01  FILLER                       PIC X(22)     ──Facilitates debugging
00029                  VALUE 'WS SUBRTN1 BEGINS HERE'.
00030
00031              01  WS-COURSE-TABLE.
00032                  05  COURSES OCCURS 1 TO 50 TIMES
00033                          DEPENDING ON WS-NUMBER-OF-COURSES
00034                          ASCENDING KEY IS COURSE-CODE
00035                          INDEXED BY COURSE-INDEX.
00036                      10  COURSE-CODE          PIC X(3).
00037                      10  COURSE-VALUE         PIC X(15).
00038
00039              01  PROGRAM-SWITCHES.
00040                  05  WS-ALREADY-EXECUTED-SWITCH PIC X(3)  VALUE 'NO'.
00041                  05  END-OF-COURSE-FILE-SWITCH  PIC X(3)  VALUE SPACES.
00042
00043              01  COUNTERS-AND-SUBSCRIPTS.
00044                  05  WS-NUMBER-OF-COURSES     PIC 9(3)   VALUE ZEROS.
00045                  05  COURSE-SUB               PIC S9(4)  COMP.
00046
00047              LINKAGE SECTION.  ──Defines passed parameters
00048              01  PASSED-PARAMETERS.
00049                  05  PASSED-COURSE-TABLE OCCURS 6 TIMES.
00050                      10  LS-CODE              PIC X(3).
00051                      10  LS-VALUE             PIC X(12).
00052
00053              PROCEDURE DIVISION
00054                  USING PASSED-PARAMETERS.
                                               ──Initializes course table only once
00055              0010-MAINLINE.
00056                  IF WS-ALREADY-EXECUTED-SWITCH = 'NO'
00057                      MOVE 'YES' TO WS-ALREADY-EXECUTED-SWITCH
00058                      PERFORM 0080-INITIALIZE-COURSE-TABLE.
00059
00060                  PERFORM 0030-EXPAND-COURSE-CODE
00061                      VARYING COURSE-SUB FROM 1 BY 1
00062                      UNTIL COURSE-SUB > 6
00063                          OR LS-CODE (COURSE-SUB) = SPACES.
00064
00065              0020-RETURN-TO-MAIN.            ──Expands a maximum of six course codes
00066                  EXIT PROGRAM.
```

FIGURE 3.19 First subprogram.

```
00067
00068           0030-EXPAND-COURSE-CODE.                          ⟋ Binary search
00069              SEARCH ALL COURSES
00070                 AT END
00071                    MOVE 'UNKNOWN' TO LS-VALUE (COURSE-SUB)
00072                 WHEN COURSE-CODE (COURSE-INDEX) = LS-CODE (COURSE-SUB)
00073                    MOVE COURSE-VALUE (COURSE-INDEX) TO LS-VALUE (COURSE-SUB).
00074
00075           0080-INITIALIZE-COURSE-TABLE.
00076              OPEN INPUT COURSE-FILE.
00077              READ COURSE-FILE
00078                 AT END MOVE 'YES' TO END-OF-COURSE-FILE-SWITCH.
00079              PERFORM 0090-READ-COURSE-FILE
00080                 VARYING COURSE-INDEX FROM 1 BY 1
00081                    UNTIL END-OF-COURSE-FILE-SWITCH = 'YES'.
00082              CLOSE COURSE-FILE.
00083                                                     ⟍ Initializes course table
00084           0090-READ-COURSE-FILE.
00085              IF WS-NUMBER-OF-COURSES > 50       ⟵ Checks that table size is not exceeded
00086                 DISPLAY 'ERROR - COURSE TABLE EXCEEDED'
00087                 MOVE 'YES' TO END-OF-COURSE-FILE-SWITCH
00088              ELSE
00089                 ADD 1 TO WS-NUMBER-OF-COURSES
00090                 MOVE IN-COURSE-CODE TO COURSE-CODE (COURSE-INDEX)
00091                 MOVE IN-COURSE-VALUE TO COURSE-VALUE (COURSE-INDEX).
00092
00093              READ COURSE-FILE
00094                 AT END MOVE 'YES' TO END-OF-COURSE-FILE-SWITCH.
```

FIGURE 3.19 *continued*

TABLE. The EXIT PROGRAM statement of line 66 returns control to the main program to the statement immediately after the original CALL.

Figure 3.20 contains the subprogram to expand the major and school codes. Both tables are initialized entirely within the subprogram, but the

```
00001           IDENTIFICATION DIVISION.
00002           PROGRAM-ID.   SUBRTN2.
00003           AUTHOR.       R. GRAUER.
00004
00005           ENVIRONMENT DIVISION.
00006           CONFIGURATION SECTION.
00007           SOURCE-COMPUTER.    IBM-4341.
00008           OBJECT-COMPUTER.    IBM-4341.
00009
00010           DATA DIVISION.                              ⟋ Facilitates debugging
00011           WORKING-STORAGE SECTION.
00012           01  FILLER                        PIC X(22)
00013               VALUE 'WS SUBRTN2 BEGINS HERE'.
00014
00015           01  SCHOOL-TABLE-AND-VALUES.
00016               05  SCHOOL-VALUES.
00017                   10  FILLER   PIC X(12)   VALUE 'BUSINESS'.
00018                   10  FILLER   PIC X(12)   VALUE 'LIBERAL ARTS'.
00019                   10  FILLER   PIC X(12)   VALUE 'ENGINEERING'.
00020                   10  FILLER   PIC X(12)   VALUE 'EDUCATION'.
00021
00022               05  SCHOOL-TABLE REDEFINES SCHOOL-VALUES.
00023                   10  SCHOOL-NAME OCCURS 4 TIMES   PIC X(12).
00024
00025           COPY TEMP.    ⟵ COPY statement brings in lines 26 - 44
```

FIGURE 3.20 Second subprogram.

```
00026 C          01  MAJOR-VALUES.
00027 C              05  FILLER          PIC X(18)   VALUE 'STASTATISTICS'.
00028 C              05  FILLER          PIC X(18)   VALUE 'FINFINANCE'.
00029 C              05  FILLER          PIC X(18)   VALUE 'MANMANAGEMENT'.
00030 C              05  FILLER          PIC X(18)   VALUE 'EDPDATA PROC'.
00031 C              05  FILLER          PIC X(18)   VALUE 'ENGENGLISH'.
00032 C              05  FILLER          PIC X(18)   VALUE 'BIOBIOLOGY'.
00033 C              05  FILLER          PIC X(18)   VALUE 'ECOECONOMICS'.
00034 C              05  FILLER          PIC X(18)   VALUE 'EENELECTRICAL ENG'.
00035 C              05  FILLER          PIC X(18)   VALUE 'MENMECHANICAL ENG'.
00036 C              05  FILLER          PIC X(18)   VALUE 'ELELEMENTARY ED'.
00037 C              05  FILLER          PIC X(18)   VALUE 'SEESECONDARY ED'.
00038 C              05  FILLER          PIC X(18)   VALUE 'SPESPECIAL ED'.
00039 C
00040 C          01  WS-MAJOR-TABLE REDEFINES MAJOR-VALUES.
00041 C              05  MAJORS OCCURS 12 TIMES
00042 C                  INDEXED BY MAJOR-INDEX.
00043 C                  10  MAJOR-CODE   PIC X(3).
00044 C                  10  MAJOR-VALUE  PIC X(15).
00045           01  COUNTERS-AND-SUBSCRIPTS.
00046               05  MAJOR-SUB                  PIC S9(4) COMP.
00047
00048           LINKAGE SECTION.
00049           01  PASSED-PARAMETERS.
00050               05  LS-MAJOR-CODE              PIC X(3).
00051               05  LS-MAJOR-VALUE             PIC X(15).
00052               05  LS-SCHOOL-CODE             PIC 9.
00053               05  LS-SCHOOL-VALUE            PIC X(12).
00054
00055           PROCEDURE DIVISION
00056               USING PASSED-PARAMETERS.
00057
00058           0010-MAINLINE.                    SET statement required prior to sequential SEARCH
00059               SET MAJOR-INDEX TO 1.
00060               SEARCH MAJORS
00061                   AT END MOVE 'UNKNOWN' TO LS-MAJOR-VALUE
00062                   WHEN LS-MAJOR-CODE = MAJOR-CODE (MAJOR-INDEX)
00063                       MOVE MAJOR-VALUE (MAJOR-INDEX) TO LS-MAJOR-VALUE.
00064
00065               IF LS-SCHOOL-CODE > 0 AND < 5         Check for invalid code
00066                   MOVE SCHOOL-NAME (LS-SCHOOL-CODE) TO LS-SCHOOL-VALUE
00067               ELSE
00068                   MOVE 'UNKNOWN' TO LS-SCHOOL-VALUE.
00069
00070           0020-RETURN-TO-MAIN.              Returns control to calling program
00071               EXIT PROGRAM.
```

FIGURE 3.20 *continued*

school codes are "hard coded," whereas the major codes are established through a COPY statement. This technique facilitates subsequent change, particularly if the major table appears in multiple programs. Only a *single* modification has to be made, to the COPY entry TEMP, which causes any program using a COPY statement to receive the new table. Realize, however, that these programs have to be *recompiled* as the COPY occurs at compile rather than execution time. *Consequently, initializing a table is best accomplished by reading values from a file* as was done in the other subprogram (Figure 3.19).

The major table is expanded via a sequential search on lines 60–63. Note well the SET statement of line 59 to initialize MAJOR-INDEX prior to the table lookup.

LS-SCHOOL-CODE is expanded via "direct access" to the school table in line 66. (The value of LS-SCHOOL-CODE is first validated in the implied IF statement of line 65.)

Summary

This chapter dealt with several "advanced" COBOL features, all of which the practitioner is expected to know. These included all forms of table processing, sorting, subprograms, and the use of dates in various calculations. Depending on the reader's background, the material may have been completely new, or simply a pleasant review. Either way, the author hopes he has answered any lingering questions.

We emphasize that the major features are effectively summarized by the programs of Figures 3.18, 3.19, and 3.20. In addition, the reader is well advised to attempt the programming projects to further solidify his or her proficiency.

True/False

1. Indexes offer a syntactical advantage over subscripts in that they permit addition and subtraction within parentheses.
2. A subscript may not be used on a table that was defined with an index.
3. The same subscript can reference many tables.
4. The same index can reference many tables.
5. DAY and DATE are equivalent.
6. JULIAN-DATE is a reserved word containing the Julian date.
7. 83001 is an example of a Julian date.
8. The COPY clause is not permitted in the Procedure Division.
9. A given entry cannot contain both an OCCURS clause and a PICTURE clause.
10. The LINKAGE SECTION appears in the calling program.
11. The order of parameters in a USING clause is unimportant.
12. A given program cannot contain more than a single CALL statement.
13. A subprogram consists of only the Data and Procedure Divisions.
14. Subscripting is more efficient than indexing.
15. A subscript of 1 refers to the first element in a table.
16. An index whose internal value (i.e., displacement) is zero refers to the first element in a table.
17. SEARCH and SEARCH ALL are interchangeable.

18. Indexes can be manipulated in a PERFORM statement.
19. Subscripts can be manipulated in a PERFORM statement.
20. ASCENDING (DESCENDING) KEY is required in an OCCURS clause if the SEARCH verb is used.
21. A binary search could be applied to a table if the elements were arranged in descending sequence.
22. A linear search over a table of 500 elements requires nine or fewer comparisons.
23. A binary search over a table of 500 elements requires nine or fewer comparisons.
24. The SORT verb cannot be used on a calculated field.
25. The SORT verb can use INPUT PROCEDURE in conjunction with GIVING.
26. The SORT verb can use OUTPUT PROCEDURE in conjunction with USING.
27. RETURN is present in the OUTPUT PROCEDURE.
28. The SORT verb cannot contain more than two sort keys.
29. The collating sequence used in a sort can be other than EBCDIC.
30. A COPY clause may appear within a COPY.
31. The USAGE clause is required when defining a subscript.
32. The EXIT statement returns control to a calling program.
33. The REDEFINES clause *must* be used to initialize a table.
34. STOP RUN should appear in either the INPUT or OUTPUT procedure.
35. The COPY statement is invoked at execution rather than compile time.

Problems

1. (a) Write the COBOL code to convert a calendar date in the form yymmdd to a Julian date in the form yyddd. (Use the entries from Figure 3.10 as appropriate.)
   (b) Develop the code necessary to compute the number of days between two calendar dates, CALENDAR-DATE (1) and CALENDAR-DATE (2), where CALENDAR-DATE (1) occurred *after* CALENDAR-DATE (2). CALENDAR-DATE is in the form yymmdd.
   (c) Given the following table definition:

   ```
   05  SERIES-OF-DATES
          OCCURS 10 TIMES
          INDEXED BY DATE-INDEX.
       10  CALENDAR-DATE        PIC 9(6).
       10  ELAPSED-DAYS         PIC 9(4).
   ```

   Compute the value of ELAPSED-DAYS where ELAPSED-DAYS (1) contains the days between CALENDAR-DATE (1) and CALENDAR-DATE (2), ELAPSED-DAYS (2) contains the days between CALENDAR-DATE (2) and (3), and so on.

Your solution should compute up to 9 possible values; i.e., ELAPSED-DAYS (9) is the number of days between CALENDAR-DATE (9) and (10).
(d) Present your solution to part (c) to the class in a structured walkthrough. (See Chapter 5 for guidelines.)

2. Given the statement:

          SORT SORT-WORK-FILE
             ASCENDING KEY SORT-LOCATION
             DESCENDING KEY SORT-DEPARTMENT
             ASCENDING KEY SORT-NAME
          USING EMPLOYEE-FILE
          OUTPUT PROCEDURE PREPARE-REPORTS.

   (a) What is the major key?
   (b) What is the minor key?
   (c) Which file will be specified in an SD?
   (d) Which file will be specified in an FD?
   (e) Which file(s) will be specified in a SELECT?
   (f) Which file contains the input data?
   (g) Which file must contain the data name SORT-LOCATION?
   (h) Is PREPARE-REPORTS a paragraph or section?

3. Draw an appropriate schematic indicating the storage assignment for the COBOL entries:

   (a) 01   SALES-TOTALS.
           05   REGION OCCURS 5 TIMES.
               10   CITY OCCURS 2 TIMES.
                   15   SALESMAN OCCURS 3 TIMES   PIC 9(4).

   (b) Given the COBOL definition in part (a), indicate whether the following entries are syntactically valid; in addition, specify which entries are syntactically valid but likely to cause problems in execution.

       i.   REGION (5)
       ii. SALESMAN (1, 2, 3)
       iii. SALESMAN (5, 3)
       iv. SALESMAN (5, 4, 3)
       v.   CITY (2)
       vi. CITY (1, 2)
       vii. SALES-TOTALS

4. How can the program of Figure 3.18 be made more efficient? Is there a difference between machine and algorithmic efficiency? How important is efficiency as a criterion of "good" programs? Is it worth the effort?

5. Given the following table definition:

       01   LOCATION-VALUE.
           05   FILLER   PIC X(16)   VALUE '010ATLANTA   '.
           05   FILLER   PIC X(16)   VALUE '020BOSTON   '.
           05   FILLER   PIC X(16)   VALUE '030CHICAGO   '.
           05   FILLER   PIC X(16)   VALUE '040DETROIT   '.
           05   FILLER   PIC X(16)   VALUE '050KANSAS CITY   '.

```
            05  FILLER                    PIC X(16)  VALUE '060LOS ANGELES   '.
            05  FILLER                    PIC X(16)  VALUE '070NEW YORK      '.
            05  FILLER                    PIC X(16)  VALUE '080PHILADELPHIA '.
            05  FILLER                    PIC X(16)  VALUE '090SAN FRANCISCO'.
            05  FILLER                    PIC X(16)  VALUE '045DENVER        '.
        01  LOCATION-TABLE REDEFINES LOCATION-VALUE.
            05  LOCATION OCCURS 10 TIMES
                ASCENDING KEY IS LOCATION-CODE
                INDEXED BY LOCATION-INDEX.
                10  LOCATION-CODE    PIC X(3).
                10  LOCATION-NAME    PIC X(13).
```

and the following Procedure Division code:

```
        SET LOCATION-INDEX TO 1.
        SEARCH LOCATION
            AT END DISPLAY  ' * ERROR IN LINEAR SEARCH FOR DENVER'
            WHEN LOCATION-CODE (LOCATION-INDEX) = '045'
            DISPLAY 'LINEAR SEARCH OK FOR DENVER'.
        SEARCH LOCATION
            AT END DISPLAY  ' * ERROR IN LINEAR SEARCH FOR NEW YORK'
            WHEN LOCATION-CODE (LOCATION-INDEX) = '070'
            DISPLAY 'LINEAR SEARCH OK FOR NEW YORK'.
```

(a) Indicate the output that will be produced.
(b) Code a *binary* search statement to expand code 045 for Denver. Do you expect any trouble in the execution of that statement?

Projects

1. Develop a program to prepare a set of employee profiles which provide detailed information on each employee. An approximate report format is shown in Figure 3.21.

			PERSONNEL PROFILE					
NAME:	JONES, A.B.		EDUCATION: 2 YR. DEGREE*			SOC-SEC-NO.: 123-45-6789		
AGE:	21.4 YEARS		HIRE DATE: 1/79			LOCATION: NEW YORK*		

				SALARY HISTORY				
SALARY	DATE	TYPE	PERCENT INCREASE	MONTHS BETWEEN INCREASE	ANNUAL RATE OF INCREASE	GRADE	GRADE MIDPOINT	PERCENT GRADE MIDPOINT
$12,100	7/80	P	10.0	6	20.0%	4	$16,000	75.6
$11,000	1/80	M	10.0	12	10.0%	3	$12,000	91.6
$10,000	1/79	H				3	$12,000	83.3

JOB DESCRIPTION	
TITLE	DATE
JR. PROGRAMMER*	7/80
TRAINEE	1/79

*Note: In this project coded values may appear for education, location, and title. The codes will be expanded in project 2.

FIGURE 3.21 Employee profile report format.

```
01  EMPLOYEE-RECORD.
    05  EMP-SOC-SEC-NUMBER              PIC X(9).
    05  EMP-NAME-AND-INITIALS           PIC X(14).
    05  EMP-DATE-OF-BIRTH.
        10  EMP-BIRTH-MONTH             PIC 99.
        10  EMP-BIRTH-YEAR              PIC 99.
    05  EMP-DATE-OF-HIRE.
        10  EMP-HIRE-MONTH              PIC 99.
        10  EMP-HIRE-YEAR               PIC 99.
    05  EMP-LOCATION-CODE               PIC 99.
    05  EMP-EDUCATION-CODE              PIC 9.
    05  EMP-TITLE-DATA OCCURS 2 TIMES.
        10  EMP-TITLE-CODE              PIC X(2).
        10  EMP-TITLE-DATE              PIC 9(4).
    05  EMP-SEX                         PIC X.
    05  EMP-SALARY-DATA OCCURS 3 TIMES.
        10  EMP-SALARY                  PIC 9(5).
        10  EMP-SALARY-TYPE             PIC X.
        10  EMP-SALARY-DATE.
            15  EMP-SALARY-MONTH        PIC 99.
            15  EMP-SALARY-YEAR         PIC 99.
        10  EMP-SALARY-GRADE            PIC 9.
```

FIGURE 3.22 Record description.

The record description is shown in Figure 3.22 and test data are provided in Figure 3.23. Employee profiles are to appear two per page with a page heading on every new page. Note well the following requirements which continue on page 90:

(a) Employee age is to be calculated from date of birth and date of program execution.
(b) The social security number requires the insertion of hyphens; accomplish this by defining an output picture containing blanks in appropriate positions, and then replace the blanks through the INSPECT verb.
(c) Percent salary increase, months between increase, and annual rate of salary increase all require two sets of salary data; present and previous, or previous and second previous. Do not attempt a calculation when there are insufficient data.

```
100000000DOE            J  12441177103551178451177 M23000M1178721500M1177500000
200000000WILCOX         PA10481177303451177         M19000M1178517500H1177400000
400000000LEVINE         S  01500876304450878        F19000H0876500000         00000
444444444LOWELL         S  01501178304451178        M18000H1178500000         00000
500000000SMITHERS       M  03460172404601177        M28000M0876726500M0575725000M05746
600000000SUPERPROG      S  04571077405451077        M39000H1077900000         00000
800000000PERSNICKETY    P  08550378403450378        M09000H0378300000         00000
900000000MILGROM        MB11550977103450977         F12000M1178410000M0578309000H09773
910000000BAKER          AA01460877056550877         M60000M1179955000M1178950000H08779
920000000MARKS          BB02470679056550680450679 F22000M0880920000H0679800000
930000000GOLDEN         CC03480980156550980         M30000H0980900000
940000000SUGRUE         DD04491079155181079         M24000H1079600000
950000000GITLOW         FF05501079408201079         F28000H1079700000
                           ↑
                           └─ column 22
```

FIGURE 3.23 Test data.

(d) Percent salary increase is found by subtracting the old salary from the new salary, dividing the result by the old salary, and multiplying by 100. For example, new and old salaries of $11,000 and $10,000, respectively, yield an increase of 10%.
(e) Months between increase is simply the number of months between two salary dates.
(f) Annual rate of salary increase is found by converting the percent salary increase to a 12-month basis; 10% after 6 months is equivalent to an annual rate of 20%, 10% after two years is an annual rate of 5%.
(g) The salary midpoint measures the average salary for all employees at a particular grade level. (All employees are assigned a grade from 1 to 9 to indicate their level of responsibility in the company; for example, a janitor might have a grade of 1, and the president a grade of 9.) The salary midpoint is found by multiplying the grade level by $4,000 (for example, a grade of 4 has a midpoint of $16,000).
(h) The percent of grade midpoint is found by dividing an individual's salary by his or her grade midpoint and multiplying by 100.
(i) Sort the incoming file so that the employee profiles appear in alphabetical order.
(j) Coded values may appear in the profiles for education, location, and title. (The codes are expanded in the second project.)

2. Enlarge the profile program of the first project to print expanded values (rather than codes) for education, location, and title. This program is to be written as a subprogram and called from the first project. It is to accept codes passed from the first project and return expanded values. There are a total of eight parameters as follows: location-code (PIC 99), expanded location (PIC X(15)), title-code (PIC XX), expanded title (PIC X(15)), previous title code (PIC XX), previous title (PIC X(15)), education code (PIC 9), and expanded education (PIC X(17)).

Education code is to be expanded via a *direct* lookup (the code itself indicates the position in the table of expanded values). Use the following table:

Code	Education
1	Some H.S.
2	H.S. diploma
3	Two-year degree
4	Four-year degree
5	Some grad school
6	Master's degree
7	Ph.D.
8	Other grad degree

Location code is to be expanded through a *sequential search*, using the table provided. The location table is to be established, using the OCCURS, VALUE, and REDEFINES clauses. Use the following data:

Code	Location
05	Atlanta
10	Boston
15	Chicago
20	Detroit
25	Kansas City

Code	Location
30	Los Angeles
35	Minneapolis
40	New York
45	Philadelphia

Title code is to be expanded, using a *binary search*, with the table initialized by *dynamically* reading values from a file in the following format: title code in columns 1 and 2, expanded title in columns 3 through 17. The maximum table length is 100 titles. Your program is to contain sufficient logic so that the file of title codes (shown below) is read only once, the first time the subprogram is called.

Code	Title
18	Sr. accountant
20	Auditor
35	Jr. programmer
45	Sr. programmer
55	Analyst
60	Manager

4 Guidelines, Techniques, and Philosophies

Overview

The word "standard" was deliberately omitted from this chapter's title in favor of the word "guideline." The author does believe in uniform coding practices within an installation, but urges that a sense of flexibility be maintained. Many rules do have a legitimate exception. For example, does anyone other than the corporate standard bearer believe that the standard, "avoid constants" means one must code ADD *ONE* TO COUNTER or MULTIPLY FEET BY *TWELVE* GIVING INCHES? Is clarity really enhanced by enforcing a standard in such instances?

In addition, blind allegiance to rigid standards is never a guarantee that the original intention behind the standard is fulfilled. Very often, nothing is gained by adhering to the letter, rather than the spirit, of the law. Consider, for example, the admonition to eliminate 77-level entries. Does a global change to 01 from 77 via a text editor accomplish anything?

Another reason for avoiding the word "standard" is that many reasonable guidelines cannot be quantified. Few would disagree that cryptic data names of one and two characters are undesirable. Does that suggest we adopt a standard that all data names be at least 10 characters in length? Isn't the *guideline* "use *meaningful* data names" more appropriate than an absolute standard?

Regardless of what they are called, individuals and installations alike develop a series of strategies to increase the readability of the programs they produce. The author divides his strategies into three groups. *Cosmetics* are concerned with the overall appearance of a program, *techniques* are a series of COBOL "dos and don'ts," and *philosophies* are attitudes about what is and isn't important. All of the following are discussed within the chapter. Specifically:

Cosmetics:

    Indent

    Choose meaningful data names

    Format the Data Division

    Space attractively

    Avoid commas

    Use columns 73-80

    Restrict switches and subscripts to a single use

    Avoid constants

    Place modules so they can be found

    Use appropriate comments

Techniques:

    Perform paragraphs not sections

    Avoid MOVE CORRESPONDING

    Eliminate 77-level entries

    Use 88-level entries to reduce compound conditions

    Use the COMPUTE verb for multiple arithmetic operations

    Avoid literals

    Initialize tables dynamically

    Use READ INTO, WRITE FROM, and WS BEGINS HERE

    Pass a single 01 parameter to a subprogram

    Consider Report Writer

Philosophies:

    Keep it simple

    Downplay efficiency, but choose the algorithm carefully

Code defensively

Think first, code later

Collectively, the guidelines in the chapter constitute a programming style. The author does not expect agreement on every item and welcomes dissenting opinion. Indeed, if you have sound and consistent reasons for objecting to an element of the style presented here, you are on your way to developing your own.

Guidelines

Indent

Almost no one argues against indenting successive level numbers within a record description in the Data Division. Why then do students and even practitioners resist indentation in the Procedure Division? Consider:

Poor Code:

```
PERFORM INITIALIZE-TABLE VARYING LOCATION-SUB FROM 1
BY 1 UNTIL LOCATION-SUB > 3 AFTER DEPARTMENT-SUB
FROM 1 BY 1 UNTIL DEPARTMENT-SUB > 5.

WRITE ISAM-RECORD INVALID KEY
    MOVE 'YES' TO INVALID-ISAM-KEY-SWITCH
PERFORM WRITE-ERROR-MESSAGE.

IF EMPLOYEE-AGE > 65 MOVE EMP-NAME TO
PRINT-RETIREMENT-NAME, ADD 1 TO
NUMBER-OF-RETIREES, PERFORM WRITE-RETIREE-REPORT.
```

Improved Code:

```
PERFORM INITIALIZE-TABLE
    VARYING LOCATION-SUB FROM 1 BY 1
        UNTIL LOCATION-SUB > 3
    AFTER DEPARTMENT-SUB FROM 1 BY 1
        UNTIL DEPARTMENT-SUB > 5.

WRITE ISAM-RECORD
    INVALID KEY
        MOVE 'YES' TO INVALID-ISAM-KEY-SWITCH
        PERFORM WRITE-ERROR-MESSAGE.

IF EMPLOYEE-AGE > 65
    MOVE EMP-NAME TO PRINT-RETIREMENT-NAME
    ADD 1 TO NUMBER-OF-RETIREES
    PERFORM WRITE-RETIREE-REPORT.
```

As can be seen from the improved code, subservient clauses should always be indented under the main verbs. The readability of PERFORM, for example, is improved immeasurably by indenting VARYING under PERFORM, and UNTIL under VARYING. Other examples in the same vein include:

>   AFTER (BEFORE) ADVANCING under WRITE
>   AT END and WHEN under SEARCH
>   AT END and INVALID KEY under READ
>   SIZE ERROR under COMPUTE
>   GIVING under ADD, MULTIPLY, SUBTRACT, and DIVIDE

Indentation should always be *consistent* with compiler interpretation. The INVALID KEY clause, for example, is terminated by a period and the indentation should reflect this. INVALID KEY is written on a line by itself in the improved code with two subservient statements (MOVE and PERFORM) indented under it. All actions taken as a result of an IF should be indented as well, as shown in the last example.

The nested IF statement is worthy of special mention. The compiler does not interpret ELSE clauses as the programmer writes them but *associates the ELSE clause with the closest unpaired previous* IF. Consider:

Poor Code:

```
IF CD-SEX IS EQUAL TO 'M'
    IF CD-AGE IS GREATER THAN 30
        MOVE CD-NAME TO MALE-OVER-30
        ADD 1 TO NUMBER-QUALIFIED-MALES
    ELSE MOVE CD-NAME TO PRT-NAME
    ADD 1 TO MALE-UNDER-30.
```

The indentation implies that CD-NAME will be moved to PRT-NAME if CD-SEX is not equal to 'M.' This is *not* the compiler interpretation. The ELSE clause is associated with the closest previous IF which is not already paired with another ELSE. Therefore, the compiler will move CD-NAME to PRT-NAME if CD-SEX equals 'M' but CD-AGE is not greater than 30.

Nested IFs should be coded as follows:

1. Indent successive IFs four columns
2. Put the word ELSE on a line by itself, and directly under its associated IF
3. Indent detail lines for both IF and ELSE four columns

The previous nested IF statement is rewritten to reflect these guidelines:

Guidelines

Improved Code:

```
IF CD-SEX IS EQUAL TO 'M'
    IF CD-AGE IS GREATER THAN 30
        MOVE CD-NAME TO MALE-OVER-30
        ADD 1 TO NUMBER-QUALIFIED-MALES
    ELSE
        MOVE CD-NAME TO PRT-NAME
        ADD 1 TO MALE-UNDER-30.
```

Choose Meaningful Names

The COBOL compiler is very lenient with its rules for programmer-chosen names. Specifically, a user-defined word may not exceed 30 characters or begin or end with a hyphen. Valid characters for inclusion in a user defined word are A through Z, 0 through 9, and the hyphen. File and data names must contain at least one alphabetic character, whereas paragraph and section names may be all numeric. It is strongly recommended that these rules be amended as follows:

1. *Data* names should be *mnemonically* significant, and two and three-character cryptic names specifically avoided. It is impossible for the maintenance programmer, or even the original author, to determine the meaning of abbreviated data names. The usual programmer response is that this guideline adds unnecessarily to the burden of writer's cramp. Realize, however, that initial coding takes only 10-15% of the total time associated with a program. (Maintenance, testing, and debugging take the vast majority of time.) Hence, the modest increase in initial coding is more than compensated by subsequent improvements in the latter activities. Some examples:

Poor Choice:

```
SWITCH-ONE
TOTAL-1
TRANS-ID
```

Improved Choice:

```
END-OF-TRANSACTION-FILE-SWITCH
TOTAL-EMPLOYEE-GROSS-PAY
TRANSACTION-ID-NUMBER
```

2. *File* names should fully indicate the purpose of the file and include the suffix-FILE. A file name should never be tied to a physical device. Some examples:

Poor Choice:

> CUSTOMER-MASTER
> PRINT-FILE
> CARD-FILE

Improved Choice:

> CUSTOMER-MASTER-FILE
> EMPLOYEE-EXCEPTION-REPORT-FILE
> TRANSACTION-FILE

3. *Paragraph* names should be *functional* in nature, and reflect the purpose of the paragraph. A paragraph name should consist of a verb, an adjective or two, and an object: READ-TRANSACTION-FILE, ADD-NEW-RECORD, and so on. If a paragraph cannot be named in this manner, it is probably not functional, and consideration should be given to redesigning the program and/or paragraph.

Paragraph names should also be sequenced. Programmers and managers alike accept the utility of this guideline to quickly locate paragraphs in the Procedure Division. There is, however, considerable disagreement on just what sequencing scheme to use; all numbers, a single letter followed by numbers, etc. We make no strong argument for one scheme over another, other than to insist a consistent sequencing rule be followed. Some examples:

Poor Choice:

> 0005-MAINLINE
> A010-READ-AND-WRITE
> READ-TRANSACTION-FILE

Improved Choice:

> A010-WRITE-NEW-MASTER-RECORD
> 1000-PRODUCE-ERROR-REPORT
> 2000-READ-TRANSACTION-FILE

Format the Data Division

Most programmers already exercise reasonable care in preparing the Data Division. Nevertheless, the author suggests the following guidelines:

- Prefix all data names within the same FD or 01 with two or three characters unique to the FD; e.g., OM-LAST-NAME, OM-BIRTH-DATE, etc. The utility of this guideline becomes apparent in the

Procedure Division if it is necessary to refer back to the definition of a data name.
- Begin all PICTURE clauses in the same column, usually between columns 36-48, but the choice is arbitrary. Do not be unduly disturbed if one or two entries stray from the designated column because of long data names and/or indentation of level numbers. (Similar guidelines apply to USAGE and VALUE clauses as well. It is generally preferable, however, to keep a long VALUE clause on one line even if it means giving up vertical alignment.)
- Choose one form of the PICTURE clause (PIC, PIC IS, PICTURE, or PICTURE IS), and follow it consistently. PIC is the shortest, and is as good as any. (Similar guidelines apply to the USAGE and VALUE clauses.)
- Indent successive level numbers under an 01 by a consistent amount; e.g., two or four columns. Leave "gaps" between adjacent levels; e.g., 01, 05, 10, 15, or 01, 04, 08, 12, instead of using consecutive numbers; i.e., avoid 01, 02, 03. Use the *same* level numbers from FD to FD to maintain consistency within a program.
- Indent successive lines of the same entry, when a particular data name has subservient clauses. For example, the INDEXED BY and ASCENDING KEY clauses should be indented under the original OCCURS clause.

Space Attractively

The adoption of various spacing conventions can go a long way toward improving the appearance and readability of a program. The author believes very strongly in the insertion of blank lines throughout a program to highlight important statements. Specific suggestions include a blank line before all paragraphs, before FDs and/or 01 entries, and even before specific verbs.

The reader can also cause various portions of a listing to begin on a new page. This is accomplished in the ANS 74 standard by putting a slash in column 7 of a source statement, and leaving the rest of the line blank. The next source statement ejects to a new page.

Avoid Commas

The compiler treats a comma as noise; it has no effect on the generated object code. Many programmers have acquired the habit of inserting commas to increase legibility. While this works rather well with prose, it can have just the opposite effect in COBOL. This is because of the blurred print chains which make it difficult to distinguish a comma from a period. As we have already seen, the presence or absence of a period is critical. Hence, the inability to distinguish a period from a comma becomes rather annoying. The best solution is to try to avoid commas altogether.

Use Columns 73-80

Although columns 73-80 are optional, they can be put to good use; e.g., to indicate program modifications. Any statement which is added or altered ought to have the maintenance programmer's initials and date of modification. Thus, RTG01/83 would indicate the programmer RTG modified (or added) this statement in January 1983.

Restrict Switches and Subscripts to a Single Use

Data names defined as switches and/or subscripts should be restricted to a single use; i.e., common coupling should be avoided. Consider:

Poor Code:

```
77  SUBSCRIPT                          PIC S9(4).
77  EOF-SWITCH                         PIC X(3)      VALUE SPACES.
 .
 . .

    PERFORM INITIALIZE-TITLE-FILE
        UNTIL EOF-SWITCH = 'YES'.

    MOVE SPACES TO EOF-SWITCH.

    PERFORM PROCESS-EMPLOYEE-RECORDS
        UNTIL EOF-SWITCH = 'YES'.

    PERFORM COMPUTE-SALARY-HISTORY
        VARYING SUBSCRIPT FROM 1 BY 1
            UNTIL SUBSCRIPT > 3.

    PERFORM FIND-MATCHING-TITLE
        VARYING SUBSCRIPT FROM 1 BY 1
            UNTIL SUBSCRIPT > 100.
```

Improved Code:

```
01  PROGRAM-SUBSCRIPTS.
    05  TITLE-SUBSCRIPT                PIC S9(4).
    05  SALARY-SUBSCRIPT               PIC S9(4).

01  END-OF-FILE-SWITCHES.
    05  END-OF-TITLE-FILE-SWITCH       PIC X(3)      VALUE SPACES.
    05  END-OF-EMPLOYEE-FILE-SWITCH    PIC X(3)      VALUE SPACES.
 .
 . .

    PERFORM INITIALIZE-TITLE-FILE
        UNTIL END-OF-TITLE-FILE-SWITCH = 'YES'.
```

```
PERFORM PROCESS-EMPLOYEE-RECORDS
    UNTIL END-OF-EMPLOYEE-FILE-SWITCH = 'YES'.

PERFORM COMPUTE-SALARY-HISTORY
    VARYING SALARY-SUBSCRIPT FROM 1 BY 1
        UNTIL SALARY-SUBSCRIPT > 3.

PERFORM FIND-MATCHING-TITLE
    VARYING TITLE-SUBSCRIPT FROM 1 BY 1
        UNTIL TITLE-SUBSCRIPT > 100.
```

At the very least, the improved code offers superior documentation. By restricting data names to a single use, one automatically avoids such nondescript entries as EOF-SWITCH or SUBSCRIPT. Of greater impact, the improved code is more apt to be correct in that a given data name is modified or tested in fewer places within a program. Finally, if bugs do occur, the final values of the unique data names (TITLE-SUBSCRIPT and SALARY-SUBSCRIPT) will be of much greater use than the simple value of SUBSCRIPT.

Avoid Constants

A significant portion of maintenance programming (and headaches) could probably be avoided if the original program were written with an eye toward future change. Consider:

Poor Code:

```
05  STATE-TABLE OCCURS 50 TIMES.
    10  STATE-POPULATION     PIC 9(8).
    10  STATE-NAME           PIC X(15).
     .
     .
    PERFORM COMPUTE-STATE-TOTALS
        VARYING STATE-SUBSCRIPT FROM 1 BY 1
            UNTIL STATE-SUBSCRIPT > 50.

    COMPUTE AVERAGE-POPULATION = TOTAL-POPULATION / 50.
```

Improved Code:

```
05  NUMBER-OF-STATES         PIC 99    VALUE 50.
     .
     .
05  STATE-TABLE OCCURS 99 TIMES.
    10  STATE-POPULATION     PIC 9(8).
    10  STATE-NAME           PIC X(15).
     .
     .
```

```
PERFORM COMPUTE-STATE-TOTALS
    VARYING STATE-SUBSCRIPT FROM 1 BY 1
        UNTIL STATE-SUBSCRIPT > NUMBER-OF-STATES.

COMPUTE AVERAGE-POPULATION = TOTAL-POPULATION / NUMBER-OF-STATES.
```

Admittedly, it has been some years since Alaska and Hawaii became states. Nevertheless, if and when another state is admitted, the improved code is decidedly easier to modify. All that needs to be changed is the value of NUMBER-OF-STATES. The poor code, however, requires changes in several places: the constant 50 has to be changed to 51 three times. The possibility of error is much greater, as the programmer is required to track down all instances where the value changes. (Remember, constants do not appear on a cross reference listing.)

A second benefit of avoiding constants in favor of variable data names is increased readability. Consider:

Poor Code:

```
ADD .04 .04 GIVING TOTAL-SALES-TAX-PERCENTAGE.
```

Improved Code:

```
ADD NEW-YORK-STATE-SALES-TAX NEW-YORK-CITY-SALES-TAX
    GIVING TOTAL-SALES-TAX-PERCENTAGE.
```

The reader is hard pressed to determine the meaning of either occurrence of .04 in the first example, whereas the meaning is obvious in the second example. True, the latter requires definition of additional data names in the Data Division and extra pencil strokes in the Procedure Division. This is a small price to pay, however, for the increased legibility and ease of maintenance.

Avoiding constants is one guideline that should *not* be taken too literally. Consider:

```
01  CONSTANT-DEFINITION.
    05  ONE            PIC 9      VALUE 1.
    05  TWELVE         PIC 99     VALUE 12.
    05  ONE-HUNDRED    PIC 9(3)   VALUE 100.
    .
    .
    ADD ONE TO COUNTER.
    DIVIDE INCHES BY TWELVE GIVING FEET.
    COMPUTE PERCENT-CHANGE = ONE-HUNDRED * (NEW - OLD) / OLD.
```

One would be hard pressed to argue that use of the data names ONE, TWELVE, and ONE-HUNDRED improves readability. Quite the contrary.

Avoiding constants is a good standard. However, constants are permitted in rare instances, when they are truly constant and their value is apparent.

Place Modules So They Can Be Found

Thought should be given to the physical placement of paragraphs within a program. Figure 4.1a contains a hierarchy chart with modules numbered according to a simple, and hopefully obvious, scheme using both letters and numbers. Two approaches for ordering these procedures in a COBOL program are shown in Figure 4.1b and c.

Figure 4.1b groups the modules in a *horizontal* manner. Modules are listed in the program as they appear in the hierarchy chart, one row at a time, from left to right. Figure 4.1c, on the other hand, is known as a *vertical* arrangement. It groups modules in the listing as they appear in the hierarchy chart, from the top down, and then from left to right. The vertical arrangement appears to offer a better view of program flow, but either technique is quite proper and common. Adoption of this convention will simplify location of individual paragraphs, particularly if followed consistently by everyone in the shop.

Use Appropriate Comments

Although there is growing disillusionment with comments in structured COBOL programs, good code does not eliminate their necessity. As

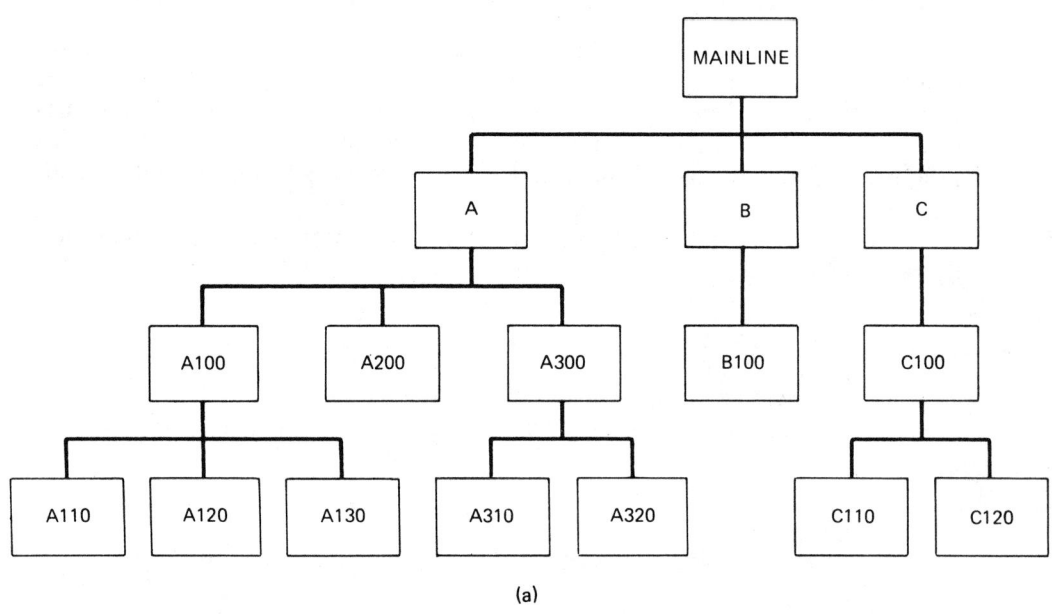

(a)

FIGURE 4.1 (a) Hierarchy chart. (b) Horizontal arrangement of modules within a COBOL program. (c) Vertical arrangement of modules within a COBOL program.

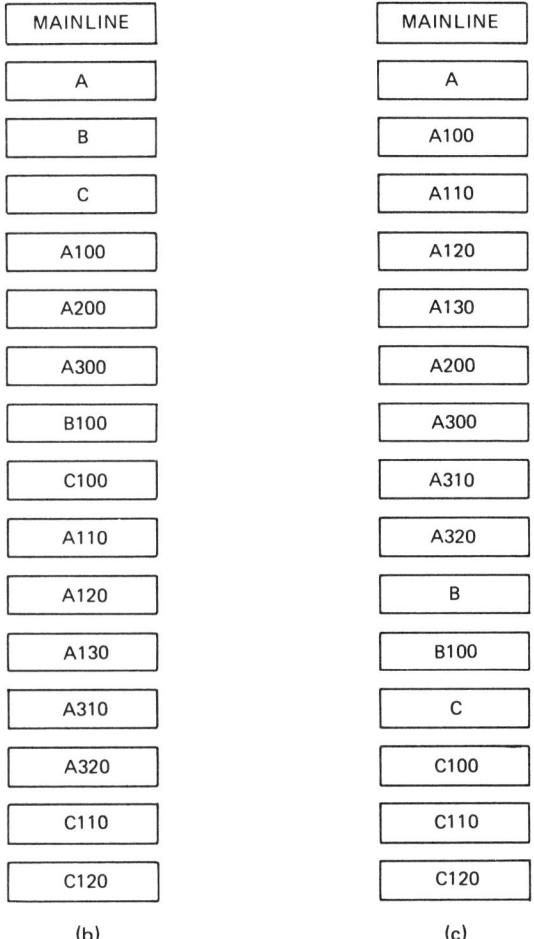

FIGURE 4.1 *continued*

Yourdon[1] has so eloquently stated, "No programmer, no matter how wise, no matter how experienced, no matter how hard pressed for time, no matter how well intentioned, should be forgiven an uncommented and undocumented program." The mere presence of comments, however, does *not* ensure a well-documented program, and poor comments are sometimes worse than no comments at all. The most common fault is *redundance* with the source code. For example, in the code:

```
*       CALCULATE NET PAY
        COMPUTE NET-PAY = GROSS-PAY - FEDERAL-TAX - VOLUNTARY-DEDUCTION.
```

[1] E. Yourdon, *Techniques of Program Structure and Design* (Englewood Cliffs, N.J.: Prentice-Hall, 1975).

the comment does not add to the readability of the program. It might even be said to detract from legibility because it breaks the logical flow as one is reading. Worse than redundant, comments may be *obsolete*, *incorrect*, or *inconsistent with the associated code*. This happens if program statements are changed during debugging or maintenance, and the comments are not correspondingly altered. *The compiler does not validate comments.* Comments may also be correct, but incomplete and hence misleading. In sum, the presence of comments is essential, but great care, *more than is commonly exercised*, should be applied to developing and maintaining comments in a program.

As a general rule, comments should be provided whenever you are doing something which is not immediately obvious to another person. When considering a comment, imagine you are turning the program over for maintenance, and insert comments whenever you would pause to explain a feature in your program. Do assume, however, that the maintenance programmer is as competent in COBOL as you are. Thus, your comments should be directed to *why* you are doing something, rather than to what you are doing.

Techniques

Perform Paragraphs, Not Sections

The motivation behind this guideline is best demonstrated by example. Given the following Procedure Division, what will be the final value of X?

```
PROCEDURE DIVISION.
MAINLINE SECTION.
    MOVE ZEROS TO X.
    PERFORM A.
    PERFORM B.
    PERFORM C.
    PERFORM D.
    STOP RUN.
A SECTION.
    ADD 1 TO X.
B.
    ADD 1 TO X.
C.
    ADD 1 TO X.
D.
    ADD 1 TO X.
```

The *correct* answer is 7, *not 4*. A common error made by many programmers is a misinterpretation of the statement PERFORM A. Since A is a *section* and not a *paragraph*, the statement PERFORM A invokes *every* paragraph in that section, namely, paragraphs B, C, and D, in addition to the unnamed paragraph immediately after the section header.

A perform statement specifies a *procedure*, which is *either* a section or a paragraph. Unfortunately, there is no way of telling the nature of the procedure from the perform statement itself. Consequently, when a section is specified as a procedure, the unfortunate result is too often execution of unintended code. Can't happen? Did you correctly compute the value of X?

A subservient guideline is to *avoid* use of PERFORM THRU; e.g., PERFORM PARAGRAPH-100 THRU PARAGRAPH-300, because its effect is dependent on the *physical* placement of paragraphs within a program. If, for example, PARAGRAPH-200 is subsequently added between PARAGRAPH-100 and PARAGRAPH-300, then the PERFORM THRU statement causes execution of an additional paragraph which may or may not be desired.

PERFORM THRU EXIT, e.g., PERFORM PARAGRAPH-A THRU PARAGRAPH-A-EXIT, should be avoided as well. Use of PERFORM THRU in this instance is in essence invoking only a single paragraph, and the author sees no gain in cluttering a program with a series of dummy EXIT paragraphs.

Avoid MOVE CORRESPONDING

The CORRESPONDING option requires *duplicate* data names in the Data Division, which precludes a unique prefix for every 01 entry. Since most shops endorse the prefix concept, use of the CORRESPONDING option is automatically eliminated. Even if this were not the case, the author suggests that CORRESPONDING be avoided because it is not clearly understood. To prove the latter point, consider Figure 4.2.

Given Figure 4.2, and the statement:

MOVE CORRESPONDING CARD-IN TO PRINT-LINE,

answer true or false for the following:

1. CREDITS will *not* be moved because it has a different level number in each record.
2. SOCIAL-SECURITY-NUM will *not* be moved because it is the second field in CARD-IN and the last field in PRINT-LINE.
3. STUDENT-NAME will *not* be moved because it has a different picture clause in CARD-IN and PRINT-LINE.
4. ZIP-CODE *will* be moved even though it has different level numbers.

The correct answer to all four questions is *false*. Essentially, the CORRESPONDING option moves *elementary* items with *identical* data names, *irrespective* of level number, position, or picture clause, provided

```
01  CARD-IN.
    05  STUDENT-NAME              PIC X(20).
    05  SOCIAL-SECURITY-NUM       PIC 9(9).
    05  STUDENT-ADDRESS.
        10  STREET                PIC X(15).
        10  CITY-STATE            PIC X(15).
    05  ZIP-CODE                  PIC X(5).
    05  CREDITS                   PIC 999.
    05  MAJOR                     PIC X(10).
    05  FILLER                    PIC X(3).
     . .
      .
01  PRINT-LINE.
    10  STUDENT-NAME              PIC X(25).
    10  FILLER                    PIC X(2).
    10  CREDITS                   PIC ZZ9.
    10  FILLER                    PIC X(2).
    10  TUITION                   PIC $$,$$9.99.
    10  FILLER                    PIC X(2).
    10  STUDENT-ADDRESS.
        15  STREET                PIC X(15).
        15  CITY-STATE            PIC X(15).
        15  ZIP-CODE              PIC X(5).
    10  FILLER                    PIC X(2).
    10  SOCIAL-SECURITY-NUM       PIC 999B99B9999.
```

FIGURE 4.2 Data Division code for duplicate data names.

the data names have *identical qualification* (up to, but not including, the 01 level). CREDITS, SOCIAL-SECURITY-NUM, and STUDENT-NAME will all be moved despite differences in level, position, or picture because these items are irrelevant. ZIP-CODE, however, will *not* be moved due to a difference in qualification. The field belongs directly to CARD-IN, but to STUDENT-ADDRESS of PRINT-LINE. The extra level of qualification in the receiving field precludes the move, i.e., ZIP-CODE is not moved.

Eliminate 77-Level Entries

In theory, a 77-level entry is an *independent* data name with no relationship to any other data name in the program. In practice, few if any data names are truly independent. The suggestion is to eliminate 77-level entries in favor of grouping related entries under a common 01 description. Consider:

Poor Code:

```
77  COUNTER-ONE                  PIC 9(3)      VALUE ZEROS.
77  COUNTER-TWO                  PIC 9(3)      VALUE ZEROS.
77  COUNTER-THREE                PIC 9(3)      VALUE ZEROS.
```

Improved Code:

```
01  RECORD-COUNTERS.
    05  NUMBER-OF-RECORDS-READ     PIC 9(3)     VALUE ZEROS.
    05  NUMBER-OF-GOOD-RECORDS     PIC 9(3)     VALUE ZEROS.
    05  NUMBER-OF-BAD-RECORDS      PIC 9(3)     VALUE ZEROS.
```

The improved code has given the three counters more descriptive names which reflect both similarities and differences among the related items. This guideline has already been accepted in a large number of shops, and it is anticipated that the next COBOL standard will officially eliminate 77-level entries—see Appendix A. It is important, however, that individuals comply with the *intended* as well as *literal* interpretation. One could use a text editor, for example, to change globally all occurrences of 77 to 01. That would comply with the literal meaning, but not the intent, in that the resulting program would now contain pages of unrelated 01 entries.

Use 88-Level Entries to Reduce Compound Conditions

Condition names (88-level entries) are useful to improve documentation. They facilitate program changes and can reduce the need for compound conditions in an IF statement. Consider the case of a political candidate seeking the names of registered Democrats in three Florida cities.

Poor Code:

```
IF (LOCATION-CODE = 48 OR 65 OR 93)
   AND POLITICAL-PARTY = 'D' ...
```

Improved Code:

```
05  LOCATION-CODE              PIC 99.
    88  MIAMI                  VALUE 48.
    88  TAMPA                  VALUE 65.
    88  FT-LAUDERDALE          VALUE 93.
    88  FLORIDA                VALUES ARE 48, 65, 93.

05  POLITICAL-PARTY            PIC X.
    88  DEMOCRAT               VALUE 'D'.
    88  REPUBLICAN             VALUE 'R'.

IF FLORIDA AND DEMOCRAT ...
```

When 88-level entries are *not* used, the IF statement is considerably harder to read. Moreover, the chances for error are greater as the condition portion is more complex to code. In the example shown, the parentheses are required, and the meaning will change if they are removed. The improved code defines the city and political party codes in the Data Division, resulting in an easier to read Procedure Division.

Condition names also facilitate maintenance in that changes to existing codes, and/or addition of new codes is done in only one place, the Data Division. When 88-level entries are not used, and the value of a given data name is tested more than once in the Procedure Division, changes are required in several places.

Use the COMPUTE Verb for Multiple Arithmetic Operators

The COMPUTE verb should always be used when *multiple* arithmetic operators are involved. Consider two sets of equivalent code:

Poor Code:

```
MULTIPLY B BY B GIVING B-SQUARED.
MULTIPLY 4 BY A GIVING FOUR-A.
MULTIPLY FOUR-A BY C GIVING FOUR-A-C.
SUBTRACT FOUR-A-C FROM B-SQUARED GIVING RESULT-1.
COMPUTE RESULT-2 = RESULT-1 ** .5.
SUBTRACT B FROM RESULT-2 GIVING NUMERATOR.
MULTIPLY 2 BY A GIVING DENOMINATOR.
DIVIDE NUMERATOR BY DENOMINATOR GIVING X.
```

Improved Code:

```
COMPUTE X = (-B + (B ** 2 - (4 * A * C)) ** .5) / (2 * A).
```

Both sets of code apply to the quadratic formula,

$$X = \frac{-B + \sqrt{B^2 - 4AC}}{2A}.$$

It is fairly easy to determine what is happening from the single COMPUTE statement. It is next to impossible to realize the cumulative effect of the eight individual arithmetic statements. Interpretation of the unacceptable code is further clouded by the mandatory definition of data names for intermediate results, RESULT-1, RESULT-2, etc.

Note well that parentheses are *required* around 2 * A in the denominator. If they had been omitted, the numerator would have been divided by 2 and then the quotient would have been multiplied by A. The parentheses around 4 * A * C are *optional*, as they do not alter the normal order of operations.

The COMPUTE statement is favored for multiple operations, but the individual arithmetic verbs are preferable when only a *single* operation is required. Hence, ADD 1 TO COUNTER is easier to code than COMPUTE COUNTER = COUNTER + 1.

Avoid Literals

The constant (literal) portion of a print line should be defined in Working-Storage, rather than moved to the print line in the Procedure Division. Consider:

Poor Code:

```
        MOVE 'STUDENT NAME    SOC SEC NUM    CREDITS    TUITION
-          'SCHOLARSHIP    FEES' TO PRINT-LINE.
        WRITE PRINT-LINE.
```

Improved Code:

```
        01   HEADING-LINE.
             05   FILLER    PIC X(12)    VALUE 'STUDENT NAME'.
             05   FILLER    PIC X(10)    VALUE SPACES.
             05   FILLER    PIC X(11)    VALUE 'SOC SEC NUM'.
             05   FILLER    PIC X(2)     VALUE SPACES.
             05   FILLER    PIC X(7)     VALUE 'CREDITS'.
             05   FILLER    PIC X(2)     VALUE SPACES.
             05   FILLER    PIC X(7)     VALUE 'TUITION'.
             05   FILLER    PIC X(3)     VALUE SPACES.
             05   FILLER    PIC X(11)    VALUE 'SCHOLARSHIP'.
             05   FILLER    PIC X(2)     VALUE SPACES.
             05   FILLER    PIC X(4)     VALUE 'FEES'.
              .
              .
             WRITE PRINT-LINE FROM HEADING-LINE.
```

The poor code illustrates continuation of a nonnumeric literal. The first line begins with a quote before STUDENT NAME, and ends *without* a closing quote in column 72. The continued line contains a hyphen in column 7, and both a beginning and ending quote.

The improved code may appear unnecessarily long in contrast to the poor code. However, it is an unwritten law that users will change column headings and/or spacing at least twice before being satisfied. Such changes are easily accommodated in the improved code, but often tedious in the original solution. Assume, for example, that four spaces are required between CREDITS and TUITION, rather than the two that are there now. Modification of the poor code requires that *both* lines in the MOVE statement be completely rewritten, whereas only a PICTURE clause changes in the improved version.

An alternative definition of HEADING-LINE is as follows:

```
01   HEADING-LINE.
     05   FILLER      PIC X(22)    VALUE 'STUDENT NAME'.
     05   FILLER      PIC X(13)    VALUE 'SOC SEC NUM'.
     05   FILLER      PIC X(9)     VALUE 'CREDITS'.
     05   FILLER      PIC X(10)    VALUE 'TUITION'.
     05   FILLER      PIC X(13)    VALUE 'SCHOLARSHIP'.
     05   FILLER      PIC X(4)     VALUE 'FEES'.
```

In this example, each VALUE clause contains fewer characters than the associated PICTURE clause. Accordingly, alignment is from left to right, with extra (low order) positions padded with blanks.

Definition of literals in the Data Division, rather than in the Procedure Division, should be extended to tables of error messages as well. Consider:

Poor Code:

```
MOVE 'TRANSACTION CODE IS NOT A, C, OR D' TO PRINT-MESSAGE.
PERFORM WRITE-ERROR-MESSAGE.
 .
 .
 .
MOVE 'TRANSACTION ID IS NOT FOUND ON MASTER FILE' TO PRINT-MESSAGE.
PERFORM WRITE-ERROR-MESSAGE.
 .
 .
 .
MOVE 'TRANSACTION ID IS ALREADY ON MASTER FILE' TO PRINT-MESSAGE.
PERFORM WRITE-ERROR-MESSAGE.
```

Improved Code:

```
01   ERROR-MESSAGES.
     05   TRANSACTION-CODE-ERROR            PIC X(45)
          VALUE 'TRANSACTION CODE IS NOT A, C, OR D'.
     05   MISSING-TRANSACTION-ERROR         PIC X(45)
          VALUE 'TRANSACTION ID IS NOT FOUND ON MASTER FILE'.
     05   DUPLICATE-TRANSACTION-ERROR       PIC X(45)
          VALUE 'TRANSACTION ID IS ALREADY ON MASTER FILE'.
      .
      .
      .
MOVE TRANSACTION-CODE-ERROR TO PRINT-MESSAGE.
PERFORM WRITE-ERROR-MESSAGE.
  .
  .
  .
MOVE MISSING-TRANSACTION-ERROR TO PRINT-MESSAGE.
PERFORM WRITE-ERROR-MESSAGE.
  .
  .
  .
MOVE DUPLICATE-TRANSACTION-ERROR TO PRINT-MESSAGE.
PERFORM WRITE-ERROR-MESSAGE.
```

The improved code is again significantly longer than the poorer version. However, it enables the programmer to see at a glance the various error checks because they are grouped together in the Data Division. Of equal importance is the ease with which the text of an existing message can be changed, and/or a new message added.

Initialize Tables Dynamically

Change is perhaps the most fundamental law of data processing, and nowhere is it more apparent than in the constant addition of new codes to various tables. It is highly desirable, therefore, to facilitate the implementation of table changes. Consider three methods for table initialization.

The least favored technique is hard coding a table within a program, because the program has to be *recompiled* and *retested* every time a new code is added. Moreover, since the table is apt to be used in several programs, the same change has to be made in *many* places, i.e., in *every* program which references the table. This leads to various problems in data integrity because some programs will not be changed, or changed incorrectly, or changed at different times, etc.

An improved technique is to use a COPY statement. Every program requiring a table has access to it, through the same COPY statement. Use of the COPY facilitates change in that additions to the table are made in only one place. The disadvantage to this technique is that all programs utilizing the COPY statement still have to be *recompiled* and *retested*.

The optimal method is to initialize a table by dynamically reading values from a file. Changes to the table are made in only one place, the file itself. Programs accessing the file need not be recompiled or retested. Sample code is shown in Figure 4.3. (This figure closely resembles Figure

```
    READ LOCATION-CODE-FILE
        AT END DISPLAY 'LOCATION FILE EMPTY'.
    PERFORM 010-INITIALIZE-LOCATION-TABLE
        VARYING LOCATION-INDEX FROM 1 BY 1
            UNTIL LOCATION-FILE-SWITCH = 'YES'.
010-INITIALIZE-LOCATION-TABLE.
    ADD 1 TO NUMBER-OF-LOCATIONS.
    IF NUMBER-OF-LOCATIONS > 500
        DISPLAY 'LOCATION TABLE TOO SMALL'
        MOVE 'YES' TO LOCATION-FILE-SWITCH
    ELSE
        MOVE INCOMING-FILE-CODE TO LOCATION-CODE (LOCATION-INDEX)
        MOVE INCOMING-FILE-NAME TO LOCATION-NAME (LOCATION-INDEX).
    READ LOCATION-CODE-FILE
        AT END MOVE 'YES' TO LOCATION-FILE-SWITCH.
```

The boxed line `IF NUMBER-OF-LOCATIONS > 500` is annotated: Ensures that table size is not exceeded and prevents subscript (index) errors.

FIGURE 4.3 Dynamic table initialization.

3.6. A subtle distinction is that the earlier example used subscripts in the PERFORM/VARYING as opposed to indexes in the present situation.)

The reader may recognize this guideline as a restatement of the discussion on *binding time* from Chapter 2.

Use READ INTO, WRITE FROM, and WS BEGINS HERE

If a program terminates prematurely, the first task is to identify the record being processed at the instant the problem occurred. Unfortunately, I/O areas are difficult to find in a dump. The problem is further compounded with blocked records when the entire physical record is in storage and one has to isolate the logical record within the physical record. The following technique is helpful:

```
         WORKING-STORAGE SECTION.
         01   FILLER                         PIC X(14)
                  VALUE 'WS BEGINS HERE'.
         01   WS-EMPLOYEE-RECORD.
              05   EMP-NAME                  PIC X(25).
              05   EMP-SOC-SEC-NUMBER        PIC 9(9).
                .
                .
         01   WS-HDG-LINE-1.
                .
                .
         READ EMPLOYEE-FILE INTO WS-EMPLOYEE-RECORD
              AT END...
         WRITE PRINT-LINE FROM WS-HDG-LINE-1
              AFTER ADVANCING...
```

The start of Working-Storage is found by scanning the alphabetic interpretation of the dump, searching for WS BEGINS HERE. The technique is not sophisticated, but it does work. Once the Working-Storage Section is found, one can easily identify the record in question as well as the values of all other data names defined in Working-Storage, e.g., switches, subscripts, etc. (See Grauer and Crawford, *The COBOL Environment*,[2] p. 199, for an illustration of this technique.)

Several variations are common with this guideline. When subprograms are used, the VALUE clause is often amended to include the program's name; e.g., WS OF SUBPROGRAM-1 BEGINS HERE. In addition, when the Working-Storage section is very large, several VALUE clauses may appear within the *same* program to delineate various areas of Working-Storage.

[2] R. Grauer and M. Crawford, *The COBOL Environment* (Englewood Cliffs, N.J.: Prentice-Hall, 1979).

Pass a Single 01 Parameter to a Subprogram

The *order* of arguments in the CALL USING and PROCEDURE DIVISION USING clauses of the calling and called program is critical. One can *guarantee* that the order and picture clauses will be identical in both calling and called program by passing only a single 01 record which is *copied* into both programs. Consider:

Poor Code:

```
CALL 'DECODER'
    USING TITLE-CODE, EXPANDED-TITLE,
        LOCATION-CODE, EXPANDED-LOCATION.
 .
 .
PROCEDURE DIVISION
    USING LS-TITLE-CODE, LS-EXPANDED-TITLE,
        LS-LOCATION-CODE, LS-EXPANDED-LOCATION.
```

Improved Code:

```
            COPY ARGUMENTS.
C   01  PARAMETER-LIST.
C       05  TITLE-CODE              PIC 9(3).
C       05  EXPANDED-TITLE          PIC X(15).
C       05  LOCATION-CODE           PIC XX.
C       05  EXPANDED-LOCATION       PIC X(12).
         .
         .
        CALL 'DECODER'
            USING PARAMETER-LIST.

        LINKAGE SECTION.
            COPY ARGUMENTS.
C   01  PARAMETER-LIST.
C       05  TITLE-CODE              PIC 9(3).
C       05  EXPANDED-TITLE          PIC X(15).
C       05  LOCATION-CODE           PIC XX.
C       05  EXPANDED-LOCATION       PIC X(12).
        PROCEDURE DIVISION
            USING PARAMETER-LIST.
```

Use of the single 01 parameter facilitates coding in the USING clauses, and also makes them immune to change. Use of the same COPY member in both programs eliminates any problem with listing arguments in the wrong order, and/or inconsistent definition through different pictures.

Consider Report Writer

Report Writer is one of the most powerful features in COBOL, yet many programmers will not even consider using it. The author views this situation as extremely unfortunate, and attributes it to notoriously poor vendor manuals. Report Writer is well worth learning because it provides automatic formation of heading, detail, and footing lines. Of greater import, it automatically and *correctly* totals, and subtotals, over various levels of control breaks.

The reader is referred to Chapter 8 for a thorough introduction to the technique. It is well worth considering!

Philosophies

Keep It Simple

Procedure Division code should be kept as straightforward as possible, and efforts at being cute or fancy should be discouraged. Beginning programmers, especially, are notorious for trying to impress their peers with "clever" code, which too often confuses the issue.

Consider the following payroll specification for hourly employees: all employees receive straight time for the first 40 hours worked, time and a half for the next 8 hours, and double time for any hours over 48. For example, an employee who worked 50 hours with an hourly rate of $5.00 should receive $280.00 (40 hours at $5.00, 8 hours at $7.50, and 2 hours at $10.00).

The following, *logically equivalent* IF statements, are partial solutions:

```
         IF HOURS-WORKED > 48
            COMPUTE GROSS-PAY
              = 40 * HOURLY-RATE
              + 8 * HOURLY-RATE * 1.5
              + (HOURS-WORKED - 48) * HOURLY-RATE * 2.

         IF HOURS-WORKED > 48
            COMPUTE GROSS-PAY
              = 52 * HOURLY-RATE
              + (HOURS-WORKED - 48) * HOURLY-RATE * 2.
```

The first statement is a line longer, but is the *preferred* solution as *it more closely represents the physical problem.* It is easy to see that individuals working more than 48 hours receive straight time for the first 40 hours, time and a half for the next 8 hours, and double time for any hours over 48. Although the second statement produces equivalent results, it deviates significantly from the physical situation. A maintenance programmer would be hard pressed to understand the meaning of the constant

52. Lest the reader think that this is a concocted example, we credit it to a math major in COBOL 1. The student was an accomplished mathematician and FORTRAN programmer. His solution may be elegant in a mathematical sense, but it is certainly undesirable in a commercial environment.

Downplay Efficiency, but Choose the Algorithm Carefully

"More computing sins are committed in the name of efficiency (without necessarily achieving it) than for any other single reason including blind stupidity."[3] Efficiency is mentioned again and again by seminar attendees when asked to list attributes of a good program. However, the notion that one must spend inordinate amounts of time trying to save a microsecond here, and a byte there, is no longer valid.

For one thing, memory is not the scarce commodity it once was. True, it is a resource to be reckoned with on microcomputers, but even there its importance is diminished. Look how far we've come, for example, when 256K are available on a microcomputer.[4]

Even when a legitimate argument can be made for trying to increase efficiency, the effort may not be worth the price. The ratio of hardware to personnel dollars has reversed completely. Twenty years ago, it made economic sense to reduce hardware requirements (through greater efficiency) because the latter cost so much more. Today, the opposite is true; *people are more expensive than machines*, and expending personnel dollars to reduce hardware costs is often counterproductive.

Simply stated, efficiency is not the primary criterion of a good program. *Correctness* is, and it is far easier to make a correct program efficient (if one insists), than an efficient program correct. Efficiency also takes a back seat to *maintainability*. A good program must be easily read and maintained by someone other than the original author. Nothing should be done, in the name of efficiency or anything else, to obscure program clarity.

Despite the preceding arguments, efficiency need not be ignored completely, provided one concentrates on the "right" kind of efficiency. To that end, the *algorithm* chosen is often far more important than the generated object code. Consider, for example, the SORT program of Figure 3.18, which listed students by grade point average (a calculated field).

The INPUT PROCEDURE calculated the grade point average of incoming records, after which *every* record was released to the work file. The OUTPUT PROCEDURE returned records from the sort work file, and *selectively* printed students with an average of 3.00 or higher. The program runs significantly faster if the selection is done in the INPUT PROCEDURE. Assume, for example, that STUDENT-FILE contains 1,000 records, of

---

[3]William A. Wulf, "A Case Against the GO TO," *25th ACM Conference Proceedings*, 1972.

[4]IBM announcement of its personal computer, August 1981.

which 100 have the necessary average. Is it not a wasted effort to sort the entire file of 1,000 records, when only 100 are of interest?

Chances are, however, that if you asked practitioners to make the original program of Figure 3.18 more efficient, most would suggest the addition of USAGE clauses and ignore the algorithm completely. That, unfortunately, is missing the boat. It is usually far better to have an *efficient algorithm coded inefficiently, than to have an inefficient algorithm painstakingly coded to utilize every machine efficiency.*

Another common example of algorithmic efficiency comes in the application of table lookups. A binary search is far faster than a sequential search for medium and large-size tables. For example, a binary search over a table of 500 elements requires a *maximum* of 9 tries whereas a sequential lookup takes an *average* of 250. Expanding the table to 1,000 elements produces numbers of 10 and 500, respectively.

One last example of algorithmic efficiency is testing the most likely condition first. Consider a file of 10,000 records in which three types of transactions are possible: A (addition), C (correction), and D (deletion). Further assume that 7,000 records are corrections, 2,500 are additions, and 500 are deletions and that this distribution remains fairly constant from run to run. If the most likely condition, i.e., corrections, is tested first, a total of 13,500 comparisons are required, as shown:

```
IF IN-CODE = 'C' ...              (executed 10,000 times)
    ELSE IF IN-CODE = 'A' ...     (executed  3,000 times)
        ELSE IF IN-CODE = 'D' ... (executed    500 times)
```

If, on the other hand, the least likely condition is tested first, then 26,500 comparisons are necessary:

```
IF IN-CODE = 'D' ...              (executed 10,000 times)
    ELSE IF IN-CODE = 'A' ...     (executed  9,500 times)
        ELSE IF IN-CODE = 'C' ... (executed  7,000 times)
```

Although this technique requires some knowledge of file characteristics, it can be used to great advantage when that information is available.

Code Defensively

A well-written program is not limited to computing answers; it should also include checks for erroneous data. The requirements of precisely what to check for are included in the specifications given to the programmer. However, in the course of coding, other situations will suggest themselves and these should be brought to the attention of the analyst and included in the program.

Installations frequently develop standards that specify overall requirements for error processing. Murphy's law is the most encompassing, and the author believes that one cannot check too much. (If incoming transactions are processed by a separate edit program, most of the programming checks suggested next are done in the edit program and need not be repeated. The essential point, however, is that incoming data are apt to be in error and must be checked; when and how this is done is of secondary importance.) The following are typical error checks:

1. *Numeric test:* Ensures that a numeric field does in fact contain numeric data. Commas, decimal points, blanks, and dollar signs, are *not* numeric and will cause problems in execution. The test is easy to implement and takes the form:

```
IF EMPLOYEE-SALARY IS NUMERIC
    PERFORM SALARY-CALCULATIONS
ELSE
    PERFORM ERROR-ROUTINE.
```

2. *Alphabetic test:* Analogous to a numeric test, except that it checks that alphabetic fields have been coded. Any errors detected here are typically less serious than for numeric fields.

3. *Reasonableness check:* Assures that a given number is within "normal" bounds. These tests often take the form of *limit* checks, that is, testing that a value does not exceed a designated upper or lower extreme. For example, a payroll program may check that no hourly worker's pay exceeds $500 per week. A weekly gross that exceeded this amount might be deemed unreasonable and the transaction flagged for further scrutiny. A *range* check ensures that a given value is within specified limits, and is another form of reasonableness check.

4. *Consistency check:* Verifies that the values in two or more fields are consistent, for example, salary and job title. Since salary is partly a function of job title, there should be a correlation between the two. Another example of a consistency check would be an individual's credit rating and the amount of credit a bank is willing to extend.

5. *Checking that a code exists:* One of the most common, yet most important tests. This author has seen countless errors compounded because this check was not implemented. For example:

```
IF SEX = 'M'
    ADD 1 TO NUMBER-OF-MEN
ELSE
    ADD 1 TO NUMBER-OF-WOMEN.
```

It is decidedly *poor* practice to assume that an incoming record is female if it is not male. Rather, *both* codes should be explicitly checked, and if neither occurs, a suitable error should be printed. Recall also the various table processing examples in Chapter 3, and the use of AT END in the SEARCH verb for this specific purpose.

6. *Sequence check:* Assures that incoming records are in proper order. It can also be used when several lines (cards) comprise one record to assure that the lines within a record are in proper sequence.

7. *Completeness check:* Verifies that all required fields are present, as when records are added to a file.

8. *Date check:* Ensures that an incoming date is acceptable, and is implemented in several ways. Birth dates can be checked to ensure that no one is hired who is younger than 16 or older than 65. Checks can be made on a date to test that the day falls between 1 and 31, the month between 1 and 12, and the year within a designated period, often just the current year.

9. *Subscript check:* Validates that a subscript or index is within a table's original definition. See, for example, Figure 4.3, which illustrated how to initialize a table dynamically.

Diligent application of defensive programming minimizes the need for subsequent debugging. Realize that any debugging technique suffers from the fact that it is applied *after* a bug has occurred. Defensive programming assumes that errors will occur (they are, after all, inevitable), and takes steps to make them apparent to the programmer and/or user *before* a program terminates.

Is it reasonable to impose the "burden" of defensive programming on the COBOL programmer? After all, the user is provided with a manual and instructions that "anyone" should be capable of following. Why then should the programmer be held responsible for the sins of the user? The COBOL compiler provides a good analogy. Programmers are given manuals, yet the compiler assumes they will make errors and rejects incorrectly coded COBOL with appropriate messages. Since we as programmers depend on the compiler's ability to check our errors, we cannot object to the user's dependence on us to validate his or her transactions.

Is defensive programming worth the extra time? It is if you have ever been called at two in the morning to be told that your program "bombed" because of invalid data.

Think First, Code Later

For whatever reason, programmers are often deemed unproductive unless they are coding. Once specifications are approved, and not uncommonly even before, programmers are subjected to a variety of pressures to begin the job. The urging may come from management, from users, and even from within. It is critical, however, that one put aside the impulse to code and simply *think*.

Do no coding whatsoever for a period of time, be it 10 minutes or 10 days. Plan your solution thoroughly; it is far easier to discard a poor approach than a poor program. Pay attention to the design; develop pseudocode; conduct walkthroughs. Do anything, and everything, but delay coding until you have analyzed at least one alternate solution. The end result will be far superior, and will be produced in less total time, than a program hastily constructed without forethought.

Summary

The most important criterion of a good program is that it work; the second is that it be easily read and maintained by someone other than the original author. This chapter contained a series of programming strategies to achieve the second objective.

The author believes strongly in the concept of *guidelines* rather than rigid standards. First, many standards do have legitimate exceptions; second, one can conform to the "letter of the law," yet miss its spirit entirely; and third, many desirable techniques are not easily quantified.

The guidelines contained herein are those of the author and evolved over time through personal growth and exposure to others' ideas. No doubt, some will change again; new techniques will suggest themselves and old standbys may be deleted. In much the same way, the reader will not agree with everything that has been said. That, too, is a natural and desirable consequence of a dynamic field.

True/False

1. Maintainability is the most important criterion of a good program.
2. It is impossible to overcomment a program.
3. Indentation is more important in the Data Division than in the Procedure Division.
4. Wherever possible, several statements should appear on the same line in the Procedure Division to save space.
5. Blank lines should never be used as they waste inordinate amounts of storage space.
6. A single switch that references multiple files is preferable to defining a separate switch for each file.
7. Adherence to structured programming assures that a program will be easy to read.
8. Machine efficiency is more important than algorithmic efficiency.
9. A program must contain at least one 77-level entry.
10. One should pay a great deal of attention to USAGE clauses.
11. Report Writer is to be avoided at all costs.

12. Constants should *never* appear in a well-written program.
13. Programming standards at AT&T and General Motors are probably identical.
14. ANS 74 COBOL requires that paragraphs be sequenced.
15. Indentation does not affect compiler interpretation.
16. A comment is indicated by a slash in column 7.
17. One should never code two COBOL statements if equivalent logic can be expressed in a single statement.
18. A comma will generally enhance readability.
19. It is completely immaterial whether one performs paragraphs or sections.
20. Data names should be short to reduce coding and/or keypunch effort.
21. Use of PERFORM THRU is to be encouraged.
22. A FILLER entry, with the VALUE 'WS BEGINS HERE', should appear in all programs.
23. Coding should begin *immediately* after one receives a program's specifications.
24. Error checks need not be included in a program if one is assured that incoming data will be valid.
25. COBOL compilers typically insert object code to ensure that table size is not exceeded during execution.

Problems

1. Do you agree with *all* of the author's guidelines? Do you agree with the concept of less than rigid guidelines, or do you prefer coding standards? Select a guideline which is most objectionable and argue against it. Can you suggest any additional techniques not mentioned in the chapter?
2. Select a program that you have recently written or have been assigned to maintain. Critique it with respect to the presence or absence of standards.
3. Can you suggest any improvements to the code in Figure 4.4?

```
       FD  CARD-FILE
           LABEL RECORDS ARE OMITTED
           RECORD CONTAINS 80 CHARACTERS
           DATA RECORD IS STUDENT-CARD
       01  STUDENT-CARD.
           05   STUDENT-NAME         PICTURE IS A(20).
           05   SOC-SEC-NO           PICTURE IS 9(9).
           05   CREDITS              PICTURE IS 9(2).
           05   UNION-MEMBER         PICTURE IS A.
           05   SCHOLARSHIP          PICTURE IS 9(4).
           05   FILLER               PICTURE IS X(44).
```

FIGURE 4.4   COBOL code for Problem 3.

```
IF INPUT-CODE = 'A', MOVE INPUT-NAME TO HOLD-NAME
IF INPUT-AMOUNT IS GREATER THAN 100
PERFORM ADJUST-AMOUNT VARYING WS-SUB
   FROM 1 BY 1 UNTIL WS-SUB IS GREATER THAN 10
   AFTER HOLD-SUB FROM 1 BY 1 UNTIL HOLD-SUB IS EQUAL TO 8
ELSE, NEXT SENTENCE ELSE, DISPLAY INPUT-NAME.
```

FIGURE 4.5 COBOL code for Problem 4.

4. Reformat the nested IF statement of Figure 4.5.

5. Does your shop have a COBOL standards manual? Is it larger than the vendor's COBOL manual? What procedures exist for standards enforcement? Are these procedures followed? If not, why not?

6. Do you have any preference for using symbols in lieu of equivalent phrases; e.g., do you prefer the greater than sign instead of the COBOL reserved words GREATER THAN? Why or why not?

Projects

There are no specific projects associated with this chapter. However, the reader should strive to incorporate these and/or other guidelines in all programming projects.

Techniques of Structured Communication

5

Overview

Chapter 2 discussed the role of the hierarchy chart as an overall design aid. The reader was urged to view individual modules as "black boxes"; i.e., to recognize which functions were necessary, but to *defer* consideration of how they would be implemented. In other words, the hierarchy chart provided a *functional* rather than *procedural* description; it stated *what* had to be done, but not *how*.

This chapter moves toward specification of the *detailed* logic *within* a module. It begins with the traditional flowchart and introduces two alternatives associated with structured methodology: *pseudocode* and *Nassi-Shneiderman* charts. It also presents *decision tables* and *decision trees* as parallel methods for stating and verifying user specifications.

It is worth noting that errors in a system are typically associated with errors in the coding phase, when in reality they are often due to problems in analysis and/or design. (See Figure 5.1.) How much simpler life would

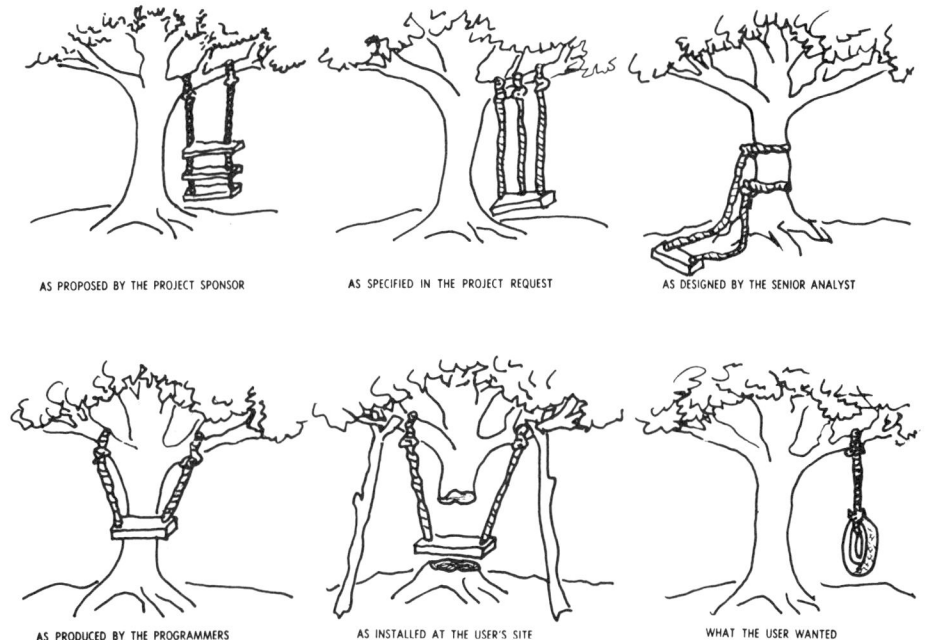

FIGURE 5.1 A failure to communicate. From the *University of London Computer Centre Newsletter* No. 53, March 1973.

be if errors could be detected *as early as possible* in the development cycle. To that end, the *structured walkthrough* is formally introduced as the last topic in the chapter.

The Traditional Flowchart

Every programmer is familiar with the traditional flowchart: a pictorial representation of the logic inherent in a computer program. In theory one is supposed to draw a flowchart *before* writing a program, so that it can be used as a development aid. In practice, the flowchart is often drawn *after* the program has been written, and then only because it is required as part of the documentation. (Proof of this phenomenon lies in the success of program products such as ADR's AUTOFLOW,[1] which accept a program as input, and produce a flowchart as output!)

To put it as gently as possible, use of the traditional flowchart as the primary means of communicating logic is on the way out, and has been for many years (although this author will still, on occasion, flowchart a *small* portion of a complex program; e.g., 8 to 10 blocks). On the whole, however, flowcharts have given way to newer techniques which are explained in a subsequent section.

[1] AUTOFLOW is a trademark of Applied Data Research, a leading software house, and has sold several thousand copies.

Flowcharts have come into disfavor for many reasons. They are time-consuming to draw and often stretch over several pages. They are difficult to follow and maintain. Of greater import is their natural affinity for expressing unconditional branches (i.e., GO TOs) which is contradictory to current programming practice. Even when flowcharts are restricted to the three basic logic structures, the results are often awkward and not very helpful. For whatever the reason, many programmers and/or students avoid flowcharts unless compelled by a manager (or instructor) to submit a flowchart with the completed program.

Individuals do, however, willingly and often, write notes to themselves prior to coding a program. A new technique, *pseudocode* can be regarded as *"neat* notes to oneself," and since programmers tend to do this anyway, the technique is gaining favor.

Pseudocode

Pseudocode, also known as *structured English* or *Program Development Language* (PDL), uses statements similar to computer instructions to describe logic. Pseudocode is not bound by formal syntactical rules as is a programming language. Nor is it bound by rules of indentation, which is strictly at the discretion of the person using it.

The only real limitation is a restriction to the elementary logic structures of sequence, selection, and iteration, causing pseudocode to flow easily from the top down. Pseudocode has a very distinct block structure which arises naturally, and is extremely conducive to structured programming. An example of pseudocode to merge two sequential files is shown in Figure 5.2. (The specifications require the merged record to contain fields from records in both files, and for an appropriate error message to appear if matching records are not present.)

The example illustrates a desirable characteristic of pseudocode; *it is sufficiently precise to serve as a real aid in writing a program, while informal enough to be intelligible to nonprogrammers* (i.e., users). It can be written quickly and easily, and hence is more likely to be maintained if modifications are necessary. The pseudocode of Figure 5.2 is an elegant example of how nontrivial logic may be expressed in clear and concise fashion.

Many programmers have requested precise rules to use in developing pseudocode. Unfortunately, the very nature of the technique prohibits such restrictions, as they imply a formalism which pseudocode does not possess. Nevertheless, the following guidelines may prove helpful:

- Indent for readability.
- Use ENDIF and ENDDO to indicate the end of a block of logic; use vertical lines to indicate the extent of a block.
- Minimize or avoid the use of adjectives and adverbs.

```
        OPEN files
        Initial reads for FILE-1 and FILE-2
     ┌─ DO WHILE data remains on either file
     │  ┌─ IF FILE-1 < FILE-2
     │  │     WRITE error message "FILE-2 record missing"
     │  │     READ FILE-1 only
     │  │  ELSE
     │  │     ┌─ IF FILE-2 < FILE-1
     │  │     │     WRITE error message "FILE-1 record missing"
     │  │     │     READ FILE-2 only
     │  │     │  ELSE (if the files are equal)
     │  │     │     Combine matching records
     │  │     │     WRITE merged record
     │  │     │     READ FILE-1 and FILE-2
     │  │     └─ ENDIF
     │  └─ ENDIF
     └─ ENDDO
        CLOSE files
        STOP RUN
```

FIGURE 5.2 Pseudocode for a two-file merge.

- Use strongly descriptive verbs; try to avoid innocuous ones such as process, handle, and so on.
- Use parenthetical expressions to clarify conditions associated with the ELSE portion of an IF statement.
- Restrict the pseudocode for a given module to a single page; if it doesn't fit, divide the module into two or more subordinate modules.

Nassi-Shneiderman Charts

Nassi-Shneiderman (or simply N-S) charts are a third technique for depicting program logic. The diagrams depict only the three control structures of sequence, selection, and iteration, and have no provision for the GO TO statement. (N-S charts are sometimes referred to as Chapin charts, in that the latter gentleman also claims credit for the technique.)

A Nassi-Shneiderman diagram for a two-file merge is shown in Figure 5.3. It corresponds closely to the pseudocode of Figure 5.2, and detractors of the technique have referred to it as "pseudocode with boxes around it."

An N-S diagram is a series of rectangles of varying size. Decisions are indicated by inverted triangles within a rectangle. Alternate logic paths are separated by a vertical line. Module names of the iteration structure are indicated vertically.

Both N-S charts and the traditional flowchart graphically depict the logic to be performed. An N-S diagram does not contain flow lines or arrow heads nor have special shapes for different functions; e.g., a parallelogram for

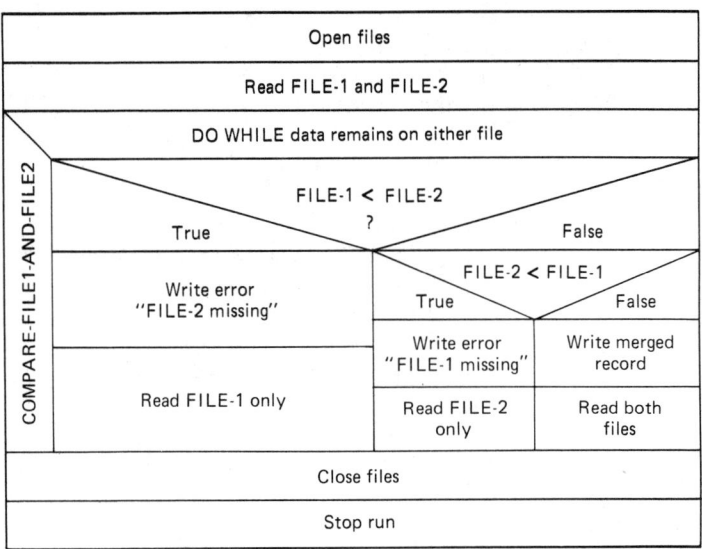

FIGURE 5.3   Nassi-Shneiderman chart for two-file merge.

I/O and so on. It is more compact and easier to draw than a flowchart, and is readily translated to structured COBOL code. This author views it as superior to a flowchart, but less desirable than pseudocode. The primary disadvantage of N-S diagrams is that they are cumbersome to maintain.

Comparison of Techniques

Let us consider an example that contrasts pseudocode, flowcharts, and Nassi-Shneiderman charts. (The problem chosen is deliberately *not* related to data processing for the following reason. We are dealing with an exercise in logic, and further with alternate means of communicating that logic. If the problem chosen were data processing oriented, then the reader would probably have already encountered it, in one form or another. However, selection of an unrelated problem eliminates any preexisting bias toward a particular solution.) Consider now the problem of the Structured Robot.

The objective of the exercise is to provide a series of commands to a robot, so that it can move through a maze, e.g., Figure 5.4, to reach a goal. It is a simple maze in that there are no dead ends; i.e., the robot enters and makes steady progress to reach its objective.

The robot understands the following commands:

STEP	Take one step forward
TURN RIGHT	Turn 90° to the right
TURN LEFT	Turn 90° to the left
STOP	Shut down

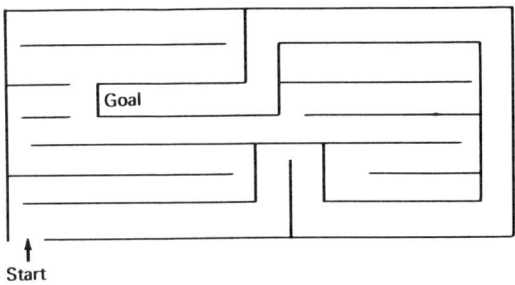

FIGURE 5.4 A typical maze.

A condition code, AT WALL or NOT AT WALL, is returned after the first three commands. If AT WALL is returned, the robot is standing directly in front of a wall and cannot proceed further. If NOT AT WALL is received, the robot can take at least one step directly ahead. The robot has reached the goal when it is confronted by a wall on three sides.

The problem is to develop the necessary logic to get the robot through *any* maze of the type shown in Figure 5.4 (i.e., a maze with no dead ends). The logic must be structured; that is, it should consist only of sequence, selection, and/or iteration blocks. The solution is expressed in Nassi-Schneiderman, flowchart, and pseudocode format for comparative purposes (Figures 5.5, 5.6, and 5.7 respectively). Observe also the dotted lines in Figure 5.6 to indicate the fundamental building blocks of sequence, selection, and iteration.

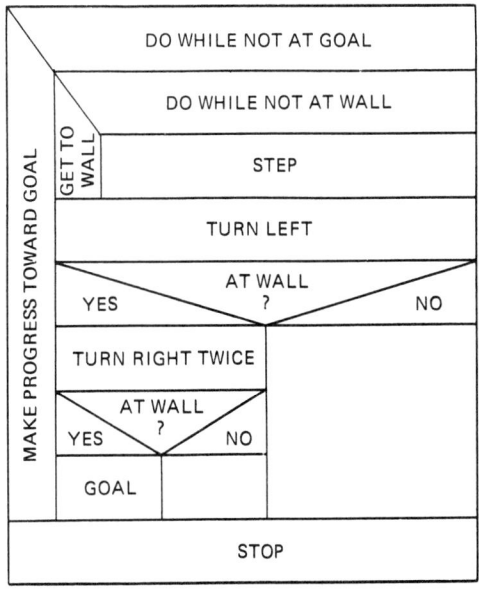

FIGURE 5.5 Nassi-Shneiderman chart for robot problem.

Comparison of Techniques 127

The author's personal preference is to use pseudocode in lieu of flowcharts and N-S diagrams. The reader is, of course, free to choose whatever method he or she likes best.

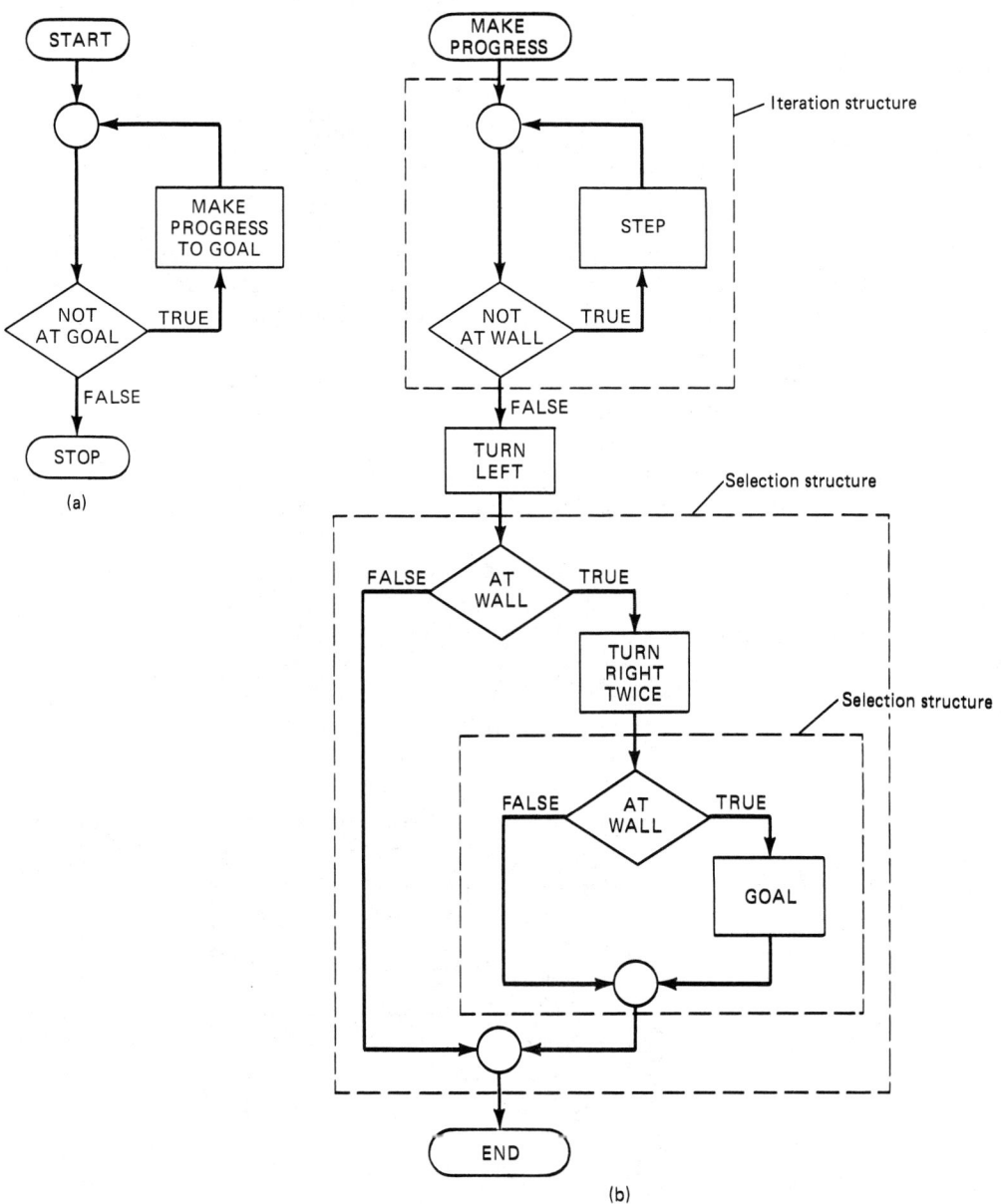

FIGURE 5.6 (a) Overall flowchart. (b) Details of the MAKE-PROGRESS-TOWARD-GOAL module.

```
┌─DO WHILE not at goal
│  ┌─DO WHILE not at wall
│  │    step
│  └─ENDDO
│    Turn left
│  ┌─IF at wall
│  │    Turn right twice
│  │  ┌─IF at wall
│  │  │    Goal is reached
│  │  └─ENDIF
│  └─ENDIF
└─ENDDO
  Stop
```

FIGURE 5.7 Pseudocode for robot problem.

Decision Tables

Flowcharts, pseudocode, and N-S diagrams are used by programmers to express detailed logic. Decision tables, on the other hand, are often used by analysts and even users to express program specifications.

A *decision table* is a graphic technique of particular value in situations with many branches and/or options. It is a chart that concisely displays *all conditions and associated actions* in the form of a matrix. Once developed, it is helpful in writing code and simultaneously provides excellent documentation. (The reader is referred to the fine book by Thomas Gildersleeve[2] for a more complete treatment of the subject.)

A decision table has four components, as shown in Figure 5.8.

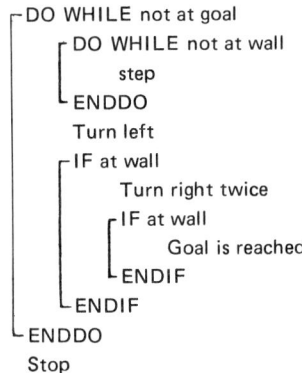

FIGURE 5.8 Parts of a decision table.

As with all techniques, the method is best illustrated by example. Consider the rather confusing specification of Figure 5.9a. In order to develop a decision table, one first has to identify the various *conditions* which can occur, and the *associated actions*. Figures 5.9b and 5.9c highlight the conditions and actions respectively.

One thing that becomes obvious from Figures 5.9b and c is that user

---

[2] Thomas R. Gildersleeve, *Decision Tables and Their Practical Application in Data Processing* (Englewood Cliffs, N.J.: Prentice-Hall, 1970).

> Customers classified as poor payers are not to have their orders shipped unless they ordered a discontinued item. Good payers, on the other hand, are to have their orders shipped immediately unless there is insufficient stock. If a stockout does occur, do not ship anything. Instead, place an order for more inventory unless the customer ordered a discontinued item, in which case back orders are not possible. Incidentally, good payers receive a 5% discount on all orders.
>
> (a)

> Customers classified as <u>poor payers</u> are not to have their orders shipped unless they ordered a <u>discontinued item</u>. <u>Good payers</u>, on the other hand, are to have their orders shipped immediately, unless there is <u>insufficient stock</u>. If a <u>stockout does occur</u>, do not ship anything. Instead, place an order for more inventory unless the customer ordered a <u>discontinued item</u>, in which case back orders are not possible. Incidentally, <u>good payers</u> receive a 5% discount on all orders.
>
> (b)

> Customers classified as poor payers are <u>not to have their orders shipped</u> unless they ordered a discontinued item. Good payers, on the other hand, are to have <u>their orders shipped</u> immediately, unless there is insufficient stock. If a stockout does occur, <u>do not ship anything</u>. Instead, <u>place an order for more inventory</u> unless the customer ordered a discontinued item, in which case <u>back orders are not possible</u>. Incidentally, good payers <u>receive a 5% discount</u> on all orders.
>
> (c)

FIGURE 5.9 (a) Specification. (b) Specification with conditions underlined. (c) Specification with actions underlined.

specifications often employ different words to say the same thing; e.g., "insufficient stock" and "stockout does occur," or "place an order for more inventory" and "back order." A cardinal rule of providing good specifications, therefore, is to *use standard language*, but try as we might to impose this suggestion, users tend to be set in their ways. Decision tables, however, bring about this standardization.

Returning to Figure 5.9b, we can identify three distinct variables, each with two possible values. Customers may be classified as good or poor payers, they may order discontinued or nondiscontinued items, and the stock on hand is either sufficient or insufficient to meet the order. All told, there are *eight* ($2 \times 2 \times 2$) possible combinations, and consequently, the decision table will have eight columns.

Figure 5.10 represents the first attempt at constructing a decision table. The upper left quadrant (the condition stub) identifies the conditions, while the upper right quadrant specifies the eight possible combinations. (The values of Y and N are strategically assigned so that all eight combinations are

	1	2	3	4	5	6	7	8
Good payer	Y	Y	Y	Y	N	N	N	N
Discontinued item	Y	Y	N	N	Y	Y	N	N
Sufficient stock	Y	N	Y	N	Y	N	Y	N
Ship order	X		X		X			
Back order				X				
Give discount	X		X					

FIGURE 5.10 Initial decision table.

covered. Various texts, Demarco[3] for example, provide different methods for generating the condition entry portion.)

The lower left quadrant (i.e., the action stub) lists the actions which are possible as extracted from Figure 5.9c. The lower right quadrant, the action entry, indicates the actions to be taken under various conditions. It is here that the decision table comes into its own as a specification checker. Note well the omissions and/or inconsistencies which are detected in the original specification.

What is to be done, for example, if there is *insufficient stock of a discontinued item* (Rules 2 and 6)? The specification clearly states that shipment is not to be made if stock is insufficient, but also states that it is not possible to order additional inventory of discontinued items. Failure to make a partial shipment in this instance would result in a lost sale, which is probably not what the user intended. A second ambiguity arises when a *poor payer orders a nondiscontinued item* (Rules 7 and 8). Again, the specification clearly states that shipment is not to be made under these circumstances, but provides no indication of what to do. Finally, should a back order be placed if a poor payer orders a nondiscontinued item for which the stock is insufficient (Rule 8)?

Armed with the original specification and decision table, the analyst can ask the user for clarification. To complete the example, the user suggests *partial shipments with no discounts to good payers who order discontinued items with insufficient stock* (Rule 2). *Prepayment is to be requested from poor payers ordering nondiscontinued items, and back orders should not be placed for poor payers* (Rules 7 and 8). The completed decision table is shown in Figure 5.11.

Once the decision table is completed, the analyst looks for ways to *reduce* the number of columns in order to simplify the eventual coding.

---

[3] Tom Demarco, *Structured Analysis and System Specification*, (Englewood Cliffs, N.J.: Prentice-Hall, 1979).

	1	2	3	4	5	6	7	8
Good payer	Y	Y	Y	Y	N	N	N	N
Discontinued item	Y	Y	N	N	Y	Y	N	N
Sufficient stock	Y	N	Y	N	Y	N	Y	N
Ship order	X		X		X			
Back order				X				
Give discount	X		X					
Ship partial order		X				X		
Ask for prepayment							X	X

FIGURE 5.11 Revised decision table.

Gildersleeve goes into the subject in detail, but we will provide only a brief indication of this kind of analysis. Specifically, we will look for *pairs of columns which have identical actions and matching conditions in all instances but one.*

Consider, for example, columns 1 and 3 of Figure 5.11. Both pertain to orders from good payers, with sufficient stock available, and differ in only *one* aspect, whether or not the item is discontinued. However, because the resulting *actions are identical*, and because the conditions *differ in only one aspect*, the two columns may be combined into one. In other words, when a good payer orders an item with sufficient stock, we are *indifferent* as to whether or not the item has been discontinued.

Examine Figure 5.11 and look for other pairs of columns which may be combined in similar fashion. You should find two sets, columns 2 and 6,

	1-3	2-6	4	5	7-8
Good payer	Y	—	Y	N	N
Discontinued item	—	Y	N	Y	N
Sufficient stock	Y	N	N	Y	—
Ship order	X			X	
Back order			X		
Give discount	X				
Ship partial order		X			
Ask for prepayment					X

FIGURE 5.12 Reduced decision table.

and columns 7 and 8. Figure 5.12 is a reduced decision table in which the number of columns has been reduced from the eight which appeared originally in Figure 5.11 to five.

Decision Trees

Decision trees contain *identical* information as decision tables, with the added advantage of requiring no user training whatsoever. Figure 5.13 contains a decision tree corresponding to the decision table of Figure 5.11. The text provides no additional explanation, because none is required. Consequently, decision trees are very useful in conversations with *nontechnical* users.

The disadvantage of decision trees is that they are not amenable to techniques of reduction, i.e., combination of columns. A useful approach, therefore, is to begin with a decision tree when speaking with users, then convert to a decision table when preparing formal programming specifications.

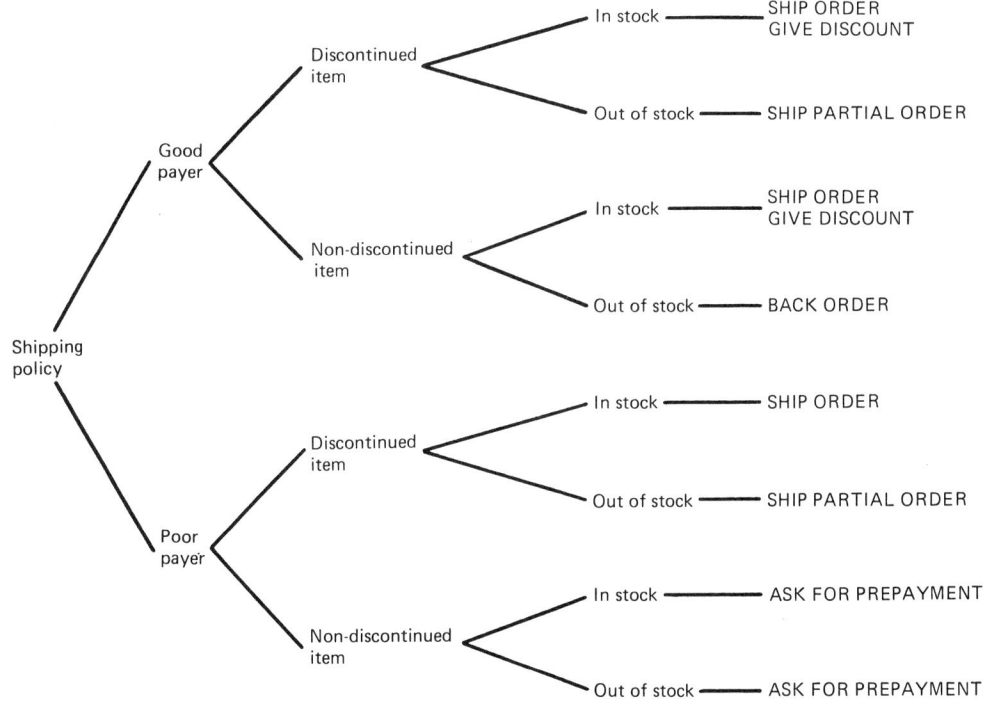

FIGURE 5.13 Decision tree (corresponds to Figure 5.11).

Structured Walkthroughs

The *structured walkthrough* is a peer evaluation technique intended to find errors at any stage in a program's life cycle. It may be applied to flowcharts, pseudocode, N-S diagrams, decision tables, test data, hierarchy charts, or even user specifications. The overriding objective of a walkthrough is *early error detection* because the sooner an error is found, the easier it is to correct. This section presents an overview of the topic, discussing when walkthroughs should be held, the walkthrough procedure itself, and suggestions for successful walkthroughs. The reader is referred to *Structured Walkthroughs*, by Edward Yourdon,[4] for a more complete discussion.

Types of Walkthroughs

Walkthroughs may be conducted at several stages in a project, with the attendees and objectives varying according to when the session is held. Smaller projects may not hold all of the listed sessions, while larger systems could require several sessions of a given type. Typical kinds of walkthroughs include the following:

Specification walkthroughs review a system's functional requirements, and are held at the beginning of the cycle. Attendees include user representatives, system analysts, and system designers. The intent is to spot omissions, ambiguities, and/or inconsistencies in the system specification. The review document may be a narrative description of the proposed system, a functional specification, one or more decision tables and/or decision trees, a data flow diagram, and so on.

Test walkthroughs ensure the adequacy and completeness of test data. The author suggests that these walkthroughs be held shortly after specification reviews as a further check on a system's requirements. Attendees include the user (who hopefully provides some or all of the test data), a systems analyst, a designer, and a programmer. The material reviewed at this session consists of *test data and anticipated results.* A common occurrence is that the programmer's view of the anticipated results is substantially different from that of the user and/or analyst (see Figure 5.1). This in turn may lead to a revision of the original specifications.

Design walkthroughs review the hierarchy chart according to the guidelines of Chapter 2. It is essential to verify *completeness* of the chart, the use of *functional* modules, proper subordination, span of control, and so on. Attendance is generally limited to designers and programmers.

Logic walkthroughs in which the "inside" of the more complex modules in a hierarchy chart are reviewed. The material presented may include pseudocode, N-S diagrams, flowcharts, or even a cleanly compiled program. Attendees include designers and programmers.

Standards walkthroughs review completed code to ensure compliance with installation standards. Technical documentation may also be checked

[4] E. Yourdon, *Structured Walkthroughs*, 2nd Ed. (Englewood Cliffs, N.J.: Prentice-Hall, 1979).

with the same objective. Attendees include programmers and an auditor or other representative of the standards group.

Operations or procedures walkthroughs are held at the end of development before a system is put into production. Attendees should include users and/or operations personnel, i.e., the people who will make the system work on a daily basis. The material reviewed should consist of procedures manuals and/or user documentation.

The Walkthrough Procedure

The underlying philosophy of the structured walkthrough is that an individual is too close to his or her own work to see adequately, and evaluate objectively, potential problems. The walkthrough brings the evaluation into the open and requires that an individual formally, and periodically, have his or her work reviewed by a peer group. Different organizations conduct walkthroughs in different ways, and consequently it is difficult to establish a system with which everyone will agree. Nevertheless, the following procedure seems typical of many shops.

The person being reviewed initiates the walkthrough by scheduling the session and selecting the reviewers. The reviewee distributes copies of his or her work *prior* to the walkthrough (at least one day in advance) with the expectation that reviewers will read and study the material.

Reviewers accept different roles during the actual walkthrough. The *moderator* (or *coordinator*) is responsible for keeping the discussion on track, avoiding conflict, resolving disputes, etc. He or she should be a person skilled in group dynamics, hopefully with a good sense of humor. A second person functions as a *secretary* (or *librarian*) and maintains an accurate list of any problems which are uncovered. The remaining attendees function as reviewers and critically analyze the material presented.

The reviewee begins the session by presenting his or her work, line by line, making sure every piece is reviewed. The attendees pose questions and/or raise objections as they occur. The coordinator keeps the session moving and the secretary notes the errors.

The session ends when the discussion is no longer fruitful. The reviewee is given the problem list and is expected to resolve all errors.

Suggestions for Successful Walkthroughs

The preceding discussion may read well in theory, but programmers often dislike the walkthrough concept. The probable reason is that individuals resent having their "private" work publicly reviewed, and regard criticism of code, intended or otherwise, as a personal affront. The attitude is natural, and stems from years of working alone.

Walkthroughs can and have become unpleasant and ego-deflating experiences. "Structured walkovers" and/or "stompthroughs" are names given to less than successful sessions. Only if the atmosphere is kept open and nondefensive, only if the discussion is restricted to major problems rather than trivial errors, and only if personality clashes are avoided can the walkthrough be an effective technique. The author suggests the following guidelines be observed to increase the chance for success:

1. *The program and not the programmer is reviewed.* Walkthroughs are intended to find problems and should never be used as a basis for employee evaluation. It is quite logical, therefore, to *exclude* the manager; i.e., the individual in charge of salaries and promotions, from attending.
2. *Emphasize error detection, not correction.* It is simply assumed that the reviewee will take the necessary corrective action *after* the session. Reviewers should not discuss corrections. (The reviewee may well require help in correcting a problem, in which case he or she should consult with the reviewer on an *individual* basis *after* the walkthrough.)
3. *Everyone, from senior analyst to trainee, has his or her work reviewed.* This avoids singling out an individual and further removes any stigma from having one's work reviewed. It also promotes the give-and-take atmosphere that is so vital to making the concept work.
4. *Establish a list of well-defined objectives for each session and do not deviate.* Adherence to this guideline keeps the discussion on track and helps to guarantee its productiveness.
5. *Encourage, or demand, participation from the reviewers.* A walkthrough will indeed become a waste of time if no one has anything to say. Let it be known that each reviewer will be expected to make at least two comments, one positive and one negative. Alternatively, require each reviewer to come to the session with a list of at least three questions.
6. *Impose a predetermined time limit*, from half an hour to two hours. Walkthroughs will eventually cease to be productive and degenerate into a discussion of last night's ball game, the new manager, or some other "hot" topic. The situation should be anticipated and avoided, perhaps by scheduling walkthroughs an hour before lunch. If all of the walkthrough's objectives have not been met when the deadline is reached, schedule a second session.

Summary

The reader should be comfortable with the parallel techniques of flowcharts, pseudocode, and N-S diagrams. All three communicate identical information, and the individual is free to choose whichever method he or she prefers.

Current thought seems to run in favor of pseudocode, but that will vary from installation to installation.

Decision tables and/or decision trees have been used for many years, and well before the advent of structured methods. Nevertheless, they are still applicable today, and are useful in communicating with users. Both methods are effective in detecting omissions and/or inconsistencies in user specifications.

Structured walkthroughs are an effective means of achieving *early* error detection. The underlying premise is that an individual is too close to his or her own work to critique it objectively, and the walkthrough is designed to bring the evaluation process into the open. Several guidelines were suggested to keep walkthroughs from becoming "walkovers." Chief among these were the *emphasis on error detection rather than error correction*, and the fact that *everyone*, from junior trainee to senior analyst, is reviewed.

True/False

1. A decision table with 4 conditions, each with 2 alternatives, has a total of 16 rules.
2. A decision table with 3 conditions, each with 3 alternatives, has a total of 27 rules.
3. A decision table and a decision tree contain identical information, but display it differently.
4. A flowchart can be drawn from a decision table.
5. A flowchart is probably the most popular way of communicating program logic.
6. Pseudocode has precise syntactical rules.
7. N-S charts are more easily modified than pseudocode.
8. Decision trees are readily understood by nontechnical users.
9. N-S charts have no provision for expressing an unconditional branch.
10. Pseudocode is normally developed after a program has been written.
11. Pseudocode and hierarchy charts express the same thing.
12. Decision tables and/or decision trees are well suited to detecting incomplete or inconsistent specifications.
13. The emphasis in a structured walkthrough is on error detection rather than error correction.
14. Walkthroughs should be held for trainees only as these are the individuals most likely to make mistakes.
15. Managers typically should not attend walkthroughs.
16. A walkthrough generally takes a minimum of two hours.
17. Walkthroughs should be restricted to the coding phase of a project.

Problems

1. Consider the Tic Tac Toe project specified at the end of Chapter 2. Develop a flowchart, pseudocode, or an N-S diagram corresponding to the *overall* hierarchy chart. Which of the three is easiest to develop? To modify? Which technique do you think is the best means of communication?

2. Repeat Problem 1 for the blackjack problem, also specified at the end of Chapter 2.

3. Has your work ever been the subject of a structured walkthrough? Did the quality of your work improve, merely because you knew you had to present it? Was the experience helpful, a waste of time, or worse? Are you looking forward to your next walkthrough?

4. Do you agree with banning managers from walkthroughs? Is it possible that the role of moderator in a walkthrough might best be filled by the project manager?

5. Do you agree with the author's suggestions for successful walkthroughs? Are there any guidelines you wish to add to the list? To remove from the list?

6. Have you ever been a reviewer at a walkthrough? Did you learn anything? Can the structured walkthrough become a vehicle for education, in addition to its primary goal of error detection?

7. The following problem is reprinted from Ed Yourdon's book, *Techniques of Program Structure and Design*, used by permission of Prentice-Hall, Inc.

    If a customer has placed an order which exceeds his credit limit, then send the order to the credit department. However, the order should always be accepted if this is one of our special customers, i.e., one who does business with us regularly. Also, if the order is less than the minimum allowable shipping quantity, it should be rejected and sent to the shipping department manager. However, the computer system should be capable of receiving exceptions to this rule, as there will be cases when a customer will insist that his order be shipped, even though it is too small.

    Construct a decision table and then reduce it. The original version will have 16 columns, but the final version can be reduced substantially. (In constructing the initial table, an additional clarification will be required; specifically, a given order should not be rejected for two reasons simultaneously. Hence, if a given set of conditions causes a rejection for both credit and shipping requirements, reject it for credit only.)

    Finally, develop a COBOL IF statement corresponding to the reduced table.

Projects

There are no specific programming projects associated with this chapter. However, it is hoped that the reader will apply the techniques covered to subsequent assignments.

Sequential File Maintenance

6

Overview

This is an important chapter for the practitioner, as it presents the *balance line algorithm* for sequential file maintenance. This *completely general* procedure permits *multiple* transactions for the same transaction key as well as *multiple* transaction files. It should be readily appreciated by anyone who has had to develop and/or modify a COBOL program for a *sequential file update*.

The algorithm is presented through pseudocode and associated hierarchy chart. It is implemented in stages through the *top down approach*, i.e., the philosophy of testing a program before it is completely coded. The requirements of a COBOL case study are presented, and two versions of a COBOL program are developed. The first contains several *program stubs*, and tests the interaction among the higher level paragraphs in the hierarchy chart. The second, and completed, version fulfills the requirements of the case study.

The chapter also considers the problem of *program maintenance*. The requirements of the original case study are altered significantly to include a second transaction file. We show, however, that *nontrivial* modifications to a program's specifications can be easily implemented if the original program adhered to principles of sound design. Accordingly, the chapter is a good illustration of how the structured theory of earlier chapters can be applied to a COBOL setting.

Finally, we consider advanced syntactical elements of COBOL per se, dealing with sequential files.

Balance Line Algorithm

Every programmer has confronted the problem of a sequential update, and virtually every COBOL book has addressed the subject. However, few, if any, programmers and/or authors have developed a truly general solution, with simultaneous simplicity of explanation. This author was impressed with a paper by Barry Dwyer,[1] which detailed a general solution to the problem. Dwyer's technique has been referred to as "the balance line algorithm," and is also described in a book by Johnson and Cooper.[2]

The *balance line algorithm* requires at least three files: an old master, a new master, and one or more transaction files. The transaction and old master files are assumed to be in sequence on the same key. Its value must be unique for every record in the old master, but need not be unique for the transaction file(s); i.e., there can be several transactions for the same master record.

Three types of transactions are permitted: additions, deletions, and changes to existing records. A given transaction affects only a single master record, and as previously stated, there can be multiple transactions for the same master record. There can also be multiple transaction files.

The concept of an *active key* is the basis for the algorithm. *The active key is the smaller of the old master and transaction keys currently being processed.* Thus, if the transaction key is less than the old master, the active key is equal to the transaction key; if the transaction and old master keys are equal, the active key is equal to either; finally, if the old master is less than the transaction key, then the active key is set to the old master. (Note how easily the technique is extended to multiple transaction files; the *active key is always defined as the smallest value of all keys currently processed.*)

Figure 6.1 contains pseudocode for the overall update process, with only a single transaction file shown for simplicity. Initially, the first record is read from each file and the first active key is determined. Johnson and Cooper liken the active key to a policeman at a busy intersection. Only

---

[1] B. Dwyer, "One More Time—How to Update a Master File," *Communications of the ACM*, vol. 24, no. 1 (January 1981).

[2] L. F. Johnson, and R. H. Cooper, *File Techniques for Data Base Organization in COBOL* (Englewood Cliffs, N.J.: Prentice-Hall, 1981).

```
OPEN FILES
READ TRANSACTION-FILE, AT END MOVE HIGH-VALUES TO TRANSACTION-KEY
READ OLD-MASTER-FILE, AT END MOVE HIGH-VALUES TO OLD-MASTER-KEY
CHOOSE FIRST ACTIVE-KEY
DO WHILE ACTIVE-KEY ≠ HIGH-VALUES
    IF OLD-MASTER-KEY = ACTIVE-KEY
        MOVE OLD-MASTER-RECORD TO NEW-MASTER-RECORD
        READ OLD-MASTER-FILE, AT END MOVE HIGH-VALUES TO OLD-MASTER-KEY
    ENDIF
    DO WHILE TRANSACTION-KEY = ACTIVE-KEY
        APPLY TRANSACTION TO NEW-MASTER-RECORD
        READ TRANSACTION-FILE, AT END MOVE HIGH-VALUES TO TRANSACTION-KEY
    ENDDO
    IF NO DELETION WAS PROCESSED
        WRITE NEW-MASTER-RECORD
    ENDIF
    CHOOSE NEXT ACTIVE-KEY
ENDDO
CLOSE FILES
STOP RUN
```

FIGURE 6.1 Balance line algorithm.

those records whose key equals the active key are allowed through the intersection (to participate in the update process). Eventually, the key on each file will equal HIGH-VALUES and the algorithm will terminate.

The major loop of Figure 6.1 executes repeatedly until the active key is equal to HIGH-VALUES; i.e., until both the old master and transaction files are out of data. If the key of the current old master record is equal to the active key, the old master record is moved to the new master, and another record is read from the old master file. A second loop applies all transactions, equal to the active key, to the current master record. (The transaction file is read repeatedly in this inner loop after each transaction is processed.) When the transaction key no longer equals the active key, a check is made to see if a deletion was processed, and if not, the new master record is written. The next active key is chosen and the outer loop continues.

Figure 6.2 expands on the basic logic of Figure 6.1 to include error processing. Although the transaction file is assumed to be valid in and of itself, there are additional errors which come to light only in the actual update process. *Specifically, the update program must reject transactions which attempt to add records that already exist in the old master (i.e., duplicate additions). It should also reject transactions which attempt to change or delete records that do not exist (i.e., a miscopied transaction key).*

Dwyer suggests that the easiest way to accomplish this error processing is through the assignment of an *allocation status* to every value of the active key; i.e., the value of the key is either allocated or it isn't. Deletion of an existing record will change the status from on to off; addition of a new

```
OPEN FILES
READ TRANSACTION-FILE, AT END MOVE HIGH-VALUES TO TRANSACTION-KEY
READ OLD-MASTER-FILE, AT END MOVE HIGH-VALUES TO OLD-MASTER-KEY
CHOOSE FIRST ACTIVE-KEY
DO WHILE ACTIVE-KEY ≠ HIGH-VALUES
    IF OLD-MASTER-KEY = ACTIVE-KEY
        MOVE 'YES' TO RECORD-KEY-ALLOCATED-SWITCH
        MOVE OLD-MASTER-RECORD TO NEW-MASTER-RECORD
        READ OLD-MASTER-FILE, AT END MOVE HIGH-VALUES TO OLD-MASTER-KEY
    ELSE (ACTIVE-KEY IS NOT IN OLD-MASTER-FILE)
        MOVE 'NO' TO RECORD-KEY-ALLOCATED-SWITCH
    ENDIF
    DO WHILE TRANSACTION-KEY = ACTIVE-KEY
        IF ADDITION
            IF RECORD-KEY-ALLOCATED-SWITCH = 'YES'
                WRITE 'ERROR – DUPLICATE ADD'
            ELSE (ACTIVE-KEY IS NOT IN OLD-MASTER-FILE)
                MOVE TRANSACTION-RECORD TO NEW-MASTER-RECORD
                MOVE 'YES' TO RECORD-KEY-ALLOCATED-SWITCH
            ENDIF
        ELSE IF CORRECTION
            IF RECORD-KEY-ALLOCATED-SWITCH = 'YES'
                PROCESS CORRECTION
            ELSE (ACTIVE-KEY IS NOT IN OLD-MASTER-FILE)
                WRITE 'ERROR – NO MATCH'
            ENDIF
        ELSE IF DELETION
            IF RECORD-KEY-ALLOCATED-SWITCH = 'YES'
                MOVE 'NO' TO RECORD-KEY-ALLOCATED-SWITCH
                PROCESS DELETION
            ELSE (ACTIVE-KEY IS NOT IN OLD-MASTER-FILE)
                WRITE 'ERROR – NO MATCH'
            ENDIF
        ENDIF
        READ TRANSACTION-FILE, AT END MOVE HIGH-VALUES TO TRANSACTION-KEY
    ENDDO
    IF RECORD-KEY-ALLOCATED-SWITCH = 'YES'
        WRITE NEW-MASTER-RECORD
    ENDIF
    CHOOSE NEXT ACTIVE-KEY
ENDDO
CLOSE FILES
STOP RUN
```

FIGURE 6.2 Expanded balance line algorithm.

record alters the status from off to on. An attempt to add a key whose status is already on signifies a duplicate addition. In similar fashion, attempting to change or delete a record whose allocation status is off also implies an error, as the transaction key is not present in the old master.

The only time a record is written to the new master file is if the RECORD-KEY-ALLOCATED-SWITCH is set to YES. In other words, deletions are accomplished simply by setting the switch to NO and not writing the record. The pseudocode of Figure 6.2 includes RECORD-KEY-ALLOCATED-SWITCH as per the previous discussion.

The reader should be convinced of the total generality of Figure 6.2 and, further, that *multiple transactions for the same key may be presented in any order*. If, for example, an addition and correction are input in that order, the record will be added and corrected in the same run. However, if the correction precedes the addition, then the correction will be flagged as a no match, and only the addition will take effect. Two additions for the same key will result in adding the first, and flagging the second, as a duplicate add. An addition, correction, and deletion may be processed in that order for the same transaction. A deletion followed by an addition may also be processed. The latter combination will, however, produce an error message, indicating an attempt to delete a record which is not in the old master. In other words, multiple transactions for the same key can be presented in any order, e.g., in *chronological* order, with no requirement for a secondary sort on transaction code.

COBOL Case Study

Implementation of the balance line algorithm is illustrated in the context of a COBOL case study. We begin with a relatively simple set of requirements and then extend the original specifications. This will demonstrate the generality of the approach, and the relative ease with which *maintenance* can be accomplished in a well-written program.

Figures 6.3 and 6.4 contain the record layouts of the old master and transaction files respectively. As can be seen, the transaction file allows for three transaction types: additions, corrections, and deletions, as explained previously. The transaction file is assumed to be valid in and of itself because it has been processed by a "stand alone" edit program. Hence, each transaction has a valid transaction code (A, C, or D), numeric fields are numeric, and so on. Nevertheless, the update program must check (and flag) two kinds of errors which could not be detected in the stand alone edit, as they require interaction with the old master file. These are:

- *Duplicate additions*—in which the social security number of a transaction coded as an addition *already* exists in the old master, and
- *No matches*—in which the social security number of either a deletion or correction transaction type does *not* exist in the old master.

The specifications of the update program are straightforward. Additions are to be added to the new master file in their entirety. Deletions are to be

```
01  OLD-MASTER-RECORD.
    05  OLD-SOC-SEC-NUMBER                 PIC X(9).
    05  OLD-NAME.
        10  OLD-LAST-NAME                  PIC X(15).
        10  OLD-INITIALS                   PIC XX.
    05  OLD-DATE-OF-BIRTH.
        10  OLD-BIRTH-MONTH                PIC 99.
        10  OLD-BIRTH-YEAR                 PIC 99.
    05  OLD-DATE-OF-HIRE.
        10  OLD-HIRE-MONTH                 PIC 99.
        10  OLD-HIRE-YEAR                  PIC 99.
    05  OLD-LOCATION-CODE                  PIC X(3).
    05  OLD-PERFORMANCE-CODE               PIC X.
    05  OLD-EDUCATION-CODE                 PIC X.
    05  OLD-TITLE-DATA OCCURS 2 TIMES.
        10  OLD-TITLE-CODE                 PIC 9(3).
        10  OLD-TITLE-DATE                 PIC 9(4).
    05  OLD-SALARY-DATA OCCURS 3 TIMES.
        10  OLD-SALARY                    PIC 9(5).
        10  OLD-SALARY-DATE               PIC 9(4).
```

FIGURE 6.3 Old master record.

```
01  TRANSACTION-RECORD.
    05  TR-SOC-SEC-NUMBER                  PIC X(9).
    05  TR-NAME.
        10  TR-LAST-NAME                   PIC X(15).
        10  TR-INITIALS                    PIC XX.
    05  TR-DATE-OF-BIRTH.
        10  TR-BIRTH-MONTH                 PIC 99.
        10  TR-BIRTH-YEAR                  PIC 99.
    05  TR-DATE-OF-HIRE.
        10  TR-HIRE-MONTH                  PIC 99.
        10  TR-HIRE-YEAR                   PIC 99.
    05  TR-LOCATION-CODE                   PIC X(3).
    05  TR-PERFORMANCE-CODE                PIC X.
    05  TR-EDUCATION-CODE                  PIC X.
    05  TR-TITLE-DATA.
        10  TR-TITLE-CODE                  PIC 9(3).
        10  TR-TITLE-DATE                  PIC 9(4).
    05  TR-SALARY-DATA.
        10  TR-SALARY                      PIC 9(5).
        10  TR-SALARY-DATE                 PIC 9(4).
    05  TR-TRANSACTION-CODE                PIC X.
        88  ADDITION             VALUE 'A'.
        88  CORRECTION           VALUE 'C'.
        88  DELETION             VALUE 'D'.
    05  FILLER                             PIC X(24).
```

FIGURE 6.4 Transaction record.

removed from the old master file, which is accomplished simply by not writing a record to the new master. Corrections are handled on a parameter by parameter basis. Transactions entered as corrections are to contain the social security number and *only* those fields which are to be changed. Assume, for example, that birth date and location code are to be corrected. The transaction will contain *only* the social security number and *corrected* values of birth date and location code in the *designated* positions on the transaction record (as per Figure 6.4). The *correction* procedure first moves the old master record to the new master, and then examines the transaction fields one at a time. Whenever a nonblank transaction parameter is found, the transaction value will replace the existing value in the master record. (Note that the old master record of Figure 6.3 contains multiple values of both salary and title data. Initially, however, only the most recent value, i.e., the *first* occurrence, may be corrected—see part e of the suggested project at the chapter's end.)

The hierarchy chart of Figure 6.5 contains the necessary *functions* to implement the balance line algorithm, and corresponds to the pseudocode of Figure 6.2 developed earlier. (Modules which are shaded in the upper left corner are called from more than one place.) Recall that pseudocode and a hierarchy chart depict *different* things. Pseudocode indicates sequence and decision making logic, whereas a hierarchy chart depicts function. It indicates what has to be done, but not necessarily when.

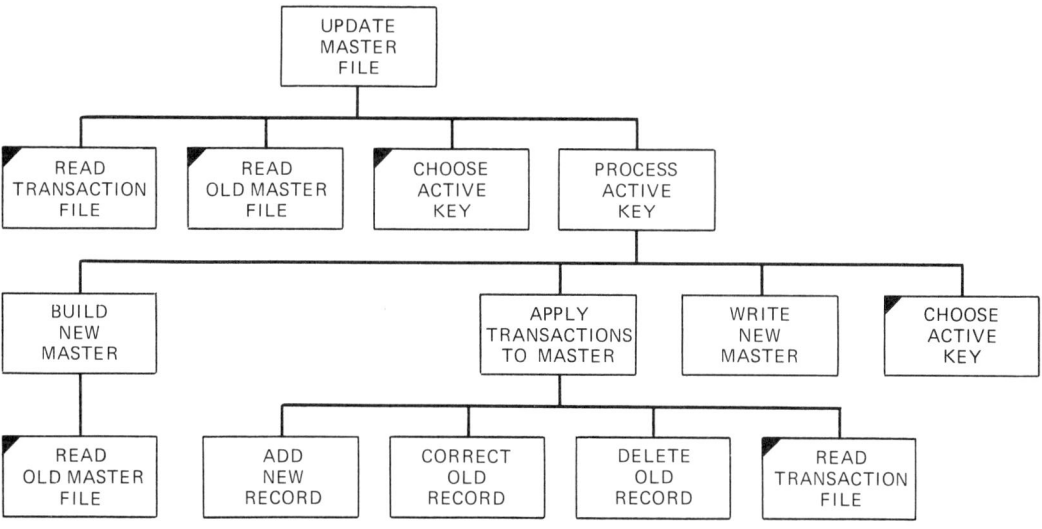

FIGURE 6.5 Hierarchy chart for balance line algorithm.

The hierarchy chart is the major tool of structured design, and was thoroughly discussed in Chapter 2. Its primary use in the present chapter is to illustrate top down testing; i.e., the philosophy of testing a program before it is completely coded.

COBOL Case Study

Top Down Testing

Top down testing imposes that *the highest (and most difficult) modules in a hierarchy chart be tested earlier, and more often, than the lower level (and often trivial) routines.* It requires that testing begin as *soon as possible*, and well before the program is actually finished. This is accomplished by initially coding lower level modules as *program stubs*, which are *abbreviated* versions of completed modules.

There are several ways to code a program stub, the most common being a single DISPLAY statement. A stub paragraph may also return a constant for use by other paragraphs, or a random number within a given range, again for use by other paragraphs. A stub may request help from an on-line terminal, asking a person to do the work the module was supposed to. Or finally, the stub may simply be a shortened version of the final module. Whichever form it takes, the details of a stub paragraph are supplied later *after* it has been established that the module is called in correct sequence.

The rationale of the top down approach was established in Chapter 2, which showed a more even distribution of testing over a program's development. (See Figure 2.4) Of greater import is the fact that *errors are found earlier, and corrected easier*, than with the conventional "bottom up" approach. (The latter technique initially finds the programmer spending inordinate amounts of time formatting various reports, with the unhappy result that production is entered with beautifully formatted, but totally erroneous, output. Correction involves an abundance of panic, overtime, and more often than not, several resignations from the programming staff.)

By contrast, top down testing concentrates on the *interaction* of a program's modules with one another. Hence, with respect to the hierarchy chart of Figure 6.5, one is more concerned that the paragraphs are called in the proper sequence, than with the details of ADD-NEW-RECORD, DELETE-OLD-RECORD, and so on. To appreciate fully the concept of top down testing, we develop a "stubs" program for the sequential update. This in turn requires preparation of test data as shown in Figure 6.6.

The reader should be convinced that Figure 6.6 contains sufficient data to test adequately the eventual update program. All transaction types are present. Multiple transactions have the same key (000000000, 400000000, and 555555555). There is a duplicate addition (200000000) which should be flagged as an error, as well as attempted corrections on erroneous social security numbers (400000001 and the first correction for 555555555).

While on the subject of test data, it is desirable that a person other than the programmer, *preferably the user*, be the one to supply the data. The latter individual does not know how the program actually works, and thus is in a better position to make up *objective* data. In addition, the user knows the *original* specification and is not subject to distortions from the analysis phase. The programmer, on the other hand, is biased, either con-

```
100000000SUGRUE        P 12450879100E533308802220879280001081260000980
200000000CRAWFORD        MA09430678100E64440678        420000680360000678
300000000MILGROM         IR06130580200E6555108140006814800000580
400000000BENJAMIN        BL10531073100E73331073        300001081280001080
500000000TATER           JS02500779200P43330779        310001081270000779
600000000GRAUER          RT11450877200E59001181800118050000118145000118 0
700000000JONES           A 09500778100G64440779333077839000088136000077 9
800000000SMITH           BB08520681300P84440681        385000681
900000000BAKER           E 064908 79100G99870879        650000881550000879
```

(a)

```
                                    Multiple transactions are permitted for the same old master record
000000000BOROW          /  JS03431281100  998712815500012 81A
000000000BOROW         /   JS        X                           C
200000000CRAWFORD     /    MA09430678100E64440680420000680A
400000000BENJAMIN          BL                                    C
400000000BENJAMIN          BL1054                                C
400000000BENJAMIN          BL    1074                            C
400000001BENJAMIN          BL        200                         C
500000000TATER             C                                     D
555555555NEW EMPLOYEE      RT1145                                C
555555555NEW EMPLOYEE      RT11440681100E64440681390000681A
555555555NEW EMPLOYEE      RT        555                         C
700000000JONES             A                      385000781C
800000000SMITH             BB        400                         C
```

(b)

FIGURE 6.6 Test data. (a) Old master file; (b) transaction file.

sciously or subconsciously, and will generate data to accommodate his or her program and/or interpretation of the specifications.

We should also mention that anticipated results are best computed *before* testing begins. Otherwise, it is too easy to assume the program works, because the output "looks right." Indeed, trainees are often so overjoyed merely to get output that they conclude the testing phase upon receiving their first printout.

Given the need for adequate test data, consider now the stubs program of Figure 6.7 and its associated output in Figure 6.8.

Stubs Program

Figure 6.7 is the stubs program for a sequential update implemented according to the balance line algorithm. It is "complete" in that it contains a paragraph for every module in the hierarchy chart of Figure 6.5. It is "incomplete" because several of the lower level modules exist only as program stubs; i.e., abbreviated paragraphs.

Upon closer examination, Figure 6.7 is seen to contain only two files, the old master and transaction, with record descriptions corresponding to Figures 6.3 and 6.4, respectively. These files are accessed through READ INTO statements and described in Working-Storage as per the guidelines in Chapter 4. The new master file is not referenced explicitly in Figure 6.7. Instead, the paragraphs 0060-BUILD-NEW-MASTER and 0080-WRITE-NEW-MASTER contain DISPLAY statements to indicate only that they

```
00001              IDENTIFICATION DIVISION.
00002              PROGRAM-ID.    SEQSTUB.
00003              AUTHOR.        R. GRAUER.
00004
00005              ENVIRONMENT DIVISION.
00006              CONFIGURATION SECTION.
00007              SOURCE-COMPUTER.    IBM-4341.
00008              OBJECT-COMPUTER.    IBM-4341.
00009
00010              INPUT-OUTPUT SECTION.
00011              FILE-CONTROL.
00012                  SELECT TRANSACTION-FILE          ←— Two input files are required
00013                      ASSIGN TO UT-S-TRANS.
00014                  SELECT OLD-MASTER-FILE
00015                      ASSIGN TO UT-S-MASTER.
00016
00017              DATA DIVISION.
00018              FILE SECTION.
00019              FD  TRANSACTION-FILE
00020                  LABEL RECORDS ARE STANDARD
00021                  BLOCK CONTAINS 0 RECORDS
00022                  RECORD CONTAINS 80 CHARACTERS
00023                  DATA RECORD IS TRANSACTION-RECORD.
00024              01  TRANSACTION-RECORD               PIC X(80).
00025
00026              FD  OLD-MASTER-FILE
00027                  LABEL RECORDS ARE STANDARD
00028                  BLOCK CONTAINS 0 RECORDS
00029                  RECORD CONTAINS 80 CHARACTERS
00030                  DATA RECORD IS OLD-MAST-RECORD.
00031              01  OLD-MAST-RECORD                  PIC X(80).
00032                                              ┌— Facilitates debugging
00033              WORKING-STORAGE SECTION.
00034              01  FILLER                           PIC X(14)
00035                      VALUE 'WS BEGINS HERE'.
00036
00037              01  WS-TRANS-RECORD.
00038                  05  TR-SOC-SEC-NUMBER            PIC X(9).
00039                  05  TR-NAME.
00040                      10  TR-LAST-NAME             PIC X(15).
00041                      10  TR-INITIALS              PIC XX.
00042                  05  TR-DATE-OF-BIRTH.
00043                      10  TR-BIRTH-MONTH           PIC 99.
00044                      10  TR-BIRTH-YEAR            PIC 99.
00045                  05  TR-DATE-OF-HIRE.
00046                      10  TR-HIRE-MONTH            PIC 99.
00047                      10  TR-HIRE-YEAR             PIC 99.
00048                  05  TR-LOCATION-CODE             PIC X(3).
00049                  05  TR-PERFORMANCE-CODE          PIC X.
00050                  05  TR-EDUCATION-CODE            PIC X.
00051                  05  TR-TITLE-DATA.
00052                      10  TR-TITLE-CODE            PIC 9(3).
00053                      10  TR-TITLE-DATE            PIC 9(4).
00054                  05  TR-SALARY-DATA.                    ┌— Three transaction types are permitted
00055                      10  TR-SALARY                PIC 9(5).
00056                      10  TR-SALARY-DATE           PIC 9(4).
00057                  05  TR-TRANSACTION-CODE          PIC X.
00058                      88  ADDITION         VALUE 'A'.
00059                      88  CORRECTION       VALUE 'C'.
00060                      88  DELETION         VALUE 'D'.
00061                  05  FILLER                       PIC X(24).
00062
00063              01  WS-OLD-MAST-RECORD.
00064                  05  OLD-SOC-SEC-NUMBER           PIC X(9).
00065                  05  OLD-NAME.
00066                      10  OLD-LAST-NAME            PIC X(15).
00067                      10  OLD-INITIALS             PIC XX.
```

FIGURE 6.7 Stubs program.

```
00068                05    OLD-DATE-OF-BIRTH.
00069                      10    OLD-BIRTH-MONTH              PIC 99.
00070                      10    OLD-BIRTH-YEAR               PIC 99.
00071                05    OLD-DATE-OF-HIRE.
00072                      10    OLD-HIRE-MONTH               PIC 99.
00073                      10    OLD-HIRE-YEAR                PIC 99.
00074                05    OLD-LOCATION-CODE                  PIC X(3).
00075                05    OLD-PERFORMANCE-CODE               PIC X.
00076                05    OLD-EDUCATION-CODE                 PIC X.
00077                05    OLD-TITLE-DATA OCCURS 2 TIMES.
00078                      10    OLD-TITLE-CODE               PIC 9(3).
00079                      10    OLD-TITLE-DATE               PIC 9(4).
00080                05    OLD-SALARY-DATA OCCURS 3 TIMES.
00081                      10    OLD-SALARY                   PIC 9(5).
00082                      10    OLD-SALARY-DATE              PIC 9(4).
00083
00084           01    WS-BALANCE-LINE-SWITCHES.
00085                05    WS-ACTIVE-KEY                      PIC X(9).
00086                05    WS-RECORD-KEY-ALLOCATED-SWITCH     PIC X(3).
00087
00088           PROCEDURE DIVISION.
00089           0010-UPDATE-MASTER-FILE.
00090               OPEN INPUT TRANSACTION-FILE
00091                          OLD-MASTER-FILE.
00092               PERFORM 0020-READ-TRANSACTION-FILE.         ⎤—Initial reads
00093               PERFORM 0030-READ-OLD-MASTER-FILE.          ⎦
00094               PERFORM 0040-CHOOSE-ACTIVE-KEY.
00095               PERFORM 0050-PROCESS-ACTIVE-KEY
00096                   UNTIL WS-ACTIVE-KEY = HIGH-VALUES.
00097               CLOSE TRANSACTION-FILE
00098                     OLD-MASTER-FILE.
00099               STOP RUN.
00100
00101           0020-READ-TRANSACTION-FILE.
00102               READ TRANSACTION-FILE INTO WS-TRANS-RECORD
00103                   AT END MOVE HIGH-VALUES TO TR-SOC-SEC-NUMBER.
00104
00105           0030-READ-OLD-MASTER-FILE.
00106               READ OLD-MASTER-FILE INTO WS-OLD-MAST-RECORD
00107                   AT END MOVE HIGH-VALUE TO OLD-SOC-SEC-NUMBER.
00108
00109           0040-CHOOSE-ACTIVE-KEY.                    ⎤—Determines active key
00110               IF TR-SOC-SEC-NUMBER LESS THAN OLD-SOC-SEC-NUMBER
00111                   MOVE TR-SOC-SEC-NUMBER TO WS-ACTIVE-KEY
00112               ELSE
00113                   MOVE OLD-SOC-SEC-NUMBER TO WS-ACTIVE-KEY.
00114
00115           0050-PROCESS-ACTIVE-KEY.              ⎤—DISPLAY statements to facilitate testing
00116               DISPLAY '       '.
00117               DISPLAY '       '.
00118               DISPLAY 'RECORDS BEING PROCESSED'.
00119               DISPLAY '   TRANSACTION SOC SEC #: ' TR-SOC-SEC-NUMBER.
00120               DISPLAY '   OLD MASTER SOC SEC #:  ' OLD-SOC-SEC-NUMBER.
00121               DISPLAY '   ACTIVE KEY:            ' WS-ACTIVE-KEY.
00122               DISPLAY '       '.
00123
00124               IF OLD-SOC-SEC-NUMBER = WS-ACTIVE-KEY
00125                   MOVE 'YES' TO WS-RECORD-KEY-ALLOCATED-SWITCH
00126                   PERFORM 0060-BUILD-NEW-MASTER
00127               ELSE
00128                   MOVE 'NO' TO WS-RECORD-KEY-ALLOCATED-SWITCH.
00129
00130               PERFORM 0070-APPLY-TRANS-TO-MASTER
00131                   UNTIL WS-ACTIVE-KEY NOT EQUAL TR-SOC-SEC-NUMBER.
00132
00133               IF WS-RECORD-KEY-ALLOCATED-SWITCH = 'YES'
00134                   PERFORM 0080-WRITE-NEW-MASTER.
```

FIGURE 6.7 *continued*

```
00135
00136             PERFORM 0040-CHOOSE-ACTIVE-KEY.
00137
00138         0060-BUILD-NEW-MASTER.
00139             DISPLAY '0060-BUILD-NEW-MASTER ENTERED'.
00140             PERFORM 0030-READ-OLD-MASTER-FILE.
00141
00142         0070-APPLY-TRANS-TO-MASTER.
00143             DISPLAY '0070-APPLY-TRANS-TO-MASTER ENTERED'
00144                 '     TRANSACTION CODE:  ' TR-TRANSACTION-CODE.
00145             IF ADDITION
00146                 PERFORM 0090-ADD-NEW-RECORD
00147             ELSE
00148                 IF CORRECTION                                    ─Determines which
00149                     PERFORM 0100-CORRECT-OLD-RECORD              lower level module
00150                 ELSE                                             to execute
00151                     IF DELETION
00152                         PERFORM 0110-DELETE-OLD-RECORD.
00153
00154             PERFORM 0020-READ-TRANSACTION-FILE.
00155
00156         0080-WRITE-NEW-MASTER.
00157             DISPLAY '0080-WRITE-NEW-MASTER ENTERED'.
00158                                              ─── Partially coded paragraphs
00159         0090-ADD-NEW-RECORD.
00160             DISPLAY '0090-ADD-NEW-RECORD ENTERED'.
00161             IF WS-RECORD-KEY-ALLOCATED-SWITCH = 'YES'
00162                 DISPLAY '    ERROR-DUPLICATE ADDITION: ' TR-SOC-SEC-NUMBER
00163             ELSE
00164                 MOVE 'YES' TO WS-RECORD-KEY-ALLOCATED-SWITCH.
00165
00166         0100-CORRECT-OLD-RECORD.
00167             DISPLAY '0100-CORRECT-OLD-RECORD ENTERED'.
00168             IF WS-RECORD-KEY-ALLOCATED-SWITCH = 'YES'
00169                 NEXT SENTENCE
00170             ELSE
00171                 DISPLAY '    ERROR-NO MATCHING RECORD: ' TR-SOC-SEC-NUMBER.
00172
00173         0110-DELETE-OLD-RECORD.
00174             DISPLAY '0110-DELETE-OLD-RECORD ENTERED'.           /Error check
00175             IF WS-RECORD-KEY-ALLOCATED-SWITCH = 'YES'
00176                 MOVE 'NO' TO WS-RECORD-KEY-ALLOCATED-SWITCH
00177             ELSE
00178                 DISPLAY '    ERROR-NO MATCHING RECORD: ' TR-SOC-SEC-NUMBER.
```

FIGURE 6.7 *continued*

have been called. Indeed, Figure 6.7 is seen to contain many such DISPLAY statements to *facilitate testing by indicating program flow.* It will be shown that significant testing can take place without providing full details of the lower level modules such as 0090-ADD-NEW-RECORD, 0100-CORRECT-OLD-RECORD, etc.

Consider the test data of Figure 6.6, in conjunction with the program of Figure 6.7 and its associated output (Figure 6.8). We begin by reading the first record from each file, social security numbers 000000000 and 100000000 for the transaction and old master, respectively. The active key is the *smaller* of the two, i.e., social security number 000000000, and corresponds to the transaction value. The paragraph 0070-APPLY-TRANS-TO-MASTER is entered for the first transaction, after which the lower level paragraph 0090-ADD-NEW-RECORD is invoked. The second transaction

```
                                              ┌─ Active key is the smaller of old master and transaction keys
RECORDS BEING PROCESSED                      /
  TRANSACTION SOC SEC #:   000000000
  OLD MASTER SOC SEC #:    100000000
  ACTIVE KEY:              000000000

0070-APPLY-TRANS-TO-MASTER ENTERED    TRANSACTION CODE: A
0090-ADD-NEW-RECORD ENTERED
0070-APPLY-TRANS-TO-MASTER ENTERED    TRANSACTION CODE: C
0100-CORRECT-OLD-RECORD ENTERED
0080-WRITE-NEW-MASTER ENTERED


RECORDS BEING PROCESSED
  TRANSACTION SOC SEC #:   200000000
  OLD MASTER SOC SEC #:    100000000
  ACTIVE KEY:              100000000

┌────────────────────────────────────┐
│ 0060-BUILD-NEW-MASTER ENTERED      │──── Existing old master with no activity is copied to new master
│ 0080-WRITE-NEW-MASTER ENTERED      │
└────────────────────────────────────┘


RECORDS BEING PROCESSED
  TRANSACTION SOC SEC #:   200000000
  OLD MASTER SOC SEC #:    200000000
  ACTIVE KEY:              200000000
                                                       ┌─ Duplicate addition is flagged
0060-BUILD-NEW-MASTER ENTERED                         /
  0070-APPLY-TRANS-TO-MASTER ENTERED    TRANSACTION CODE: A
  0090-ADD-NEW-RECORD ENTERED
  ERROR-DUPLICATE ADDITION: 200000000
0080-WRITE-NEW-MASTER ENTERED


RECORDS BEING PROCESSED
  TRANSACTION SOC SEC #:   400000000
  OLD MASTER SOC SEC #:    300000000
  ACTIVE KEY:              300000000

0060-BUILD-NEW-MASTER ENTERED
0080-WRITE-NEW-MASTER ENTERED


RECORDS BEING PROCESSED
  TRANSACTION SOC SEC #:   400000000
  OLD MASTER SOC SEC #:    400000000
  ACTIVE KEY:              400000000
                                           ┌─ Three transactions are applied to same master record
0060-BUILD-NEW-MASTER ENTERED             /
  0070-APPLY-TRANS-TO-MASTER ENTERED    TRANSACTION CODE: C
  0100-CORRECT-OLD-RECORD ENTERED
  0070-APPLY-TRANS-TO-MASTER ENTERED    TRANSACTION CODE: C
  0100-CORRECT-OLD-RECORD ENTERED
  0070-APPLY-TRANS-TO-MASTER ENTERED    TRANSACTION CODE: C
  0100-CORRECT-OLD-RECORD ENTERED
0080-WRITE-NEW-MASTER ENTERED


RECORDS BEING PROCESSED
  TRANSACTION SOC SEC #:   400000001
  OLD MASTER SOC SEC #:    500000000
  ACTIVE KEY:              400000001

0070-APPLY-TRANS-TO-MASTER ENTERED    TRANSACTION CODE: C
0100-CORRECT-OLD-RECORD ENTERED
  ERROR-NO MATCHING RECORD: 400000001 ──── Error message indicating a miscopied social
                                           security number
```

FIGURE 6.8 Output of stubs program.

```
RECORDS BEING PROCESSED
   TRANSACTION SOC SEC #:   500000000
   OLD MASTER SOC SEC #:    500000000
   ACTIVE KEY:              500000000

0060-BUILD-NEW-MASTER ENTERED
0070-APPLY-TRANS-TO-MASTER ENTERED       TRANSACTION CODE: D
0110-DELETE-OLD-RECORD ENTERED


RECORDS BEING PROCESSED
   TRANSACTION SOC SEC #:   555555555
   OLD MASTER SOC SEC #:    600000000
   ACTIVE KEY:              555555555

0070-APPLY-TRANS-TO-MASTER ENTERED       TRANSACTION CODE: C
0100-CORRECT-OLD-RECORD ENTERED
   ERROR-NO MATCHING RECORD: 555555555
0070-APPLY-TRANS-TO-MASTER ENTERED       TRANSACTION CODE: A
0090-ADD-NEW-RECORD ENTERED
0070-APPLY-TRANS-TO-MASTER ENTERED       TRANSACTION CODE: C
0100-CORRECT-OLD-RECORD ENTERED
0080-WRITE-NEW-MASTER ENTERED
```

Attempted correction is flagged before addition is accomplished

Correction successfully applied *after* addition

```
RECORDS BEING PROCESSED
   TRANSACTION SOC SEC #:   700000000
   OLD MASTER SOC SEC #:    600000000
   ACTIVE KEY:              600000000

0060-BUILD-NEW-MASTER ENTERED
0080-WRITE-NEW-MASTER ENTERED


RECORDS BEING PROCESSED
   TRANSACTION SOC SEC #:   700000000
   OLD MASTER SOC SEC #:    700000000
   ACTIVE KEY:              700000000

0060-BUILD-NEW-MASTER ENTERED
0070-APPLY-TRANS-TO-MASTER ENTERED       TRANSACTION CODE: C
0100-CORRECT-OLD-RECORD ENTERED
0080-WRITE-NEW-MASTER ENTERED


RECORDS BEING PROCESSED
   TRANSACTION SOC SEC #:   800000000
   OLD MASTER SOC SEC #:    800000000
   ACTIVE KEY:              800000000

0060-BUILD-NEW-MASTER ENTERED
0070-APPLY-TRANS-TO-MASTER ENTERED       TRANSACTION CODE: C
0100-CORRECT-OLD-RECORD ENTERED
0080-WRITE-NEW-MASTER ENTERED
```

Transaction key has been set to HIGH-VALUES and does not print

```
RECORDS BEING PROCESSED
   TRANSACTION SOC SEC #:   
   OLD MASTER SOC SEC #:    900000000
   ACTIVE KEY:              900000000

0060-BUILD-NEW-MASTER ENTERED
0080-WRITE-NEW-MASTER ENTERED
```

FIGURE 6.8 *continued*

in the test data also has social security number 000000000, so that 0070-APPLY-TRANS-TO-MASTER is executed a second time, followed by 0100-CORRECT-OLD-RECORD. When the transaction key no longer equals the active key; i.e., when the third transaction (CRAWFORD, social security number 200000000) is read from Figure 6.6, the paragraph 0080-WRITE-NEW-MASTER is invoked, implying that a new master record will be written.

The second determination of the active key compares transaction and old master social security numbers of 200000000 and 100000000, producing an active key of 100000000. There is no activity for the existing old master, causing it to be copied to the new master, as implied by the paragraphs 0060-BUILD-NEW-MASTER and 0080-WRITE-NEW-MASTER.

The third determination of the active key finds the *same* social security number in both files, producing an error message for a duplicate addition. The fourth active key, 300000000, indicates a second inactive master record with appropriate action as previously discussed. Multiple corrections are processed for the next active key 400000000, followed by an error message for the miscopied transaction social security number of 400000001.

By this time, the reader should have the feeling *that the program of Figure 6.7 appears to be working*. In other words, paragraphs are executed in the correct sequence for the test data of Figure 6.6. A critical analysis of the output of Figure 6.8 can be construed as initial program testing. A successful conclusion, i.e., correspondence between the output of Figure 6.8 and the anticipated output for the test data leads one to believe that the overall logic of the update program is correct. (The remainder of Figure 6.8 is left to the reader as an exercise.)

Completed Program

Once the stubs program has been tested and debugged, it is relatively easy to "fill in the blanks" and complete the maintenance program. In other words, the most difficult portion of the maintenance program is the *interaction* between modules; i.e., whether to read from the old master or transaction file or both, how to hold the current old master record to apply multiple transactions, which lower level module to call: add, correct or delete, and so on.

Figure 6.9 is the completed version of Figure 6.7. The most obvious difference between the two programs is the increased length of Figure 6.9, which has been achieved by expanding the earlier program stubs. The completed program contains an added paragraph, 0105-CORRECT-INDIVIDUAL-FIELDS, which is called from 0100-CORRECT-OLD-RECORD. This extra paragraph is necessary because COBOL does not have an "inline" perform capability. The completed program references NEW-MASTER-FILE explicitly and contains the requisite COBOL entries: SELECT, FD, etc.

Output produced by the program of Figure 6.9 using the test data of Figure 6.6 is shown in Figure 6.10. The reader should carefully verify the

```
00001              IDENTIFICATION DIVISION.
00002              PROGRAM-ID.    SEQUPDT.
00003              AUTHOR.        R. GRAUER.
00004
00005              ENVIRONMENT DIVISION.
00006              CONFIGURATION SECTION.
00007              SOURCE-COMPUTER.      IBM-4341.
00008              OBJECT-COMPUTER.      IBM-4341.
00009
00010              INPUT-OUTPUT SECTION.
00011              FILE-CONTROL.
00012                  SELECT TRANSACTION-FILE
00013                      ASSIGN TO UT-S-TRANS.
00014                  SELECT OLD-MASTER-FILE              ←Output file has been added
00015                      ASSIGN TO UT-S-MASTER.
00016                  SELECT NEW-MASTER-FILE
00017                      ASSIGN TO UT-S-NEWMAST.
00018
00019              DATA DIVISION.
00020              FILE SECTION.
00021              FD  TRANSACTION-FILE
00022                  LABEL RECORDS ARE STANDARD
00023                  BLOCK CONTAINS 0 RECORDS
00024                  RECORD CONTAINS 80 CHARACTERS
00025                  DATA RECORD IS TRANSACTION-RECORD.
00026              01  TRANSACTION-RECORD               PIC X(80).
00027
00028              FD  OLD-MASTER-FILE
00029                  LABEL RECORDS ARE STANDARD
00030                  BLOCK CONTAINS 0 RECORDS
00031                  RECORD CONTAINS 80 CHARACTERS
00032                  DATA RECORD IS OLD-MAST-RECORD.
00033              01  OLD-MAST-RECORD                  PIC X(80).
00034                                                        IBM OS feature to indicate block
00035              FD  NEW-MASTER-FILE                       size is entered in JCL
00036                  LABEL RECORDS ARE STANDARD
00037                  BLOCK CONTAINS 0 RECORDS
00038                  RECORD CONTAINS 80 CHARACTERS
00039                  DATA RECORD IS NEW-MAST-RECORD.
00040              01  NEW-MAST-RECORD                  PIC X(80).
00041
00042              WORKING-STORAGE SECTION.
00043              01  FILLER                           PIC X(14)
00044                     VALUE 'WS BEGINS HERE'.
00045
00046              01  WS-TRANS-RECORD.
00047                  05  TR-SOC-SEC-NUMBER            PIC X(9).
00048                  05  TR-NAME.
00049                      10  TR-LAST-NAME             PIC X(15).
00050                      10  TR-INITIALS              PIC XX.
00051                  05  TR-DATE-OF-BIRTH.
00052                      10  TR-BIRTH-MONTH           PIC 99.
00053                      10  TR-BIRTH-YEAR            PIC 99.
00054                  05  TR-DATE-OF-HIRE.
00055                      10  TR-HIRE-MONTH            PIC 99.
00056                      10  TR-HIRE-YEAR             PIC 99.
00057                  05  TR-LOCATION-CODE             PIC X(3).
00058                  05  TR-PERFORMANCE-CODE          PIC X.
00059                  05  TR-EDUCATION-CODE            PIC X.
00060                  05  TR-TITLE-DATA.
00061                      10  TR-TITLE-CODE            PIC 9(3).
00062                      10  TR-TITLE-DATE            PIC 9(4).
00063                  05  TR-SALARY-DATA.
00064                      10  TR-SALARY                PIC 9(5).
00065                      10  TR-SALARY-DATE           PIC 9(4).
00066                  05  TR-TRANSACTION-CODE          PIC X.
00067                      88  ADDITION        VALUE 'A'.
00068                      88  CORRECTION      VALUE 'C'.        ←Three transaction types
00069                      88  DELETION        VALUE 'D'.
```

FIGURE 6.9 Completed sequential update.

```
00070              05  FILLER                           PIC X(24).
00071
00072          01  WS-OLD-MAST-RECORD.
00073              05  OLD-SOC-SEC-NUMBER               PIC X(9).
00074              05  OLD-NAME.
00075                  10  OLD-LAST-NAME                PIC X(15).
00076                  10  OLD-INITIALS                 PIC XX.
00077              05  OLD-DATE-OF-BIRTH.
00078                  10  OLD-BIRTH-MONTH              PIC 99.
00079                  10  OLD-BIRTH-YEAR               PIC 99.
00080              05  OLD-DATE-OF-HIRE.                     Record layouts are identical
00081                  10  OLD-HIRE-MONTH               PIC 99.
00082                  10  OLD-HIRE-YEAR                PIC 99.
00083              05  OLD-LOCATION-CODE                PIC X(3).
00084              05  OLD-PERFORMANCE-CODE             PIC X.
00085              05  OLD-EDUCATION-CODE               PIC X.
00086              05  OLD-TITLE-DATA OCCURS 2 TIMES.
00087                  10  OLD-TITLE-CODE               PIC 9(3).
00088                  10  OLD-TITLE-DATE               PIC 9(4).
00089              05  OLD-SALARY-DATA OCCURS 3 TIMES.
00090                  10  OLD-SALARY                   PIC 9(5).
00091                  10  OLD-SALARY-DATE              PIC 9(4).
00092
00093          01  WS-NEW-MAST-RECORD.
00094              05  NEW-SOC-SEC-NUMBER               PIC X(9).
00095              05  NEW-NAME.
00096                  10  NEW-LAST-NAME                PIC X(15).
00097                  10  NEW-INITIALS                 PIC XX.
00098              05  NEW-DATE-OF-BIRTH.
00099                  10  NEW-BIRTH-MONTH              PIC 99.
00100                  10  NEW-BIRTH-YEAR               PIC 99.
00101              05  NEW-DATE-OF-HIRE.
00102                  10  NEW-HIRE-MONTH               PIC 99.
00103                  10  NEW-HIRE-YEAR                PIC 99.
00104              05  NEW-LOCATION-CODE                PIC X(3).
00105              05  NEW-PERFORMANCE-CODE             PIC X.
00106              05  NEW-EDUCATION-CODE               PIC X.
00107              05  NEW-TITLE-DATA OCCURS 2 TIMES.
00108                  10  NEW-TITLE-CODE               PIC 9(3).
00109                  10  NEW-TITLE-DATE               PIC 9(4).
00110              05  NEW-SALARY-DATA OCCURS 3 TIMES.
00111                  10  NEW-SALARY                   PIC 9(5).
00112                  10  NEW-SALARY-DATE              PIC 9(4).
00113
00114          01  WS-BALANCE-LINE-SWITCHES.
00115              05  WS-ACTIVE-KEY                    PIC X(9).
00116              05  WS-RECORD-KEY-ALLOCATED-SWITCH   PIC X(3).
00117
00118          PROCEDURE DIVISION.
00119          0010-UPDATE-MASTER-FILE.
00120              OPEN INPUT TRANSACTION-FILE
00121                         OLD-MASTER-FILE
00122                   OUTPUT NEW-MASTER-FILE.
00123              PERFORM 0020-READ-TRANSACTION-FILE.
00124              PERFORM 0030-READ-OLD-MASTER-FILE.
00125              PERFORM 0040-CHOOSE-ACTIVE-KEY.
00126              PERFORM 0050-PROCESS-ACTIVE-KEY
00127                  UNTIL WS-ACTIVE-KEY = HIGH-VALUES.      Processing terminates when the active
00128              CLOSE TRANSACTION-FILE                      key is HIGH-VALUES; i.e., when both
00129                    OLD-MASTER-FILE                       files are empty
00130                    NEW-MASTER-FILE.
00131              STOP RUN.
00132
00133          0020-READ-TRANSACTION-FILE.
00134              READ TRANSACTION-FILE INTO WS-TRANS-RECORD
00135                  AT END MOVE HIGH-VALUES TO TR-SOC-SEC-NUMBER.
00136
```

FIGURE 6.9 *continued*

```
00137           0030-READ-OLD-MASTER-FILE.
00138               READ OLD-MASTER-FILE INTO WS-OLD-MAST-RECORD
00139                   AT END MOVE HIGH-VALUE TO OLD-SOC-SEC-NUMBER.
00140
00141           0040-CHOOSE-ACTIVE-KEY.
00142               IF TR-SOC-SEC-NUMBER LESS THAN OLD-SOC-SEC-NUMBER
00143                   MOVE TR-SOC-SEC-NUMBER TO WS-ACTIVE-KEY
00144               ELSE
00145                   MOVE OLD-SOC-SEC-NUMBER TO WS-ACTIVE-KEY.
00146
00147           0050-PROCESS-ACTIVE-KEY.
00148               IF OLD-SOC-SEC-NUMBER = WS-ACTIVE-KEY
00149                   MOVE 'YES' TO WS-RECORD-KEY-ALLOCATED-SWITCH
00150                   PERFORM 0060-BUILD-NEW-MASTER
00151               ELSE
00152                   MOVE 'NO' TO WS-RECORD-KEY-ALLOCATED-SWITCH.
00153
00154               PERFORM 0070-APPLY-TRANS-TO-MASTER
00155                   UNTIL WS-ACTIVE-KEY NOT EQUAL TR-SOC-SEC-NUMBER.
00156
00157               IF WS-RECORD-KEY-ALLOCATED-SWITCH = 'YES'
00158                   PERFORM 0080-WRITE-NEW-MASTER.
00159
00160               PERFORM 0040-CHOOSE-ACTIVE-KEY.
00161
00162           0060-BUILD-NEW-MASTER.
00163               MOVE WS-OLD-MAST-RECORD TO WS-NEW-MAST-RECORD.
00164               PERFORM 0030-READ-OLD-MASTER-FILE.
00165
00166           0070-APPLY-TRANS-TO-MASTER.
00167               IF ADDITION
00168                   PERFORM 0090-ADD-NEW-RECORD
00169               ELSE
00170                   IF CORRECTION
00171                       PERFORM 0100-CORRECT-OLD-RECORD
00172                   ELSE
00173                       IF DELETION
00174                           PERFORM 0110-DELETE-OLD-RECORD.
00175
00176               PERFORM 0020-READ-TRANSACTION-FILE.
00177
00178           0080-WRITE-NEW-MASTER.
00179               WRITE NEW-MAST-RECORD FROM WS-NEW-MAST-RECORD.
00180
00181           0090-ADD-NEW-RECORD.
00182               IF WS-RECORD-KEY-ALLOCATED-SWITCH = 'YES'
00183                   DISPLAY '   ERROR-DUPLICATE ADDITION: ' TR-SOC-SEC-NUMBER
00184               ELSE
00185                   MOVE 'YES' TO WS-RECORD-KEY-ALLOCATED-SWITCH
00186                   MOVE SPACES TO WS-NEW-MAST-RECORD
00187                   MOVE TR-SOC-SEC-NUMBER TO NEW-SOC-SEC-NUMBER
00188                   MOVE TR-NAME TO NEW-NAME
00189                   MOVE TR-DATE-OF-BIRTH TO NEW-DATE-OF-BIRTH
00190                   MOVE TR-DATE-OF-HIRE TO NEW-DATE-OF-HIRE
00191                   MOVE TR-LOCATION-CODE TO NEW-LOCATION-CODE
00192                   MOVE TR-PERFORMANCE-CODE TO NEW-PERFORMANCE-CODE
00193                   MOVE TR-EDUCATION-CODE TO NEW-EDUCATION-CODE
00194                   MOVE TR-TITLE-DATA TO NEW-TITLE-DATA (1)
00195                   MOVE TR-SALARY-DATA TO NEW-SALARY-DATA (1).
00196
00197           0100-CORRECT-OLD-RECORD.
00198               IF WS-RECORD-KEY-ALLOCATED-SWITCH = 'YES'
00199                   PERFORM 0105-CORRECT-INDIVIDUAL-FIELDS
00200               ELSE
00201                   DISPLAY '   ERROR-NO MATCHING RECORD: ' TR-SOC-SEC-NUMBER.
00202
```

Applies multiple transactions to a single master record

Expanded from a program stub

FIGURE 6.9 *continued*

```
00203              0105-CORRECT-INDIVIDUAL-FIELDS.
00204                  IF TR-NAME NOT EQUAL SPACES
00205                      MOVE TR-NAME TO NEW-NAME.
00206                  IF TR-DATE-OF-BIRTH NOT EQUAL SPACES
00207                      MOVE TR-DATE-OF-BIRTH TO NEW-DATE-OF-BIRTH.
00208                  IF TR-DATE-OF-HIRE NOT EQUAL SPACES
00209                      MOVE TR-DATE-OF-HIRE TO NEW-DATE-OF-HIRE.
00210                  IF TR-LOCATION-CODE NOT EQUAL SPACES
00211                      MOVE TR-LOCATION-CODE TO NEW-LOCATION-CODE.
00212                  IF TR-PERFORMANCE-CODE NOT EQUAL SPACES
00213                      MOVE TR-PERFORMANCE-CODE TO NEW-PERFORMANCE-CODE.
00214                  IF TR-EDUCATION-CODE NOT EQUAL SPACES
00215                      MOVE TR-EDUCATION-CODE TO NEW-EDUCATION-CODE.
00216                  IF TR-TITLE-CODE IS NUMERIC
00217                      MOVE TR-TITLE-CODE TO NEW-TITLE-CODE (1).
00218                  IF TR-TITLE-DATE IS NUMERIC
00219                      MOVE TR-TITLE-DATE TO NEW-TITLE-DATE (1).
00220                  IF TR-SALARY IS NUMERIC
00221                      MOVE TR-SALARY TO NEW-SALARY (1).
00222                  IF TR-SALARY-DATE IS NUMERIC
00223                      MOVE TR-SALARY-DATE TO NEW-SALARY-DATE (1).
00224
00225              0110-DELETE-OLD-RECORD.
```

Precludes writing new master and deletes record (see lines 157 - 158)

```
00226                  IF WS-RECORD-KEY-ALLOCATED-SWITCH = 'YES'
00227                      MOVE 'NO' TO WS-RECORD-KEY-ALLOCATED-SWITCH
00228                  ELSE
00229                      DISPLAY '  ERROR-NO MATCHING RECORD: ' TR-SOC-SEC-NUMBER.
```

FIGURE 6.9 *continued*

correctness of the output with respect to the original test data. Observe in particular how multiple transactions were applied to a single old master record (BENJAMIN), how BOROW was successfully added to the new master, and how TATER was deleted. The error messages successfully

This record has been added   *Two fields have been corrected from two different transactions*

```
000000000BOROW         JS0343128100X99871281         550001281
100000000SUGRUE       P 1245087910 0E5333088022208792800010812600 00980
200000000CRAWFORD      MA09430678100E64440678         4200006803600 00678
300000000MILGROM       IR06130580200E6555108140006814800 00580
400000000BENJAMIN      BL10541074100E73331073         3000010812800 01080
555555555NEW EMPLOYEE  RT11440681100E65550681         390000681
600000000GRAUER        RT11450877200E5900118180011805000011814500 01180
700000000JONES        A 09500778100G644407793330778385000781360000779
800000000SMITH         BB08520681300P84000681         385000681
900000000BAKER        E 06490879100G99870879         6500008815500 00879
```

Social security number 500000000 has been deleted

(a)

Pertains to first transaction for this record

```
ERROR-DUPLICATE ADDITION: 200000000
ERROR-NO MATCHING RECORD: 400000001
ERROR-NO MATCHING RECORD: 555555555
```

(b)

FIGURE 6.10 Output of sequential update (see test data of Figure 6.6). (a) New master; (b) error messages.

reflect both erroneous conditions; i.e., a duplicate addition and miscopied social security number.

The error message associated with employee 555555555 further illustrates the power of the balance line algorithm. The first transaction is correctly flagged as an error because the social security number is not present in the old master. The second transaction adds the record, and the third and last transaction changes title from 444 to 555.

Program Maintenance

We have stated repeatedly that a well-written program must be easily read and maintained, and have argued that adherence to the structured methodology brings this goal closer to reality. This section puts the theory to the acid test of program maintenance. Specifically, we consider a number of nontrivial changes to the completed program of Figure 6.9. These are:

1. Inclusion of a *second* transaction (i.e., a promotion) file to accommodate promotions and/or salary increases. The record layout for this file is shown in Figure 6.11.

```
01  PROMOTION-RECORD.
    05  PR-SOC-SEC-NUMBER          PIC X(9).
    05  PR-NAME.
        10  PR-LAST-NAME           PIC X(15).
        10  PR-INITIALS            PIC XX.
    05  PR-SALARY-DATA.
        10  PR-SALARY              PIC 9(5).
        10  PR-SALARY-DATE         PIC 9(4).
    05  PR-TITLE-DATA.
        10  PR-TITLE-CODE          PIC 9(3).
        10  PR-TITLE-DATE          PIC 9(4).
    05  PR-PROMOTION-CODE          PIC X.
        88  SALARY-RAISE           VALUE 'R'.
        88  PROMOTION              VALUE 'P'.
    05  FILLER                     PIC X(37).
```

FIGURE 6.11 Promotion record.

2. Salary increases are to be handled in the following manner: The transaction salary becomes the present salary in the new master, causing the present salary in the old master to become the previous salary in the new master. In similar fashion, the previous salary in the old master becomes the second previous salary in the new master. (The record layout of the master file in Figure 6.3 allowed three salary levels.) The situation is shown schematically in Figure 6.12.

Each occurrence of salary is accompanied by a salary date in both

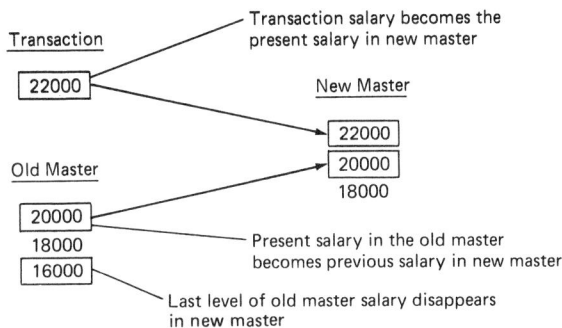

FIGURE 6.12 Salary increases.

the old master and promotion record layouts (see Figures 6.3 and 6.11). Accordingly, the salary dates are to be adjusted simultaneously with the salaries.

3. Promotions (i.e., title changes in the new file) are to be handled in a manner analogous to salary increases. Hence, the transaction title, PR-TITLE-CODE, becomes the present title in the new master, causing the present title in the old master to become the previous title in the new master. The associated dates are to be adjusted simultaneously.

4. Deletions (in the original transaction file) are to be written in their entirety to a new file, DELETED-RECORD-FILE for possible recall at a future date.

5. All error messages are to be expanded to print the entire transaction which is in error.

The implementation of these modifications is best accomplished by considering the necessary changes in the program's hierarchy chart. Figure 6.5 contained the chart for the original problem, and Figure 6.13 depicts the expanded version. Dotted lines in Figure 6.13 denote additional modules mandated by the required changes.

It should be apparent that a new module, APPLY-PROMOTIONS-TO-MASTER, is necessary to process the additional file. It in turn has three subordinates, DO-TITLE-UPDATE, DO-SALARY-UPDATE, and READ-PROMOTION-FILE. The latter is called from two places; in UPDATE-MASTER-FILE to provide the priming read for the promotion file, and from APPLY-PROMOTIONS-TO-MASTER to read the next promotion record.

The true generality of the balance line algorithm is appreciated from the expanded chart of Figure 6.13. Even though a second transaction file has been added, there are no new modules required for the algorithm per se. It is, of course, necessary to change the logic of CHOOSE-ACTIVE-KEY, in that active key is now the smaller of *three* values (old master, transaction,

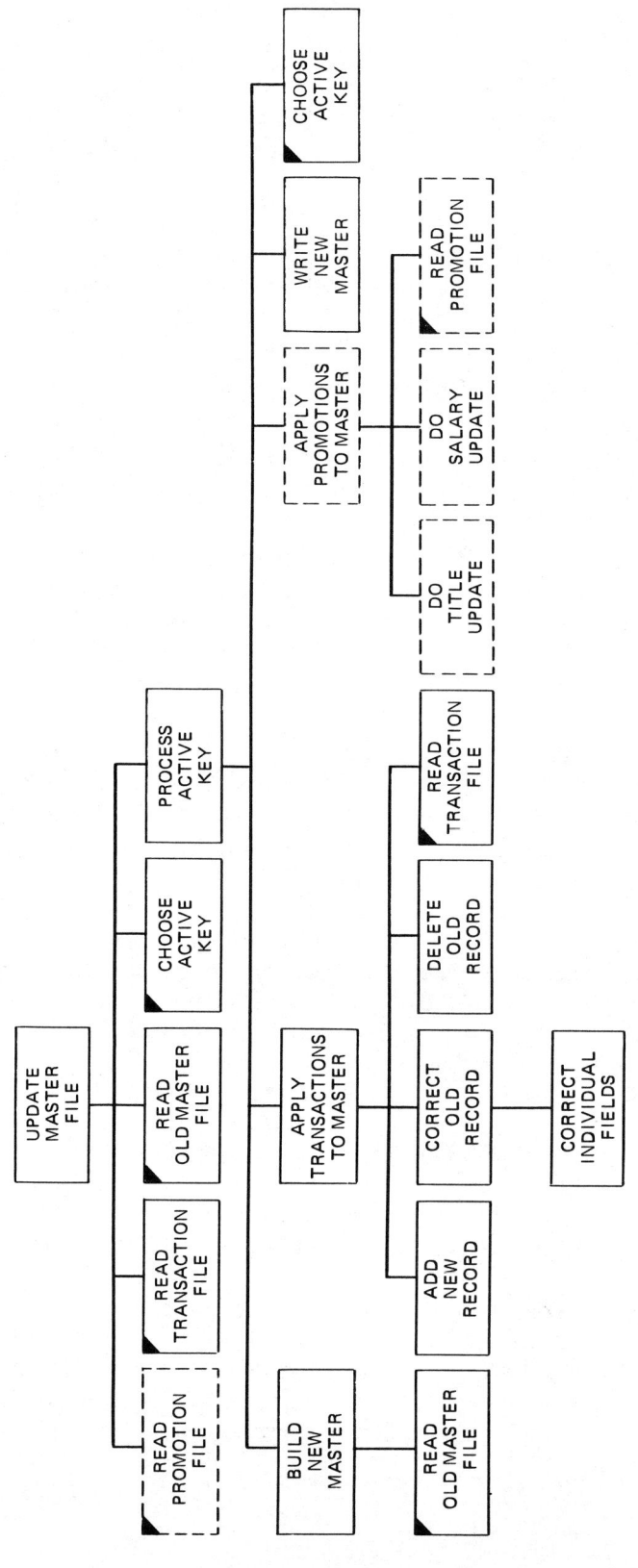

FIGURE 6.13 Expanded hierarchy chart. Notes: 1. Dotted lines indicate new modules which must be added as a consequence of the modification requirements. 2. The internal logic of CHOOSE-ACTIVE-KEY, and DELETE-OLD-RECORD will change. 3. Shading in upper left corner indicates a module which is called from more than one place.

and promotion social security numbers), rather than two as before. However, it is relatively simple to make this change, and further, we are confident it will work. (Could the same degree of confidence be achieved if you were suddenly asked to modify the last maintenance program you wrote?)

It is also necessary to change the internal code of DELETE-OLD-RECORD in order to write deleted transactions to a special file. Again, we are confident that the change will work, and further, that *the change will not affect any other modules in the program.* This is because the modules in the hierarchy chart were carefully developed to be *highly cohesive*, but *loosely coupled*, COBOL paragraphs. In other words, each paragraph in the maintenance program accomplishes a *single* function, and further, the paragraphs are relatively independent of one another. We are able to make changes easily, and avoid the almost universal condition of fixing one problem but creating two new ones in its stead.

The modified program is shown in Figure 6.14. The author expects the program to be self-explanatory, and says nothing further. Test data and associated output are shown in Figure 6.15. (The transaction and old master files of Figure 6.15 are the same as in Figure 6.6.)

```
00001              IDENTIFICATION DIVISION.
00002              PROGRAM-ID.    SEQUPEX.
00003              AUTHOR.        R. GRAUER.
00004
00005              ENVIRONMENT DIVISION.
00006              CONFIGURATION SECTION.
00007              SOURCE-COMPUTER.      IBM-4341.
00008              OBJECT-COMPUTER.      IBM-4341.
00009
00010              INPUT-OUTPUT SECTION.
00011              FILE-CONTROL.
00012                  SELECT TRANSACTION-FILE
00013                      ASSIGN TO UT-S-TRANS.
00014                  SELECT OLD-MASTER-FILE
00015                      ASSIGN TO UT-S-MASTER.      /Promotion file has been added
00016                  SELECT PROMOTION-FILE
00017                      ASSIGN TO UT-S-PROMOTE.
00018                  SELECT DELETED-RECORD-FILE
00019                      ASSIGN TO UT-S-DELETE.
00020                  SELECT NEW-MASTER-FILE
00021                      ASSIGN TO UT-S-NEWMAST.
00022
00023              DATA DIVISION.
00024              FILE SECTION.
00025              FD  TRANSACTION-FILE
00026                  LABEL RECORDS ARE STANDARD
00027                  BLOCK CONTAINS 0 RECORDS
00028                  RECORD CONTAINS 80 CHARACTERS
00029                  DATA RECORD IS TRANSACTION-RECORD.
00030              01  TRANSACTION-RECORD                PIC X(80).
00031
00032              FD  OLD-MASTER-FILE
00033                  LABEL RECORDS ARE STANDARD
00034                  BLOCK CONTAINS 0 RECORDS
00035                  RECORD CONTAINS 80 CHARACTERS
00036                  DATA RECORD IS OLD-MAST-RECORD.
00037              01  OLD-MAST-RECORD                   PIC X(80).
00038
```

FIGURE 6.14 Modified sequential update.

```
00039             FD  PROMOTION-FILE
00040                 LABEL RECORDS ARE STANDARD
00041                 BLOCK CONTAINS 0 RECORDS
00042                 RECORD CONTAINS 80 CHARACTERS
00043                 DATA RECORD IS PROMOTION-RECORD.
00044             01  PROMOTION-RECORD                        PIC X(80).
00045
00046             FD  DELETED-RECORD-FILE
00047                 LABEL RECORDS ARE STANDARD
00048                 BLOCK CONTAINS 0 RECORDS
00049                 RECORD CONTAINS 80 CHARACTERS
00050                 DATA RECORD IS DELETED-RECORD.
00051             01  DELETED-RECORD                          PIC X(80).
00052
00053             FD  NEW-MASTER-FILE
00054                 LABEL RECORDS ARE STANDARD
00055                 BLOCK CONTAINS 0 RECORDS
00056                 RECORD CONTAINS 80 CHARACTERS
00057                 DATA RECORD IS NEW-MAST-RECORD.
00058             01  NEW-MAST-RECORD                         PIC X(80).
00059
00060             WORKING-STORAGE SECTION.
00061             01  FILLER                                  PIC X(14)
00062                     VALUE 'WS BEGINS HERE'.
00063
00064             01  WS-TRANS-RECORD.
00065                 05  TR-SOC-SEC-NUMBER                   PIC X(9).
00066                 05  TR-NAME.
00067                     10  TR-LAST-NAME                    PIC X(15).
00068                     10  TR-INITIALS                     PIC XX.
00069                 05  TR-DATE-OF-BIRTH.
00070                     10  TR-BIRTH-MONTH                  PIC 99.
00071                     10  TR-BIRTH-YEAR                   PIC 99.
00072                 05  TR-DATE-OF-HIRE.
00073                     10  TR-HIRE-MONTH                   PIC 99.
00074                     10  TR-HIRE-YEAR                    PIC 99.
00075                 05  TR-LOCATION-CODE                    PIC X(3).
00076                 05  TR-PERFORMANCE-CODE                 PIC X.
00077                 05  TR-EDUCATION-CODE                   PIC X.
00078                 05  TR-TITLE-DATA.
00079                     10  TR-TITLE-CODE                   PIC 9(3).
00080                     10  TR-TITLE-DATE                   PIC 9(4).
00081                 05  TR-SALARY-DATA.
00082                     10  TR-SALARY                       PIC 9(5).
00083                     10  TR-SALARY-DATE                  PIC 9(4).
00084                 05  TR-TRANSACTION-CODE                 PIC X.
00085                     88  ADDITION         VALUE 'A'.
00086                     88  CORRECTION       VALUE 'C'.
00087                     88  DELETION         VALUE 'D'.
00088                 05  FILLER                              PIC X(24).
00089
00090             01  WS-PROMOTION-RECORD.
00091                 05  PR-SOC-SEC-NUMBER                   PIC X(9).
00092                 05  PR-NAME.
00093                     10  PR-LAST-NAME                    PIC X(15).
00094                     10  PR-INITIALS                     PIC XX.
00095                 05  PR-SALARY-DATA.
00096                     10  PR-SALARY                       PIC 9(5).
00097                     10  PR-SALARY-DATE                  PIC 9(4).
00098                 05  PR-TITLE-DATA.
00099                     10  PR-TITLE-CODE                   PIC 9(3).
00100                     10  PR-TITLE-DATE                   PIC 9(4).
00101                 05  PR-PROMOTION-CODE                   PIC X.
00102                     88  SALARY-RAISE     VALUE 'R'.
00103                     88  PROMOTION        VALUE 'P'.
00104                 05  FILLER                              PIC X(37).
00105
```

FIGURE 6.14 *continued*

```
00106           01  WS-OLD-MAST-RECORD.
00107               05  OLD-SOC-SEC-NUMBER              PIC X(9).
00108               05  OLD-NAME.
00109                   10  OLD-LAST-NAME               PIC X(15).
00110                   10  OLD-INITIALS                PIC XX.
00111               05  OLD-DATE-OF-BIRTH.
00112                   10  OLD-BIRTH-MONTH             PIC 99.
00113                   10  OLD-BIRTH-YEAR              PIC 99.
00114               05  OLD-DATE-OF-HIRE.
00115                   10  OLD-HIRE-MONTH              PIC 99.
00116                   10  OLD-HIRE-YEAR               PIC 99.
00117               05  OLD-LOCATION-CODE               PIC X(3).
00118               05  OLD-PERFORMANCE-CODE            PIC X.
00119               05  OLD-EDUCATION-CODE              PIC X.
00120               05  OLD-TITLE-DATA OCCURS 2 TIMES.    ──Two levels of title data
00121                   10  OLD-TITLE-CODE              PIC 9(3).
00122                   10  OLD-TITLE-DATE              PIC 9(4).
00123               05  OLD-SALARY-DATA OCCURS 3 TIMES.   ──Three levels of salary data
00124                   10  OLD-SALARY                  PIC 9(5).
00125                   10  OLD-SALARY-DATE             PIC 9(4).
00126
00127           01  WS-NEW-MAST-RECORD.
00128               05  NEW-SOC-SEC-NUMBER              PIC X(9).
00129               05  NEW-NAME.
00130                   10  NEW-LAST-NAME               PIC X(15).
00131                   10  NEW-INITIALS                PIC XX.
00132               05  NEW-DATE-OF-BIRTH.
00133                   10  NEW-BIRTH-MONTH             PIC 99.
00134                   10  NEW-BIRTH-YEAR              PIC 99.
00135               05  NEW-DATE-OF-HIRE.
00136                   10  NEW-HIRE-MONTH              PIC 99.
00137                   10  NEW-HIRE-YEAR               PIC 99.
00138               05  NEW-LOCATION-CODE               PIC X(3).
00139               05  NEW-PERFORMANCE-CODE            PIC X.
00140               05  NEW-EDUCATION-CODE              PIC X.
00141               05  NEW-TITLE-DATA OCCURS 2 TIMES.
00142                   10  NEW-TITLE-CODE              PIC 9(3).
00143                   10  NEW-TITLE-DATE              PIC 9(4).
00144               05  NEW-SALARY-DATA OCCURS 3 TIMES.
00145                   10  NEW-SALARY                  PIC 9(5).
00146                   10  NEW-SALARY-DATE             PIC 9(4).
00147
00148           01  WS-BALANCE-LINE-SWITCHES.
00149               05  WS-ACTIVE-KEY                   PIC X(9).
00150               05  WS-RECORD-KEY-ALLOCATED-SWITCH  PIC X(3).
00151
00152           PROCEDURE DIVISION.
00153           0010-UPDATE-MASTER-FILE.
00154               OPEN INPUT TRANSACTION-FILE
00155                          PROMOTION-FILE
00156                          OLD-MASTER-FILE
00157                    OUTPUT NEW-MASTER-FILE
00158                           DELETED-RECORD-FILE.
00159               PERFORM 0015-READ-PROMOTION-FILE.
00160               PERFORM 0020-READ-TRANSACTION-FILE.
00161               PERFORM 0030-READ-OLD-MASTER-FILE.
00162               PERFORM 0040-CHOOSE-ACTIVE-KEY.
00163               PERFORM 0050-PROCESS-ACTIVE-KEY
00164                   UNTIL WS-ACTIVE-KEY = HIGH-VALUES.
00165               CLOSE TRANSACTION-FILE
00166                     PROMOTION-FILE
00167                     OLD-MASTER-FILE
00168                     NEW-MASTER-FILE
00169                     DELETED-RECORD-FILE.
00170               STOP RUN.
00171
00172           0015-READ-PROMOTION-FILE.
00173               READ PROMOTION-FILE INTO WS-PROMOTION-RECORD
00174                   AT END MOVE HIGH-VALUES TO PR-SOC-SEC-NUMBER.
00175
```

FIGURE 6.14 *continued*

```
00176      0020-READ-TRANSACTION-FILE.
00177          READ TRANSACTION-FILE INTO WS-TRANS-RECORD
00178              AT END MOVE HIGH-VALUES TO TR-SOC-SEC-NUMBER.
00179
00180      0030-READ-OLD-MASTER-FILE.
00181          READ OLD-MASTER-FILE INTO WS-OLD-MAST-RECORD
00182              AT END MOVE HIGH-VALUE TO OLD-SOC-SEC-NUMBER.
00183
00184      0040-CHOOSE-ACTIVE-KEY.
00185          IF TR-SOC-SEC-NUMBER LESS THAN OLD-SOC-SEC-NUMBER
00186              IF TR-SOC-SEC-NUMBER LESS THAN PR-SOC-SEC-NUMBER
00187                  MOVE TR-SOC-SEC-NUMBER TO WS-ACTIVE-KEY
00188              ELSE
00189                  MOVE PR-SOC-SEC-NUMBER TO WS-ACTIVE-KEY
00190          ELSE
00191              IF PR-SOC-SEC-NUMBER LESS THAN OLD-SOC-SEC-NUMBER
00192                  MOVE PR-SOC-SEC-NUMBER TO WS-ACTIVE-KEY
00193              ELSE
00194                  MOVE OLD-SOC-SEC-NUMBER TO WS-ACTIVE-KEY.
00195                                           ⎯ Logic expanded to include PROMOTION-FILE
00196      0050-PROCESS-ACTIVE-KEY.
00197          IF OLD-SOC-SEC-NUMBER = WS-ACTIVE-KEY
00198              MOVE 'YES' TO WS-RECORD-KEY-ALLOCATED-SWITCH
00199              PERFORM 0060-BUILD-NEW-MASTER
00200          ELSE
00201              MOVE 'NO' TO WS-RECORD-KEY-ALLOCATED-SWITCH.
00202
00203          PERFORM 0070-APPLY-TRANS-TO-MASTER
00204              UNTIL WS-ACTIVE-KEY NOT EQUAL TR-SOC-SEC-NUMBER.
00205
00206          PERFORM 0075-APPLY-PROMO-TO-MASTER
00207              UNTIL WS-ACTIVE-KEY NOT EQUAL PR-SOC-SEC-NUMBER.
00208
00209          IF WS-RECORD-KEY-ALLOCATED-SWITCH = 'YES'
00210              PERFORM 0080-WRITE-NEW-MASTER.
00211
00212          PERFORM 0040-CHOOSE-ACTIVE-KEY.
00213
00214      0060-BUILD-NEW-MASTER.
00215          MOVE WS-OLD-MAST-RECORD TO WS-NEW-MAST-RECORD.
00216          PERFORM 0030-READ-OLD-MASTER-FILE.
00217
00218      0070-APPLY-TRANS-TO-MASTER.
00219          IF ADDITION
00220              PERFORM 0090-ADD-NEW-RECORD
00221          ELSE
00222              IF CORRECTION
00223                  PERFORM 0100-CORRECT-OLD-RECORD
00224              ELSE
00225                  IF DELETION
00226                      PERFORM 0110-DELETE-OLD-RECORD.
00227
00228          PERFORM 0020-READ-TRANSACTION-FILE.
00229
00230      0075-APPLY-PROMO-TO-MASTER.     ⎯ Intermediate level module has been added
00231          IF PROMOTION
00232              PERFORM 0120-DO-TITLE-UPDATE
00233          ELSE
00234              IF SALARY-RAISE
00235                  PERFORM 0130-DO-SALARY-RAISE.
00236
00237          PERFORM 0015-READ-PROMOTION-FILE.
00238
00239      0080-WRITE-NEW-MASTER.
00240          WRITE NEW-MAST-RECORD FROM WS-NEW-MAST-RECORD.
00241
00242      0090-ADD-NEW-RECORD.               ⎯ Error messages are
00243          IF WS-RECORD-KEY-ALLOCATED-SWITCH = 'YES'   better formatted
00244              DISPLAY '   '
00245              DISPLAY '   ERROR DUPLICATE ADDITION: '
00246              DISPLAY '   TRANSACTION IN ERROR: ' WS-TRANS-RECORD
```

FIGURE 6.14 *continued*

```
00247                   ELSE
00248                       MOVE 'YES' TO WS-RECORD-KEY-ALLOCATED-SWITCH
00249                       MOVE SPACES TO WS-NEW-MAST-RECORD
00250                       MOVE TR-SOC-SEC-NUMBER TO NEW-SOC-SEC-NUMBER
00251                       MOVE TR-NAME TO NEW-NAME
00252                       MOVE TR-DATE-OF-BIRTH TO NEW-DATE-OF-BIRTH
00253                       MOVE TR-DATE-OF-HIRE TO NEW-DATE-OF-HIRE
00254                       MOVE TR-LOCATION-CODE TO NEW-LOCATION-CODE
00255                       MOVE TR-PERFORMANCE-CODE TO NEW-PERFORMANCE-CODE
00256                       MOVE TR-EDUCATION-CODE TO NEW-EDUCATION-CODE
00257                       MOVE TR-TITLE-DATA TO NEW-TITLE-DATA (1)
00258                       MOVE TR-SALARY-DATA TO NEW-SALARY-DATA (1).
00259
00260               0100-CORRECT-OLD-RECORD.
00261                   IF WS-RECORD-KEY-ALLOCATED-SWITCH = 'YES'
00262                       PERFORM 0105-CORRECT-INDIVIDUAL-FIELDS
00263                   ELSE
00264                       DISPLAY ' '
00265                       DISPLAY '   ERROR-NO MATCHING RECORD: '
00266                       DISPLAY '     TRANSACTION IN ERROR: ' WS-TRANS-RECORD.
00267
00268               0105-CORRECT-INDIVIDUAL-FIELDS.
00269                   IF TR-NAME NOT EQUAL SPACES
00270                       MOVE TR-NAME TO NEW-NAME.
00271                   IF TR-DATE-OF-BIRTH NOT EQUAL SPACES
00272                       MOVE TR-DATE-OF-BIRTH TO NEW-DATE-OF-BIRTH.
00273                   IF TR-DATE-OF-HIRE NOT EQUAL SPACES
00274                       MOVE TR-DATE-OF-HIRE TO NEW-DATE-OF-HIRE.
00275                   IF TR-LOCATION-CODE NOT EQUAL SPACES
00276                       MOVE TR-LOCATION-CODE TO NEW-LOCATION-CODE.
00277                   IF TR-PERFORMANCE-CODE NOT EQUAL SPACES
00278                       MOVE TR-PERFORMANCE-CODE TO NEW-PERFORMANCE-CODE.
00279                   IF TR-EDUCATION-CODE NOT EQUAL SPACES
00280                       MOVE TR-EDUCATION-CODE TO NEW-EDUCATION-CODE.
00281                   IF TR-TITLE-CODE IS NUMERIC
00282                       MOVE TR-TITLE-CODE TO NEW-TITLE-CODE (1).
00283                   IF TR-TITLE-DATE IS NUMERIC
00284                       MOVE TR-TITLE-DATE TO NEW-TITLE-DATE (1).
00285                   IF TR-SALARY IS NUMERIC
00286                       MOVE TR-SALARY TO NEW-SALARY (1).
00287                   IF TR-SALARY-DATE IS NUMERIC
00288                       MOVE TR-SALARY-DATE TO NEW-SALARY-DATE (1).
00289
00290               0110-DELETE-OLD-RECORD.
00291                   IF WS-RECORD-KEY-ALLOCATED-SWITCH = 'YES'
00292                       MOVE 'NO' TO WS-RECORD-KEY-ALLOCATED-SWITCH
00293                       WRITE DELETED-RECORD FROM WS-NEW-MAST-RECORD
00294                   ELSE                              ─ Deleted records are written to a new file
00295                       DISPLAY ' '
00296                       DISPLAY '   ERROR-NO MATCHING RECORD: '
00297                       DISPLAY '     TRANSACTION IN ERROR: ' WS-TRANS-RECORD.
00298
00299               0120-DO-TITLE-UPDATE.
00300                   IF WS-RECORD-KEY-ALLOCATED-SWITCH = 'YES'
00301                       MOVE NEW-TITLE-CODE (1) TO NEW-TITLE-CODE (2)
00302                       MOVE NEW-TITLE-DATE (1) TO NEW-TITLE-DATE (2)
00303                       MOVE PR-TITLE-CODE TO NEW-TITLE-CODE (1)
00304                       MOVE PR-TITLE-DATE TO NEW-TITLE-DATE (1)
00305                   ELSE
00306                       DISPLAY ' '                    ─ Low level modules have been added
00307                       DISPLAY '   ERROR-NO MATCHING RECORD: '
00308                       DISPLAY '     PROMOTION IN ERROR: ' WS-PROMOTION-RECORD.
00309
00310               0130-DO-SALARY-RAISE.
00311                   IF WS-RECORD-KEY-ALLOCATED-SWITCH = 'YES'
00312                       MOVE NEW-SALARY (2) TO NEW-SALARY (3)
00313                       MOVE NEW-SALARY-DATE (2) TO NEW-SALARY-DATE (3)
```

FIGURE 6.14 *continued*

```
00314                MOVE NEW-SALARY (1) TO NEW-SALARY (2)
00315                MOVE NEW-SALARY-DATE (1) TO NEW-SALARY-DATE (2)
00316                MOVE PR-SALARY TO NEW-SALARY (1)
00317                MOVE PR-SALARY-DATE TO NEW-SALARY-DATE (1)
00318           ELSE
00319                DISPLAY '  '
00320                DISPLAY ' ERROR-NO MATCHING RECORD: '
00321                DISPLAY '    PROMOTION IN ERROR: ' WS-PROMOTION-RECORD.
```

FIGURE 6.14 *continued*

```
000000000BOROW          JS03431281100 99871281550001281A
000000000BOROW          JS           X                  C
200000000CRAWFORD       MA09430678100E64440680420000680A
400000000BENJAMIN       BL                              C
400000000BENJAMIN       BL1054                          C
400000000BENJAMIN       BL    1074                      C
400000001BENJAMIN       BL          200                 C
500000000TATER          C                               D
555555555NEW EMPLOYEE   RT1145                          C
555555555NEW EMPLOYEE   RT11440681100E64440681390000681A
555555555NEW EMPLOYEE   RT          555                 C
700000000JONES          A                      385000781C
800000000SMITH          BB         400                  C
```
(a)

Benjamin's salary will be updated in the new master

```
400000000BENJAMIN       350000182          R
400000000BENJAMIN              4440182P
500000000TATER          330000182          R
600000000GRAUER                9990182P
800000000SMITH          900000182          R
888888888JOHNSON        400000182          R
```
(b)

```
100000000SUGRUE    P  12450879100E5333088022208792800010812600009800
200000000CRAWFORD  MA09430678100E64440678    42000680360000678
300000000MILGROM   IR06130580200E65551081400068148000058 0
400000000BENJAMIN  BL10531073100E73331073    300010812800010800
500000000TATER     JS02500779200P43330779    310001081270000779
600000000GRAUER    RT11450877200E5900118180011805000011814500011800
700000000JONES     A 09500778100G64440779333077839000088136000077 9
800000000SMITH     BB08520681300P84440681    385000681
900000000BAKER     E  06490879100G99870879   6500008815500008799
```
(c)

Benjamin now has three salary levels to indicate that a salary update has taken place

```
000000000BOROW      JS03431281100X99871281    550001281
100000000SUGRUE     P  12450879100E5333088022208792800010812600009800
200000000CRAWFORD   MA09430678100E64440678    42000680360000678
300000000MILGROM    IR06130580200E65551081400068148000058 0
400000000BENJAMIN   BL10541074100E74440182333107335000018230000108128000108 0
555555555NEW EMPLOYEE RT11440681100E65550681  390000681
600000000GRAUER     RT11450877200E5999018290011815000011814500011800
700000000JONES      A 09500778100G64440779333077838500007813600007799
800000000SMITH      BB08520681300P84000681    900001823850006810 0
900000000BAKER      E  06490879100G99870879   6500008815500008799
```
(d)

FIGURE 6.15 (a) Transaction file (repeated from Figure 6.6b). (b) Promotion file. (c) Old master file (repeated from Figure 6.6a). (d) New master file. (e) Deleted record file. (f) Error messages.

Deleted records are now written to a separate file

```
500000000TATER        JS02500779200P43330779        310001081270000779
```
(e)

Error message is better formatted than in Figure 6.10b

```
ERROR DUPLICATE ADDITION:
  TRANSACTION IN ERROR: 200000000CRAWFORD        MA09430678100E64440680420000680A

ERROR-NO MATCHING RECORD:
  TRANSACTION IN ERROR: 400000001BENJAMIN        BL         200                    C

ERROR-NO MATCHING RECORD:
  PROMOTION IN ERROR: 500000000TATER             330000182        R

ERROR-NO MATCHING RECORD:
  TRANSACTION IN ERROR: 555555555NEW EMPLOYEE    RT1145                            C

ERROR-NO MATCHING RECORD:
  PROMOTION IN ERROR: 888888888JOHNSON           400000182        R
```
(f)

FIGURE 6.15 *continued*

COBOL Extensions

The illustrations of Figures 6.7, 6.9, and 6.14 were well-written and complete COBOL programs. They served to demonstrate the balance line algorithm, top down testing, and program maintenance. Nevertheless, there are additional COBOL constructs which are useful in processing sequential files in a commercial setting. Accordingly, we cover the SELECT statement in detail, the I-O-CONTROL paragraph, the complete FD entry, and extensions of the OPEN and CLOSE statements. The reader is referred to the 1974 ANS COBOL language summary[3] for additional information.

SELECT Statement

The 1974 standard recognizes three types of file organization (sequential, relative, and indexed), with three distinct SELECT statements. The complete SELECT statement for sequential files has the format:

> SELECT [OPTIONAL] file-name
>   ASSIGN TO implementor-name-1 [, implementor-name-2] ...
>
> [RESERVE integer-1 $\begin{bmatrix} \text{AREA} \\ \text{AREAS} \end{bmatrix}$]
>
> [ORGANIZATION IS SEQUENTIAL]
>
> [ACCESS MODE IS SEQUENTIAL]
>
> [FILE STATUS IS data-name-1]

---

[3] *American National Standard Programming Language COBOL*, X3.23-1974 (New York: American National Standards Institute, 1974).

The OPTIONAL clause means that the file need not be present when the program is run, e.g., the first cycle of sequential maintenance during which the old master file does not exist. The RESERVE clause increases processing efficiency by providing alternate I/O areas (buffers), and unless otherwise instructed, most compilers reserve at least one alternate area. The ORGANIZATION and ACCESS MODE clauses default to sequential, and consequently, these clauses are often omitted for sequential files. They are required, however, for other types of file organization; e.g., indexed files. The FILE STATUS clause allows one to monitor the execution of each I/O request, and is further discussed in Chapter 7.

I-O-CONTROL Paragraph

The I-O-CONTROL paragraph specifies points for rerun, common memory areas for different files, and the location of multiple files on tape. It has the general form

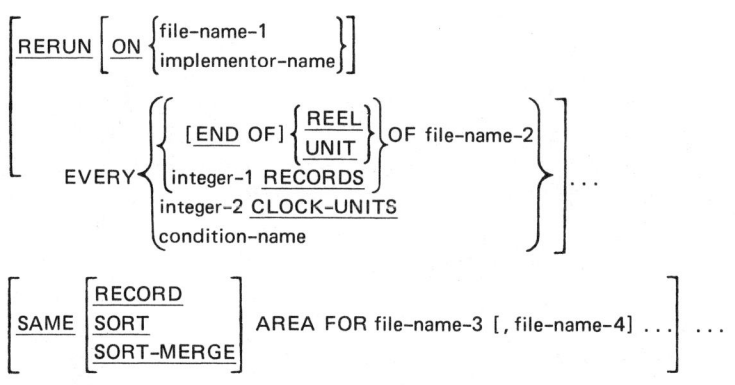

The RERUN clause establishes a checkpoint, i.e., a snapshot of a program's status at a given point during execution. The intended use is for *long-running* programs, so that if a program terminates abnormally, it can be restarted from the checkpoint, rather than the beginning. It is relatively easy to create a checkpoint, but often difficult to restart the job from the checkpoint. Moreover, the problem may have occurred *before* the checkpoint was taken, in which case the restart would be worthless. The facility is there, but should be used with discretion.

The SAME AREA clause causes the listed files to share the same storage locations for their I/O routines. While that capability may have been useful 10 or 15 years ago when storage was at a premium, it is less essential today. Moreover, its use may introduce unnecessary complications in program logic in that the listed files cannot be open at the same time.

The MULTIPLE FILE clause is used when there are multiple files on a reel of tape to indicate the position of the file in question. (The identical function can also be accomplished through the LABEL parameter in OS JCL.)

FD Entry

The FD for sequential files has the form:

$$\underline{FD} \text{ file-name}$$

$$\left[\underline{BLOCK} \text{ CONTAINS [integer-1 \underline{TO}] integer-2 } \left\{\begin{matrix}\underline{RECORDS} \\ \underline{CHARACTERS}\end{matrix}\right\}\right]$$

$$[\underline{RECORD} \text{ CONTAINS [integer-3 \underline{TO}] integer-4 CHARACTERS}]$$

$$\text{LABEL} \left\{\begin{matrix}\underline{RECORDS} \text{ ARE} \\ \underline{RECORD} \text{ IS}\end{matrix}\right\} \left\{\begin{matrix}\underline{STANDARD} \\ \underline{OMITTED}\end{matrix}\right\}$$

$$\left[\underline{VALUE} \text{ } \underline{OF} \left\{\text{implementor-name IS } \left\{\begin{matrix}\text{data-name-1} \\ \text{literal-1}\end{matrix}\right\}\right\} \ldots \right]$$

$$\left[\text{DATA} \left\{\begin{matrix}\underline{RECORD} \text{ IS} \\ \underline{RECORDS} \text{ ARE}\end{matrix}\right\} \text{ record-name-1 [record-name-2]} \ldots \right]$$

The BLOCK and RECORD CONTAINS clauses provide for variable as well as fixed-length records with four distinct formats possible: fixed-length records, both blocked and unblocked, and variable-length records, both blocked and unblocked. Considerable flexibility is permitted, and one must take care to express exact intent. Note, for example, that the following pairs of entries are *not* equivalent:

        BLOCK CONTAINS 5 RECORDS
        RECORD CONTAINS 42 TO 342 CHARACTERS

versus

        BLOCK CONTAINS 210 TO 1710 CHARACTERS
        RECORD CONTAINS 42 TO 342 CHARACTERS

The first pair states that the block contains exactly 5 records. The second pair states that the block contains from 210 to 1710 characters and thus could contain many more than 5 records if most of the records were of the smaller size.

Omission of the BLOCK CONTAINS clause causes the compiler to assume that the records are unblocked and is equivalent to BLOCK CONTAINS 1 RECORD. (The entry BLOCK CONTAINS 0 RECORDS is common under IBM OS operating systems, and means that the block size will be entered at execution time in the JCL.)

The LABEL RECORDS clause is the only required clause in the FD. LABEL RECORDS ARE STANDARD implies that standard labels are used and label processing is to be performed. LABEL RECORDS ARE OMITTED means either labels are omitted or they are nonstandard (i.e., user labels); in either case, no label processing is to be performed.

When labels are used, the system must have additional information to enable it to perform label processing. Under an IBM operating system, the information is specified in the JCL. In other systems, it is supplied in the VALUE clause of the FD. Consider the entry:

```
FD  OLD-MASTER-FILE
        .
        .
    LABEL RECORDS ARE STANDARD
    VALUE OF TAPE-LABEL IS 123456.
```

TAPE-LABEL is an implementor-name (i.e., a system-name that refers to a particular feature available in a given vendor's system. The SPECIAL-NAMES paragraph of the Environment Division relates implementor names to programmer-specified mnemonic names). The intent of these entries is to ensure that the COBOL file, OLD-MASTER-FILE, will be read from a specific tape volume.

OPEN and CLOSE Statements

General formats for sequential files are shown:

$$\underline{\text{OPEN}} \left\{ \begin{array}{l} \underline{\text{INPUT}} \text{ file-name-1} \left[\begin{array}{l} \underline{\text{REVERSED}} \\ \text{WITH } \underline{\text{NO}} \text{ REWIND} \end{array} \right] \ldots \\ \underline{\text{OUTPUT}} \text{ file-name-2 [WITH } \underline{\text{NO}} \text{ REWIND]} \ldots \\ \underline{\text{EXTEND}} \text{ file-name-3} \ldots \end{array} \right\} \ldots$$

$$\underline{\text{CLOSE}} \text{ file-name-1} \left[\left\{ \begin{array}{l} \underline{\text{REEL}} \\ \underline{\text{UNIT}} \end{array} \right\} \left[\begin{array}{l} \text{WITH } \underline{\text{NO}} \text{ REWIND} \\ \text{FOR } \underline{\text{REMOVAL}} \end{array} \right] \right] \ldots$$

The action of the OPEN and CLOSE verbs depends on the specifications of the LABEL RECORDS clause in the file FD. If standard labels are used, the OPEN initiates label processing. In an input file, the header label is checked against information in the JCL (IBM systems) or in the FD VALUE clause (non-IBM). When an output file is opened, an appropriate header label is written. The CLOSE statement initiates similar procedures for trailer labels; i.e., it checks the trailer label of an input file and causes a new trailer label to be written for an output file. Label processing is not performed if the FD contains LABEL RECORDS ARE OMITTED.

The simplest form of an OPEN statement for an input file is OPEN INPUT file-name, which automatically causes a tape to be rewound. If NO REWIND is specified, rewinding is suppressed. (The latter is used when many files are contained on the same reel.) The REVERSED option causes the file to be processed in reverse order, starting with the last record. (This is not possible on all tape drives; further, the option is available only for single-reel files.)

The EXTEND option in the OPEN statement is restricted to single-reel files. If this mode is specified, subsequent write statements will add records after the last existing record in the file, as though the file were in the OUTPUT mode. (The same effect can be accomplished by coding DISP=MOD in OS JCL.)

The simplest form of the CLOSE statement is CLOSE file-name, which automatically rewinds a tape at the end of processing. The NO REWIND option is used for multiple file volumes and prevents the automatic rewinding associated with the CLOSE. The REEL or UNIT specification causes the volume, but not the file, to close and is used with multivolume files.

Summary

The chapter began with discussion of the balance line algorithm, a truly general approach to sequential file maintenance. The algorithm allows multiple transactions to reference a single master record, as well as multiple transaction files. The flexibility of the approach was further demonstrated by the example on program maintenance in which the original specifications were significantly altered.

The author made a point of the ease with which he was able to modify the program of Figure 6.9 to accommodate revised specifications. Attention was drawn to the expanded hierarchy chart in which new modules were added and existing modules enlarged. Program maintenance was also facilitated by the attention paid to programming style, in particular the use of meaningful data names and indentation, which is present in all illustrative programs.

The concept of top down testing was demonstrated through the stubs program of Figure 6.7 and its associated output in Figure 6.8. Early testing ensures that modules are called in proper sequence, and facilitates the correction of any errors which are detected. The preparation of test data was discussed. It was suggested that *anyone but the programmer* provide the data, and that the anticipated results be calculated *before* the program is actually run.

The chapter concluded with a discussion of advanced syntactical features for sequential files. The SELECT statement was covered in detail, as were the I-O-CONTROL paragraph, complete FD, and the OPEN and CLOSE statements.

True/False

1. The balance line algorithm requires a unique key for every record in the old master file.
2. Transactions to the balance line algorithm must be presented in the order: additions, changes, deletions.
3. The balance line algorithm permits multiple transactions for the same master record and can be generalized to any number of transaction files.
4. A program must be completely coded before any testing can begin.
5. The highest level modules in a hierarchy chart should be tested first.
6. One can logically assume that input to a maintenance program will be valid.
7. One need not check for duplicate additions if the transaction file has been run through a "stand alone" edit program.
8. A module in a hierarchy chart can be called from more than one place.
9. Pseudocode and hierarchy charts depict the same thing.
10. A "program stub" may consist of a one-line DISPLAY paragraph.
11. Test data should be designed by the programmer writing the program.
12. Top down testing can be applied to complete systems as well as individual programs.
13. All records in a sequential file must be the same length.
14. Variable length records may be blocked.
15. "Physical record" and "logical record" are synonymous.
16. A blocking factor of 3 implies that 3 buffers will be used to process the file.
17. The ORGANIZATION and ACCESS MODE clauses are optional in the SELECT statement for sequential files.
18. BLOCK CONTAINS 0 RECORDS is a valid entry under IBM's OS operating system.
19. Use of FILE STATUS and DECLARATIVES is not permitted with sequential files.
20. Sequential files may be stored on either tape or disk.

Problems

1. Modify the pseudocode of Figure 6.2 to accommodate the change in specifications associated with the additional file. Does the additional pseudocode make the overall figure unwieldy? Do you think the resulting pseudocode should be subdivided into more than one page? If so, how?

2. Redraw the hierarchy chart of Figure 6.13 as a Yourdon structure chart by including control couples and indicating the major loops and decisions. Which do you find easier to read—the original figure or its Yourdon counterpart?

3. The transaction file of Figure 6.6b has both name and initials entered on "C" type transactions in addition to the social security number. Is this necessary according to the specifications and subsequent COBOL implementation (Figure 6.9)? Describe both an advantage and a disadvantage for entering the name and initials.

4. The specifications of the update program do not discuss how to change, i.e., correct the social security number of an *existing* record. With respect to Figure 6.6a, for example, how could the social security number of Sugrue, who already exists in the old master file, be changed to 100000001? Discuss two different approaches, with an advantage and a disadvantage for each. (See part (f) in the programming project for one suggestion.)

Projects

1. This rather substantial project involves *maintenance*, and as such is typical of what entry-level programmers are apt to encounter in the "real world." Accordingly, the author believes this project to be especially important. The reader is asked to implement the following changes to the program of Figure 6.14:

   (a) Salary increases are to be *rejected* with an appropriate error message if any of the following conditions occur:
      i. The new salary matches the present salary in the old master,
      ii. The new salary date matches the present salary date in the old master,
      iii. The performance code in the old master is P,
      iv. The name and initials on the salary increase record do *not* match the name and initials in the old master.

   (b) Promotions (i.e., title changes) are to be *rejected* if any of the following conditions occur:
      i. The new title matches the present title in the old master,
      ii. The new title date matches the present title date in the old master,
      iii. The name and initials in the promotion record do not match the name and initials in the old master.

   (c) Any transaction coded as an addition must contain every field in the record layout in Figure 6.4, else the transaction is to be rejected with an appropriate message. (A single error message, ATTEMPTED ADDITION HAS INCOMPLETE DATA, is acceptable.)

   (d) Transactions coded as deletions are to contain a date in the TR-TITLE-DATE field and should be rejected if the date is missing. Records deleted from the old master file are still to be written to DELETED-RECORD-FILE. However, the deleted record should contain the transaction date as its present title date, and the title code 999 as its present title. (This in turn causes the present title data from the old master to become the previous title data in the deleted record.)

   (e) A new one-position numeric field is to be included at the end of the transaction record (in column 57) to permit historical corrections on title or salary data. Specifically, a 1 indicates that the present level is to be corrected, a 2 the previous level, and so on. (Valid values are 1, 2, and 3, since 3 levels of salary data are defined in Figure 6.3. Valid levels for a title correction are 1 and 2.) Corrections to either title or salary data must have a valid level entered, or else the transaction is to be rejected, with an appropriate error message.

(f) A new transaction type, S, is to be permitted to accommodate a change in social security number to an existing record. The existing (but incorrect) social security number is to appear in columns 1-9 of the transaction record, while the corrected social security number appears in columns 58-66. The change is *not* to take place, however, if it would produce two records in the new master with the same social security number. Realize also that *if* any social security number is changed the new master file will be out of sequence and must be resorted. Sorting is not to take place, however, if no social security numbers are changed. Finally, if multiple transactions are included, all transactions should reference the *old* social security number. (The social security modification is *by far the most difficult* portion in the assignment.)

(g) Incoming transactions can no longer be assumed to have valid transaction codes, i.e., A, C, D, or S (as per the social security modification). Reject any transactions containing an invalid code through an appropriate error message.

(h) Incoming promotions can no longer be assumed to have a valid code, i.e., P or R. Reject invalid transactions with an appropriate message.

(i) Separate counts are to be maintained for the number of old master records, for the number of *valid* additions processed, and for the number of *valid* deletions processed. Display the anticipated number of new master records (equal to the number of records in the old master, plus the number of additions, minus the number of deletions) at the end of the update.

In spite of the substantial nature and number of changes, the author is convinced the reader will be able to make the necessary modifications. However, it is critical that one follow the admonition of Chapter 4, to *think first and code later*. To that end, it is strongly suggested that the following activities be done *before* actual coding takes place.

(a) Expand the hierarchy chart of Figure 6.13 to include any new modules which are necessary. In addition, indicate the existing modules which must be altered. *Present the results to the class in a structured walkthrough.*

(b) Expand the test data and results of Figure 6.15 to accommodate the modifications, and simultaneously clarify any ambiguity in the specifications. *Present these results in a structured walkthrough.* It is strongly suggested that the entire class use the *same* test data.

(c) Develop pseudocode for some of the more involved modules; e.g., **DO-SALARY-UPDATE, APPLY-TRANSACTIONS-TO-MASTER**, etc. *Again, present the results in a structured walkthrough.*

Finally, the reader may recognize that some of the modifications could better be implemented in a stand alone edit, e.g., checking for a valid transaction code in parts (g) or (h), checking for a deletion date in part (d), and so on. Nevertheless, *all* changes are to be done in the maintenance program of Figure 6.14. Good luck.

7 Indexed Files

Overview

This chapter continues the discussion of file maintenance begun in Chapter 6. It opens with a conceptual view of indexed files, and covers all COBOL elements necessary for this type of file organization. It includes two COBOL programs to illustrate fully the use of indexed files. The first creates an indexed file, and the second is a nonsequential update with parallel requirements to the program of Chapter 6.

The opening section provides an intuitive discussion of how an indexed file works. The example chosen is IBM's VSAM implementation, and the terminology and physical characteristics are unique to VSAM. Different vendors have different vocabulary and/or other means of implementation, but the underlying concepts are the same; namely, a series of indexes which access individual records on a sequential or random basis. Of greater import, *the COBOL syntax is identical for all vendors who adhere to the ANS 74 standard*.

The opening section is followed by complete coverage of COBOL syntax. Material is included on SEQUENTIAL, RANDOM, and DYNAMIC ACCESS; FILE STATUS bytes and DECLARATIVES; ALTERNATE RECORD KEY; and the DELETE, START, READ, WRITE, and REWRITE statements. There is also brief mention of the coding differences between IBM's VSAM and ISAM implementation. *The former adheres to the ANS 74 standard, whereas the latter does not.*

Concepts of File Organization

As stated in the overview, different vendors have different *physical* implementations of indexed files, and consequently different terminology. Nevertheless, the principles are the same; namely, a series of indexes which allow individual records to be accessed either sequentially or nonsequentially. This section provides an intuitive discussion of how an indexed file actually works.

In reality, the physical implementation of an indexed file is of little or no concern to the programmer. The operating system automatically establishes and maintains the indexes, and the programmer is concerned primarily with accessing the file through the appropriate COBOL elements. Nevertheless, a conceptual understanding is of benefit in developing a more competent and better rounded individual. Accordingly, we consider IBM's VSAM implementation.

A VSAM file or data set is divided into *control areas* and *control intervals*. A control interval is a continuous area of auxiliary storage. A control area contains one or more control intervals. A control interval is independent of the physical device on which it resides (i.e., a control interval which takes exactly one track of a given direct access device may require more or less than one track if the file were moved to another type of device). That situation is of no concern to the user.

The length of a control interval is fixed, either by VSAM or the user. VSAM will determine an optimum length based on record size, type of device, and the amount of space required for an I/O buffer. All control intervals in a given file are the same length and cannot be changed without creating an entirely new data set.

A VSAM file is defined with an index so that individual records may be located on a random basis. (In actuality, there are two kinds of VSAM data sets, *key sequenced* and *entry sequenced*. This discussion concerns only the former, and entry sequenced data sets are not mentioned further.) Entries in the index are known as index records. The lowest level index is called the *sequence set*. Records in all higher levels are collectively called the *index set*.

An entry in a sequence set contains the *highest* key in a control interval and a vertical pointer to that interval. An entry in an index set contains the *highest* key in the index record at the next lower level and a vertical pointer to that index record. These concepts are made clearer by examination of Figure 7.1.

Figure 7.1 shows 28 records hypothetically distributed in a VSAM data set. The entire file consists of three control areas; each area in turn contains three control intervals. The shaded areas shown at the end of each control interval contain information required by VSAM. The index set has only one level of indexing. There are three entries in the index set, one for each control area. Each entry in the index set contains the highest key in the corresponding control area; thus, 377, 619, and 800 are the highest keys in the first, second, and third control areas, respectively. Each control area has its own sequence set. The entries in the first sequence set show the highest keys of the control intervals in the first control area to be 280, 327, and 377, respectively. Note that the highest entry in the third control interval, 377, corresponds to the highest entry in the first control area of the index set.

Figure 7.1 alludes to two kinds of pointers, vertical and horizontal. Vertical pointers are used for direct access to an individual record. For example, assume that the record with a key of 449 is to be retrieved. VSAM begins at the highest level of index (i.e., at the index set). It concludes that record key 449, *if it is present*, is in the second control area (377 is the highest key in the first area, whereas 619 is the highest key in the second

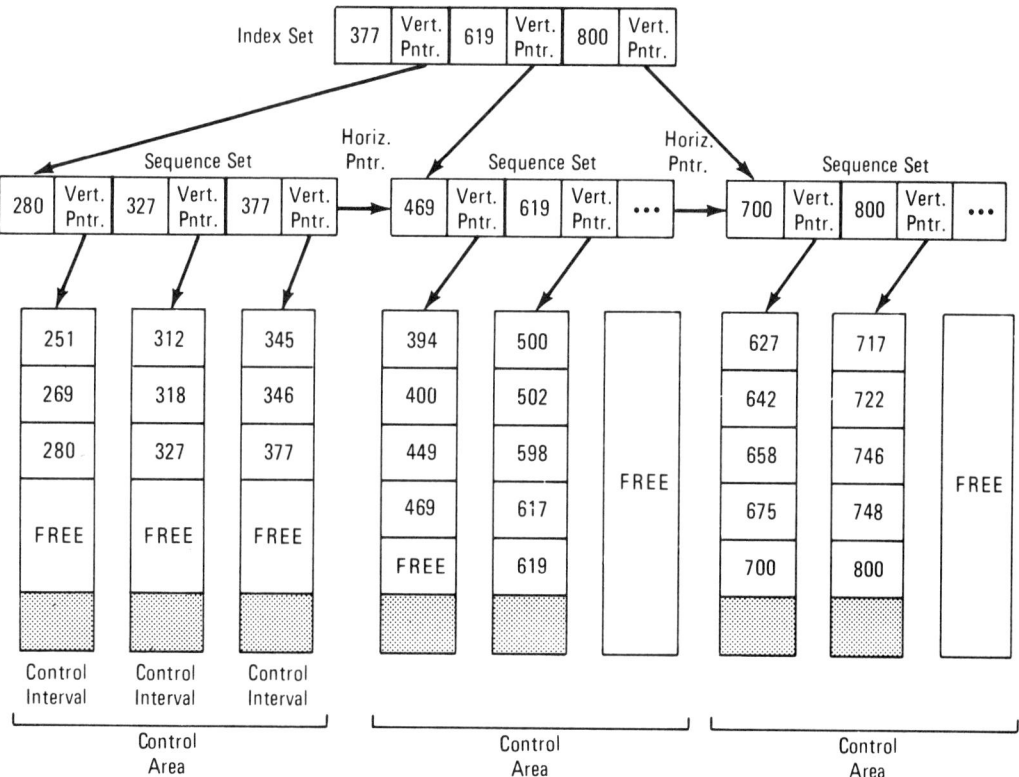

FIGURE 7.1 Initial distribution of records in a VSAM data set.

Concepts of File Organization 177

control area). VSAM follows the vertical pointer to the sequence set for the second control area and draws its final conclusion: record key 449, if it exists, will be in the first control interval of the second control area.

Horizontal pointers are used for sequential access only. In this instance, VSAM begins at the first sequence set and uses the horizontal pointer to get from that sequence set record to the one containing the next highest key. Put another way, the vertical pointer in a sequence set record points to data; the horizontal pointer indicates the sequence set record containing the next highest record.

Figure 7.1 contains several allocations of *free space*, which is distributed in one of two ways: as free space within a control interval, or as a free control interval within a control area. In other words, as VSAM loads a file, empty space is deliberately left throughout the file. This is done to facilitate subsequent insertion of new records. By employing this technique, VSAM eliminates the need for the overflow areas of IBM's ISAM implementation. (Retrieval of records is generally faster under VSAM because there is no need to chain through the overflow areas as in ISAM.)

Figure 7.2 shows the changes brought about by the addition of two

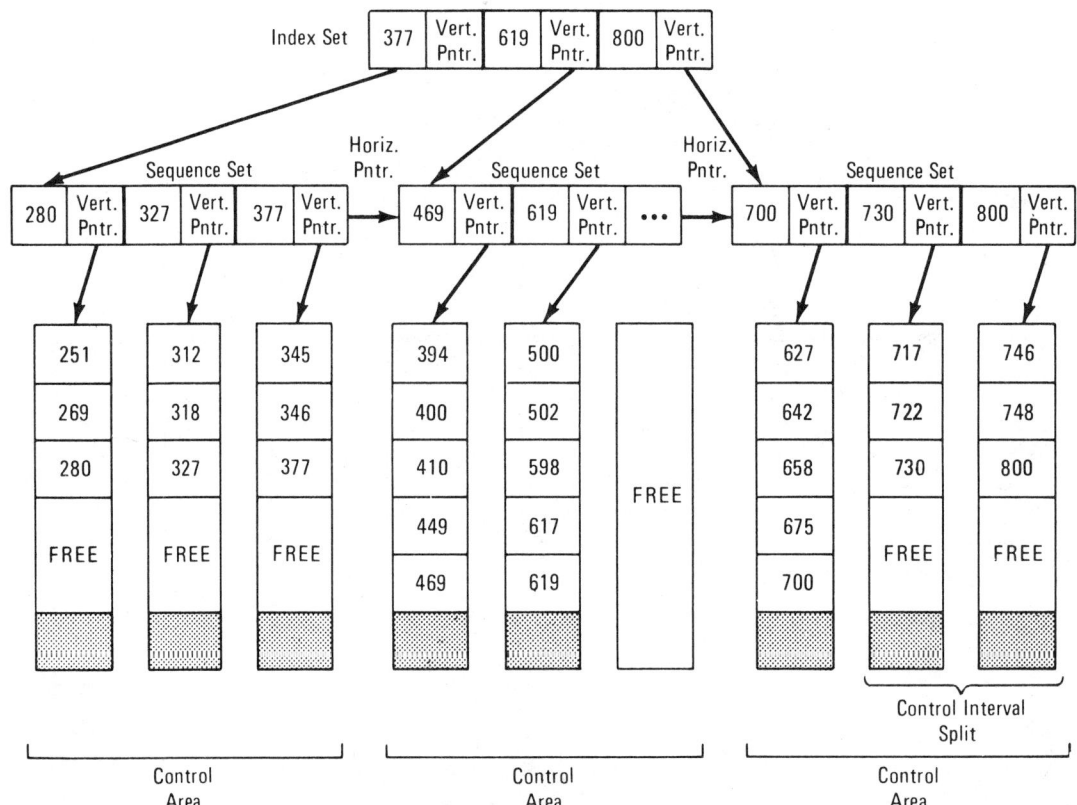

FIGURE 7.2 Illustration of control interval split.

178   Chapter 7—Indexed Files

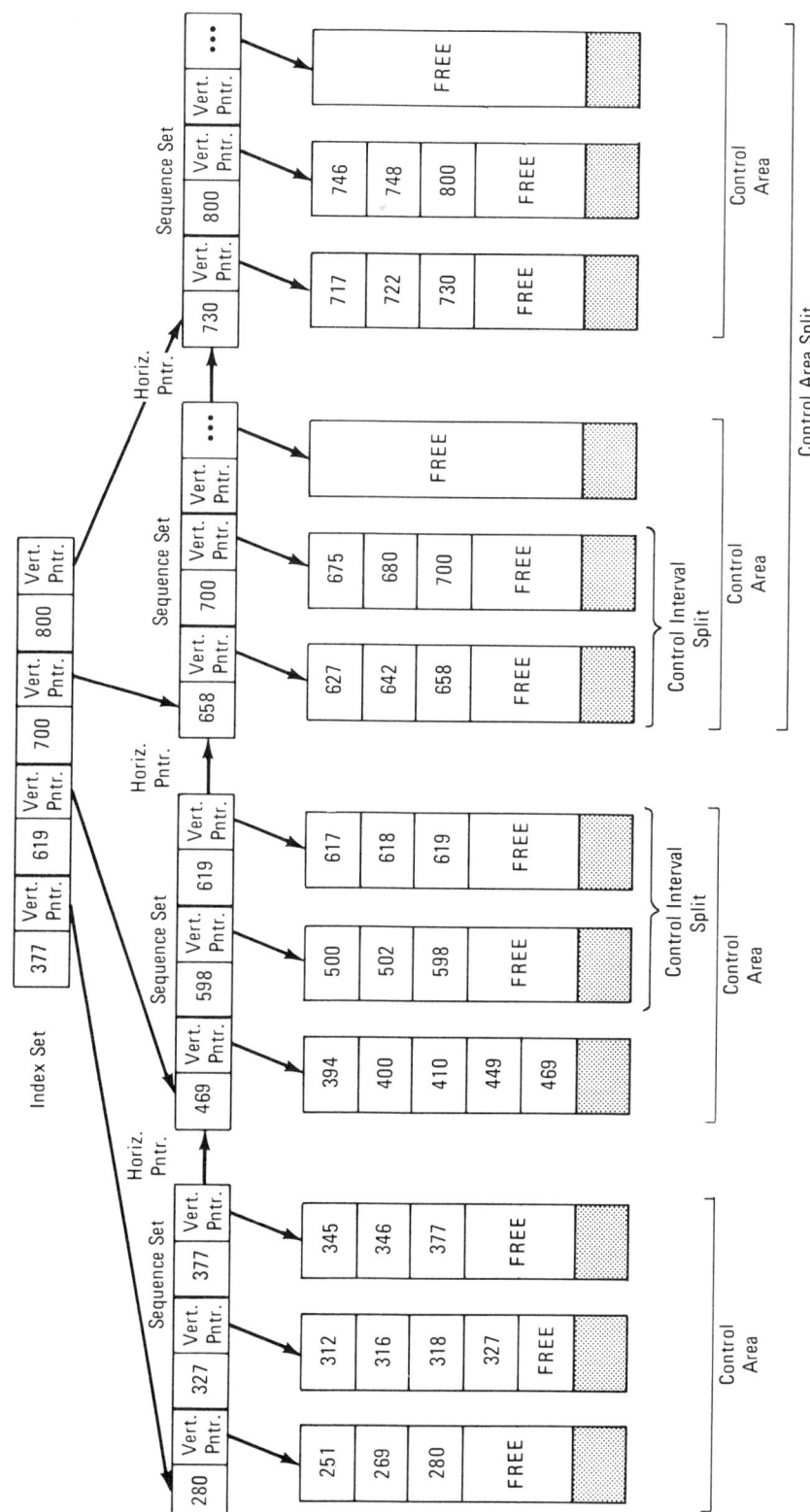

FIGURE 7.3 Illustration of control area split.

new records, with keys of 410 and 730, to the file of Figure 7.1. Addition of the first record, key 410, poses no problem, as free space is available in the control interval where the record belongs. Record 410 is inserted into its proper place and the other records in that control interval are moved down.

The addition of record key 730 requires different action. The control interval that should contain this record is full in Figure 7.1. Consequently, VSAM causes a *control interval split*, in which some of the records in the previously filled control interval are moved to an empty control interval in the same control area. Entries in the sequence set for the third control area will change, as shown in Figure 7.2. This makes considerable sense when we realize that each record in a sequence set contains the key of the highest record in the corresponding control interval. Thus, the records in the sequence set must reflect the control interval split. Note that after a control interval split, subsequent additions are facilitated, as free space is again readily available.

Figure 7.3 shows the results of including three additional records, with keys of 316, 618, and 680. Record 316 is inserted into free space in the second control interval of the first control area, with the other records initially in this interval shifted down. Record 618 causes a control interval split in the second control area.

Record 680 also requires a control interval split except that there are no longer any free control intervals in the third control area. Accordingly, a *control area split* is initiated, in which some of the records in the old control area are moved into a new control area at the end of the data set. Both the old and the new control areas will have free control intervals as a result of the split. In addition, the index set has a fourth entry, indicating the presence of a new control area. The sequence set is also expanded to allow for the fourth control area.

COBOL Requirements

Indexed files have additional COBOL requirements that center on the Environment and Procedure Divisions. The former uses an expanded SELECT statement, while the latter employs new forms of the OPEN, READ, and WRITE, and introduces the START, REWRITE, and DELETE verbs. In addition, DECLARATIVES are frequently coded to monitor the result of I/O operations. (DECLARATIVES can also be used with sequential files.) This section presents the COBOL syntax in detail.

It must be emphasized that *this section discusses the ANS 74 syntax exclusively*. (IBM users should realize that IBM has *two* distinct implementations of indexed files, VSAM and ISAM. The COBOL requirements are similar, but not identical. *VSAM adheres to the ANS 74 syntax, but ISAM does not.* IBM ISAM users should consult an appropriate reference for COBOL differences.)

Environment Division

The COBOL requirements for indexed files in the Environment Division are concerned exclusively with the SELECT statement.

SELECT

The complete syntax of the SELECT statement for ANS 74 indexed files is shown:

```
SELECT file-name
    ASSIGN TO implementor-name-1 [, implementor-name-2] ...
    
    [ RESERVE integer-1  [ AREA  ] ]
    [                    [ AREAS ] ]
    
    ORGANIZATION IS INDEXED
    
    [                    { SEQUENTIAL } ]
    [ ACCESS MODE IS     { RANDOM     } ]
    [                    { DYNAMIC    } ]
    
    RECORD KEY IS data-name-1
    
    [ALTERNATE RECORD KEY IS data-name-2 [WITH DUPLICATES]] ...
    
    [FILE STATUS IS data-name-3] .
```

Three clauses, ASSIGN, ORGANIZATION IS INDEXED, and RECORD KEY, are *required* for indexed files. Two other clauses, RESERVE AREA and FILE STATUS, may be specified for sequential as well as indexed files.

The ASSIGN clause ties a programmer-chosen file-name to a system (i.e., implementor) name. The control language links the system-name to a physical device. (On IBM OS systems, for example, the ASSIGN clause references a DDname which is repeated on a JCL DD statement to specify the actual file.)

The RESERVE AREA clause increases processing efficiency by allocating alternate I/O areas (or buffers) for the file. If the clause is omitted, the number of alternate areas defaults to the vendor's implementation. Specification of RESERVE 0 AREAS will slow processing but save an amount of storage equal to the buffer size. This is generally done only on smaller systems when the amount of main memory is limited.

ORGANIZATION IS INDEXED is mandatory for indexed files and requires no further explanation.

The meaning of ACCESS MODE is readily apparent when either SEQUENTIAL or RANDOM is specified. ACCESS IS DYNAMIC allows a file to be read either sequentially or nonsequentially in the *same* program.

The format of the READ statement determines the access method and is further discussed in that section.

The RECORD KEY clause references a field *defined in the indexed record whose value must be unique for each record in the file.* The value of the RECORD KEY is used by the operating system to establish the necessary indexes for the file.

ALTERNATE RECORD KEY provides a *second* path for random access. Unlike the RECORD KEY which must be unique for every record, the ALTERNATE KEY may contain duplicate values. This capability is extremely powerful and gives COBOL some limited facility for data base management. A common application is to specify social security or account number as the RECORD KEY, and name as the ALTERNATE KEY. This is useful in on-line applications where a customer, e.g., Grauer, doesn't know his account number. A *random* read on name would locate the first Grauer followed by a series of *sequential* reads to locate the proper record (ACCESS IS DYNAMIC is required to allow both sequential and random access in the same program). Realize also that while the ALTERNATE KEY is powerful, it is quite *expensive* in that a second set of indexes must be maintained by the operating system. Consequently, the feature should *not* be used indiscriminately but only when absolutely required by the application.

The FILE STATUS clause defines a two-byte area to indicate the success or failure of every I/O operation. It is used in conjunction with DECLARATIVES and is explained in that section.

Procedure Division

Several verbs in the Procedure Division are uniquely associated with indexed files, and/or have extended formats for indexed files. These include: OPEN, READ, WRITE, REWRITE, DELETE, and START. In addition, DECLARATIVE procedures are used frequently with such files.

OPEN

A new option of the OPEN verb, OPEN I-O, is required when updating indexed files. Consider first the syntax of the OPEN statement:

$$\text{OPEN} \left\{ \begin{array}{l} \underline{\text{INPUT}} \\ \underline{\text{OUTPUT}} \\ \underline{\text{I-O}} \end{array} \right\} \text{file-name}$$

INPUT and OUTPUT are used when an indexed file is accessed or created, respectively. However, when only a single master file is specified, as for nonsequential maintenance, OPEN I-O is necessary. In other words, the single master file functions as both an input and an output file.

READ

The READ statement has two distinct syntaxes, for sequential and nonsequential access, respectively. These are:

Format 1 (Sequential Access):

>READ file-name [NEXT] RECORD [INTO identifier-1]
>   [AT END imperative-statement-1]

Format 2 (Random Access):

>READ file-name RECORD [INTO identifier-1]
>   [KEY IS data-name-1]
>   [INVALID KEY imperative-statement-1]

Format 1, for sequential access, has been used throughout the text and should present no difficulty. The NEXT phrase is required if a sequential read is called for, and ACCESS IS DYNAMIC was specified. Use of READ INTO is strongly suggested to simplify debugging as recommended in Chapter 4.

A *random* READ is preceded by a MOVE statement, in which the key of the desired record is moved to the data name designated as the RECORD KEY in the SELECT statement. *The INVALID KEY clause is activated if the specified key cannot be found in the indexed file.* For example,

>MOVE 888888888 TO SOC-SEC-NUMBER.
>READ INDEXED-FILE INTO WS-WORK-AREA
>INVALID KEY DISPLAY 'RECORD NOT FOUND'.

The indexed file is randomly accessed for the record with social security number 888 88 8888 (assuming SOC-SEC-NUMBER was designated as the RECORD KEY in the file's SELECT statement). If record 888888888 does not exist in the indexed file, the INVALID KEY condition is raised.

If ALTERNATE RECORD KEY was specified in the SELECT statement, the KEY IS clause is used in the READ statement to indicate which field will be used to retrieve the record. For example,

>MOVE 'SMITH' TO EMP-NAME.
>READ INDEXED-FILE INTO WS-WORK-AREA
>   KEY IS EMP-NAME
>INVALID KEY DISPLAY 'RECORD NOT FOUND'.

The indexed file is randomly accessed for the *first* record with EMP-NAME of Smith (assuming EMP-NAME was designated as the ALTERNATE RECORD KEY). If no Smith can be found, the INVALID KEY condition is raised.

WRITE

The WRITE statement includes an additional clause for indexed files. Consider,

> WRITE record-name [FROM identifier-1]
> [INVALID KEY imperative statement]

If ACCESS IS SEQUENTIAL is specified when an indexed file is created, then incoming records are required to be in sequential order, and further each record is required to have a unique key. The INVALID KEY condition is raised if either of these requirements is violated.

One should also realize that *once a WRITE statement has been successfully executed, the record that was just written is no longer available in the file's record area.* This point is illustrated in R. Grauer, *A COBOL Book of Practice and Reference*, (Englewood Cliffs, N.J.: Prentice-Hall, 1981) pp. 185-86, 213-14.

REWRITE

The REWRITE verb replaces existing records when a file has been opened as an I-O file. Its syntax is similar to that of the WRITE verb, as shown:

> REWRITE record-name [FROM identifier-1]
> [INVALID KEY imperative statement]

The INVALID KEY condition is raised if the record key of the last record read does not match the key of the record to be replaced.

DELETE

The DELETE statement removes a record from an indexed file. Its syntax is simply:

> DELETE file-name RECORD
> [INVALID KEY imperative statement]

When a DELETE statement is successfully executed, the record that was deleted is logically removed from the file and can no longer be accessed. The DELETE statement can be used only on a file that was opened in the I-O mode.

START

The START statement causes the file to be positioned to the first record whose value is equal to, greater than, or not less than the value contained in the identifier. INVALID KEY is raised if no record is found that meets the specified criterion. Syntactically, the START statement has the form:

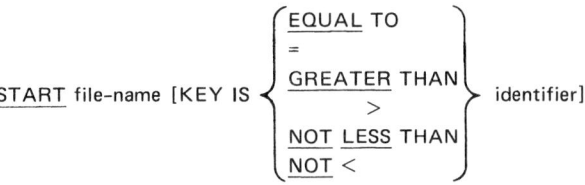

[INVALID KEY imperative statement]

DECLARATIVES

DECLARATIVES consist of one or more special purpose *sections*, which appear at the *beginning* of the Procedure Division, before the first executable statement. The purpose of DECLARATIVES is to expand the normal error-handling procedures of the operating system, and/or to aid in debugging. (DECLARATIVES can also be used in conjunction with Report Writer and is discussed further in Chapter 8.)

Declarative sections contain a USE verb to specify when the procedure is to take effect. Consider the first format which enables the programmer to specify his or her own error handling procedure for indexed files:

$$\text{USE AFTER STANDARD} \begin{Bmatrix} \text{EXCEPTION} \\ \text{ERROR} \end{Bmatrix} \text{PROCEDURE ON} \begin{Bmatrix} \{\text{file-name-1}\}\dots \\ \text{INPUT} \\ \text{OUTPUT} \\ \text{I-O} \\ \text{EXTEND} \end{Bmatrix}$$

The user's error procedure generally interrogates the two-byte area designated in the FILE STATUS clause of the SELECT statement. The operating system automatically updates the value of the FILE STATUS bytes after *every* I/O operation, according to Table 7.1.

TABLE 7.1 File Status Codes

Key-1	Key-2	Cause
0	0	Successful completion
1	0	End-of-file
2	1	Invalid key: Sequence error
	2	Duplicate key
	3	No record found
	4	Boundary violation
3	0	Permanent I/O error: No further information
	4	Boundary violation
9	1	Other error: Password failure
	2	Logic error
	3	Resource not available
	4	Sequential record not available
	5	Invalid or incomplete file information
	6	No DD statement

The entries in Table 7.1 correspond to the ANS 74 standard for key-1 equal to 0, 1, 2, or 3. The standard also allows the vendor to define additional codes when key-1 equals 9, and the entries in Table 7.1 match IBM's VSAM implementation. The advantage of DECLARATIVES is that the user can gain more information than with the standard error routine. Consider, for example, Figure 7.4, and assume that there is an error associated with the statement WRITE VSAM-RECORD.

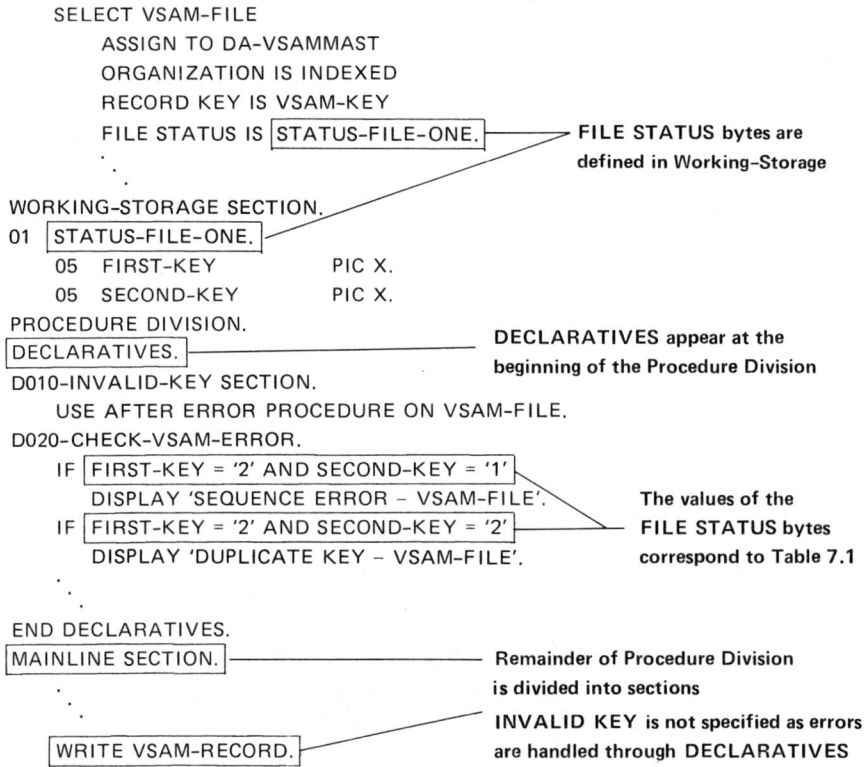

FIGURE 7.4 Use of declarative procedures.

If the programmer had specified the INVALID KEY clause in the WRITE statement, then the associated imperative statement would execute when the error occurred. The programmer would know that there was a problem in the attempted WRITE, but would *not* know the reason. If, however, a declarative procedure is established, as in Figure 7.4, then the file status bytes can be examined to determine *why* the error occurred.

Several features of Figure 7.4 bear mention.

1. The word DECLARATIVES immediately follows the Procedure Division header, and in turn is followed by the declarative procedures. END DECLARATIVES precedes the remainder of the Procedure Division.

2. Declarative procedures must be *sections*, and consequently the remainder of the Procedure Division should be divided into sections as well. (D020-CHECK-VSAM-ERROR is a paragraph name in the declarative section D010-INVALID-KEY. The paragraph name is included because ANS 74 COBOL does not permit unnamed paragraphs.)
3. Declarative procedures are executed by the input-output control system after completing the standard input-output error routine, or upon recognition of the INVALID KEY or AT END conditions when these phrases have not been specified in the associated input-output statement. When the USE procedures are finished, control implicitly returns to the routine that caused the USE procedures to be invoked.
4. Declarative procedures may not reference any procedures appearing outside of the DECLARATIVE section.

A second format of the USE statement is for *debugging*. Consider:

$$\underline{\text{USE}} \text{ FOR } \underline{\text{DEBUGGING}} \text{ ON } \left\{ \begin{array}{l} \text{cd-name-1} \\ [\underline{\text{ALL}} \text{ REFERENCES OF] identifier-1} \\ \text{file-name-1} \\ \text{procedure-name-1} \\ \underline{\text{ALL}} \text{ } \underline{\text{PROCEDURES}} \end{array} \right\} \dots$$

A USE FOR DEBUGGING statement is the first statement in a debugging section, and *requires the DEBUGGING MODE clause in the SOURCE-COMPUTER paragraph*. Whenever a debugging section is executed, a special register, DEBUG-ITEM, is filled with information describing why the section was called. DEBUG-ITEM is a reserved word with the following description:

```
01  DEBUG-ITEM.
    02  DEBUG-LINE          PIC X(6).
    02  FILLER              PIC X VALUE SPACE.
    02  DEBUG-NAME          PIC X(30).
    02  FILLER              PIC X VALUE SPACE.
    02  DEBUG-SUB-1         PIC S9999.
    02  FILLER              PIC X VALUE SPACE.
    02  DEBUG-SUB-2         PIC S9999.
    02  FILLER              PIC X VALUE SPACE.
    02  DEBUG-SUB-3         PIC S9999.
    02  FILLER              PIC X VALUE SPACE.
    02  DEBUG-CONTENTS      PIC X(n).
```

The value of the various entries, DEBUG-NAME, DEBUG-LINE, etc., depends on why the section was called in the first place. DEBUG-NAME, for example, will contain a file name if USE FOR DEBUGGING ON file-name was specified, and a procedure name if USE FOR DEBUGGING ON procedure-name was indicated. The reader is urged to consult the vendor's manual for a complete description. Nevertheless, the meaning of the various entries is fairly intuitive and the reader should have little difficulty in following the illustrative programs.

All debugging sections *must appear together at the beginning of DECLARATIVES*.

Creating an Indexed File

Figure 7.5 contains a COBOL program to create an indexed file, using the data of Figure 7.6. Output produced by the program is shown in Figure 7.7 (on pages 192 and 193). Although the logic is trivial (i.e., read a record from an incoming transaction file and write it to the output indexed file), the program illustrates many of the statements just discussed.

The SELECT statement includes ORGANIZATION IS INDEXED to denote an indexed file. ACCESS is specified as SEQUENTIAL as the file is being created. (The ACCESS clause could have been omitted as the default access mode is sequential.) The RECORD KEY entry references a field defined *within* the indexed record (line 39), the value of which must be *unique* for every record in the file. FILE STATUS specifies a two-byte field which in turn is defined in Working-Storage (lines 47-49).

DECLARATIVES follow immediately after the Procedure Division header (line 57) and end on line 78. There are three declarative sections, each with a USE statement. The USE FOR DEBUGGING sections *require* that DEBUGGING MODE be specified in the SOURCE-COMPUTER paragraph of the Environment Division (line 7).

The entry on line 59, USE FOR DEBUGGING ON ALL PROCEDURES, produces a *trace* of the program. (The same result could also have been achieved by the READY TRACE statement, but the latter is not part of the ANS 74 standard, and hence is not available on all compilers. Use of DECLARATIVES is therefore the preferred method of obtaining a trace.) The DISPLAY statements of lines 61-63 reference DEBUG-LINE, DEBUG-NAME, and DEBUG-CONTENTS, respectively. The first produces the line number causing the procedure to be executed, the second the name of the procedure, and the last an indication of why the procedure was called; e.g., START PROGRAM for the *first* executable statement, PERFORM LOOP for a performed paragraph, USE PROCEDURE when a declarative section is called, and so on.

The RESOLVE-ERROR section (lines 73-77) is invoked *whenever an error occurs in an I/O operation for INDEXED-FILE*. Accordingly, the WRITE statement of line 105 omitted the INVALID KEY clause in order that error processing be handled explicitly in DECLARATIVES. The test data of Figure 7.6 contain two records, social security numbers 400000000 and 500000000, which are out of sequence. The RESOLVE-ERROR section is called twice, each time indicating FILE-STATUS bytes

```
00001              IDENTIFICATION DIVISION.
00002              PROGRAM-ID.    CREATE2.
00003              AUTHOR.        R. GRAUER.
00004
00005              ENVIRONMENT DIVISION.                  Debugging mode is required with DECLARATIVE
00006              CONFIGURATION SECTION.                 debugging sections
00007              SOURCE-COMPUTER.      IBM-4341   WITH DEBUGGING MODE.
00008              OBJECT-COMPUTER.      IBM-4341.
00009
00010              INPUT-OUTPUT SECTION.
00011              FILE-CONTROL.
00012                  SELECT TRANSACTION-FILE
00013                      ASSIGN TO UT-S-TRANS.
00014
00015                  SELECT INDEXED-FILE
00016                      ASSIGN TO DA-VSAMMAST          Required entry for indexed file
00017                      ORGANIZATION IS INDEXED
00018                      ACCESS IS SEQUENTIAL
00019                      RECORD KEY IS INDEX-SOC-SEC-NUMBER
00020                      FILE STATUS IS FILE-STATUS-BYTES.
00021
00022              DATA DIVISION.
00023              FILE SECTION.
00024              FD  TRANSACTION-FILE
00025                  LABEL RECORDS ARE STANDARD
00026                  BLOCK CONTAINS 0 RECORDS
00027                  RECORD CONTAINS 80 CHARACTERS
00028                  DATA RECORD IS TRANSACTION-RECORD.
00029              01  TRANSACTION-RECORD.
00030                  05  TRANS-SOC-SEC-NUMBER            PIC X(9).
00031                  05  TRANS-NAME                      PIC X(20).
00032                  05  REST-OF-TRANS-RECORD            PIC X(51).
00033
00034              FD  INDEXED-FILE                       File status bytes are defined in Working-Storage
00035                  LABEL RECORDS ARE STANDARD
00036                  RECORD CONTAINS 80 CHARACTERS
00037                  DATA RECORD IS INDEXED-RECORD.
00038              01  INDEXED-RECORD.
00039                  05  INDEX-SOC-SEC-NUMBER            PIC X(9).
00040                  05  INDEX-NAME                      PIC X(20).
00041                  05  REST-OF-INDEXED-RECORD          PIC X(51).
00042
00043              WORKING-STORAGE SECTION.
00044              01  FILLER                              PIC X(14)
00045                  VALUE 'WS BEGINS HERE'.
00046
00047              01  FILE-STATUS-BYTES.
00048                  05  FIRST-STATUS-BYTE               PIC X.
00049                  05  SECOND-STATUS-BYTE              PIC X.
00050
00051              01  END-OF-FILE-SWITCH                  PIC X(3)  VALUE SPACES.
00052
00053              01  DISPLAY-MESSAGES.
00054                  05  I-O-OPERATION                   PIC X(15) VALUE SPACES.
00055
00056              PROCEDURE DIVISION.            DECLARATIVES appears at the start
00057              DECLARATIVES.                  of the Procedure Division
00058              DISPLAY-PROCEDURE SECTION.
00059                  USE FOR DEBUGGING ON ALL PROCEDURES.
00060              DISPLAY-PARAGRAPH.                      Traces program execution
00061                  DISPLAY DEBUG-LINE.
00062                  DISPLAY DEBUG-NAME.
00063                  DISPLAY DEBUG-CONTENTS.
00064                  DISPLAY '  '.
00065
00066              DISPLAY-FILE-REFERENCE SECTION.
00067                  USE FOR DEBUGGING ON INDEXED-FILE.
```

FIGURE 7.5 Program to create an indexed file.

```
00068          WRITE-STATUS-CODE.
00069              DISPLAY 'OPERATION: ' I-O-OPERATION
00070                     'STATUS CODE: ' FILE-STATUS-BYTES.
00071              DISPLAY ' '.
00072
00073          RESOLVE-ERROR SECTION.            ⟋Supplements WRITE statement of line 105
00074              USE AFTER ERROR PROCEDURE ON INDEXED-FILE.
00075          DISPLAY-ERRORS.
00076              DISPLAY 'INPUT RECORD READ ' TRANSACTION-RECORD
00077                     'STATUS CODE: ' FILE-STATUS-BYTES.
00078          END DECLARATIVES.
00079
00080          REST-OF-PROCEDURE-DIVISION SECTION.
00081          MAINLINE.
00082              MOVE 'OPEN' TO I-O-OPERATION.
00083              OPEN INPUT TRANSACTION-FILE
00084                   OUTPUT INDEXED-FILE.
00085
00086              PERFORM READ-TRANSACTION-FILE.
00087              PERFORM WRITE-INDEXED-FILE
00088                  UNTIL END-OF-FILE-SWITCH = 'YES'.
00089
00090              MOVE 'CLOSE' TO I-O-OPERATION.
00091              CLOSE TRANSACTION-FILE
00092                    INDEXED-FILE.
00093
00094          TERMINATION.
00095              STOP RUN.
00096
00097          READ-TRANSACTION-FILE.
00098              READ TRANSACTION-FILE
00099                  AT END MOVE 'YES' TO END-OF-FILE-SWITCH.
00100
00101          WRITE-INDEXED-FILE.      ⟋Error processing is handled by DECLARATIVES
00102              MOVE TRANS-SOC-SEC-NUMBER TO INDEX-SOC-SEC-NUMBER.
00103              MOVE TRANS-NAME TO INDEX-NAME.
00104              MOVE REST-OF-TRANS-RECORD TO REST-OF-INDEXED-RECORD.
00105              WRITE INDEXED-RECORD.
00106              PERFORM READ-TRANSACTION-FILE.
00107
```

FIGURE 7.5 *continued*

of 21, which are consistent with the Table 7.1. (The program of Figure 7.5 writes records to the indexed file sequentially as they are read from the transaction file. The first three records, 100000000, 300000000, and 600000000 are in ascending sequence, and are written to the indexed file *before* records 400000000 and 500000000 are read. Hence, the *latter* two are judged out of sequence rather than record 600000000, which may have been the reader's assumption from viewing Figure 7.6 alone.)

Figure 7.5 also contains a declarative section for the data-name INDEXED-FILE. Accordingly, execution of the OPEN and CLOSE state-

```
100000000SUGRUE        P  12450079100C533308802220879280
300000000MILGROM       IR06130580200E655510814000681480
600000000GRAUER        RT11450877200E590011818001180500
400000000BENJAMIN      BL10531073100E73331073         300
500000000TATER         JS02500779200P43330779         310
```
↖Records are out of sequence and are displayed as errors in Figure 7.7

FIGURE 7.6 Input to program creating indexed file.

ments of lines 83 and 91 invokes this procedure, and produces the associated output in Figure 7.7, in which the status bytes are 00.

COBOL Case Study—Nonsequential File Maintenance

Much of Chapter 6 was dedicated to the balance line algorithm, a truly general technique for *sequential* file maintenance. This section extends that technique to a *nonsequential* update.

Before proceeding further, let us distinguish between the two methods of file maintenance. In a sequential update, there are *two* distinct master files, an old and a new master. *Every record in the old master is rewritten to the new master regardless of whether it changes.* In a nonsequential update, however, there is a *single* file which functions as both the old and new master, and *only those records which change are rewritten.* In addition, a sequential update is driven by the *relationship between the old master and transaction files*, whereas a nonsequential update is driven by the transaction file(s) only; i.e., transactions are processed until the file(s) is empty.

The choice between the two techniques is governed by the *activity* of the file to be updated. An active file, one with a "high" percentage of records to be changed, is best updated sequentially. An inactive file, on the other hand, i.e., one with a "low" percentage of changed records, should be updated nonsequentially. Unfortunately, quantitative guidelines as to what constitutes a high or low percentage of activity are not easily available.

Our case study assumes that incoming transactions have been sorted. (This is perfectly acceptable if the update is done in a batch environment, but not if it is done in real time.) It is in fact desirable to presort the transaction file, particularly when multiple transactions are applied to a single master record. In this way, the indexed file is read (and written or rewritten) *only once* for each value of the record key.

This section develops a COBOL program to update an indexed file nonsequentially and follows the requirements of the expanded maintenance program of Chapter 6, i.e., Figure 6.14. Test data and associated output match Figure 6.15, and are not repeated. A hierarchy chart and pseudocode are shown in Figures 7.8 and 7.9, respectively.

Compare the hierarchy chart of Figure 7.8 to the sequential version of Chapter 6, noting the following changes:

1. The READ-OLD-MASTER module has disappeared from the second level of the hierarchy chart; i.e., the key of the old master record is *not* used in determining the active key.

2. The BUILD-NEW-MASTER and READ-OLD-MASTER-FILE modules from levels 3 and 4 have been replaced by a single module READ-INDEXED-FILE.

```
000082
REST-OF-PROCEDURE-DIVISION
START PROGRAM

000080
MAINLINE
FALL THROUGH              ┌─ Status code of 00 indicates successful OPEN operation
                          │
OPERATION: OPEN        STATUS CODE: 00

000086
READ-TRANSACTION-FILE
PERFORM LOOP

000087
WRITE-INDEXED-FILE
PERFORM LOOP

000106
READ-TRANSACTION-FILE
PERFORM LOOP

┌──────────────────────┐     DEBUG - LINE, NAME, and CONTENTS indicate
│ 000087               │     line number, procedure name, and reason for
│ WRITE-INDEXED-FILE   │     execution
│ PERFORM LOOP         │
└──────────────────────┘

000106
READ-TRANSACTION-FILE
PERFORM LOOP

000087
WRITE-INDEXED-FILE
PERFORM LOOP

000106
READ-TRANSACTION-FILE
PERFORM LOOP

000087
WRITE-INDEXED-FILE
PERFORM LOOP
```

FIGURE 7.7 Output produced by Figure 7.5.

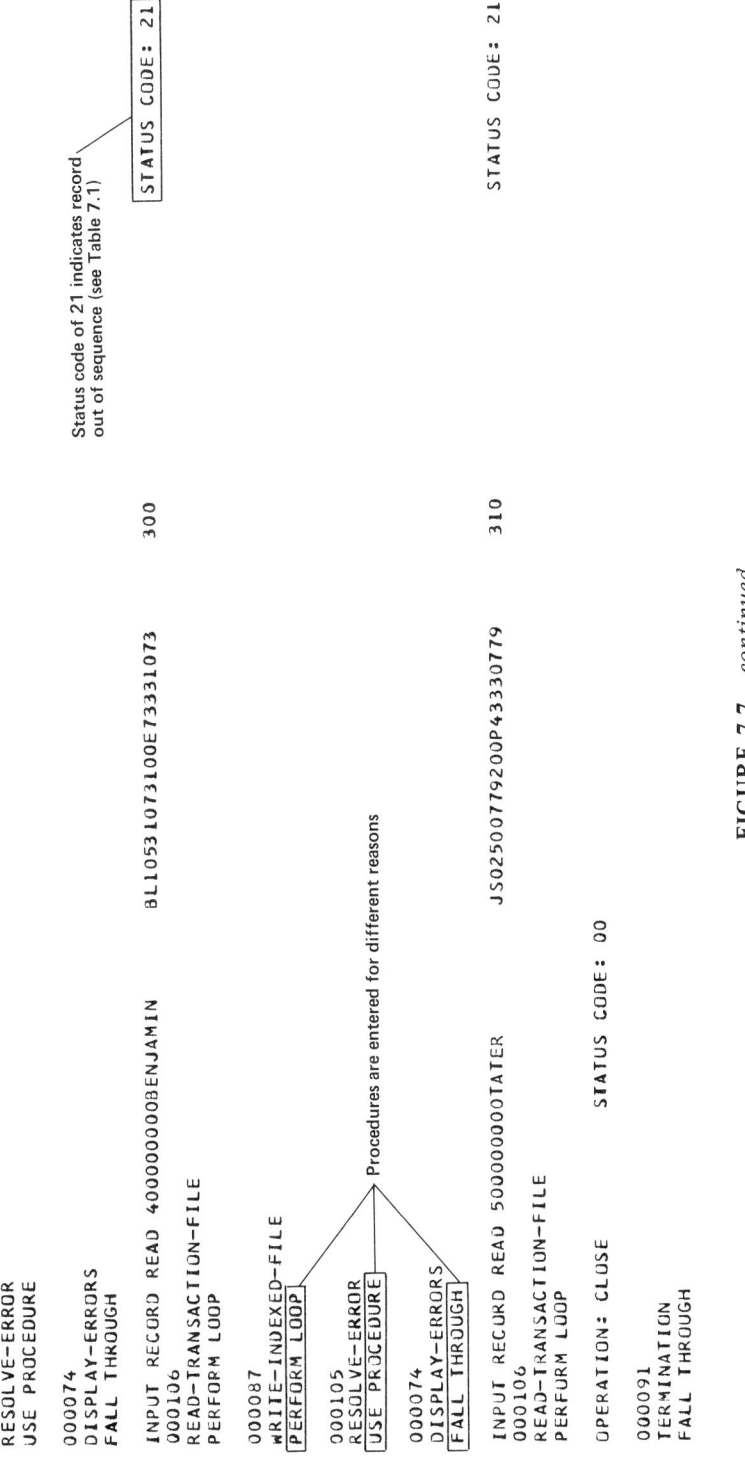

FIGURE 7.7 *continued*

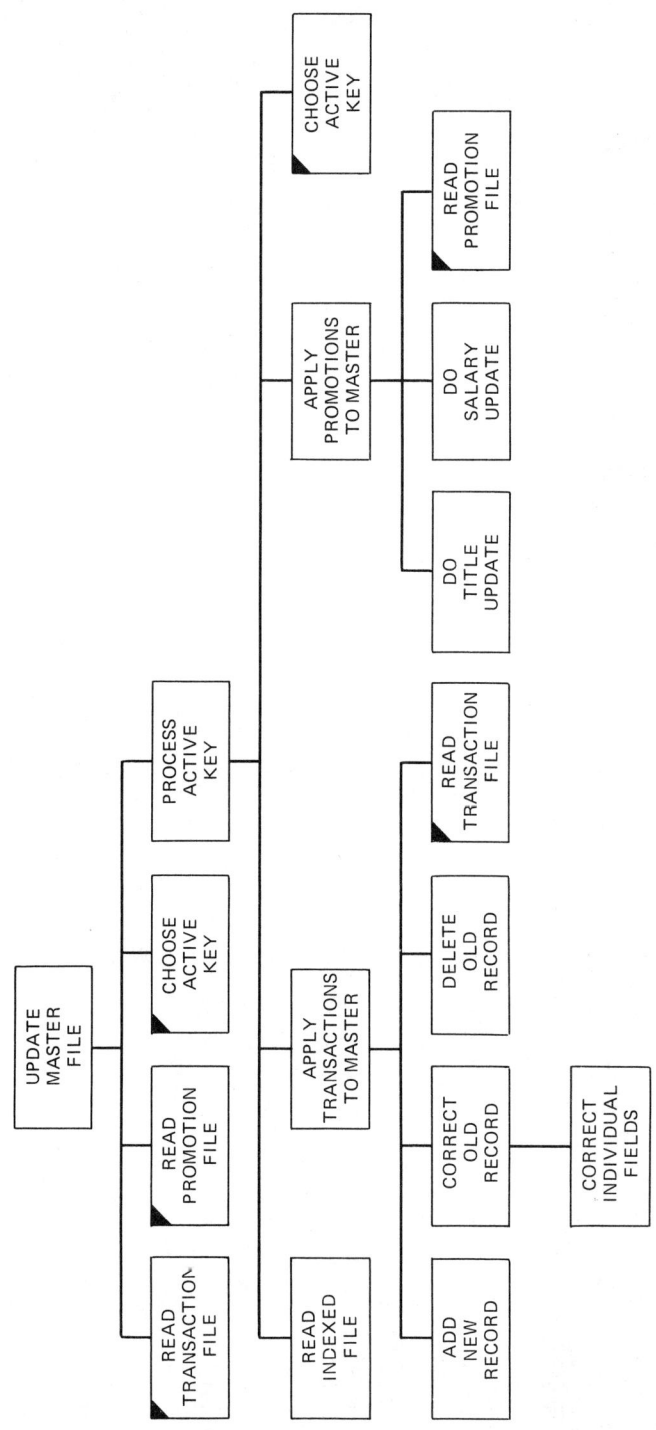

FIGURE 7.8 Hierarchy chart for nonsequential update.

194   Chapter 7—Indexed Files

In spite of these differences, the two hierarchy charts have more similarities than differences. The *logic of most modules is unchanged*, and the only module which changes significantly is CHOOSE-ACTIVE-KEY. The active key is now the smaller of *two* values, the transaction and promotion keys (as opposed to three: transaction, promotion, and old master).

Figure 7.9 contains pseudocode corresponding to the overall hierarchy chart. Figures 7.10 and 7.11 amplify the logic for processing transactions and promotions, respectively.

RECORD-KEY-ALLOCATED-SWITCH serves the same function as in the sequential version; i.e., it checks for duplicate additions and/or no matches. A second switch, RECORD-ORIGINALLY-THERE-SWITCH, is

```
OPEN FILES
READ TRANSACTION-FILE, AT END MOVE HIGH-VALUES TO TRANSACTION-KEY
READ PROMOTION-FILE, AT END MOVE HIGH-VALUES TO PROMOTION-KEY
CHOOSE FIRST ACTIVE-KEY
DO WHILE ACTIVE-KEY ≠ HIGH-VALUES
   MOVE ACTIVE-KEY TO INDEX-SOCIAL-SECURITY-NUMBER
   MOVE 'YES' TO RECORD-KEY-ALLOCATED-SWITCH
   MOVE 'YES' TO RECORD-ORIGINALLY-THERE-SWITCH
   READ INDEXED-FILE
        INVALID KEY MOVE 'NO' TO RECORD-KEY-ALLOCATED-SWITCH
                   MOVE 'NO' TO RECORD-ORIGINALLY-THERE-SWITCH
   DO WHILE TRANSACTION-KEY = ACTIVE-KEY
      APPLY TRANSACTION TO INDEXED-RECORD
      READ TRANSACTION-FILE, AT END MOVE HIGH-VALUES TO TRANSACTION-KEY
   ENDDO
   DO WHILE PROMOTION-KEY = ACTIVE-KEY
      APPLY PROMOTION TO INDEXED-RECORD
      READ PROMOTION-FILE, AT END MOVE HIGH-VALUES TO PROMOTION-KEY
   ENDDO
   IF RECORD-KEY-ALLOCATED-SWITCH = 'YES'
      IF RECORD-ORIGINALLY-THERE-SWITCH = 'YES'
          REWRITE RECORD
      ELSE (RECORD WAS ADDED TO INDEXED-FILE)
          WRITE RECORD
      ENDIF
   ELSE (RECORD IS NOT TO APPEAR IN INDEXED-FILE)
      IF RECORD-ORIGINALLY-THERE-SWITCH = 'YES'
          DELETE RECORD
      ELSE (A NO MATCH WAS PROCESSED)
          NEXT SENTENCE
      ENDIF
   ENDIF
   CHOOSE NEXT ACTIVE-KEY
ENDDO
CLOSE FILES
STOP RUN
```

APPLY TRANSACTION TO INDEXED-RECORD — Expanded in Figure 7.10
APPLY PROMOTION TO INDEXED-RECORD — Expanded in Figure 7.11

FIGURE 7.9 Pseudocode for nonsequential update.

```
 ┌─ IF ADDITION
 │    ┌─ IF RECORD-KEY-ALLOCATED-SWITCH = 'YES'
 │    │     WRITE 'ERROR – DUPLICATE ADD'
 │    │  ELSE (ACTIVE-KEY IS NOT IN INDEXED-FILE)
 │    │     MOVE TRANSACTION-RECORD TO INDEXED-RECORD
 │    │     MOVE 'YES' TO RECORD-KEY-ALLOCATED-SWITCH
 │    └─ ENDIF
 │  ELSE IF CORRECTION
 │    ┌─ IF RECORD-KEY-ALLOCATED-SWITCH = 'YES'
 │    │     PROCESS CORRECTION
 │    │  ELSE (ACTIVE-KEY IS NOT IN INDEXED-FILE)
 │    │     WRITE 'ERROR – NO MATCH'
 │    └─ ENDIF
 │  ELSE IF DELETION
 │    ┌─ IF RECORD-KEY-ALLOCATED-SWITCH = 'YES'
 │    │     MOVE 'NO' TO RECORD-KEY-ALLOCATED-SWITCH
 │    │     PROCESS DELETION
 │    │  ELSE (ACTIVE-KEY IS NOT IN INDEXED-FILE)
 │    │     WRITE 'ERROR – NO MATCH'
 │    └─ ENDIF
 └─ ENDIF
```

FIGURE 7.10   Pseudocode for APPLY-TRANSACTION-TO-INDEXED-RECORD.

also required to decide if an updated indexed-record is to be written, rewritten, or deleted. Both switches are initially set to YES for each value of the active key. A random read of the indexed file sets both switches to NO if the value of the active key is not in the indexed file.

RECORD-KEY-ALLOCATED-SWITCH is manipulated by itself on subsequent additions or deletions. It is set to YES when a record is added and set to NO when a record is deleted. RECORD-ORIGINALLY-THERE-SWITCH is set only by the random read of the indexed file.

```
 ┌─ IF PROMOTION
 │    ┌─ IF RECORD-KEY-ALLOCATED-SWITCH = 'YES'
 │    │     PROCESS PROMOTION
 │    │  ELSE (ACTIVE KEY IS NOT IN INDEXED-FILE)
 │    │     WRITE 'ERROR – NO MATCH'
 │    └─ ENDIF
 │  ELSE IF SALARY-RAISE
 │    ┌─ IF RECORD-KEY-ALLOCATED-SWITCH = 'YES'
 │    │     PROCESS SALARY-RAISE
 │    │  ELSE (ACTIVE KEY IS NOT IN INDEXED-FILE)
 │    │     WRITE 'ERROR – NO MATCH'
 │    └─ ENDIF
 └─ ENDIF
```

FIGURE 7.11   Pseudocode for APPLY-PROMOTION-TO-INDEXED-RECORD.

Figure 7.12 contains the completed program. The SELECT statement for INDEXED-FILE (lines 15–19) has the required ORGANIZATION IS INDEXED and RECORD KEY clauses, and specifies ACCESS IS RANDOM. INDEXED-FILE is opened as I-O in line 135 because it serves as both the old and new master files; i.e., it is read from *and* written to.

```
00001              IDENTIFICATION DIVISION.
00002              PROGRAM-ID.    NONSEQUP.
00003              AUTHOR.        R. GRAUER.
00004
00005              ENVIRONMENT DIVISION.
00006              CONFIGURATION SECTION.
00007              SOURCE-COMPUTER.     IBM-4341.
00008              OBJECT-COMPUTER.     IBM-4341.
00009
00010              INPUT-OUTPUT SECTION.
00011              FILE-CONTROL.
00012                  SELECT TRANSACTION-FILE
00013                      ASSIGN TO UT-S-TRANS.
00014
00015                  SELECT INDEXED-FILE
00016                      ASSIGN TO DA-VSAMMAST
00017                      ORGANIZATION IS INDEXED          ── Indicates nonsequential access
00018                      ACCESS IS RANDOM
00019                      RECORD KEY IS INDEX-SOC-SEC-NUMBER.
00020
00021                  SELECT PROMOTION-FILE
00022                      ASSIGN TO UT-S-PROMOTE.
00023
00024                  SELECT DELETED-RECORD-FILE
00025                      ASSIGN TO UT-S-DELETE.
00026
00027              DATA DIVISION.
00028              FILE SECTION.
00029              FD  TRANSACTION-FILE
00030                  LABEL RECORDS ARE STANDARD           ⟩ Record key is defined within
00031                  BLOCK CONTAINS 0 RECORDS               the index record
00032                  RECORD CONTAINS 80 CHARACTERS
00033                  DATA RECORD IS TRANSACTION-RECORD.
00034              01  TRANSACTION-RECORD                 PIC X(80).
00035
00036              FD  INDEXED-FILE
00037                  LABEL RECORDS ARE STANDARD
00038                  RECORD CONTAINS 80 CHARACTERS
00039                  DATA RECORD IS INDEXED-RECORD.
00040              01  INDEXED-RECORD.
00041                  05  INDEX-SOC-SEC-NUMBER           PIC X(9).
00042                  05  REST-OF-INDEXED-RECORD         PIC X(71).
00043
00044              FD  PROMOTION-FILE
00045                  LABEL RECORDS ARE STANDARD
00046                  BLOCK CONTAINS 0 RECORDS
00047                  RECORD CONTAINS 80 CHARACTERS
00048                  DATA RECORD IS PROMOTION-RECORD.
00049              01  PROMOTION-RECORD                   PIC X(80).
00050
00051              FD  DELETED-RECORD-FILE
00052                  LABEL RECORDS ARE STANDARD
00053                  BLOCK CONTAINS 0 RECORDS
00054                  RECORD CONTAINS 80 CHARACTERS
00055                  DATA RECORD IS DELETED-RECORD.
00056              01  DELETED-RECORD                     PIC X(80).
00057
```

FIGURE 7.12 Nonsequential update.

```
00058              WORKING-STORAGE SECTION.
00059              01  FILLER                              PIC X(14)
00060                      VALUE 'WS BEGINS HERE'.
00061
00062              01  WS-TRANS-RECORD.
00063                  05  TR-SOC-SEC-NUMBER               PIC X(9).
00064                  05  TR-NAME.
00065                      10   TR-LAST-NAME               PIC X(15).
00066                      10   TR-INITIALS                PIC XX.
00067                  05  TR-DATE-OF-BIRTH.
00068                      10   TR-BIRTH-MONTH             PIC 99.
00069                      10   TR-BIRTH-YEAR              PIC 99.
00070                  05  TR-DATE-OF-HIRE.
00071                      10   TR-HIRE-MONTH              PIC 99.
00072                      10   TR-HIRE-YEAR               PIC 99.
00073                  05  TR-LOCATION-CODE                PIC X(3).
00074                  05  TR-PERFORMANCE-CODE             PIC X.
00075                  05  TR-EDUCATION-CODE               PIC X.
00076                  05  TR-TITLE-DATA.
00077                      10   TR-TITLE-CODE              PIC 9(3).
00078                      10   TR-TITLE-DATE              PIC 9(4).
00079                  05  TR-SALARY-DATA.
00080                      10   TR-SALARY                  PIC 9(5).
00081                      10   TR-SALARY-DATE             PIC 9(4).
00082                  05  TR-TRANSACTION-CODE             PIC X.
00083                      88   ADDITION         VALUE 'A'.
00084                      88   CORRECTION       VALUE 'C'.
00085                      88   DELETION         VALUE 'D'.
00086                  05  FILLER                          PIC X(24).
00087
00088              01  WS-NDX-MAST-RECORD.
00089                  05  NDX-SOC-SEC-NUMBER              PIC X(9).
00090                  05  NDX-NAME.
00091                      10   NDX-LAST-NAME              PIC X(15).
00092                      10   NDX-INITIALS               PIC XX.
00093                  05  NDX-DATE-OF-BIRTH.
00094                      10   NDX-BIRTH-MONTH            PIC 99.
00095                      10   NDX-BIRTH-YEAR             PIC 99.
00096                  05  NDX-DATE-OF-HIRE.
00097                      10   NDX-HIRE-MONTH             PIC 99.
00098                      10   NDX-HIRE-HEAR              PIC 99.
00099                  05  NDX-LOCATION-CODE               PIC X(3).
00100                  05  NDX-PERFORMANCE-CODE            PIC X.
00101                  05  NDX-EDUCATION-CODE              PIC X.
00102                  05  NDX-TITLE-DATA OCCURS 2 TIMES.
00103                      10   NDX-TITLE-CODE             PIC 9(3).
00104                      10   NDX-TITLE-DATE             PIC 9(4).
00105                  05  NDX-SALARY-DATA OCCURS 3 TIMES.
00106                      10   NDX-SALARY                 PIC 9(5).
00107                      10   NDX-SALARY-DATE            PIC 9(4).
00108
00109              01  WS-PROMOTION-RECORD.
00110                  05  PR-SOC-SEC-NUMBER               PIC X(9).
00111                  05  PR-NAME.
00112                      10   PR-LAST-NAME               PIC X(15).
00113                      10   PR-INITIALS                PIC XX.
00114                  05  PR-SALARY-DATA.
00115                      10   PR-SALARY                  PIC 9(5).
00116                      10   PR-SALARY-DATE             PIC 9(4).
00117                  05  PR-TITLE-DATA.
00118                      10   PR-TITLE-CODE              PIC 9(3).
00119                      10   PR-TITLE-DATE              PIC 9(4).
00120                  05  PR-PROMOTION-CODE               PIC X.
00121                      88   SALARY-RAISE     VALUE 'R'.
00122                      88   PROMOTION        VALUE 'P'.
00123                  05  FILLER                          PIC X(37).
00124
```

FIGURE 7.12 *continued*

```
00125
00126             01  WS-BALANCE-LINE-SWITCHES.
00127                 05  WS-ACTIVE-KEY                       PIC X(9).
00128                 05  WS-RECORD-KEY-ALLOCATED-SWITCH      PIC X(3).
00129                 05  WS-RECORD-ORIGINALLY-THERE-SW       PIC X(3).
00130
00131             PROCEDURE DIVISION.
00132             0010-UPDATE-MASTER-FILE.
00133                 OPEN INPUT TRANSACTION-FILE
00134                            PROMOTION-FILE              ┌─ Indexed file serves as both
00135                      I-O INDEXED-FILE                     old and new master
00136                      OUTPUT DELETED-RECORD-FILE.
00137                 PERFORM 0015-READ-PROMOTION-FILE.
00138                 PERFORM 0020-READ-TRANSACTION-FILE.
00139                 PERFORM 0040-CHOOSE-ACTIVE-KEY.
00140                 PERFORM 0050-PROCESS-ACTIVE-KEY
00141                     UNTIL WS-ACTIVE-KEY = HIGH-VALUES.
00142                 CLOSE TRANSACTION-FILE
00143                       PROMOTION-FILE
00144                       INDEXED-FILE
00145                       DELETED-RECORD-FILE.
00146                 STOP RUN.
00147
00148             0015-READ-PROMOTION-FILE.
00149                 READ PROMOTION-FILE INTO WS-PROMOTION-RECORD
00150                     AT END MOVE HIGH-VALUES TO PR-SOC-SEC-NUMBER.
00151
00152             0020-READ-TRANSACTION-FILE.
00153                 READ TRANSACTION-FILE INTO WS-TRANS-RECORD
00154                     AT END MOVE HIGH-VALUES TO TR-SOC-SEC-NUMBER.
00155
00156             0030-READ-INDEXED-FILE.
00157                 MOVE WS-ACTIVE-KEY TO INDEX-SOC-SEC-NUMBER.
00158                 MOVE 'YES' TO WS-RECORD-KEY-ALLOCATED-SWITCH.
00159                 MOVE 'YES' TO WS-RECORD-ORIGINALLY-THERE-SW.
00160
00161                 READ INDEXED-FILE INTO WS-NDX-MAST-RECORD
00162                     INVALID KEY
00163                         MOVE 'NO' TO WS-RECORD-KEY-ALLOCATED-SWITCH
00164                         MOVE 'NO' TO WS-RECORD-ORIGINALLY-THERE-SW.
00165                                                        └─ Nonsequential read
00166             0040-CHOOSE-ACTIVE-KEY.
00167                 IF TR-SOC-SEC-NUMBER LESS THAN PR-SOC-SEC-NUMBER
00168                     MOVE TR-SOC-SEC-NUMBER TO WS-ACTIVE-KEY
00169                 ELSE
00170                     MOVE PR-SOC-SEC-NUMBER TO WS-ACTIVE-KEY.
00171
00172             0050-PROCESS-ACTIVE-KEY.               ┌─ Active key is determined from
00173                 PERFORM 0030-READ-INDEXED-FILE.       transaction and promotion files
00174
00175                 PERFORM 0070-APPLY-TRANS-TO-MASTER
00176                     UNTIL WS-ACTIVE-KEY NOT EQUAL TR-SOC-SEC-NUMBER.
00177
00178                 PERFORM 0075-APPLY-PROMO-TO-MASTER
00179                     UNTIL WS-ACTIVE-KEY NOT EQUAL PR-SOC-SEC-NUMBER.
00180
00181                 IF WS-RECORD-KEY-ALLOCATED-SWITCH = 'YES'    ┌─ Existing records
00182                     IF WS-RECORD-ORIGINALLY-THERE-SW = 'YES'    are rewritten
00183                         REWRITE INDEXED-RECORD FROM WS-NDX-MAST-RECORD
00184                     ELSE
00185                         WRITE INDEXED-RECORD FROM WS-NDX-MAST-RECORD
00186                 ELSE
00187                     IF WS-RECORD-ORIGINALLY-THERE-SW = 'YES'
00188                         DELETE INDEXED-FILE.       ┌─ Old records are removed through
00189                                                       DELETE verb
00190                 PERFORM 0040-CHOOSE-ACTIVE-KEY.
00191
```

FIGURE 7.12 *continued*

```
00192
00193             0070-APPLY-TRANS-TO-MASTER.
00194                 IF ADDITION
00195                     PERFORM 0090-ADD-NDX-RECORD
00196                 ELSE
00197                     IF CORRECTION
00198                         PERFORM 0100-CORRECT-NDX-RECORD
00199                     ELSE                          ⟩ Identical modules as in sequential update
00200                         IF DELETION
00201                             PERFORM 0110-DELETE-NDX-RECORD.
00202
00203                 PERFORM 0020-READ-TRANSACTION-FILE.
00204
00205             0075-APPLY-PROMO-TO-MASTER.
00206                 IF PROMOTION
00207                     PERFORM 0120-DO-TITLE-UPDATE
00208                 ELSE
00209                     IF SALARY-RAISE
00210                         PERFORM 0130-DO-SALARY-RAISE.
00211
00212                 PERFORM 0015-READ-PROMOTION-FILE.
00213
00214             0090-ADD-NDX-RECORD.
00215                 IF WS-RECORD-KEY-ALLOCATED-SWITCH = 'YES'
00216                     DISPLAY '    '
00217                     DISPLAY '    ERROR DUPLICATE ADDITION: '
00218                     DISPLAY '    TRANSACTION IN ERROR: ' WS-TRANS-RECORD
00219                 ELSE
00220                     MOVE 'YES' TO WS-RECORD-KEY-ALLOCATED-SWITCH
00221                     MOVE SPACES TO WS-NDX-MAST-RECORD
00222                     MOVE TR-SOC-SEC-NUMBER TO NDX-SOC-SEC-NUMBER
00223                     MOVE TR-NAME TO NDX-NAME
00224                     MOVE TR-DATE-OF-BIRTH TO NDX-DATE-OF-BIRTH
00225                     MOVE TR-DATE-OF-HIRE TO NDX-DATE-OF-HIRE
00226                     MOVE TR-LOCATION-CODE TO NDX-LOCATION-CODE
00227                     MOVE TR-PERFORMANCE-CODE TO NDX-PERFORMANCE-CODE
00228                     MOVE TR-EDUCATION-CODE TO NDX-EDUCATION-CODE
00229                     MOVE TR-TITLE-DATA TO NDX-TITLE-DATA (1)
00230                     MOVE TR-SALARY-DATA TO NDX-SALARY-DATA (1).
00231
00232             0100-CORRECT-NDX-RECORD.
00233                 IF WS-RECORD-KEY-ALLOCATED-SWITCH = 'YES'
00234                     PERFORM 0105-CORRECT-INDIVIDUAL-FIELDS
00235                 ELSE
00236                     DISPLAY '    '
00237                     DISPLAY '    ERROR-NO MATCHING RECORD: '
00238                     DISPLAY '    TRANSACTION IN ERROR: ' WS-TRANS-RECORD.
00239
00240             0105-CORRECT-INDIVIDUAL-FIELDS.
00241                 IF TR-NAME NOT EQUAL SPACES
00242                     MOVE TR-NAME TO NDX-NAME.
00243                 IF TR-DATE-OF-BIRTH NOT EQUAL SPACES
00244                     MOVE TR-DATE-OF-BIRTH TO NDX-DATE-OF-BIRTH.
00245                 IF TR-DATE-OF-HIRE NOT EQUAL SPACES
00246                     MOVE TR-DATE-OF-HIRE TO NDX-DATE-OF-HIRE.
00247                 IF TR-LOCATION-CODE NOT EQUAL SPACES
00248                     MOVE TR-LOCATION-CODE TO NDX-LOCATION-CODE.
00249                 IF TR-PERFORMANCE-CODE NOT EQUAL SPACES
00250                     MOVE TR-PERFORMANCE-CODE TO NDX-PERFORMANCE-CODE.
00251                 IF TR-EDUCATION-CODE NOT EQUAL SPACES
00252                     MOVE TR-EDUCATION-CODE TO NDX-EDUCATION-CODE.
00253                 IF TR-TITLE-CODE IS NUMERIC
00254                     MOVE TR-TITLE-CODE TO NDX-TITLE-CODE (1).
00255                 IF TR-TITLE-DATE IS NUMERIC
00256                     MOVE TR-TITLE-DATE TO NDX-TITLE-DATE (1).
00257                 IF TR-SALARY IS NUMERIC
00258                     MOVE TR-SALARY TO NDX-SALARY (1).
```

FIGURE 7.12 *continued*

```
00259              IF TR-SALARY-DATE IS NUMERIC
00260                  MOVE TR-SALARY-DATE TO NDX-SALARY-DATE (1).
00261
00262          0110-DELETE-NDX-RECORD.
00263              IF WS-RECORD-KEY-ALLOCATED-SWITCH = 'YES'
00264                  MOVE 'NO' TO WS-RECORD-KEY-ALLOCATED-SWITCH
00265                  WRITE DELETED-RECORD FROM WS-NDX-MAST-RECORD
00266              ELSE
00267                  DISPLAY '   '
00268                  DISPLAY '   ERROR-NO MATCHING RECORD: '
00269                  DISPLAY '   TRANSACTION IN ERROR: ' WS-TRANS-RECORD.
00270                                           Same modules as in sequential update
00271          0120-DO-TITLE-UPDATE.
00272              IF WS-RECORD-KEY-ALLOCATED-SWITCH = 'YES'
00273                  MOVE NDX-TITLE-CODE (1) TO NDX-TITLE-CODE (2)
00274                  MOVE NDX-TITLE-DATE (1) TO NDX-TITLE-DATE (2)
00275                  MOVE PR-TITLE-CODE TO NDX-TITLE-CODE (1)
00276                  MOVE PR-TITLE-DATE TO NDX-TITLE-DATE (1)
00277              ELSE
00278                  DISPLAY '   '
00279                  DISPLAY '   ERROR-NO MATCHING RECORD: '
00280                  DISPLAY '   PROMOTION IN ERROR: ' WS-PROMOTION-RECORD.
00281
00282          0130-DO-SALARY-RAISE.
00283              IF WS-RECORD-KEY-ALLOCATED-SWITCH = 'YES'
00284                  MOVE NDX-SALARY (2) TO NDX-SALARY (3)
00285                  MOVE NDX-SALARY-DATE (2) TO NDX-SALARY-DATE (3)
00286                  MOVE NDX-SALARY (1) TO NDX-SALARY (2)
00287                  MOVE NDX-SALARY-DATE (1) TO NDX-SALARY-DATE (2)
00288                  MOVE PR-SALARY TO NDX-SALARY (1)
00289                  MOVE PR-SALARY-DATE TO NDX-SALARY-DATE (1)
00290              ELSE
00291                  DISPLAY '   '
00292                  DISPLAY '   ERROR-NO MATCHING RECORD: '
00293                  DISPLAY '   PROMOTION IN ERROR: ' WS-PROMOTION-RECORD.
```

FIGURE 7.12 *continued*

The logic of 0010-UPDATE-MASTER-FILE closely parallels that of the sequential update except that an initial read is not done for the old master. Consequently, the logic of 0040-CHOOSE-ACTIVE-KEY has been modified to take the lesser of two values as the active key.

As in the sequential update, 0050-PROCESS-ACTIVE-KEY is executed repeatedly until the active key equals HIGH-VALUES. The first task in processing each value of the active key is to read the indexed file to determine if the current value is already allocated; i.e., whether the value of the active key exists in the indexed file. Note well the use of switches in the INVALID KEY clause (lines 162–164), and how the switches are set to YES immediately prior to the random read. Observe also that WS-ACTIVE-KEY is moved to INDEX-SOC-SEC-NUMBER (i.e., the field defined as the RECORD KEY in line 19) prior to the random read.

The contents of the intermediate and lower level modules; 0070-APPLY-TRANS-TO-MASTER, 0075-APPLY-PROMO-TO-MASTER, 0090-ADD-NDX-RECORD, 0100-CORRECT-NDX-RECORD, 0105-CORRECT-INDIVIDUAL-FIELDS, 0110-DELETE-NDX-RECORD, 0120-DO-TITLE-UPDATE, and 0130-DO-SALARY-RAISE are the same as in the sequential update. However, the mechanics of writing, rewriting and/or deleting indexed records are more complicated than with a sequential file; hence, the need for lines 181-188.

IBM Differences (ISAM versus VSAM)

As stated in the chapter overview, different vendors have different physical implementations for indexed files. The actual method, however, is of little concern to the programmer, *provided the associated COBOL elements adhere to the ANS 74 standard.* Unfortunately, not all vendors follow the standard, and consequently there are subtle differences from compiler to compiler. The author cannot cover all vendors for lack of space, but he does highlight differences in the IBM implementations for VSAM and ISAM.

Simply stated, *IBM's VSAM implementation follows the ANS 74 standard exactly, whereas ISAM does not.* Hence, the preceding discussion pertained directly to VSAM, but not to ISAM. The major ISAM coding differences are summarized, beginning with the ISAM SELECT statement:

```
SELECT file-name
    ASSIGN TO DA-I-ddname
    [RESERVE {NO / integer-1} ALTERNATE AREAS]
    [ACCESS MODE IS {SEQUENTIAL / RANDOM}]
    [NOMINAL KEY IS data-name-1]
    RECORD KEY is data-name-2
```

The ORGANIZATION IS INDEXED clause is *not* used with an ISAM file, whereas it is required under VSAM. In addition, the powerful VSAM options of ACCESS IS DYNAMIC, ALTERNATE RECORD KEY, and FILE STATUS are not permitted.

Observe also the use of NOMINAL KEY for ISAM and its *omission* for VSAM. A random read is accomplished under VSAM by moving the key of the record to be found to the field defined as the RECORD KEY; *under ISAM, one moves the key of the record to be found to the NOMINAL KEY*, which in turn is defined in Working-Storage.

Records in a VSAM file are removed through the DELETE statement. In ISAM, this is accomplished by moving HIGH-VALUES to the first byte of the ISAM record (also known as the delete byte) and *rewriting* the record. This mandates the *additional* ISAM requirement of moving LOW-VALUES to the delete byte when ISAM records are initially created.

ISAM is the older, and less efficient, means of indexed organization. In all probability, most IBM installations have already converted from ISAM to VSAM, in which case the preceding section is of little interest. If not, however, then the discussion may prove useful as a *starting* point in the conversion. The reader is referred to the appropriate IBM manuals for more complete information.

Summary

The chapter discussed all necessary COBOL elements for processing indexed files and illustrated them in two complete programs. The first created an indexed file and the second updated it nonsequentially. The latter extended the balance line algorithm of Chapter 6 and was accompanied by pseudocode and a hierarchy chart.

DECLARATIVES were covered in depth, with specific illustrations for debugging and for interrogating the FILE STATUS bytes. (DECLARATIVES may be used with sequential files as well.)

Finally, the COBOL differences for the IBM ISAM and VSAM implementations were highlighted.

True/False

1. ALTERNATE RECORD KEY should *always* be specified for indexed files to allow for future expansion.
2. The FILE STATUS clause is permitted only for indexed files.
3. A READ statement *must* contain either the AT END or INVALID KEY clause.
4. Declarative procedures may appear *anywhere* within the Procedure Division.
5. Inclusion of the INTO clause in a READ statement is not recommended as it requires additional storage space.
6. RESERVE 0 AREAS is highly recommended to speed up processing.
7. Declarative procedures can be specified for both sequential and indexed files.
8. The value of RECORD KEY must be unique for every record in an indexed file.
9. The value of ALTERNATE RECORD KEY must be unique for every record in an indexed file.
10. DEBUG-ITEM is a COBOL reserved word, with a predetermined format.
11. The FILE STATUS clause is a mandatory entry in the SELECT statement for an indexed file.
12. An indexed file can be accessed sequentially and nonsequentially in the same program.
13. The first byte of an indexed record should contain either LOW or HIGH VALUES.
14. WRITE and REWRITE can be used interchangeably.
15. Records in an indexed file are deleted by moving HIGH-VALUES to the first byte.
16. The COBOL syntax for IBM VSAM files conforms to the ANS 74 standard.
17. The COBOL syntax for IBM ISAM files conforms to the ANS 74 standard.
18. Active files are best updated nonsequentially.
19. READY TRACE is part of the ANS 74 standard.

Problems

1. Describe the changes to Figure 7.3 if record keys 401, 723, 724, and 725 were added. What would happen if record keys 502 and 619 were deleted?

2. Indicate whether the following statements apply to ISAM only, VSAM only, or both:
   (a) Uses the first byte to denote active or inactive status.
   (b) Removes inactive records through the DELETE verb.
   (c) Requires the RECORD KEY clause in its SELECT statement.
   (d) Has the NOMINAL KEY clause in its SELECT statement.
   (e) Requires ORGANIZATION IS INDEXED in its SELECT statement.
   (f) Conforms to the ANS 74 standard.
   (g) Can access records either sequentially or nonsequentially.
   (h) Can *access* records either sequentially or nonsequentially in the *same* program.
   (i) Can be opened as an I/O file.
   (j) Uses the REWRITE verb to change existing records.
   (k) Uses control areas and control intervals.
   (l) Uses track and cylinder indexes.
   (m) Can be accessed through the START verb.
   (n) Can have an ALTERNATE RECORD KEY.
   (o) Can specify ACCESS IS DYNAMIC.

3. Assume that record key 289 is to be inserted in the first control area of the VSAM data set of Figure 7.3. Logically, it could be added as the *last* record in the first control interval, or the *first* record in the second control interval. Is there a preference?

   In similar fashion, should record 620 be inserted as the *last* record in the third interval of the second area, or as the *first* record in the first interval of the third area?

   Finally, will record 900 be inserted as the *last* record in the fourth control area, or will it require *creation of a fifth control area?* Can you describe in general terms how VSAM adds records at the end of control areas and/or control intervals?

4. A bank uses an indexed file for its outstanding loans. The record key is CUSTOMER-LOAN-NUMBER which consists of a unique six-digit customer number and a three-digit sequence number. Each loan a customer receives is assigned a new sequence number. Customer 111111, for example, may have two outstanding loans with keys of 111111001 and 111111002. Develop code to retrieve all outstanding loans for a given customer. (Hint: use the START verb.)

Projects

1. Modify the program of Figure 7.12 to accommodate the specifications of Project 1 in Chapter 6 with the exception of parts (f) and (i). In addition, expand the SELECT statement of lines 15-19 to include the FILE STATUS clause. Delete the INVALID KEY entry of line 162, replacing it with a check of the FILE STATUS bytes for the appropriate value (see Table 7.1). Delete the AT END clauses in lines 150 and 154 as well, substituting a check for the equivalent FILE STATUS bytes. This in turn requires that a different set of status bytes be defined for each sequential file.

8 Report Writer

Overview

This book is written with two major objectives. The first is to present aspects of structured methodology in a way that can be easily understood and applied by COBOL programmers. The second is to develop proficiency in COBOL through adequate coverage of advanced language elements. This chapter covers Report Writer, and is directed toward the second objective. Inclusion of this topic is entirely consistent with the overall goals of the book. The examples are fully structured, and as we shall see, Report Writer produces programs that work and are easily maintained.

Report Writer is paradoxically one of the most powerful, yet least used facilities in COBOL. Practitioners list several reasons for its disfavor, including:

1. "I find Report Writer statements difficult to code and modify...."
2. "Maintenance is impossible because no one in the shop knows it. What will happen when you leave....?"

3. "I tried it, and it didn't work; it seems that the Report Writer modules of most COBOL compilers contain one or more bugs. . . ."
4. "I never learned it in school; I tried to teach myself from the vendor's manual but couldn't follow the discussion. . . ."
5. "I used it successfully a few times until my program ABENDed in the middle of Report Writer; debugging was a joke. . . ."
6. "I would like to try it, but it's not available on the compiler we have. . . ."
7. "I can't use it because my manager has banned it from the shop. . . ."

These comments were made to the author during seminars to some 1,000 programmers in 40 cities during 1980 and 1981. The groups he addressed ranged in experience from six months to 15 years, and they form the basis for a very *informal* survey. Prior to the seminar, approximately one person in 10 used Report Writer on a regular basis. However, after a two hour lecture, upwards of 75% expressed serious interest in using the facility.

For the time being, let us refute the preceding arguments simply by stating that Report Writer works and works well; that it is no more difficult to code, debug, and maintain than other COBOL statements, and that there is no reason not to use it. A more elegant argument in favor of Report Writer will be the three COBOL listings in the chapter itself.

We begin with a definition of terms associated with Report Writer, then progress immediately to a program for processing two levels of control breaks. We modify the program to process a third-level control break, and substitute summary for detail reporting. We conclude with a third Report Writer program containing many fine points of the module.

The overall approach is to teach Report Writer through example, and to avoid becoming bogged down with syntax and other technical considerations. We do, however, conclude with a more formal discussion of how Report Writer works, and end with rigid presentation of the syntax. The reader should consult a vendor's Reference Manual for additional information.

Vocabulary

Report Writer is best used for problems involving control breaks. A *control break* is defined as a change in a designated field. For example, if an incoming file is sorted by location, and location is the control field, a control break occurs every time location changes. If the file is sorted by location, and department within location, it is possible to designate two control fields, department and location.

Let us assume a file has been sorted on location, and department within location. Hence, all employees in department 100 in Atlanta precede the Atlanta employees in department 200, who precede those in department

300, etc. Next come the employees in department 100 in Boston, followed by department 200 in Boston and so forth. A single control break occurs as departments change within the *same* location; e.g., from department 100 in Atlanta to department 200 in Atlanta. A double control break, on location and department, arises when we go from department 300 in Atlanta to department 100 in Boston.

Our second definition has to do with the way Report Writer generates output. Every line in every report belongs to one of seven kinds of *report groups*. It is not necessary that a given report contain all seven report groups. Moreover control headings, control footings, and detail report groups may occur more than once. The seven categories are:

1. *Report heading:* one or more lines appearing once at the beginning (initiation) of a report.
2. *Report footing:* one or more lines appearing once at the conclusion (termination) of a report.
3. *Page heading:* one or more lines appearing at the beginning of each page after the report heading.
4. *Page footing:* one or more lines appearing at the end of each page.
5. *Control heading:* one or more lines appearing before a control break; i.e., when the contents of a designated field change.
6. *Control footing:* one or more lines appearing after a control break.
7. *Detail:* one or more lines for each selected record.

A given report may contain multiple *control headings*, *footings*, and/or *detail* report groups. A report may *not* contain more than one report heading or report footing, and/or more than one page heading or page footing.

Example 1—Two Control Breaks

For better understanding of control breaks, report groups, and Report Writer in general, we proceed to a complete COBOL program. Input to the program consists of a transaction file, a portion of which is shown in Figure 8.1.

Each record contains a transaction number and amount, the salesman responsible, and his or her location. Note well that the data have been sorted by location, and by salesman within location. A *single control break* occurs from salesman to salesman within the same location; i.e., from Lavor to Tater within Chicago. A *double control break* occurs when salesman and location switch simultaneously; e.g., from Tater in Chicago to Jaffee in Detroit.

The problem is to obtain a sales total for each individual salesman, for each location, and for the company as a whole. Figure 8.2 shows two pages from a report produced by the COBOL program developed later in the

Location	Salesman	Transaction #	Amount
. .			
Chicago	Lavor	151100	8000
Chicago	Lavor	256777	7500
Chicago	Lavor	321456	1000
Chicago	Tater	050000	0500
Chicago	Tater	112278	2430
Detroit	Jaffee	800000	7700
Detroit	Lee	888888	8800
Detroit	Lee	905432	9500
. .			

FIGURE 8.1 Input to Report Writer program.

chapter. Note in particular, the presence of a *page heading, control heading* on a location change, and *control footings* on both salesman and location.

Data Division Requirements

The essence of Report Writer is to describe what a report should look like in the Data Division, rather than specify how it is generated in the Procedure Division. The happy consequence is that the latter is typically quite short, because much of the logic is generated automatically. The programmer is relieved of mundane tasks including: page headings and/or footings, spacing, initializing and reinitializing, and so on. Consider now Figure 8.3, the COBOL program which produced the output of Figure 8.2. At first, its Data Division may appear unduly long and complex. In reality it is no longer than that of any meaningful COBOL program, with or without Report Writer.

A report is written to a file defined in a SELECT statement. The FD for this file contains an additional entry, REPORT IS (line 26 in Figure 8.3), which specifies the name of the report. Note that there are no 01 entries for this FD since the description of the file is handled in the Report Section. The entry in the REPORT IS clause has a corresponding RD (Report Description) in the Report Section (line 49) of the Data Division.

The CONTROLS clause (line 50 in Figure 8.3) identifies the control breaks as FINAL, TR-SALESMAN-LOCATION, and TR-SALESMAN-NAME. Subsequent specification of control headings and/or control footings will cause information to print before and/or after control breaks in these fields. Specification of CONTROL IS FINAL causes a control break at the end of the report. Note well that the identifier(s) in the CONTROL clause, i.e., TR-SALESMAN-LOCATION and TR-SALESMAN-NAME, exist in each incoming record.

The remaining clauses of the RD physically describe the pages of the report. One can specify the maximum number of lines per page (PAGE LIMIT), the first line on which anything may be printed (HEADING),

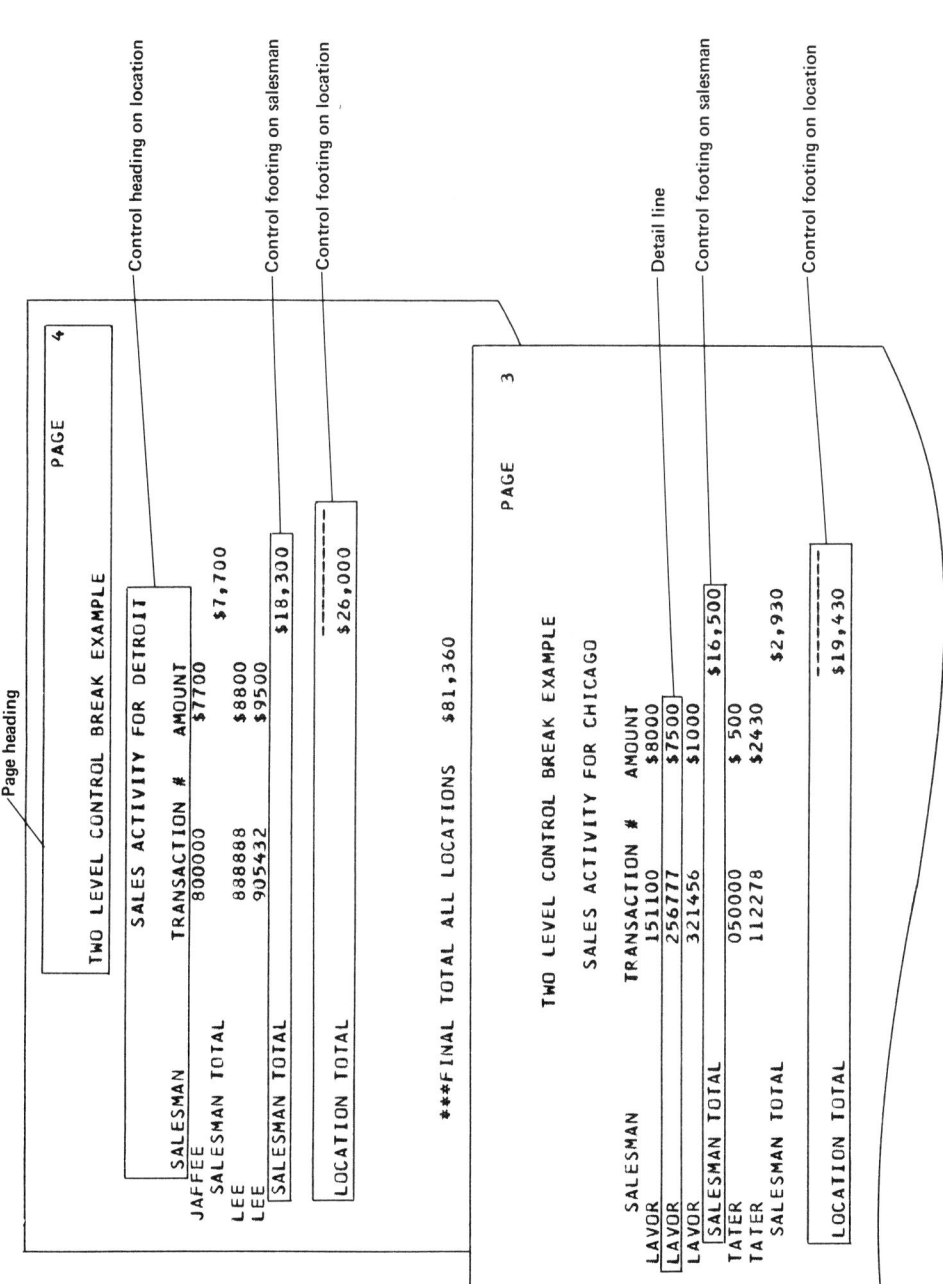

FIGURE 8.2 Output produced by Report Writer.

Example 1—Two Control Breaks   **209**

```
00001              IDENTIFICATION DIVISION.
00002              PROGRAM-ID.  RWONE.
00003              AUTHOR.    R. GRAUER.
00004
00005              ENVIRONMENT DIVISION.
00006              CONFIGURATION SECTION.
00007              SOURCE-COMPUTER.    IBM-4341.
00008              OBJECT-COMPUTER.    IBM-4341.
00009              INPUT-OUTPUT SECTION.
00010              FILE-CONTROL.
00011                  SELECT SALES-FILE
00012                      ASSIGN TO UT-S-SALES.
00013                  SELECT PRINT-FILE
00014                      ASSIGN TO UT-S-REPORT.
00015
00016              DATA DIVISION.
00017              FILE SECTION.
00018              FD  SALES-FILE
00019                  LABEL RECORDS ARE OMITTED
00020                  BLOCK CONTAINS 0 RECORDS
00021                  RECORD CONTAINS 80 CHARACTERS
00022                  DATA RECORD IS SALES-RECORD.
00023              01  SALES-RECORD                    PIC X(80).
00024
00025              FD  PRINT-FILE
00026                  REPORT IS CONTROL-BREAK           ─ Identifies report name in subsequent RD
00027                  LABEL RECORDS ARE OMITTED
00028                  RECORD CONTAINS 133 CHARACTERS.   ─ Facilitates debugging in conjunction
00029                                                      with READ INTO statements
00030              WORKING-STORAGE SECTION.
00031              01  FILLER                          PIC X(14)
00032                  VALUE 'WS BEGINS HERE'.
00033              01  WS-DATA-FLAG                    PIC X(3)     VALUE SPACES.
00034
00035              01  TRANSACTION-AREA.
00036                  05  TR-SALESMAN-NAME            PIC X(20).
00037                  05  TR-AMOUNT                   PIC S9(4).
00038                  05  FILLER                      PIC XX.
00039                  05  TR-NUMBER                   PIC X(6).        Fields designated as
00040                  05  TR-TYPE                     PIC X.           control breaks in
00041                  05  TR-SALESMAN-REGION          PIC X(17).       Report Section
00042                  05  TR-SALESMAN-LOCATION        PIC X(20).
00043                  05  FILLER                      PIC X(10).
00044
00045              01  FILLER                          PIC X(12)
00046                  VALUE 'WS ENDS HERE'.
00047                                              ─ Beginning of Report Section
00048              REPORT SECTION.
00049              RD  CONTROL-BREAK               ─ Report name matches entry in line 26
00050                  CONTROLS ARE FINAL TR-SALESMAN-LOCATION TR-SALESMAN-NAME
00051                  PAGE LIMIT 50 LINES
00052                  HEADING 1                                 ─ Establishes control breaks
00053                  FIRST DETAIL 5
00054                  LAST DETAIL 45
00055                  FOOTING 48.
00056
00057              01  TYPE IS PAGE HEADING.  ─ Indicates absolute line number
00058                  05  LINE NUMBER 1.
00059                      10  COLUMN NUMBER 61        PIC X(4)
00060                          VALUE 'PAGE'.
00061                      10  COLUMN NUMBER 66        PIC ZZZZZ9
00062                          SOURCE PAGE-COUNTER.
00063                  05  LINE NUMBER PLUS 2.
00064                      10  COLUMN NUMBER 22        PIC X(31)
00065                          VALUE 'TWO LEVEL CONTROL BREAK EXAMPLE'.
00066
```

FIGURE 8.3 Report writer program.

```
00067        01   TYPE IS CONTROL HEADING TR-SALESMAN-LOCATION.
00068             05   LINE NUMBER 5.
00069                  10   COLUMN NUMBER 25        PIC X(18)
00070                       VALUE 'SALES ACTIVITY FOR'.
00071                  10   COLUMN NUMBER 44        PIC X(20)
00072                       SOURCE TR-SALESMAN-LOCATION.
00073             05   LINE NUMBER 7.
00074                  10   COLUMN NUMBER 6         PIC X(8)
00075                       VALUE 'SALESMAN'.
00076                  10   COLUMN NUMBER 24        PIC X(13)
00077                       VALUE 'TRANSACTION #'.
00078                  10   COLUMN NUMBER 40        PIC X(7)
00079                       VALUE 'AMOUNT'.
00080
00081        01   TRANSACTION-LINE TYPE IS DETAIL.
00082             05   LINE NUMBER PLUS 1.
00083                  10   COLUMN NUMBER 2         PIC X(20)
00084                       SOURCE TR-SALESMAN-NAME.
00085                  10   COLUMN NUMBER 27        PIC X(6)
00086                       SOURCE TR-NUMBER.
00087                  10   COLUMN NUMBER 41        PIC $ZZZ9
00088                       SOURCE TR-AMOUNT.
00089
00090        01   TYPE IS CONTROL FOOTING TR-SALESMAN-NAME.
00091             05   LINE NUMBER PLUS 1.
00092                  10   COLUMN NUMBER 4         PIC X(15)
00093                       VALUE 'SALESMAN TOTAL'.
00094                  10   SALESMAN-TOTAL
00095                       COLUMN NUMBER 48        PIC $$$,$$9
00096                       SUM TR-AMOUNT.
00097
00098        01   TYPE IS CONTROL FOOTING TR-SALESMAN-LOCATION.
00099             05   LINE NUMBER PLUS 2.
00100                  10   COLUMN NUMBER 48        PIC X(10)
00101                       VALUE ALL '-'.
00102             05   LINE NUMBER PLUS 1.
00103                  10   COLUMN NUMBER 4         PIC X(14)
00104                       VALUE 'LOCATION TOTAL'.
00105                  10   LOCATION-TOTAL
00106                       COLUMN NUMBER 48        PIC $$$,$$9
00107                       SUM SALESMAN-TOTAL.
00108
00109        01   TYPE IS CONTROL FOOTING FINAL.
00110             05   LINE NUMBER PLUS 5.
00111                  10   COLUMN NUMBER 10        PIC X(28)
00112                       VALUE '***FINAL TOTAL ALL LOCATIONS'.
00113                  10   COLUMN NUMBER 40        PIC $$$$,$$9
00114                       SUM LOCATION-TOTAL.
00115
00116        PROCEDURE DIVISION.
00117        0010-CREATE-REPORTS.
00118             OPEN INPUT SALES-FILE
00119                  OUTPUT PRINT-FILE.
00120             INITIATE CONTROL-BREAK.
00121             READ SALES-FILE INTO TRANSACTION-AREA
00122                  AT END MOVE 'NO' TO WS-DATA-FLAG.
00123             PERFORM 0020-PROCESS-ALL-TRANSACTIONS
00124                  UNTIL WS-DATA-FLAG = 'NO'.
00125             TERMINATE CONTROL-BREAK.
00126             CLOSE SALES-FILE
00127                  PRINT-FILE.
00128             STOP RUN.
00129
00130        0020-PROCESS-ALL-TRANSACTIONS.
00131             GENERATE TRANSACTION-LINE.
00132             READ SALES-FILE INTO TRANSACTION-AREA
00133                  AT END MOVE 'NO' TO WS-DATA-FLAG.
```

Describes two fields on line 5

Detail report group is referenced in GENERATE statement of line 131

Control footing prints whenever a break occurs on TR-SALESMAN-NAME

FINAL control footing prints at report termination

INITIATE and TERMINATE reference report name on line 26

GENERATE references detail report group of line 81

FIGURE 8.3 *continued*

the first line for a detail (FIRST DETAIL), the last line for a control heading or detail (LAST DETAIL), and the last line for a footing (FOOTING).

The RD is followed by several 01 entries to describe report groups within that report (just as an FD is followed by 01 entries to describe records within a file). Recall that there are seven types of report groups. A given report need not contain all seven, and can contain multiple entries for the same type report group. Figure 8.3, for example, does not contain either a page or report footing, but does contain three control footings (lines 90, 98, and 109).

The most unusual aspect of Report Writer Data Division formats is that the *data-name is optional*. Hence, when reading a Report Section for the first time, it is somewhat startling to find level numbers followed immediately by clauses other than data-names. For example, there are six 01 entries in the Report Section of Figure 8.3, but only one includes a data-name, TRANSACTION-LINE (line 81), and that is because of a requirement in a subsequent Procedure Division statement (GENERATE in line 131).

The TYPE clause is required for an 01 entry in the Report Section, and cannot be specified at any other level. The program of Figure 8.3 contains six TYPE clauses, one for each report group. Consider, for example, the control heading for TR-SALESMAN-LOCATION (COBOL lines 67–79). It begins with a TYPE clause (line 67) to identify the nature of the report group. It in turn consists of two lines of output, which print every time there is a control break on TR-SALESMAN-LOCATION. The first line will appear on line 5 of the page. This in turn is a group entry, consisting of two fields beginning in columns 25 and 44 respectively. The second group item of the control heading specifies line 7 and in turn has 3 elementary items, beginning in columns 6, 24, and 40 respectively.

The value of an elementary item is obtained in one of three ways; by the SOURCE, VALUE, or SUM clauses. Specification of SOURCE; e.g., SOURCE IS TR-SALESMAN-LOCATION (in line 72) causes the current value of TR-SALESMAN-LOCATION to be moved to the output field. Specification of VALUE, e.g., VALUE 'SALESMAN' (in line 75) moves a literal to the output field. Finally, specification of SUM, e.g., SUM TR-AMOUNT (line 96) causes Report Writer to increment SALESMAN-TOTAL (line 94) by the value of TR-AMOUNT for each generated record (see Procedure Division requirements).

When a control break occurs on TR-SALESMAN-NAME, the salesman total is *rolled forward* into the next highest level counter, i.e., into LOCATION-TOTAL (line 105). The control footing for TR-SALESMAN-NAME is presented, after which SALESMAN-TOTAL is reset to zero.

In similar fashion, when a control break occurs in TR-SALESMAN-LOCATION, the value of LOCATION-TOTAL (line 105) is *rolled forward* into the next highest level total, i.e., into the FINAL total (line 114). The control footing for TR-SALESMAN-LOCATION is presented, and LOCATION-TOTAL is reset to zero.

Procedure Division Requirements

The Procedure Division of Figure 8.3 is remarkably short and contains three new verbs: INITIATE, GENERATE, and TERMINATE, all uniquely associated with Report Writer.

INITIATE is used to begin processing of a given report. Execution of this statement initializes counters, totals, etc. Its syntax is simply:

$$\underline{\text{INITIATE}} \text{ report-name-1 [report-name-2]} \ldots$$

Note that the report-name, CONTROL-BREAK, appearing in the INITIATE statement of line 120 matches the entry in the REPORT clause of the FD for PRINT-FILE (line 26). The report-name also appears in the RD entry in the Report Section (line 49) in the Data Division.

The GENERATE statement (line 131) causes Report Writer to produce automatically any of the seven report groups where and when they are needed. It has the general syntax:

$$\underline{\text{GENERATE}} \left\{ \begin{array}{l} \text{report-name} \\ \text{data-name} \end{array} \right\}$$

Two types of reporting are possible: *summary reporting* in which only heading and footing groups are produced, and *detail reporting* in which the detail report group named in the GENERATE statement is produced each time the statement is executed.

The GENERATE statement in Figure 8.3 calls for detail reporting by specifying the data-name of a report group, i.e., TRANSACTION-LINE. (Note the latter was designated as a DETAIL report group in line 81.) Figure 8.5, shown later in this chapter, illustrates summary reporting.

The TERMINATE statement (line 125) completes report processing as if a control break at the highest level occurred. All footing groups up to the highest level are produced, all counters are reset, and report processing is ended. The statement has the syntax:

$$\underline{\text{TERMINATE}} \text{ report-name-1 [report-name-2]} \ldots$$

Example 2—Three Control Breaks

The program of Figure 8.3 provided a rapid introduction to Report Writer. We continue with a second example designed (1) to integrate SORT and Report Writer, and (2) to show the ease with which a Report Writer program can be modified. Three control breaks (on region, location, and salesman) are now required rather than two. In addition, it is no longer necessary to show all transactions for a given salesman, but only his or her total. Figure 8.4 shows a page from the modified report. It contains output cor-

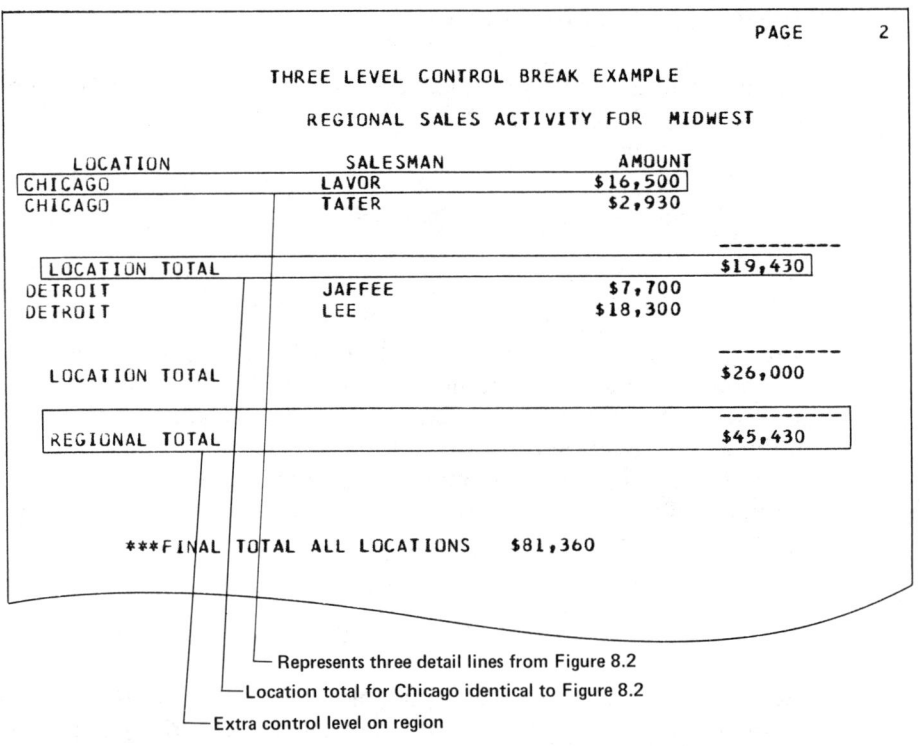

FIGURE 8.4 Output from three control break program.

responding to Figure 8.2, except that Chicago and Detroit have been combined into the Midwest region.

Sorting is accomplished within the program of Figure 8.5 through the SORT statement of lines 147–150:

```
SORT SORT-FILE
    ASCENDING KEY SORT-REGION SORT-LOCATION SORT-NAME
    USING SALES-FILE
    OUTPUT PROCEDURE 0008-REPORT.
```

Three sort keys are indicated, with SORT-REGION as the major (i.e., most important) and SORT-NAME as the minor (i.e., least important). The clause, USING SALES-FILE, indicates that SALES-FILE contains the records to be sorted and causes the SORT verb to do the necessary I/O. Hence, SALES-FILE is opened, its records are released to sort, and the file is closed, all without programmer action. (This is in contrast to the technique employed in Figure 3.18, in which the programmer selected the records to be 'released' to sort.)

After the sort is completed, control passes to the *section* specified as the OUTPUT PROCEDURE. This in turn reads (i.e., returns) records from

```
00001              IDENTIFICATION DIVISION.
00002              PROGRAM-ID.  RWTWO.
00003              AUTHOR.      R. GRAUER.
00004
00005              ENVIRONMENT DIVISION.
00006              CONFIGURATION SECTION.
00007              SOURCE-COMPUTER.     IBM-4341.
00008              OBJECT-COMPUTER.     IBM-4341.
00009              INPUT-OUTPUT SECTION.
00010              FILE-CONTROL.
00011                  SELECT SORT-FILE
00012                      ASSIGN TO UT-S-SORTWORK.
00013                  SELECT SALES-FILE
00014                      ASSIGN TO UT-S-SALES.
00015                  SELECT PRINT-FILE
00016                      ASSIGN TO UT-S-REPORT.
00017
00018              DATA DIVISION.
00019              FILE SECTION.
00020              FD  SALES-FILE
00021                  LABEL RECORDS ARE OMITTED
00022                  BLOCK CONTAINS 0 RECORDS
00023                  RECORD CONTAINS 80 CHARACTERS
00024                  DATA RECORD IS SALES-RECORD.
00025              01  SALES-RECORD                 PIC X(80).
00026
00027              FD  PRINT-FILE
00028                  REPORT IS CONTROL-BREAK
00029                  LABEL RECORDS ARE OMITTED
00030                  RECORD CONTAINS 133 CHARACTERS.
00031
00032              SD  SORT-FILE
00033                  RECORD CONTAINS 80 CHARACTERS
00034                  DATA RECORD IS SORT-RECORD.
00035              01  SORT-RECORD.
00036                  05  SORT-NAME                PIC X(20).
00037                  05  FILLER                   PIC X(13).
00038                  05  SORT-REGION              PIC X(17).
00039                  05  SORT-LOCATION            PIC X(20).
00040                  05  FILLER                   PIC X(10).
00041
00042              WORKING-STORAGE SECTION.
00043              01  FILLER                       PIC X(14)
00044                      VALUE 'WS BEGINS HERE'.
00045              01  WS-DATA-FLAG                 PIC X(3)     VALUE SPACES.
00046
00047              01  TRANSACTION-AREA.
00048                  05  TR-SALESMAN-NAME         PIC X(20).
00049                  05  TR-AMOUNT                PIC S9(4).
00050                  05  FILLER                   PIC XX.
00051                  05  TR-NUMBER                PIC X(6).
00052                  05  TR-TYPE                  PIC X.
00053                  05  TR-SALESMAN-REGION       PIC X(17).
00054                  05  TR-SALESMAN-LOCATION     PIC X(20).
00055                  05  FILLER                   PIC X(10).
00056
00057              01  FILLER                       PIC X(12)
00058                      VALUE 'WS ENDS HERE'.
00059
00060              REPORT SECTION.
00061              RD  CONTROL-BREAK
00062                  CONTROLS ARE FINAL
00063                               TR-SALESMAN-REGION
00064                               TR-SALESMAN-LOCATION
00065                               TR-SALESMAN-NAME
00066                  PAGE LIMIT 50 LINES
00067                  HEADING 1
00068                  FIRST DETAIL 5
00069                  LAST DETAIL 45
00070                  FOOTING 48.
```

FIGURE 8.5 Modified Report Writer program.

```
00071
00072          01   TYPE IS PAGE HEADING.
00073               05   LINE NUMBER 1.
00074                    10   COLUMN NUMBER 61        PIC X(4)
00075                         VALUE 'PAGE'.
00076                    10   COLUMN NUMBER 66        PIC ZZZZZ9
00077                         SOURCE PAGE-COUNTER.
00078               05   LINE NUMBER PLUS 2.
00079                    10   COLUMN NUMBER 22        PIC X(33)
00080                         VALUE 'THREE LEVEL CONTROL BREAK EXAMPLE'.
00081
00082          01   TYPE IS CONTROL HEADING TR-SALESMAN-REGION.
00083               05   LINE NUMBER 5.
00084                    10   COLUMN NUMBER 25        PIC X(27)
00085                         VALUE 'REGIONAL SALES ACTIVITY FOR'.
00086                    10   COLUMN NUMBER 54        PIC X(20)
00087                         SOURCE TR-SALESMAN-REGION.
00088               05   LINE NUMBER 7.
00089                    10   COLUMN NUMBER 6         PIC X(8)
00090                         VALUE 'LOCATION'.
00091                    10   COLUMN NUMBER 28        PIC X(15)
00092                         VALUE 'SALESMAN'.
00093                    10   COLUMN NUMBER 50        PIC X(7)
00094                         VALUE 'AMOUNT'.
00095                                                      ⟵ Control heading on region
00096          01   TRANSACTION-LINE TYPE IS DETAIL.            has been added
00097               05   LINE NUMBER PLUS 1.
00098                    10   COLUMN NUMBER 2         PIC X(20)
00099                         SOURCE TR-SALESMAN-NAME.
00100                    10   COLUMN NUMBER 27        PIC X(6)
00101                         SOURCE TR-NUMBER.
00102                    10   COLUMN NUMBER 41        PIC $ZZZ9
00103                         SOURCE TR-AMOUNT.
00104
00105          01   TYPE IS CONTROL FOOTING TR-SALESMAN-NAME.
00106               05   LINE NUMBER PLUS 1.
00107                    10   COLUMN NUMBER 2         PIC X(15)
00108                         SOURCE TR-SALESMAN-LOCATION.
00109                    10   COLUMN NUMBER 26        PIC X(20)
00110                         SOURCE TR-SALESMAN-NAME.
00111                    10   SALESMAN-TOTAL
00112                         COLUMN NUMBER 48        PIC $$$,$$9
00113                         SUM TR-AMOUNT.
00114
00115          01   TYPE IS CONTROL FOOTING TR-SALESMAN-LOCATION.
00116               05   LINE NUMBER PLUS 2.
00117                    10   COLUMN NUMBER 58        PIC X(10)
00118                         VALUE ALL '-'.
00119               05   LINE NUMBER PLUS 1.
00120                    10   COLUMN NUMBER 4         PIC X(14)
00121                         VALUE 'LOCATION TOTAL'.
00122                    10   LOCATION-TOTAL
00123                         COLUMN NUMBER 58        PIC $$$,$$9
00124                         SUM SALESMAN-TOTAL.
00125
00126          01   TYPE IS CONTROL FOOTING TR-SALESMAN-REGION.
00127               05   LINE NUMBER PLUS 2.
00128                    10   COLUMN NUMBER 58        PIC X(10)
00129                         VALUE ALL '-'.
00130               05   LINE NUMBER PLUS 1.
00131                    10   COLUMN NUMBER 4         PIC X(14)
00132                         VALUE 'REGIONAL TOTAL'.
00133                    10   REGION-TOTAL
00134                         COLUMN NUMBER 58        PIC $$$,$$9
00135                         SUM LOCATION-TOTAL.
00136                                                      ⟵ Control footing on region
00137          01   TYPE IS CONTROL FOOTING FINAL.              has been added
00138               05   LINE NUMBER PLUS 5.
00139                    10   COLUMN NUMBER 10        PIC X(28)
00140                         VALUE '***FINAL TOTAL ALL LOCATIONS'.
```

FIGURE 8.5 *continued*

```
00141              10  COLUMN NUMBER 40         PIC $$$$,$$9
00142                  SUM REGION-TOTAL.
00143
00144          PROCEDURE DIVISION.
00145          0000-SORT SECTION.                Sort keys are consistent with control
00146          0005-SORT.                        breaks of lines 63-65
00147              SORT SORT-FILE
00148                  ASCENDING KEY SORT-REGION SORT-LOCATION SORT-NAME
00149                  USING SALES-FILE
00150                  OUTPUT PROCEDURE 0008-REPORT.
00151              STOP RUN.
00152                                         Output procedure must be a section
00153          0008-REPORT SECTION.
00154          0010-CREATE-REPORTS.
00155              OPEN OUTPUT PRINT-FILE.
00156              INITIATE CONTROL-BREAK.
00157              RETURN SORT-FILE INTO TRANSACTION-AREA
00158                  AT END MOVE 'NO' TO WS-DATA-FLAG.
00159              PERFORM 0020-PROCESS-ALL-TRANSACTIONS
00160                  UNTIL WS-DATA-FLAG = 'NO'.
00161              TERMINATE CONTROL-BREAK.
00162              CLOSE PRINT-FILE.
00163              GO TO 0030-SORT-EXIT.
00164
00165          0020-PROCESS-ALL-TRANSACTIONS.   Report name implies summary reporting
00166              GENERATE CONTROL-BREAK.
00167              RETURN SORT-FILE INTO TRANSACTION-AREA
00168                  AT END MOVE 'NO' TO WS-DATA-FLAG.
00169
00170          0030-SORT-EXIT.
00171              EXIT.
```

FIGURE 8.5 *continued*

the sorted file and invokes Report Writer via INITIATE, GENERATE, and TERMINATE statements.

A second objective of Figure 8.5 is to demonstrate the ease with which changes can be made using Report Writer. The specifications have been amended to include a third control break on region. In addition, it is no longer necessary to show all transactions for a given salesman, but only his or her total.

The modifications in the program begin with specification of a control break on region (COBOL line 63). A control heading on region (line 82) is added to effect a page break on region, and the control heading on location from Figure 8.3 is eliminated. A control footing on region (line 126) is also added to achieve region totals. The GENERATE statement (line 166) reflects *summary* reporting by specifying the *report name*, CONTROL-BREAK, rather than a detail report group as was done in Figure 8.3. (The detail report group, lines 96–103, is *still required* even though summary reporting is performed.)

A single page of output was shown in Figure 8.4 for the MIDWEST region. The data reflected on this page are consistent with that of Figure 8.2. The three detail lines for LAVOR of Figure 8.2 have been replaced by a single summary line in Figure 8.4. The two location totals from Figure 8.2 have been grouped into a regional total in Figure 8.4. Finally, the page break is no longer on location (as was done in Figure 8.2) but on region.

Example 3—Finer Points of Report Writer

We have seen two complete programs using Report Writer. The first was intended as an introduction, to demystify the subject, and to demonstrate that it could be learned easily. The second showed the ease of modifying existing Report Writer programs, and the parallel use of SORT. In this third and last example, we illustrate some subtle features of the technique. Specifically, we include selective use of the GENERATE statement; the SUM UPON, GROUP INDICATE, NEXT GROUP, and RESET clauses; rolling totals forward; and the use of DECLARATIVES.

We return to the first program of the chapter and its associated output (Figure 8.2), and make the following changes:

1. The salesman's name is to appear *only once* with the *first* transaction in the group. Detail lines are to be single spaced, except for the first detail after a control footing, which is to be tripled spaced.
2. The *average* dollar amount per transaction is to be computed for each location. In addition, the number of transactions in each location is to be printed.
3. A *cumulative* total (within a location) is to appear every time a break on salesman occurs. (Individual salesman totals are no longer required.)
4. Only salesmen in Chicago and Detroit are to appear in the report.

A copy of the new output appears in Figure 8.6 and the reader may want to compare this figure to the previous report of Figure 8.2. Figure 8.7 contains the COBOL program which produced the modified report, and several items bear mention:

1. The GROUP INDICATE clause (line 88)—specifies that an elementary item print only on the *first* occurrence after a control break. Hence, the name LAVOR appeared only once in Figure 8.6, with the *first* of the three transactions associated with that salesman. GROUP INDICATE may appear only in a detail report group, and must apply to an elementary item.

2. The NEXT GROUP clause (line 96)—controls line spacing *after* the report group in which it is specified has been produced. In Figure 8.6, detail lines are single spaced, *except the first detail line after a control break on salesman which is triple spaced*. This is neatly accomplished by including NEXT GROUP in the control footing for salesman. The syntax of the NEXT GROUP clause is:

$$\text{NEXT GROUP IS} \begin{Bmatrix} \text{integer-1} \\ \text{PLUS integer-2} \\ \text{NEXT PAGE} \end{Bmatrix}$$

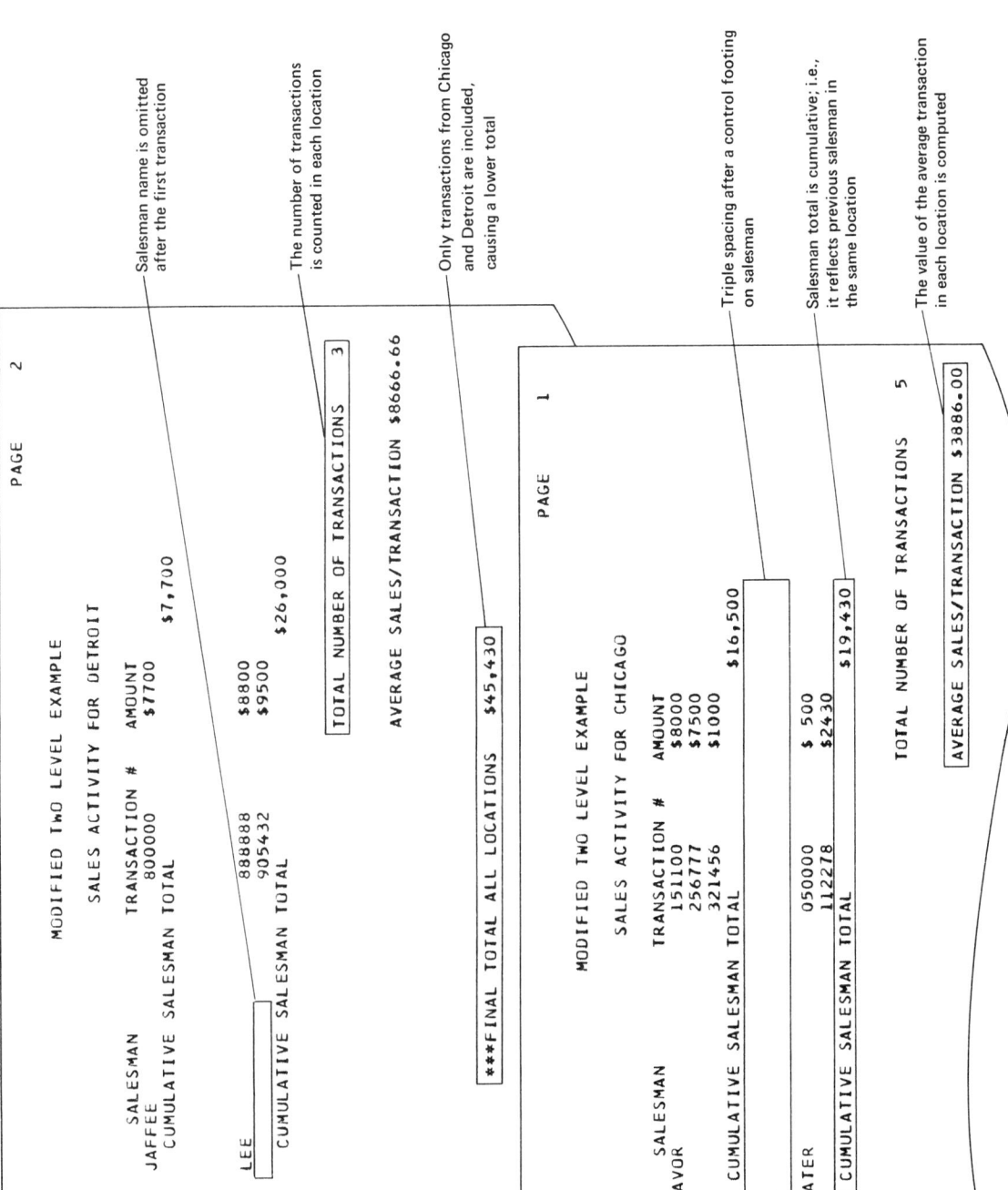

FIGURE 8.6 Modified output for two control breaks.

Example 3 – Finer Points of Report Writer

```
00001              IDENTIFICATION DIVISION.
00002              PROGRAM-ID.   RWTHR.
00003              AUTHOR.       R. GRAUER.
00004
00005              ENVIRONMENT DIVISION.
00006              CONFIGURATION SECTION.
00007              SOURCE-COMPUTER.    IBM-4341.
00008              OBJECT-COMPUTER.    IBM-4341.
00009              INPUT-OUTPUT SECTION.
00010              FILE-CONTROL.
00011                  SELECT SALES-FILE
00012                      ASSIGN TO UT-S-SALES.
00013                  SELECT PRINT-FILE
00014                      ASSIGN TO UT-S-REPORT.
00015
00016              DATA DIVISION.
00017              FILE SECTION.
00018              FD  SALES-FILE
00019                  LABEL RECORDS ARE OMITTED
00020                  BLOCK CONTAINS 0 RECORDS
00021                  RECORD CONTAINS 80 CHARACTERS
00022                  DATA RECORD IS SALES-RECORD.
00023              01  SALES-RECORD                     PIC X(80).
00024
00025              FD  PRINT-FILE
00026                  REPORT IS CONTROL-BREAK
00027                  LABEL RECORDS ARE OMITTED
00028                  RECORD CONTAINS 133 CHARACTERS.
00029
00030              WORKING-STORAGE SECTION.
00031              01  FILLER                           PIC X(14)
00032                  VALUE 'WS BEGINS HERE'.
00033              01  WS-DATA-FLAG                     PIC X(3)      VALUE SPACES.
00034
00035              01  TRANSACTION-AREA.
00036                  05  TR-SALESMAN-NAME             PIC X(20).
00037                  05  TR-AMOUNT                    PIC S9(4).
00038                  05  FILLER                       PIC XX.
00039                  05  TR-NUMBER                    PIC X(6).
00040                  05  TR-TYPE                      PIC X.
00041                  05  TR-SALESMAN-REGION           PIC X(17).
00042                  05  TR-SALESMAN-LOCATION         PIC X(20).
00043                  05  FILLER                       PIC X(10).
00044                                                         Used in SUM UPON clause of line 111
00045              01  PROGRAM-COUNTERS.
00046                  05  NUMBER-OF-TRANSACTIONS       PIC 9(3)   VALUE 1.
00047                  05  AVG-SALES-PER-TRANSACTION    PIC 9(4)V99.
00048
00049              01  FILLER                           PIC X(12)
00050                  VALUE 'WS ENDS HERE'.
00051
00052              REPORT SECTION.
00053              RD  CONTROL-BREAK
00054                  CONTROLS ARE FINAL TR-SALESMAN-LOCATION TR-SALESMAN-NAME
00055                  PAGE LIMIT 50 LINES
00056                  HEADING 1
00057                  FIRST DETAIL 5
00058                  LAST DETAIL 45
00059                  FOOTING 48.
00060
00061              01  TYPE IS PAGE HEADING.
00062                  05  LINE NUMBER 1.
00063                      10  COLUMN NUMBER 61         PIC X(4)
00064                          VALUE 'PAGE'.
00065                      10  COLUMN NUMBER 66         PIC ZZZZZ9
00066                          SOURCE PAGE-COUNTER.
00067                  05  LINE NUMBER PLUS 2.
00068                      10  COLUMN NUMBER 22         PIC X(31)
00069                          VALUE 'MODIFIED TWO LEVEL EXAMPLE'.
00070
```

FIGURE 8.7 Program containing finer points of Report Writer.

```
00071          01   TYPE IS CONTROL HEADING TR-SALESMAN-LOCATION.
00072               05   LINE NUMBER 5.
00073                    10   COLUMN NUMBER 25       PIC X(18)
00074                         VALUE 'SALES ACTIVITY FOR'.
00075                    10   COLUMN NUMBER 44       PIC X(20)
00076                         SOURCE TR-SALESMAN-LOCATION.
00077               05   LINE NUMBER 7.
00078                    10   COLUMN NUMBER 6        PIC X(8)
00079                         VALUE 'SALESMAN'.
00080                    10   COLUMN NUMBER 24       PIC X(13)
00081                         VALUE 'TRANSACTION #'.
00082                    10   COLUMN NUMBER 40       PIC X(7)
00083                         VALUE 'AMOUNT'.
00084
00085          01   TRANSACTION-LINE TYPE IS DETAIL.
00086               05   LINE NUMBER PLUS 1.
00087                    10   COLUMN NUMBER 2        PIC X(20)
00088                         GROUP INDICATE
00089                         SOURCE TR-SALESMAN-NAME.
00090                    10   COLUMN NUMBER 27       PIC X(6)
00091                         SOURCE TR-NUMBER.
00092                    10   COLUMN NUMBER 41       PIC $ZZZ9
00093                         SOURCE TR-AMOUNT.
00094
00095          01   TYPE IS CONTROL FOOTING TR-SALESMAN-NAME
00096               NEXT GROUP IS PLUS 3.
00097               05   LINE NUMBER PLUS 1.
00098                    10   COLUMN NUMBER 4        PIC X(27)
00099                         VALUE 'CUMULATIVE SALESMAN TOTAL'.
00100                    10   CUM-SALESMAN-TOTAL
00101                         COLUMN NUMBER 48       PIC $$$,$$9
00102                         SUM TR-AMOUNT RESET ON TR-SALESMAN-LOCATION.
00103
00104          01   LOCATION-TOTAL-LINE
00105               TYPE IS CONTROL FOOTING TR-SALESMAN-LOCATION.
00106               05   LINE NUMBER PLUS 3.
00107                    10   COLUMN NUMBER 40       PIC X(29)
00108                         VALUE 'TOTAL NUMBER OF TRANSACTIONS'.
00109                    10   TRANSACTIONS-IN-LOCATION
00110                         COLUMN NUMBER 70       PIC Z(3)
00111                         SUM NUMBER-OF-TRANSACTIONS UPON TRANSACTION-LINE.
00112               05   LINE NUMBER PLUS 3.
00113                    10   COLUMN NUMBER 40       PIC X(26)
00114                         VALUE 'AVERAGE SALES/TRANSACTION '.
00115                    10   COLUMN NUMBER 66       PIC $$$$9.99
00116                         SOURCE AVG-SALES-PER-TRANSACTION.
00117
00118          01   TYPE IS CONTROL FOOTING FINAL.
00119               05   LINE NUMBER PLUS 5.
00120                    10   COLUMN NUMBER 10       PIC X(28)
00121                         VALUE '***FINAL TOTAL ALL LOCATIONS'.
00122                    10   COLUMN NUMBER 40       PIC $$$$,$$9
00123                         SUM TR-AMOUNT.
00124
00125       PROCEDURE DIVISION.
00126       DECLARATIVES.
00127       A-COMPUTE-LOCATION-AVERAGE SECTION.
00128            USE BEFORE REPORTING LOCATION-TOTAL-LINE.
00129
00130       A010-COMPUTE-LOCATION-AVERAGE.
00131            DIVIDE CUM-SALESMAN-TOTAL BY TRANSACTIONS-IN-LOCATION
00132                GIVING AVG-SALES-PER-TRANSACTION.
00133       END DECLARATIVES.
00134
00135       B-MAINLINE SECTION.
00136       B010-CREATE-REPORTS.
00137            OPEN INPUT SALES-FILE
00138                 OUTPUT PRINT-FILE.
```

FIGURE 8.7 *continued*

```
00139              INITIATE CONTROL-BREAK.
00140              READ SALES-FILE INTO TRANSACTION-AREA
00141                  AT END MOVE 'NO' TO WS-DATA-FLAG.
00142              PERFORM B020-PROCESS-ALL-TRANSACTIONS
00143                  UNTIL WS-DATA-FLAG = 'NO'.
00144              TERMINATE CONTROL-BREAK.
00145              CLOSE SALES-FILE
00146                    PRINT-FILE.
00147              STOP RUN.                              Only certain transactions are
00148                                                     included in the report
00149          B020-PROCESS-ALL-TRANSACTIONS.
00150              IF TR-SALESMAN-LOCATION = 'CHICAGO' OR 'DETROIT'
00151                  GENERATE TRANSACTION-LINE.
00152              READ SALES-FILE INTO TRANSACTION-AREA
00153                  AT END MOVE 'NO' TO WS-DATA-FLAG.
```

FIGURE 8.7 *continued*

indicating that the next group may begin on either a designated line or a new page.

3. The SUM UPON clause (line 111)—is a convenient way to count the number of records in a file, or within a control group. The SUM statement of line 111 specifies NUMBER-OF-TRANSACTIONS, a data name defined and initialized to one in Working-Storage (line 46). The SUM statement references TRANSACTION-LINE, which is the name of a detail report group. The SUM UPON clause increments an internally defined counter by one (the value of NUMBER-OF-TRANSACTIONS) every time the detail report group is generated. (Hindsight is 20/20 in that ONE would have been preferable as a data name to NUMBER-OF-TRANSACTIONS.)

4. The SUM RESET clause (line 102)—prevents the automatic zeroing out of summation counters by telling Report Writer *when* the initialization is to take place. Recall that the original program of Figure 8.3 produced both salesman and location totals. Two SUM clauses were coded, and the associated counters were reset to zero at the appropriate time.

In this example, a *cumulative* location total is required for a control break on salesman; in other words, the salesman total should print as a *running* total and not be continually reset to zero. The RESET clause indicates that the associated SUM counter is to be reinitialized to zero only when location changes. (RESET must reference a *higher* level of control than the control group in which it is coded, which is consistent with the concept of a cumulative total.)

5. Use of DECLARATIVES (lines 126–133)—DECLARATIVES were introduced in Chapter 7, in conjunction with I/O error handling. A second application is in association with Report Writer.

Recall that declarative sections define procedures that are executed as a result of some condition which cannot be tested using regular language elements. If declaratives are used, they must be coded together at the beginning of the Procedure Division, be assigned *section* names, and appear between the headers DECLARATIVES and END DECLARATIVES.

The USE BEFORE REPORTING statement of line 128 causes the

declarative section to be executed before producing the control footing report group, LOCATION-TOTAL-LINE. It in turn contains the logic necessary to determine the average sale per transaction within a given location.

A declaratives procedure may contain any COBOL verb except INITIATE, GENERATE, or TERMINATE. In addition, perform statements within declaratives may not reference nondeclarative procedures; nor can declarative procedures be referenced in the nondeclarative portion of the Procedure Division.

6. Selective use of GENERATE (lines 150 and 151)—It is possible, and indeed commonplace, to include records in a report selectively. This is accomplished by making GENERATE the object of an IF statement as was done in Figure 8.7.

How Report Writer Works

The author believes that the programs of Figures 8.3, 8.5, and 8.7 are very effective in teaching fundamentals of Report Writer. Nevertheless, the practicing programmer and/or advanced student may feel a need for a better understanding of the internal workings of the module. To that end, we include a more technical discussion of the GENERATE statement. The user is referred to the vendor's Reference Manual (e.g., *VS COBOL for OS/VS*, GC26-3857) for additional information.

The GENERATE statement produces a report as specified in the Report Section. As was shown previously, one obtains *either detail or summary reporting* by specifying a data or report-name respectively. The action of the GENERATE statement is the key to understanding how Report Writer works. Its *initial* execution causes the following events to occur in order:

1. REPORT HEADING report group (if specified) is produced.
2. PAGE HEADING report group (if specified) is produced.
3. CONTROL HEADINGs are produced in the order FINAL, major, intermediate, minor.
4. The DETAIL report group is produced, provided detail reporting was requested (i.e., a data-name was specified in the GENERATE statement).

The action of *subsequent* GENERATE statements is described with the aid of Figure 8.8. The sequence of operations is as follows:

1. If a control break is detected, SUM counters are incremented, control footings are produced using *old* control values, new control values are stored, control headings are written with the *new* control values, and the SUM clauses are reset. (Any specified declarative

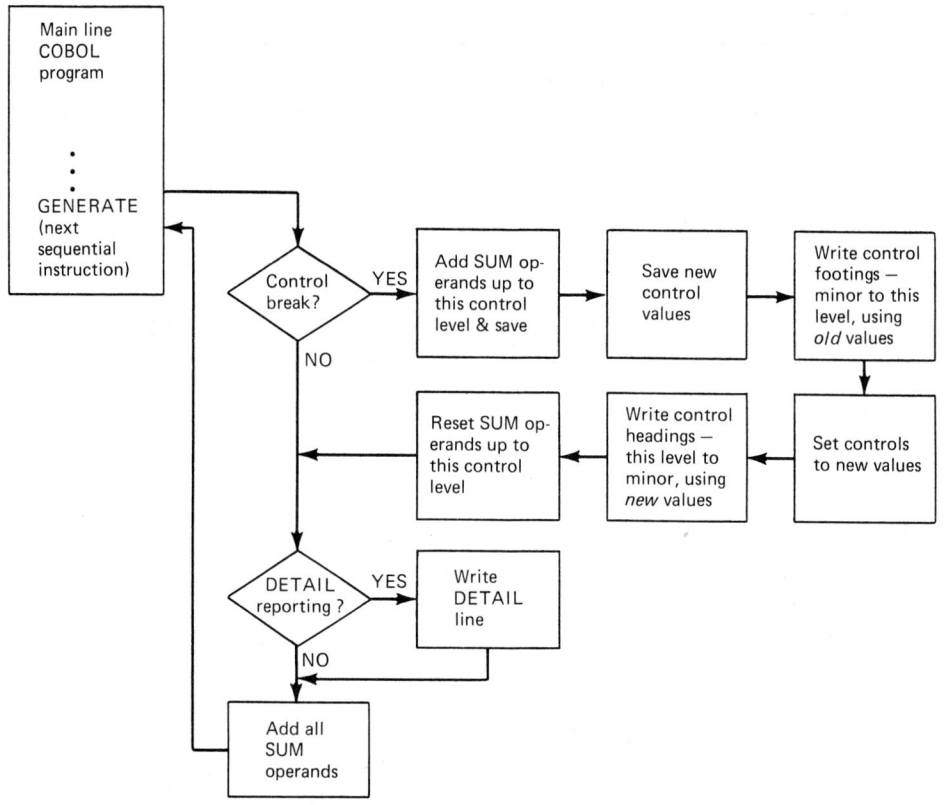

FIGURE 8.8 Action of subsequent GENERATE statements. (Courtesy of IBM Corporation.) Note: If a USE BEFORE REPORTING DECLARATIVE is specified, it is executed just before its associated control group is produced, whether or not a control break or page break occurred.

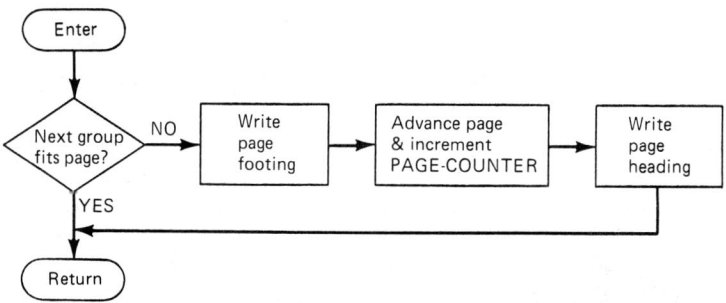

FIGURE 8.9 Effect of the PAGE clause.

procedures are executed before the associated report group is produced.)

2. Detail report groups are produced if necessary; i.e., if a data-name was specified in the GENERATE statement.

Realize also that specification of the PAGE clause within the report RD, causes additional processing to take place before each printable report group is produced. This is detailed in Figure 8.9.

Report Writer Syntax

The author's technique is to teach by example. Occasionally, however, questions arise which can only be answered by consulting the Reference Manual. To that end, various syntactical elements have been extracted to provide additional information.

TYPE Clause

The TYPE clause *must* be specified for an 01 entry in the Report Section. It has the following syntax:

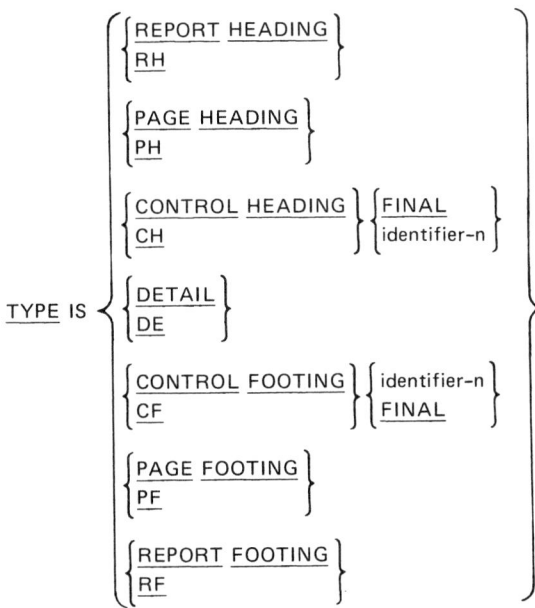

Although the options are self-explanatory, Table 8.1 further summarizes the nature of each report group.

TABLE 8.1 Report Group Types

Type	Number of Groups per Report	Criteria for Printing
Report heading (RH)	Maximum of 1 per report	Printed once, before any other groups, at the beginning of the report
Page heading (PH)	Maximum of 1 per report	Printed at the beginning of each page before all other groups except the report heading group
Control heading (CH)	Maximum of 1 per identifier (including FINAL) named in the CONTROL clause	Printed at the beginning of a control group for a designated identifier or, in the case of FINAL, before the first control group
Detail (DE)	No limit, but each detail group must have a unique 01-level data-name	Printed with each execution of the GENERATE statement, provided detail reporting was requested
Control footing (CF)	Maximum of 1 per identifier (including FINAL) named in the CONTROL clause	Printed at the end of a control group for a designated identifier
Page footing (PF)	Maximum of 1 per report	Printed at the end of each page after all other groups, except the report footing group
Report footing (RF)	Maximum of 1 per report	Printed at the termination of the report, after all other groups

RD (Report Description)

The RD (Report Description) has the following format:

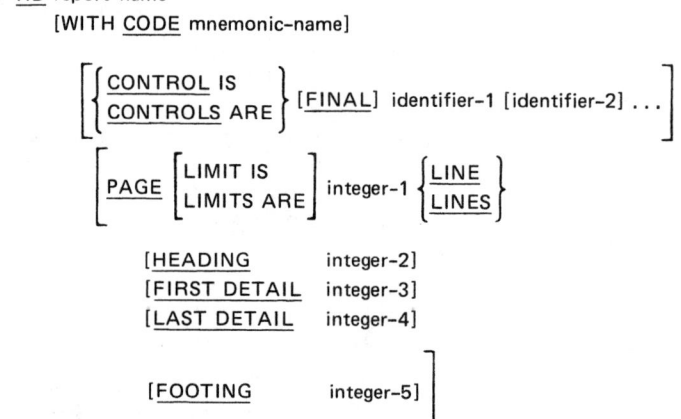

The CODE clause specifies an identifying character placed at the be-

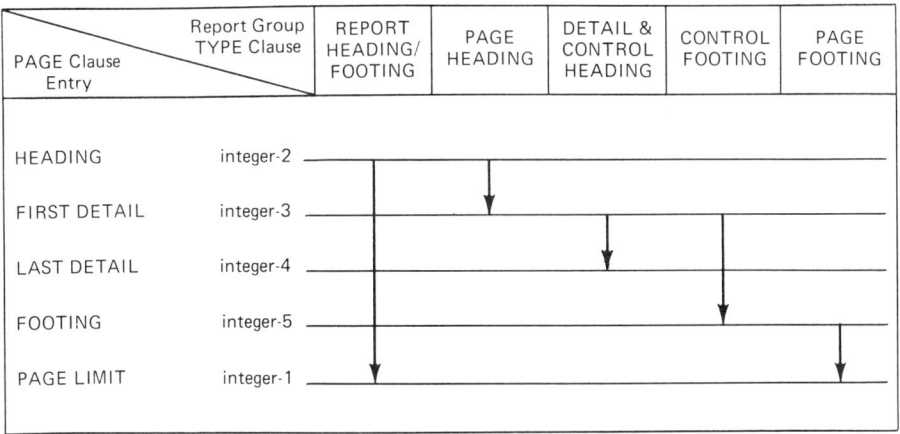

FIGURE 8.10 Effects of the PAGE clause. (Courtesy of IBM Corporation.)

ginning of each report line, and is meaningful only when multiple reports are written to the same file. It is not covered further. The CONTROL clause references the order of the control breaks and was adequately discussed in the chapter.

The PAGE LIMIT clause described in Figure 8.10, establishes the physical characteristics of a report by specifying where each report group should appear. Although various defaults are assumed for integers 1 through 5, the reader is advised to code all entries explicitly.

Report Groups

A report group consists of one or more printable lines which are treated as a unit. Four general syntaxes are possible as shown by Figure 8.11. Examples of the various formats have appeared earlier in the illustrative programs.

- Format 1 specifies the beginning of a report group and is the first entry of any group.
- Format 2 establishes the line numbers of subordinate entries, and groups subordinate elementary items together; e.g., listing several entries on a single line.
- Format 3 denotes an elementary item and is probably the most common. It has numerous options and subtleties which have been depicted.
- Format 4 describes a report group consisting of a single elementary item.

General Format 1—level-01 Group Entry

```
01  [data-name]
        TYPE Clause
        [LINE Clause]
        [NEXT GROUP Clause]
        [USAGE Clause].
```

General Format 2—Group Entry

```
level-number [data-name]
        [LINE Clause]
        [USAGE Clause].
```

General Format 3—Elementary Entry

```
level-number [data-name]
        [COLUMN NUMBER IS integer]
        [GROUP INDICATE]
        [LINE Clause]
```

$$\left\{ \begin{array}{l} \underline{\text{SOURCE}} \text{ IS identifier} \\ \underline{\text{SUM}} \text{ identifier-1 [identifier-2]} \ldots [\underline{\text{UPON}} \text{ data-name-2}] \\ \qquad [\underline{\text{RESET}} \text{ ON } \left\{ \begin{array}{l} \text{FINAL} \\ \text{identifier-3} \end{array} \right\}] \\ \underline{\text{VALUE}} \text{ IS literal} \end{array} \right\}$$

```
        PICTURE Clause
        [USAGE Clause]
        [BLANK WHEN ZERO Clause]
        [JUSTIFIED Clause]
```

General Format 4—level-01 Elementary Entry

```
01  [data-name]
        TYPE Clause
        [LINE Clause]
        [NEXT GROUP Clause]
        [COLUMN Clause]
        [GROUP INDICATE Clause]

        { SOURCE Clause  }
        { SUM Clause     }
        { VALUE Clause   }

        PICTURE Clause
        [USAGE Clause]
        [BLANK WHEN ZERO Clause]
        [JUSTIFIED Clause].
```

FIGURE 8.11 Report group syntax.

Summary

Three programs were presented illustrating the use of Report Writer. *In essence, Report Writer produces a report by describing its physical characteristics in the Data Division, rather than by specifying detailed instructions in the Procedure Division.* This philosophy simplifies the involved logic in computing subtotals and rolling them forward. The Report Section is divided into distinct report groups for control headings, footings, etc. Hence, modification of existing programs through the addition (or deletion) of report groups is easier than with ordinary COBOL programs.

The author is convinced of the merits of the facility, and hopes that he has influenced the reader to some extent. To that end, let us review the opening arguments against Report Writer from the perspective of the completed chapter.

It is purely a matter of personal opinion as to whether Report Writer statements are more difficult to code than ordinary COBOL. This author certainly doesn't think so. In fact, a strong case could be made for the opposite argument; namely, that programs involving control breaks are developed more easily using Report Writer than conventional COBOL. Compare, for example, the programs in this chapter versus the one in Figure 2.5.

The argument that no one else in a shop knows Report Writer, causing potential maintenance problems, is a case of Catch-22. No one will know Report Writer unless programmers take the initiative to learn it, and/or enlightened managers insist that they do. Continued insistence not to use the facility, because few people know it, is self-defeating.

The lack of availability on some compilers cannot be denied, *although Report Writer is part of the ANS 74 standard.* The larger vendors have implemented the facility, but it doesn't yet exist on most minis and/or micros. (Radio Shack and Microsoft, for example, have fine COBOL compilers, but without Report Writer.) However, if the facility gains acceptance, then additional vendors may feel the need to make it available, in much the same way they were compelled to support COBOL in the first place.

The related argument of error-prone compilers originally had some validity, because the module had not been used sufficiently to have been thoroughly debugged. (This was especially true for those brave souls who used previous versions in the early 1970s.) However, the author has recently used both the IBM OS/VS and Univac compilers, without difficulty.

As to debugging, Report Writer will indeed "blow up" on invalid numeric data, but so does a conventional program. The reader may note inclusion of WS BEGINS HERE, and READ INTO statements in the author's programs to pinpoint the invalid records. Use of this technique was described in Chapter 4 and pertains equally well to Report Writer programs.

In conclusion, Report Writer may not fit every application, nor is there a need to use it 100% of the time. *However, it is ideally suited to programs with multiple control breaks, and/or precisely aligned forms.* Report Writer is a powerful tool with a logic and beauty all its own, and it should be in the realm of any COBOL programmer.

True/False

1. If Report Writer is used, the COBOL program must contain a minimum of seven report groups; i.e., at least one of all seven types.
2. Report Writer requires that control headings and control footings occur in pairs.
3. A report group is limited to a single print line.
4. Report Writer is not included in all ANS 74 implementations.
5. A given COBOL program cannot contain both the SORT and Report Writer features.
6. The Procedure Division of a program containing Report Writer is typically quite short.
7. INITIATE, PROPAGATE, and TERMINATE are all associated with Report Writer.
8. Report Writer automatically sorts the incoming file if necessary.
9. A COBOL program that calls a subprogram cannot use Report Writer.
10. The Report Writer entries LINE NUMBER 2 and LINE NUMBER PLUS 2 are equivalent.
11. Data-names are frequently omitted (following the level number) when using Report Writer.
12. It is possible for an FD not to have any 01 entries defined under it.
13. The GENERATE statement determines whether summary or detail reporting will result.
14. Report Writer computes *totals* only, and is unsuitable if averages are required.
15. The SUM RESET clause prevents the automatic zeroing out of summation counters.
16. DECLARATIVES can be used with Report Writer.
17. Report Writer is an IBM extension to the ANS 74 standard.
18. If an elementary item prints after the first occurrence of a control break, it must print for *all* occurrences.
19. A detail report group description may be omitted if summary reporting is performed.

Problems

1. Consider the SUM clauses in the program of Figure 8.3. Specifically, line 107, SUM SALESMAN-TOTAL, is used to compute a location total, and line 114, SUM LOCATION-TOTAL, is used to obtain the final total. Could either or both of these clauses have been replaced by SUM TR-AMOUNT? Is there any advantage in the original approach?

Projects

1. Develop a Report Writer program corresponding to the logic of Figure 2.5. Use the same data as Figure 2.6a and produce identical output as Figure 2.6b. Which approach to control breaks do you like better: the standard COBOL of Figure 2.5 or the Report Writer solution?

2. Process a file of student records to determine enrollment totals for the School of Business. The records have been sorted by major and year within major. The record layout and test data are shown in Figures 8.12 and 8.13 respectively, and the approximate report format in Figure 8.14. Specifications continue on page 233.

```
01  STUDENT-RECORD.
    05  ST-NAME         PIC X(15).
    05  ST-MAJOR        PIC X(15).
    05  ST-YEAR         PIC XX.
    05  ST-CREDITS      PIC 99.
    05  ST-COLLEGE      PIC X(10).
```

FIGURE 8.12 STUDENT-RECORD layout.

```
ADAMS           ACCOUNTING      FR18BUSINESS
BAKER           ACCOUNTING      FR18BUSINESS
BROWN           ACCOUNTING      FR15BUSINESS
CALDWELL        ACCOUNTING      SO18BUSINESS
DAVIS           ACCOUNTING      SO17BUSINESS
FRANK           ACCOUNTING      JR16BUSINESS
GREENE          ACCOUNTING      JR16BUSINESS
HAINES          ACCOUNTING      SR19BUSINESS
MILLER          ACCOUNTING      SR15BUSINESS
NEWTON          ACCOUNTING      SR20BUSINESS
COULTER         INFO SYS        FR18BUSINESS
DREW            INFO SYS        FR18BUSINESS
ELLIOTT         INFO SYS        FR18BUSINESS
FORMAN          INFO SYS        FR18BUSINESS
GERBER          INFO SYS        SO18BUSINESS
HEWITT          INFO SYS        SO21BUSINESS
KENDALL         INFO SYS        SO21BUSINESS
LEVIN           INFO SYS        JR17BUSINESS
MOORE           INFO SYS        JR16BUSINESS
OBERMAN         INFO SYS        SR20BUSINESS
PRUITT          INFO SYS        SR18BUSINESS
CARSON          MANAGEMENT      FR15BUSINESS
DALTON          MANAGEMENT      FR15BUSINESS
ENGLAND         MANAGEMENT      SO15BUSINESS
FLANDERS        MANAGEMENT      JR12BUSINESS
TROOPER         MANAGEMENT      SR18BUSINESS
CRANDEL         MARKETING       FR15BUSINESS
```

FIGURE 8.13 Report Writer test data.

CULVER	MARKETING	FR15BUSINESS
DAWSON	MARKETING	FR18BUSINESS
ECKERD	MARKETING	SO18BUSINESS
FRIENDLY	MARKETING	SO15BUSINESS
GANDY	MARKETING	SO15BUSINESS
HALPERN	MARKETING	JR20BUSINESS
ISAACS	MARKETING	JR18BUSINESS
JUMP	MARKETING	JR15BUSINESS
LACKLAND	MARKETING	SR12BUSINESS
MONROE	MARKETING	SR15BUSINESS
NEWLEY	MARKETING	SR15BUSINESS

FIGURE 8.13 *continued*

```
                                    PAGE 2
   MAJOR:  INFO SYS

         NAME        YEAR       CREDITS
         COULTER     FR         18
         DREW        FR         18
         ELLIOTT     FR         18
         FORMAN      FR         18

         TOTAL CREDITS FOR FRESHMEN = 72

         GERBER      SO         18
         HEWITT      SO         21
         KENDALL     SO         21

         TOTAL CREDITS FOR SOPHOMORES = 60
```

```
                                    PAGE 1
   MAJOR:  ACCOUNTING

         NAME        YEAR       CREDITS
         ADAMS       FR         18
         BAKER       FR         18
         BROWN       FR         15

         TOTAL CREDITS FOR FRESHMEN = 51

         CALDWELL    SO         18
         DAVIS       SO         17

         TOTAL CREDITS FOR SOPHOMORES = 35
                    •
                 •
         TOTAL CREDITS FOR SENIORS = 54

         TOTAL CREDITS FOR ACCOUNTING = 172

         NUMBER OF STUDENTS IN ACCOUNTING = 10
```

FIGURE 8.14 Report layout.

Note well the following requirements:

(a) A control heading on major, with each major beginning on a *new* page.
(b) A control footing on year, containing the total number of credits for each year. (Observe that the year is spelled out in the control footing.)
(c) A control footing on major, containing the total number of credits in the major, and the number of students in that major.

3. Add a report heading and report footing to Project 2. The latter contains the total number of credits for each major, requires the use of DECLARATIVES, and is more difficult than it may seem initially. (See Figure 8.15.)

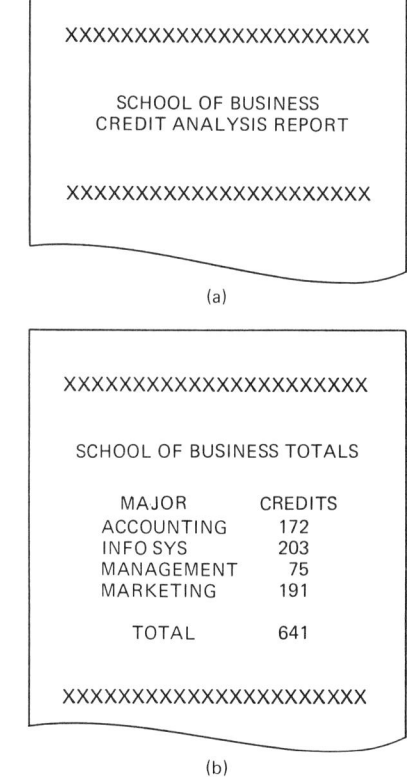

FIGURE 8.15 (a) Report heading and (b) report footing (see Project 3).

4. Revise the specifications of Project 2 to include the following changes:

(a) Assume the incoming data have not been sorted, and include the SORT verb in your program, prior to Report Writer.
(b) Assume that incoming records contain a three-position major code, rather than a 15-position expanded major. Develop a *subprogram* which will be called prior to reporting a control heading on major to expand the major code. (The subprogram should be called from a DECLARATIVES section.)

The test data of Figure 8.13 are still applicable. However, the 15-byte field ST-MAJOR has to be redefined as a 3-position code, ST-MAJOR-CODE, and a 12-byte FILLER.

9 Source Level Debugging

Overview

The beginning COBOL programmer is primarily concerned with the many compilation errors that accompany his or her first few attempts. When these errors disappear, he or she typically assumes that the execution results are correct. While this is often the case with early assignments that are logically simple, the initial euphoria disappears quickly with advanced assignments and unexpected results. Although there are those in the programming community who argue that programs can be made to run correctly on the first attempt, this author believes that logic errors will remain with us for the foreseeable future. This chapter is designed to provide realistic debugging experience over a wide range of programming projects.

The examples in this chapter are slightly modified versions of programs which appeared earlier in the book. However, the present listings produce invalid results, and the reader is asked to find and correct the errors. In each exercise there are only a few statements, in programs of two or three hundred statements, which cause the problems. The errors are subtle but not contrived, and typical of beginning (and practicing) programmers.

It is important to emphasize that each exercise is new, and has not appeared previously in any of the author's other books. (The reader may, for example, be familiar with R. Grauer, *A COBOL Book of Practice and Reference*, Prentice-Hall, 1981, which contains a similar chapter, "Source Level Debugging," with 17 additional exercises. However, *there is no overlap* in the exercises.)

The chapter begins with a list of common execution errors, reasons for their occurrence, and ways to prevent them. The author believes that the same kinds of errors continually occur, albeit in different disguises, and that the debugging skill of the individual is enhanced by knowing what to look for. Accordingly, errors on the list are tied to specific exercises in the chapter to provide meaningful examples, and correspondingly to increase the pedagogical nature of the exercises. Not every problem in this section (or the real world) can be traced to the list, but it is a good starting place.

Every attempt has been made to simulate field conditions as closely as possible. The programs are of modest length, neither trivial nor unduly complex. The errors are noted objectively, with no hint as to what the problem may be. There is one major difference, however, from the real world. The correct version of each exercise is found elsewhere in the book, and the reader need only to turn to the appropriate chapter to relieve his frustration. (The solutions are also provided at the end of this chapter.) No peeking, however, at least not until you have made an honest effort at debugging.

We begin by listing a series of common execution errors.

Common Execution Errors

1. *Failure to initialize (reinitialize) a counter.* All programmers have at one time forgotten to initialize a data-name used as a counter. The usual result is an 0C7 ABEND (data exception on IBM systems) which is relatively easy to find. A more subtle error is the failure to *reinitialize* counters when control breaks are called for. Consider the following sales report, sorted by location first, then by salesman within location.

```
LOCATION: ATLANTA
    SALESMAN        YEAR-TO-DATE-SALES
    ADAMS                $10,000
    BAKER                $50,000
    SMITH                $40,000
        TOTAL SALES FOR ATLANTA = $100,000
LOCATION: BOSTON
    SALESMAN        YEAR-TO-DATE-SALES
    BROWN                $15,000
    JONES                $20,000
    TURNER               $ 8,000
    YOUNG                $60,000
        TOTAL SALES FOR BOSTON = $203,000
```

The correct total for Boston should be $103,000, *not* $203,000. The problem was caused by failure to reinitialize the location sales total when a new location was encountered. See Exercise 9.1.

2. *Errors in looping.* The establishment of a loop requires four basic steps:

(a) Initialization of a counter

(b) Incrementing of a counter

(c) Comparison of the counter to a predetermined value

(d) An appropriate branch

Regardless of whether the programmer establishes his own loop or utilizes various features of COBOL to do it for him, these four basic steps must be accomplished in one way or another.

A frequent error occurs when a loop is executed an improper number of times, often one too many or too few. Consider the PERFORM statement:

```
PERFORM COMPUTE-YEAR-TOTAL
    VARYING MONTH-SUB FROM 1 BY 1 UNTIL MONTH-SUB = 12.
```

The routine COMPUTE-YEAR-TOTAL will be performed 11 times, *not* 12, because COBOL does the comparison *before* the branch. Thus, after the routine has been performed 11 times, MONTH-SUB is incremented from 11 to 12. Then since MONTH-SUB = 12, the perform is terminated.

An associated error occurs when the last record in a file is processed twice. This can happen if the initial (or priming) read of a structured program is not handled correctly. See Exercise 9.2.

3. *Improper use of the SEARCH verb.* SEARCH and SEARCH ALL, for linear and binary searches, respectively, greatly simplify life for the COBOL programmer. SEARCH requires that the starting search position be initialized through a SET statement, while SEARCH ALL requires codes in a table to be in sequence. Failure to conform causes erroneous results. See Exercise 9.2.

4. *Incorrect use of MOVE.* MOVE is perhaps the most frequently used statement in COBOL. It is apparently quite simple yet misunderstandings can occur, particularly when the sending and receiving fields have different lengths and/or decimal alignments. Another problem arises when the receiving field is a group item which causes the entire move to be treated as alphanumeric even though the elementary items may be numeric.

5. *Difficulty with signed numbers.* Negative numbers can only be held by *signed* numeric data names. Consider:

```
05  FIELD-A    PIC 99      VALUE 10.
05  FIELD-B    PIC S99     VALUE -12.
05  FIELD-C    PIC 99      VALUE 10.
05  FIELD-D    PIC S99     VALUE -12.

ADD FIELD-A TO FIELD-B.
ADD FIELD-D TO FIELD-C.
```

Numerically one expects the sum of 10 and -12 to be -2. The value of FIELD-B is indeed -2, but the value of FIELD-C will *incorrectly* be 2, because FIELD-C was defined without a sign. See Exercise 9.1.

6. *Improper use of nested IF statements.* A nested IF occurs when there are two or more IFs within a period. The compiler associates the ELSE clause with the closest previous IF which is not already paired with another ELSE. Consistent indentation in coding is essential if the programmer is to understand what is going on. A related problem is the misuse of Boolean functions in the condition portion of an IF. See Exercise 9.3.

7. *Missing and/or extra period.* When the IF statement is used without an ELSE, it is terminated by the period, that is, all statements between the condition and the period are executed whenever the condition is satisfied. When a period is omitted, it results in additional statements being executed, and conversely, if a period is added fewer statements are executed. While this sounds simple, it is not always easy to tell whether a period is actually present. Periods sometimes wind up in column 73, which makes them appear present, but in reality they are absent, as the compiler does not interpret columns 73-80.

The period also terminates the ELSE clause, AT END and INVALID KEY clauses in a READ or WRITE, and the SIZE ERROR clause in a COMPUTE. Similar cautions apply here as well. Exercise 9.3 contains *subtle* errors dealing with the presence or absence of a period.

8. *Access of an FD area after a WRITE.* Simply stated, one may not access an I-O area after a WRITE statement has been executed, as the buffers are switched. This is an error that many beginners make once and then learn not to do again.

9. *Improper exit from a performed routine.* One may perform out of a perform, or one may go to an exit paragraph within a range of performed paragraphs (PERFORM PAR-A THRU PAR-A-EXIT with a *forward* GO TO to PAR-A-EXIT). One may *not use GO TO to leave a performed routine* as this results in object code being altered. No example of this is shown, however, as this error so violates structured programming as to be unconscionable in today's environment.

10. *Failure to set/reset switches.* This is a common difficulty in structured programs since these are heavily dependent on logic switches. Errors of this type are usually difficult to find, because their effects can take many

forms. There is not much the author can offer in the way of advice, except a rule of thumb: whenever specific action is taken because a switch is turned on, the switch should be immediately turned off. Bear in mind, however, this is only a rule of thumb and undoubtedly has many exceptions. See Exercise 9.3.

11. *Improper linkage to a subroutine.* Although the COBOL statement to call a subprogram presents no great difficulty in and of itself, improper linkage often leads to trouble. Specifically, the arguments in both the calling and called program must appear in the same order and should have identical pictures. Moreover, if a group item, for example, an 01 record, is passed as a parameter, it is essential that the elementary items in the group item be defined identically in both programs. See Exercise 9.2.

12. *End and/or beginning file conditions.* These errors are prevalent in file maintenance applications, particularly where multiple input files are used. The author has seen untold examples of complex maintenance programs which "work" 99% of the time but fail if a unique combination of events occur; for example, the key of the last record on the transaction file is higher than the last record in the old master file, etc. A common error is that processing ceases prematurely when using multiple input files whenever the first file becomes empty. Another common error involves processing the last record twice.

13. *Invalid subscript or index.* This is one of the most common errors, and most difficult to find, because the result can take many forms. For example, one can exceed the bounds of a table during a table lookup. One can also exceed the declared size of a table during its initialization and thereby overlay a portion of code. Both problems stem from the freedom permitted by the compiler generated instructions. Consider:

```
        05   TABLE-ENTRY OCCURS 20 TIMES      PIC X(10).
```

The OCCURS clause sets aside a 200 (20 X 10) byte table in storage. Logically, one should be permitted to reference only entries with subscripts of 1 to 20. Most compilers, however, *do not* insert machine code to check on the validity of a subscript. Thus, if one tried to reference TABLE-ENTRY (21) one would access the first 10 bytes of storage *beyond* the table. In similar fashion, TABLE-ENTRY (0) points to the 10 bytes immediately before the actual table. The best defense against errors of this sort is for the programmer to insert Procedure Division code to check on the validity of subscripts, with appropriate error messages. Errors of this kind frequently result in a premature end of job in which the program fails to go to a normal end of job.

14. *Improper use of comments.* Comments in COBOL (denoted by an asterisk in column 7) are nonexecutable, but the presence (or absence) of these statements can adversely affect a program. This is especially true if a

programmer "asterisks out" executable code, as when statements in a program are no longer deemed necessary. Of course, all such statements should be deleted, but the programmer may have reason to believe that the statements will again be required at a future date. Accordingly they are turned into comments and made nonexecutable (and easily recallable). The resulting code is extremely difficult to read and often leads to subsequent errors. See Exercise 9.1.

Debugging Exercises

There are four exercises in this chapter as follows:

Exercise 9.1 *Control Breaks*, a modified version of Figure 2.5.
Exercise 9.2 *Subprograms*, a modified version of Figures 3.18, 3.19, and 3.20.
Exercise 9.3 *Sequential File Maintenance*, a modified version of Figure 6.14.
Exercise 9.4 *Report Writer*, a modified version of Figure 8.3.

Each listing is accompanied by its associated *invalid* output which is to be contrasted with the valid output from the original chapter. One final piece of advice before getting started; *make a determined effort to slow down when debugging in order to read the listings carefully*. In other words, the human eye is generally "uncritical" and sees what it wants or expects to see. For example, try reading the sentence in the box, once and only once, and as you do count the number of F's.

> Finished files are the result of years
> of scientific study combined with
> the experience of years.

There are six F's in the sentence and if you got all six you are good. The average person spots only three and you can feel reasonably proud if you got four or five. The point in this seemingly trivial example is that our eyes are less discriminating than we would like to believe. Accordingly, one must consciously slow down when debugging.

Exercise 9.1—Control Breaks

This problem is based on the listing of Figure 2.5. Input data were shown in Figure 2.6a, and the intended output in Figure 2.6b. The *erroneous* output of Figure 9.1 was produced by the listing in Figure 9.2. Indicate the necessary corrections to the program in order to resolve the following errors:

1. Salesman totals with negative balances are computed incorrectly and omit the CR editing characters; e.g., Baker's total should print as $400.00CR rather than $200.00.
2. One salesman is misplaced; i.e., Smith, with transaction 878787,

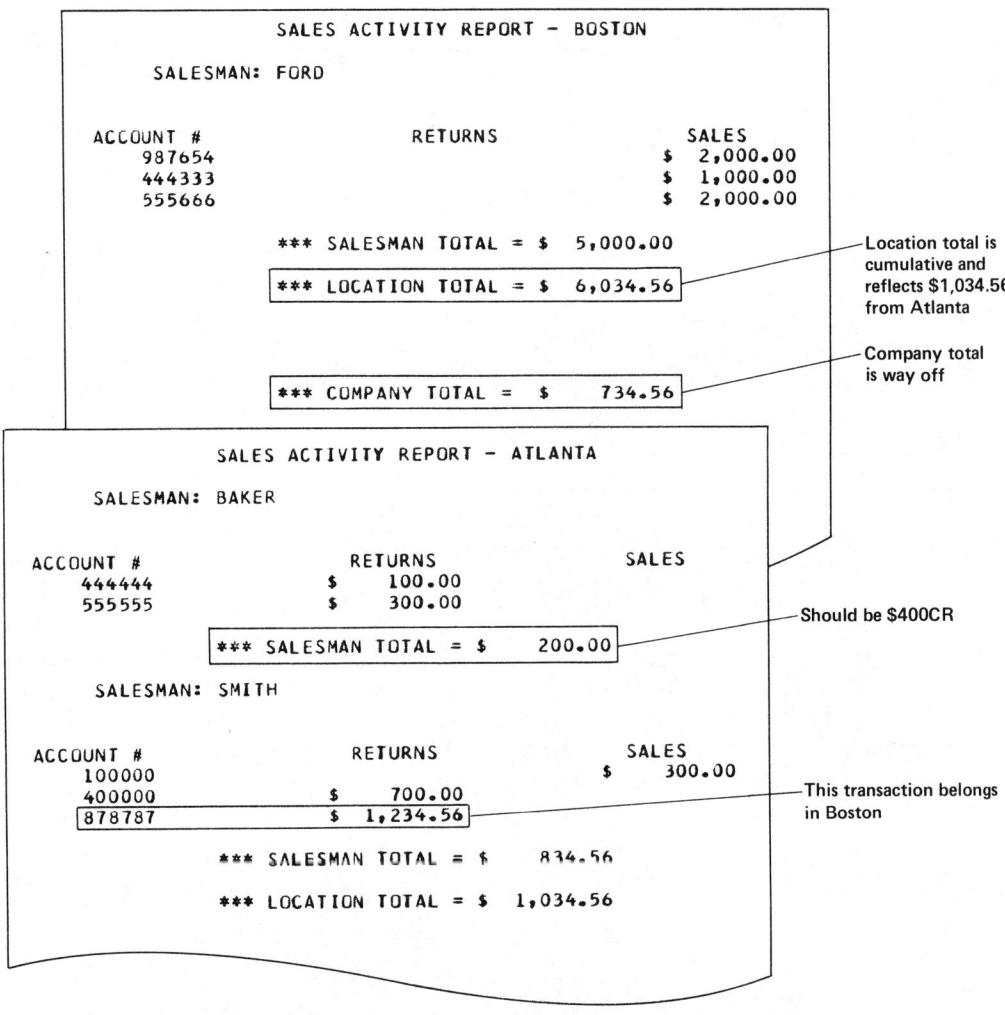

FIGURE 9.1 Erroneous output (produced by Figure 9.2).

belongs as the first transaction in Boston rather than the last transaction in Atlanta.

3. The company total of $734.56 is a fraction of what it should be.
4. Location totals are cumulative; i.e., the total for Boston should be $5,000; instead, it prints as $6,034.56, reflecting $1,034.56 from Atlanta.

Find and correct all errors in the program of Figure 9.2.

```
00001              IDENTIFICATION DIVISION.
00002              PROGRAM-ID.    ECBREAK.
00003              AUTHOR.        R. GRAUER.
00004
00005              ENVIRONMENT DIVISION.
00006              CONFIGURATION SECTION.
00007              SOURCE-COMPUTER.     IBM-4341.
00008              OBJECT-COMPUTER.     IBM-4341.
00009
00010              INPUT-OUTPUT SECTION.
00011              FILE-CONTROL.
00012                  SELECT SALES-FILE
00013                      ASSIGN TO UT-S-SYSIN.
00014                  SELECT PRINT-FILE
00015                      ASSIGN TO UT-S-PRINT.
00016
00017              DATA DIVISION.
00018              FILE SECTION.
00019              FD  SALES-FILE
00020                  LABEL RECORDS ARE STANDARD
00021                  BLOCK CONTAINS 0 RECORDS
00022                  RECORD CONTAINS 80 CHARACTERS
00023                  DATA RECORD IS SALES-RECORD.
00024              01  SALES-RECORD          PIC X(80).
00025
00026              FD  PRINT-FILE
00027                  LABEL RECORDS ARE STANDARD
00028                  RECORD CONTAINS 133 CHARACTERS
00029                  DATA RECORD IS PRINT-LINE.
00030              01  PRINT-LINE            PIC X(133).
00031
00032              WORKING-STORAGE SECTION.
00033              01  PROGRAM-SWITCHES.
00034                  05  WS-DATA-REMAINS-SW    PIC X(3)  VALUE 'YES'.
00035                  05  WS-PREVIOUS-SALESMAN  PIC X(15) VALUE SPACES.
00036                  05  WS-PREVIOUS-LOCATION  PIC X(15) VALUE SPACES.
00037
00038              01  CONTROL-BREAK-TOTALS.
00039                  05  THIS-SALESMAN-TOTAL   PIC  9(6)V99 VALUE ZEROS.
00040                  05  THIS-LOCATION-TOTAL   PIC  9(6)V99 VALUE ZEROS.
00041                  05  COMPANY-TOTAL         PIC  9(6)V99 VALUE ZEROS.
00042
00043              01  TRANSACTION-WORK-AREA.
00044                  05  TR-SALESMAN-NAME      PIC X(15).
00045                  05  TR-ACCOUNT-NUMBER     PIC 9(6).
00046                  05  TR-AMOUNT             PIC 9(4)V99.
00047                  05  TR-CODE               PIC X.
00048                      88  RETURNS      VALUE 'R'.
00049                      88  SALE         VALUE 'S'.
00050                  05  TR-LOCATION           PIC X(15).
00051                  05  FILLER                PIC X(37).
00052
```

FIGURE 9.2 Erroneous control break program.

```
00053             01  HDG-LINE-ONE.
00054                 05  FILLER                  PIC X(25)      VALUE SPACES.
00055                 05  FILLER                  PIC X(24)
00056                     VALUE 'SALES ACTIVITY REPORT - '.
00057                 05  HDG-LOCATION            PIC X(15)      VALUE SPACES.
00058                 05  FILLER                  PIC X(69)      VALUE SPACES.
00059
00060             01  HDG-LINE-TWO.
00061                 05  FILLER                  PIC X(15)      VALUE SPACES.
00062                 05  FILLER                  PIC X(10)      VALUE 'SALESMAN: '.
00063                 05  HDG-NAME                PIC X(15).
00064                 05  FILLER                  PIC X(25)      VALUE SPACES.
00065                 05  FILLER                  PIC X(78)      VALUE SPACES.
00066
00067             01  HDG-LINE-THREE.
00068                 05  FILLER                  PIC X(10)      VALUE SPACES.
00069                 05  FILLER                  PIC X(11)      VALUE 'ACCOUNT # '.
00070                 05  FILLER                  PIC X(15)      VALUE SPACES.
00071                 05  FILLER                  PIC X(7)       VALUE 'RETURNS'.
00072                 05  FILLER                  PIC X(15)      VALUE SPACES.
00073                 05  FILLER                  PIC X(5)       VALUE 'SALES'.
00074                 05  FILLER                  PIC X(70)      VALUE SPACES.
00075
00076             01  DETAIL-LINE.
00077                 05  FILLER                  PIC X(14)      VALUE SPACES.
00078                 05  DET-ACCOUNT-NUMBER      PIC 9(6).
00079                 05  FILLER                  PIC X(14)      VALUE SPACES.
00080                 05  DET-RETURNS             PIC $Z(3),ZZ9.99.
00081                 05  FILLER                  PIC X(11)      VALUE SPACES.
00082                 05  DET-SALES               PIC $Z(3),ZZ9.99.
00083                 05  FILLER                  PIC X(70)      VALUE SPACES.
00084
00085             01  SALESMAN-TOTAL-LINE.
00086                 05  FILLER                  PIC X(25)      VALUE SPACES.
00087                 05  FILLER                  PIC X(21)
00088                     VALUE '*** SALESMAN TOTAL = '.
00089                 05  PRT-SALESMAN-TOTAL      PIC $Z(3),ZZ9.99CR.
00090                 05  FILLER                  PIC X(74)      VALUE SPACES.
00091
00092             01  LOCATION-TOTAL-LINE.
00093                 05  FILLER                  PIC X(25)      VALUE SPACES.
00094                 05  FILLER                  PIC X(21)
00095                     VALUE '*** LOCATION TOTAL = '.
00096                 05  PRT-LOCATION-TOTAL      PIC $Z(3),ZZ9.99CR.
00097                 05  FILLER                  PIC X(73)      VALUE SPACES.
00098
00099             01  COMPANY-TOTAL-LINE.
00100                 05  FILLER                  PIC X(25)      VALUE SPACES.
00101                 05  FILLER                  PIC X(21)
00102                     VALUE '*** COMPANY TOTAL = '.
00103                 05  PRT-COMPANY-TOTAL       PIC $Z(3),ZZ9.99CR.
00104                 05  FILLER                  PIC X(74)      VALUE SPACES.
00105
00106             PROCEDURE DIVISION.
00107             010-CALCULATE-CONTROL-BREAKS.
00108                 OPEN INPUT SALES-FILE
00109                     OUTPUT PRINT-FILE.
00110                 READ SALES-FILE INTO TRANSACTION-WORK-AREA
00111                     AT END MOVE 'NO' TO WS-DATA-REMAINS-SW.
00112                 PERFORM 015-PROCESS-ALL-LOCATIONS
00113                     UNTIL WS-DATA-REMAINS-SW = 'NO'.
00114                 PERFORM 080-WRITE-COMPANY-TOTAL.
00115                 CLOSE SALES-FILE
00116                       PRINT-FILE.
00117                 STOP RUN.
00118
```

FIGURE 9.2 *continued*

```
00119          015-PROCESS-ALL-LOCATIONS.
00120              PERFORM 065-WRITE-LOCATION-HEADING.
00121              MOVE TR-LOCATION TO WS-PREVIOUS-LOCATION.
00122              PERFORM 020-PROCESS-ALL-SALESMEN
00123                  UNTIL TR-LOCATION NOT EQUAL WS-PREVIOUS-LOCATION
00124                  OR WS-DATA-REMAINS-SW = 'NO'.
00125              PERFORM 075-WRITE-LOCATION-TOTAL.
00126
00127          020-PROCESS-ALL-SALESMEN.
00128              MOVE TR-SALESMAN-NAME TO WS-PREVIOUS-SALESMAN.
00129              MOVE ZEROS TO THIS-SALESMAN-TOTAL.
00130              PERFORM 060-WRITE-SALESMAN-HEADING.
00131              PERFORM 030-PROCESS-ONE-SALESMAN
00132                  UNTIL TR-SALESMAN-NAME NOT EQUAL WS-PREVIOUS-SALESMAN
00133                  OR WS-DATA-REMAINS-SW = 'NO'.
00134              PERFORM 070-WRITE-SALESMAN-TOTAL.
00135
00136          030-PROCESS-ONE-SALESMAN.
00137              MOVE SPACES TO DETAIL-LINE.
00138              MOVE TR-ACCOUNT-NUMBER TO DET-ACCOUNT-NUMBER.
00139
00140              IF SALE
00141                  MOVE TR-AMOUNT TO DET-SALES
00142                  ADD TR-AMOUNT TO THIS-SALESMAN-TOTAL
00143                  ADD TR-AMOUNT TO THIS-LOCATION-TOTAL
00144      *           ADD TR-AMOUNT TO COMPANY-TOTAL
00145              ELSE
00146                  MOVE TR-AMOUNT TO DET-RETURNS
00147                  SUBTRACT TR-AMOUNT FROM THIS-SALESMAN-TOTAL
00148                  SUBTRACT TR-AMOUNT FROM THIS-LOCATION-TOTAL
00149                  SUBTRACT TR-AMOUNT FROM COMPANY-TOTAL.
00150
00151              WRITE PRINT-LINE FROM DETAIL-LINE
00152                  AFTER ADVANCING 1 LINE.
00153              READ SALES-FILE INTO TRANSACTION-WORK-AREA
00154                  AT END MOVE 'NO' TO WS-DATA-REMAINS-SW.
00155
00156          060-WRITE-SALESMAN-HEADING.
00157              MOVE TR-SALESMAN-NAME TO HDG-NAME.
00158              WRITE PRINT-LINE FROM HDG-LINE-TWO
00159                  AFTER ADVANCING 2 LINES.
00160              WRITE PRINT-LINE FROM HDG-LINE-THREE
00161                  AFTER ADVANCING 3 LINES.
00162
00163          065-WRITE-LOCATION-HEADING.
00164              MOVE TR-LOCATION TO HDG-LOCATION.
00165              WRITE PRINT-LINE FROM HDG-LINE-ONE
00166                  AFTER ADVANCING PAGE.
00167
00168          070-WRITE-SALESMAN-TOTAL.
00169              MOVE THIS-SALESMAN-TOTAL TO PRT-SALESMAN-TOTAL.
00170              WRITE PRINT-LINE FROM SALESMAN-TOTAL-LINE
00171                  AFTER ADVANCING 2 LINES.
00172
00173          075-WRITE-LOCATION-TOTAL.
00174              MOVE THIS-LOCATION-TOTAL TO PRT-LOCATION-TOTAL.
00175              WRITE PRINT-LINE FROM LOCATION-TOTAL-LINE
00176                  AFTER ADVANCING 2 LINES.
00177
00178          080-WRITE-COMPANY-TOTAL.
00179              MOVE COMPANY-TOTAL TO PRT-COMPANY-TOTAL.
00180              WRITE PRINT-LINE FROM COMPANY-TOTAL-LINE
00181                  AFTER ADVANCING 5 LINES.
```

FIGURE 9.2 *continued*

Exercise 9.2—Subprograms

This exercise is based on the programs from Chapter 3 (Figures 3.18, 3.19, and 3.20). The data were shown in Figure 3.16 and the intended output in Figure 3.17. The erroneous results are presented in Figure 9.3. Note the following errors:

1. Ages are calculated incorrectly in Figure 9.3, although they are close to being correct; e.g., Baker's age prints as 25.0 rather than 24.9 in Figure 3.17.
2. *All* table lookups have failed, but for *different* reasons. Note that all courses print as UNKNOWN, majors appear mysteriously as N, and Baker's school is RAL ARTS.
3. Only five courses rather than six were printed for Brown, although both of Baker's appeared correctly.

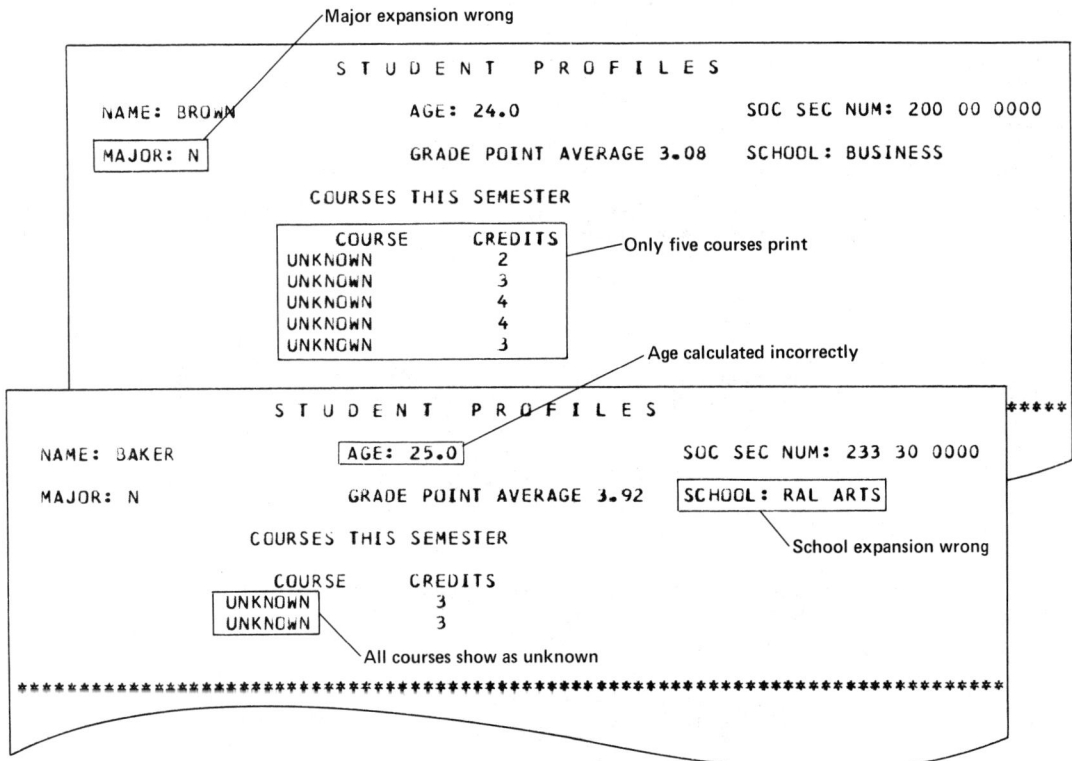

FIGURE 9.3 Erroneous student profiles (produced by Figures 9.4, 9.5, and 9.6). In addition to the errors shown, the program terminated improperly (i.e., ABENDed).

4. The program terminated abnormally with a dump after printing the last profile.

Find and correct all errors in the programs of Figures 9.4, 9.5, and 9.6.

```
00001              IDENTIFICATION DIVISION.
00002              PROGRAM-ID.    EMAIN.
00003              AUTHOR.        R. GRAUER.
00004
00005              ENVIRONMENT DIVISION.
00006              CONFIGURATION SECTION.
00007              SOURCE-COMPUTER.    IBM-4341.
00008              OBJECT-COMPUTER.    IBM-4341.
00009
00010              INPUT-OUTPUT SECTION.
00011              FILE-CONTROL.
00012                  SELECT STUDENT-FILE
00013                      ASSIGN TO UT-S-STUD.
00014                  SELECT PRINT-FILE
00015                      ASSIGN TO UT-S-PRINT.
00016                  SELECT SORT-FILE
00017                      ASSIGN TO UT-S-SORTWORK.
00018
00019              DATA DIVISION.
00020              FILE SECTION.
00021              FD  STUDENT-FILE
00022                  LABEL RECORDS ARE STANDARD
00023                  BLOCK CONTAINS 0 RECORDS
00024                  RECORD CONTAINS 80 CHARACTERS
00025                  DATA RECORD IS STUDENT-RECORD.
00026              01  STUDENT-RECORD              PIC X(80).
00027
00028              FD  PRINT-FILE
00029                  LABEL RECORDS ARE STANDARD
00030                  RECORD CONTAINS 133 CHARACTERS
00031                  DATA RECORD IS PRINT-LINE.
00032              01  PRINT-LINE                  PIC X(133).
00033
00034              SD  SORT-FILE
00035                  RECORD CONTAINS 80 CHARACTERS
00036                  DATA RECORD IS SORT-RECORD.
00037              01  SORT-RECORD.
00038                  05  SRT-SOC-SEC-NUMBER      PIC X(9).
00039                  05  SRT-NAME-AND-INITIALS.
00040                      10  SRT-LAST-NAME       PIC X(18).
00041                      10  SRT-INITIALS        PIC XX.
00042                  05  SRT-DATE-OF-BIRTH.
00043                      10  SRT-BIRTH-MONTH     PIC 99.
00044                      10  SRT-BIRTH-YEAR      PIC 99.
00045                  05  SRT-SEX                 PIC X.
00046                  05  SRT-MAJOR-CODE          PIC X(3).
00047                  05  SRT-SCHOOL-CODE         PIC 9.
00048                  05  SRT-CUMULATIVE-CREDITS  PIC 9(3).
00049                  05  SRT-CUMULATIVE-POINTS   PIC 9(3).
00050                  05  SRT-UNION-MEMBER        PIC X.
00051                  05  SRT-SCHOLARSHIP         PIC 999.
00052                  05  SRT-COURSES-THIS-SEMESTER
00053                      OCCURS 6 TIMES.
00054                      10  SRT-COURSE-NUMBER   PIC XXX.
00055                      10  SRT-COURSE-CREDITS  PIC 9.
00056                  05  SRT-GRADE-POINT-AVERAGE PIC 9V999.
00057                  05  FILLER                  PIC X(4).
```

FIGURE 9.4 Erroneous main program.

```
00058
00059           WORKING-STORAGE SECTION.
00060           01  FILLER                       PIC X(27)
00061               VALUE 'WS-MAIN PROGRAM BEGINS HERE'.
00062
00063           01  PROGRAM-SUBSCRIPTS.
00064               05  WS-COURSE-SUB            PIC S9(4)  COMP.
00065
00066           01  PROGRAM-SWITCHES.
00067               05  WS-DATA-REMAINS-SWITCH   PIC X(3) VALUE SPACES.
00068               05  WS-END-OF-SORT-FILE-SW   PIC X(3) VALUE SPACES.
00069
00070           01  WS-STUDENT-RECORD.
00071               05  STU-SOC-SEC-NUMBER       PIC X(9).
00072               05  STU-NAME-AND-INITIALS.
00073                   10  STU-LAST-NAME        PIC X(18).
00074                   10  STU-INITIALS         PIC XX.
00075               05  STU-DATE-OF-BIRTH.
00076                   10  STU-BIRTH-MONTH      PIC 99.
00077                   10  STU-BIRTH-YEAR       PIC 99.
00078               05  STU-SEX                  PIC X.
00079               05  STU-MAJOR-CODE           PIC X(3).
00080               05  STU-SCHOOL-CODE          PIC 9.
00081               05  STU-CUMULATIVE-CREDITS   PIC 9(3).
00082               05  STU-CUMULATIVE-POINTS    PIC 9(3).
00083               05  STU-UNION-MEMBER         PIC X.
00084               05  STU-SCHOLARSHIP          PIC 999.
00085               05  STU-COURSES-THIS-SEMESTER
00086                   OCCURS 6 TIMES.
00087                   10  STU-COURSE-NUMBER    PIC XXX.
00088                   10  STU-COURSE-CREDITS   PIC 9.
00089               05  FILLER                   PIC X(8).
00090
00091           01  WS-SUBROUTINE-PARAMETERS.
00092               05  WS-MAJOR-CODE            PIC X(3).
00093               05  WS-MAJOR-VALUE           PIC X(15).
00094               05  WS-SCHOOL-CODE           PIC 9.
00095               05  WS-SCHOOL-VALUE          PIC X(12).
00096
00097           01  WS-PASSED-COURSE-TABLE.
00098               05  CODE-AND-VALUE OCCURS 6 TIMES.
00099                   10  PASSED-COURSE-CODE   PIC X(3).
00100                   10  PASSED-COURSE-VALUE  PIC X(12).
00101
00102           01  WS-AGE                       PIC 99V9.
00103
00104           01  DATE-WORK-AREA.
00105               05  TODAYS-YEAR              PIC 99   VALUE ZEROS.
00106               05  TODAYS-MONTH             PIC 99   VALUE ZEROS.
00107               05  TODAYS-DAY               PIC 99   VALUE ZEROS.
00108
00109           01  PROFILE-LINE-ONE.
00110               05  FILLER                   PIC X       VALUE SPACES.
00111               05  FILLER                   PIC X(21) VALUE SPACES.
00112               05  FILLER                   PIC X(31)
00113                   VALUE 'S T U D E N T    P R O F I L E S'.
00114               05  FILLER                   PIC X(80) VALUE SPACES.
00115
00116           01  ASTERISK-LINE.
00117               05  FILLER                   PIC X       VALUE SPACES.
00118               05  FILLER                   PIC X(80) VALUE ALL '*'.
00119               05  FILLER                   PIC X(32) VALUE SPACES.
00120
00121           01  PROFILE-LINE-TWO.
00122               05  FILLER                   PIC X(3)    VALUE SPACES.
00123               05  FILLER                   PIC X(6)    VALUE 'NAME: '.
```

FIGURE 9.4 *continued*

```
00124              05  PL2-NAME                 PIC X(18).
00125              05  FILLER                   PIC X          VALUE SPACES.
00126              05  FILLER                   PIC X(5)       VALUE 'AGE: '.
00127              05  PL2-AGE                  PIC Z9.9.
00128              05  FILLER                   PIC X(18)      VALUE SPACES.
00129              05  FILLER                   PIC X(13)
00130                  VALUE 'SOC SEC NUM: '.
00131              05  PL2-SOC-SEC-NUMBER       PIC 999B99B9999.
00132              05  FILLER                   PIC X(54)      VALUE SPACES.
00133
00134          01  PROFILE-LINE-THREE.
00135              05  FILLER                   PIC X(3)       VALUE SPACES.
00136              05  FILLER                   PIC X(7)       VALUE 'MAJOR:'
00137              05  PL3-MAJOR                PIC X(15)      VALUE SPACES.
00138              05  FILLER                   PIC X(3)       VALUE SPACES.
00139              05  FILLER                   PIC X(20)
00140                  VALUE 'GRADE POINT AVERAGE '.
00141              05  PL3-GRADE-POINT-AVERAGE  PIC 9.99.
00142              05  FILLER                   PIC X(3)       VALUE SPACES.
00143              05  FILLER                   PIC X(8)       VALUE 'SCHOOL:'
00144              05  PL3-SCHOOL               PIC X(12)      VALUE SPACES.
00145              05  FILLER                   PIC X(58)      VALUE SPACES.
00146
00147          01  PROFILE-LINE-FOUR.
00148              05  FILLER                   PIC X(20)      VALUE SPACES.
00149              05  FILLER                   PIC X(22)
00150                  VALUE 'COURSES THIS SEMESTER'.
00151              05  FILLER                   PIC X(91)      VALUE SPACES.
00152
00153          01  PROFILE-LINE-FIVE.
00154              05  FILLER                   PIC X(22)      VALUE SPACES.
00155              05  FILLER                   PIC X(18)
00156                  VALUE 'COURSE      CREDITS'.
00157              05  FILLER                   PIC X(93)      VALUE SPACES.
00158
00159          01  PROFILE-LINE-SIX.
00160              05  FILLER                   PIC X(18)      VALUE SPACES.
00161              05  PL6-COURSE               PIC X(12).
00162              05  FILLER                   PIC X(5)       VALUE SPACES.
00163              05  PL6-CREDITS              PIC 9.
00164              05  FILLER                   PIC X(97)      VALUE SPACES.
00165
00166       PROCEDURE DIVISION.
00167       SORTING SECTION.
00168       0000-MAINLINE.
00169           SORT SORT-FILE
00170               DESCENDING KEY SRT-GRADE-POINT-AVERAGE
00171             INPUT PROCEDURE A-PROCESS-INPUT-FILE
00172             OUTPUT PROCEDURE B-PREPARE-REPORTS.
00173
00174       A-PROCESS-INPUT-FILE SECTION.
00175       A100-MAINLINE.
00176           OPEN INPUT STUDENT-FILE.
00177           READ STUDENT-FILE INTO WS-STUDENT-RECORD
00178               AT END MOVE 'NO' TO WS-DATA-REMAINS-SWITCH.
00179           PERFORM A200-READ-STUDENT-RECORDS
00180               UNTIL WS-DATA-REMAINS-SWITCH = 'NO'.
00181           CLOSE STUDENT-FILE.
00182           GO TO A300-EXIT.
00183
00184       A200-READ-STUDENT-RECORDS.
00185           MOVE WS-STUDENT-RECORD TO SORT-RECORD.
00186           COMPUTE SRT-GRADE-POINT-AVERAGE
00187             = SRT-CUMULATIVE-POINTS / SRT-CUMULATIVE-CREDITS.
00188           RELEASE SORT-RECORD.
00189           READ STUDENT-FILE INTO WS-STUDENT-RECORD
00190               AT END MOVE 'NO' TO WS-DATA-REMAINS-SWITCH.
```

FIGURE 9.4 *continued*

```
00191
00192            A300-EXIT.
00193                EXIT.
00194
00195            B-PREPARE-REPORTS SECTION.
00196            B100-MAINLINE.
00197                OPEN OUTPUT PRINT-FILE.
00198                RETURN SORT-FILE
00199                    AT END MOVE 'YES' TO WS-END-OF-SORT-FILE-SW.
00200                PERFORM B200-PROCESS-SORTED-RECORDS
00201                    UNTIL WS-END-OF-SORT-FILE-SW = 'YES'.
00202                CLOSE PRINT-FILE.
00203                STOP RUN.
00204
00205            B200-PROCESS-SORTED-RECORDS.
00206                IF SRT-GRADE-POINT-AVERAGE > 3.00 OR = 3.00
00207                    PERFORM B300-EXPAND-CODES
00208                    PERFORM B400-PRINT-STUDENT-PROFILE.
00209                RETURN SORT-FILE
00210                    AT END MOVE 'YES' TO WS-END-OF-SORT-FILE-SW.
00211
00212            B300-EXPAND-CODES.
00213                MOVE SRT-MAJOR-CODE TO WS-MAJOR-CODE.
00214                MOVE SRT-SCHOOL-CODE TO WS-SCHOOL-CODE.
00215                CALL 'ESUB2'
00216                    USING WS-SUBROUTINE-PARAMETERS.
00217                MOVE SPACES TO WS-PASSED-COURSE-TABLE.
00218                PERFORM B350-BUILD-COURSE-TABLE
00219                    VARYING WS-COURSE-SUB FROM 1 BY 1
00220                        UNTIL WS-COURSE-SUB > 6
00221                        OR SRT-COURSE-NUMBER (WS-COURSE-SUB) = SPACES.
00222                CALL 'ESUB1'
00223                    USING WS-PASSED-COURSE-TABLE.
00224
00225            B350-BUILD-COURSE-TABLE.
00226                MOVE SRT-COURSE-NUMBER (WS-COURSE-SUB)
00227                    TO PASSED-COURSE-CODE (WS-COURSE-SUB).
00228
00229            B400-PRINT-STUDENT-PROFILE.
00230                WRITE PRINT-LINE FROM PROFILE-LINE-ONE
00231                    AFTER ADVANCING PAGE.
00232
00233                MOVE SRT-LAST-NAME TO PL2-NAME.
00234                MOVE SRT-SOC-SEC-NUMBER TO PL2-SOC-SEC-NUMBER.
00235                ACCEPT DATE-WORK-AREA FROM DAY.
00236                COMPUTE WS-AGE = TODAYS-YEAR - SRT-BIRTH-YEAR
00237                    + (TODAYS-MONTH - SRT-BIRTH-MONTH) / 12.
00238                MOVE WS-AGE TO PL2-AGE.
00239                WRITE PRINT-LINE FROM PROFILE-LINE-TWO
00240                    AFTER ADVANCING 2 LINES.
00241
00242                MOVE WS-MAJOR-VALUE TO PL3-MAJOR.
00243                MOVE SRT-GRADE-POINT-AVERAGE TO PL3-GRADE-POINT-AVERAGE.
00244                MOVE WS-SCHOOL-VALUE TO PL3-SCHOOL.
00245                WRITE PRINT-LINE FROM PROFILE-LINE-THREE
00246                    AFTER ADVANCING 2 LINES.
00247
00248                WRITE PRINT-LINE FROM PROFILE-LINE-FOUR
00249                    AFTER ADVANCING 2 LINES.
00250
00251                WRITE PRINT-LINE FROM PROFILE-LINE-FIVE
00252                    AFTER ADVANCING 2 LINES.
00253
00254                PERFORM B450-WRITE-COURSE-LINE
00255                    VARYING WS-COURSE-SUB FROM 1 BY 1
00256                        UNTIL WS-COURSE-SUB = 6
00257                        OR PASSED-COURSE-VALUE (WS-COURSE-SUB) = SPACES.
```

FIGURE 9.4 *continued*

```
00258
00259              WRITE PRINT-LINE FROM ASTERISK-LINE
00260                  AFTER ADVANCING 3 LINES.
00261
00262          B450-WRITE-COURSE-LINE.
00263              MOVE PASSED-COURSE-VALUE (WS-COURSE-SUB) TO PL6-COURSE.
00264              MOVE SRT-COURSE-CREDITS (WS-COURSE-SUB) TO PL6-CREDITS.
00265              WRITE PRINT-LINE FROM PROFILE-LINE-SIX
00266                  AFTER ADVANCING 1 LINE.
00267
```

FIGURE 9.4 *continued*

```
00001          IDENTIFICATION DIVISION.
00002          PROGRAM-ID.    ESUB1.
00003          AUTHOR.        R. GRAUER.
00004
00005          ENVIRONMENT DIVISION.
00006          CONFIGURATION SECTION.
00007          SOURCE-COMPUTER.    IBM-4341.
00008          OBJECT-COMPUTER.    IBM-4341.
00009
00010          INPUT-OUTPUT SECTION.
00011          FILE-CONTROL.
00012              SELECT COURSE-FILE
00013                  ASSIGN TO UT-S-COURSE.
00014
00015          DATA DIVISION.
00016          FILE SECTION.
00017          FD  COURSE-FILE
00018              LABEL RECORDS ARE STANDARD
00019              BLOCK CONTAINS 0 RECORDS
00020              RECORD CONTAINS 80 CHARACTERS
00021              DATA RECORD IS COURSE-RECORD.
00022          01  COURSE-RECORD.
00023              05  IN-COURSE-CODE              PIC X(3).
00024              05  IN-COURSE-VALUE             PIC X(15).
00025              05  FILLER                      PIC X(62).
00026
00027          WORKING-STORAGE SECTION.
00028          01  FILLER                          PIC X(22)
00029              VALUE 'WS SUBRTN1 BEGINS HERE'.
00030
00031          01  WS-COURSE-TABLE.
00032              05  COURSES OCCURS 1 TO 50 TIMES
00033                  DEPENDING ON WS-NUMBER-OF-COURSES
00034                  ASCENDING KEY IS COURSE-CODE
00035                  INDEXED BY COURSE-INDEX.
00036                  10  COURSE-CODE             PIC X(3).
00037                  10  COURSE-VALUE            PIC X(15).
00038
00039          01  PROGRAM-SWITCHES.
00040              05  WS-ALREADY-EXECUTED-SWITCH PIC X(3) VALUE 'NO'.
00041              05  END-OF-COURSE-FILE-SWITCH  PIC X(3) VALUE SPACES.
00042
00043          01  COUNTERS-AND-SUBSCRIPTS.
00044              05  WS-NUMBER-OF-COURSES        PIC 9(3) VALUE ZEROS.
00045              05  COURSE-SUB                  PIC S9(4) COMP.
00046
00047          LINKAGE SECTION.
00048          01  PASSED-PARAMETERS.
00049              05  PASSED-COURSE-TABLE OCCURS 6 TIMES.
00050                  10  LS-CODE                 PIC X(3).
00051                  10  LS-VALUE                PIC X(12).
00052
```

FIGURE 9.5 Erroneous subroutine.

```
00053            PROCEDURE DIVISION
00054                USING PASSED-PARAMETERS.
00055            0010-MAINLINE.
00056                IF WS-ALREADY-EXECUTED-SWITCH = 'NO'
00057                    MOVE 'YES' TO WS-ALREADY-EXECUTED-SWITCH
00058                    PERFORM 0080-INITIALIZE-COURSE-TABLE.
00059
00060                PERFORM 0030-EXPAND-COURSE-CODE
00061                    VARYING COURSE-SUB FROM 1 BY 1
00062                        UNTIL COURSE-SUB > 6
00063                        OR LS-CODE (COURSE-SUB) = SPACES.
00064
00065            0020-RETURN-TO-MAIN.
00066                EXIT PROGRAM.
00067
00068            0030-EXPAND-COURSE-CODE.
00069                SEARCH ALL COURSES
00070                    AT END
00071                        MOVE 'UNKNOWN' TO LS-VALUE (COURSE-SUB)
00072                    WHEN COURSE-CODE (COURSE-INDEX) = LS-CODE (COURSE-SUB)
00073                        MOVE COURSE-VALUE (COURSE-INDEX) TO LS-VALUE (COURSE-SUB).
00074
00075            0080-INITIALIZE-COURSE-TABLE.
00076                OPEN INPUT COURSE-FILE.
00077                READ COURSE-FILE
00078                    AT END MOVE 'YES' TO END-OF-COURSE-FILE-SWITCH.
00079                PERFORM 0090-READ-COURSE-FILE
00080                    VARYING COURSE-INDEX FROM 1 BY 1
00081                        UNTIL END-OF-COURSE-FILE-SWITCH = 'YES'.
00082                CLOSE COURSE-FILE.
00083
00084            0090-READ-COURSE-FILE.
00085                IF WS-NUMBER-OF-COURSES > 50
00086                    DISPLAY 'ERROR - COURSE TABLE EXCEEDED'
00087                    MOVE 'YES' TO END-OF-COURSE-FILE-SWITCH
00088                ELSE
00089                    MOVE IN-COURSE-CODE TO COURSE-CODE (COURSE-INDEX)
00090                    MOVE IN-COURSE-VALUE TO COURSE-VALUE (COURSE-INDEX).
00091
00092                READ COURSE-FILE
00093                    AT END MOVE 'YES' TO END-OF-COURSE-FILE-SWITCH.
```

FIGURE 9.5 *continued*

```
00001            IDENTIFICATION DIVISION.
00002            PROGRAM-ID.    ESUB2.
00003            AUTHOR.        R. GRAUER.
00004
00005            ENVIRONMENT DIVISION.
00006            CONFIGURATION SECTION.
00007            SOURCE-COMPUTER.      IBM-4341.
00008            OBJECT-COMPUTER.      IBM-4341.
00009
00010            DATA DIVISION.
00011            WORKING-STORAGE SECTION.
00012            01  FILLER                          PIC X(22)
00013                VALUE 'WS SUBRTN2 BEGINS HERE'.
00014
00015            01  SCHOOL-TABLE-AND-VALUES.
00016                05  SCHOOL-VALUES.
00017                    10  FILLER    PIC X(12)    VALUE 'BUSINESS'.
00018                    10  FILLER    PIC X(12)    VALUE 'LIBERAL ARTS'.
00019                    10  FILLER    PIC X(12)    VALUE 'ENGINEERING'.
00020                    10  FILLER    PIC X(12)    VALUE 'EDUCATION'.
00021
```

FIGURE 9.6 Erroneous subroutine.

```
00022              05  SCHOOL-TABLE REDEFINES SCHOOL-VALUES.
00023                  10  SCHOOL-NAME OCCURS 6 TIMES    PIC X(8).
00024
00025          COPY TEMP.
00026 C    01  MAJOR-VALUES.
00027 C        05  FILLER            PIC X(18)     VALUE 'STASTATISTICS'.
00028 C        05  FILLER            PIC X(18)     VALUE 'FINFINANCE'.
00029 C        05  FILLER            PIC X(18)     VALUE 'MANMANAGEMENT'.
00030 C        05  FILLER            PIC X(18)     VALUE 'EDPDATA PROC'.
00031 C        05  FILLER            PIC X(18)     VALUE 'ENGENGLISH'.
00032 C        05  FILLER            PIC X(18)     VALUE 'BIOBIOLOGY'.
00033 C        05  FILLER            PIC X(18)     VALUE 'ECOECONOMICS'.
00034 C        05  FILLER            PIC X(18)     VALUE 'EENELECTRICAL ENG'.
00035 C        05  FILLER            PIC X(18)     VALUE 'MENMECHANICAL ENG'.
00036 C        05  FILLER            PIC X(18)     VALUE 'ELEELEMENTARY ED'.
00037 C        05  FILLER            PIC X(18)     VALUE 'SEESECONDARY ED'.
00038 C        05  FILLER            PIC X(18)     VALUE 'SPESPECIAL ED'.
00039 C
00040 C    01  WS-MAJOR-TABLE REDEFINES MAJOR-VALUES.
00041 C        05  MAJORS OCCURS 12 TIMES
00042 C                INDEXED BY MAJOR-INDEX.
00043 C            10  MAJOR-CODE            PIC X(3).
00044 C            10  MAJOR-VALUE           PIC X(15).
00045      01  COUNTERS-AND-SUBSCRIPTS.
00046          05  MAJOR-SUB                 PIC S9(4) COMP.
00047
00048  LINKAGE SECTION.
00049  01  PASSED-PARAMETERS.
00050      05  LS-MAJOR-CODE                 PIC X(4).
00051      05  LS-MAJOR-VALUE                PIC X(14).
00052      05  LS-SCHOOL-CODE                PIC 9.
00053      05  LS-SCHOOL-VALUE               PIC X(12).
00054
00055  PROCEDURE DIVISION
00056      USING PASSED-PARAMETERS.
00057
00058  0010-MAINLINE.
00059      SET MAJOR-INDEX TO 1.
00060      SEARCH MAJORS
00061          AT END MOVE 'UNKNOWN' TO LS-MAJOR-CODE
00062          WHEN LS-MAJOR-CODE = MAJOR-CODE (MAJOR-INDEX)
00063              MOVE MAJOR-VALUE (MAJOR-INDEX) TO LS-MAJOR-VALUE.
00064
00065      IF LS-SCHOOL-CODE > 0 AND < 5
00066          MOVE SCHOOL-NAME (LS-SCHOOL-CODE) TO LS-SCHOOL-VALUE
00067      ELSE
00068          MOVE 'UNKNOWN' TO LS-SCHOOL-VALUE.
00069
00070  0020-RETURN-TO-MAIN.
00071      EXIT PROGRAM.
```

FIGURE 9.6 *continued*

Exercise 9.3—Sequential File Maintenance

This exercise is based on the specifications associated with the program of Figure 6.14. There are three input files: a transaction, promotion, and old master, as shown in Figure 6.15a, b, and c, respectively. Desired output is to consist of a new master file, a deleted record file, and a set of error messages shown in Figures 6.15d, e, and f. Actual and *incorrect* output is displayed in Figure 9.7. Note well the following errors:

1. All salary raises in the promotion file are ignored; hence, the new master record for Benjamin does not reflect the new salary of $35,000. Error messages associated with salary raises for Tater and Johnson are also missing.
2. Title updates (i.e., promotions) do take effect, but erase historical information. Benjamin, for example, shows 444 as both the present and previous title code.
3. Tater was correctly written to the deleted record file, but *incorrectly* remained in the new master.
4. NEW EMPLOYEE is missing a location code in the new master, although the transaction to add this record contained a location code of 100.
5. NEW EMPLOYEE failed to have his title code corrected to 555, although there was a valid transaction to this effect.

Find and correct all errors in Figure 9.8.

FIGURE 9.7 Erroneous output from sequential update. (a) New master; (b) deleted record file; (c) error messages.

```
00001              IDENTIFICATION DIVISION.
00002              PROGRAM-ID.    ESEQUP.
00003              AUTHOR.        R. GRAUER.
00004
00005              ENVIRONMENT DIVISION.
00006              CONFIGURATION SECTION.
00007              SOURCE-COMPUTER.     IBM-4341.
00008              OBJECT-COMPUTER.     IBM-4341.
00009
00010              INPUT-OUTPUT SECTION.
00011              FILE-CONTROL.
00012                  SELECT TRANSACTION-FILE
00013                      ASSIGN TO UT-S-TRANS.
00014                  SELECT OLD-MASTER-FILE
00015                      ASSIGN TO UT-S-MASTER.
00016                  SELECT PROMOTION-FILE
00017                      ASSIGN TO UT-S-PROMOTE.
00018                  SELECT DELETED-RECORD-FILE
00019                      ASSIGN TO UT-S-DELETE.
00020                  SELECT NEW-MASTER-FILE
00021                      ASSIGN TO UT-S-NEWMAST.
00022
00023              DATA DIVISION.
00024              FILE SECTION.
00025              FD  TRANSACTION-FILE
00026                  LABEL RECORDS ARE STANDARD
00027                  BLOCK CONTAINS 0 RECORDS
00028                  RECORD CONTAINS 80 CHARACTERS
00029                  DATA RECORD IS TRANSACTION-RECORD.
00030              01  TRANSACTION-RECORD              PIC X(80).
00031
00032              FD  OLD-MASTER-FILE
00033                  LABEL RECORDS ARE STANDARD
00034                  BLOCK CONTAINS 0 RECORDS
00035                  RECORD CONTAINS 80 CHARACTERS
00036                  DATA RECORD IS OLD-MAST-RECORD.
00037              01  OLD-MAST-RECORD                 PIC X(80).
00038
00039              FD  PROMOTION-FILE
00040                  LABEL RECORDS ARE STANDARD
00041                  BLOCK CONTAINS 0 RECORDS
00042                  RECORD CONTAINS 80 CHARACTERS
00043                  DATA RECORD IS PROMOTION-RECORD.
00044              01  PROMOTION-RECORD                PIC X(80).
00045
00046              FD  DELETED-RECORD-FILE
00047                  LABEL RECORDS ARE STANDARD
00048                  BLOCK CONTAINS 0 RECORDS
00049                  RECORD CONTAINS 80 CHARACTERS
00050                  DATA RECORD IS DELETED-RECORD.
00051              01  DELETED-RECORD                  PIC X(80).
00052
00053              FD  NEW-MASTER-FILE
00054                  LABEL RECORDS ARE STANDARD
00055                  BLOCK CONTAINS 0 RECORDS
00056                  RECORD CONTAINS 80 CHARACTERS
00057                  DATA RECORD IS NEW-MAST-RECORD.
00058              01  NEW-MAST-RECORD                 PIC X(80).
00059
00060              WORKING-STORAGE SECTION.
00061              01  FILLER                          PIC X(14)
00062                      VALUE 'WS BEGINS HERE'.
00063
00064              01  WS-TRANS-RECORD.
00065                  05  TR-SOC-SEC-NUMBER           PIC X(9).
00066                  05  TR-NAME.
00067                      10  TR-LAST-NAME            PIC X(15).
```

FIGURE 9.8 Erroneous sequential update.

```
00068              10    TR-INITIALS                    PIC XX.
00069        05    TR-DATE-OF-BIRTH.
00070              10    TR-BIRTH-MONTH                 PIC 99.
00071              10    TR-BIRTH-YEAR                  PIC 99.
00072        05    TR-DATE-OF-HIRE.
00073              10    TR-HIRE-MONTH                  PIC 99.
00074              10    TR-HIRE-YEAR                   PIC 99.
00075        05    TR-LOCATION-CODE                     PIC X(3).
00076        05    TR-PERFORMANCE-CODE                  PIC X.
00077        05    TR-EDUCATION-CODE                    PIC X.
00078        05    TR-TITLE-DATA.
00079              10    TR-TITLE-CODE                  PIC 9(3).
00080              10    TR-TITLE-DATE                  PIC 9(4).
00081        05    TR-SALARY-DATA.
00082              10    TR-SALARY                      PIC 9(5).
00083              10    TR-SALARY-DATE                 PIC 9(4).
00084        05    TR-TRANSACTION-CODE                  PIC X.
00085              88    ADDITION           VALUE 'A'.
00086              88    CORRECTION         VALUE 'C'.
00087              88    DELETION           VALUE 'D'.
00088        05    FILLER                               PIC X(24).
00089
00090  01  WS-PROMOTION-RECORD.
00091        05    PR-SOC-SEC-NUMBER                    PIC X(9).
00092        05    PR-NAME.
00093              10    PR-LAST-NAME                   PIC X(15).
00094              10    PR-INITIALS                    PIC XX.
00095        05    PR-SALARY-DATA.
00096              10    PR-SALARY                      PIC 9(5).
00097              10    PR-SALARY-DATE                 PIC 9(4).
00098        05    PR-TITLE-DATA.
00099              10    PR-TITLE-CODE                  PIC 9(3).
00100              10    PR-TITLE-DATE                  PIC 9(4).
00101        05    PR-PROMOTION-CODE                    PIC X.
00102              88    SALARY-RAISE       VALUE 'S'.
00103              88    PROMOTION          VALUE 'P'.
00104        05    FILLER                               PIC X(37).
00105
00106  01  WS-OLD-MAST-RECORD.
00107        05    OLD-SOC-SEC-NUMBER                   PIC X(9).
00108        05    OLD-NAME.
00109              10    OLD-LAST-NAME                  PIC X(15).
00110              10    OLD-INITIALS                   PIC XX.
00111        05    OLD-DATE-OF-BIRTH.
00112              10    OLD-BIRTH-MONTH                PIC 99.
00113              10    OLD-BIRTH-YEAR                 PIC 99.
00114        05    OLD-DATE-OF-HIRE.
00115              10    OLD-HIRE-MONTH                 PIC 99.
00116              10    OLD-HIRE-YEAR                  PIC 99.
00117        05    OLD-LOCATION-CODE                    PIC X(3).
00118        05    OLD-PERFORMANCE-CODE                 PIC X.
00119        05    OLD-EDUCATION-CODE                   PIC X.
00120        05    OLD-TITLE-DATA OCCURS 2 TIMES.
00121              10    OLD-TITLE-CODE                 PIC 9(3).
00122              10    OLD-TITLE-DATE                 PIC 9(4).
00123        05    OLD-SALARY-DATA OCCURS 3 TIMES.
00124              10    OLD-SALARY                     PIC 9(5).
00125              10    OLD-SALARY-DATE                PIC 9(4).
00126
00127  01  WS-NEW-MAST-RECORD.
00128        05    NEW-SOC-SEC-NUMBER                   PIC X(9).
00129        05    NEW-NAME.
00130              10    NEW-LAST-NAME                  PIC X(15).
00131              10    NEW-INITIALS                   PIC XX.
00132        05    NEW-DATE-OF-BIRTH.
00133              10    NEW-BIRTH-MONTH                PIC 99.
00134              10    NEW-BIRTH-YEAR                 PIC 99.
```

FIGURE 9.8 *continued*

```
00135              05   NEW-DATE-OF-HIRE.
00136                   10   NEW-HIRE-MONTH            PIC 99.
00137                   10   NEW-HIRE-YEAR             PIC 99.
00138              05   NEW-LOCATION-CODE              PIC X(3).
00139              05   NEW-PERFORMANCE-CODE           PIC X.
00140              05   NEW-EDUCATION-CODE             PIC X.
00141              05   NEW-TITLE-DATA OCCURS 2 TIMES.
00142                   10   NEW-TITLE-CODE            PIC 9(3).
00143                   10   NEW-TITLE-DATE            PIC 9(4).
00144              05   NEW-SALARY-DATA OCCURS 3 TIMES.
00145                   10   NEW-SALARY                PIC 9(5).
00146                   10   NEW-SALARY-DATE           PIC 9(4).
00147
00148         01   WS-BALANCE-LINE-SWITCHES.
00149              05   WS-ACTIVE-KEY                  PIC X(9).
00150              05   WS-RECORD-KEY-ALLOCATED-SWITCH PIC X(3).
00151
00152         PROCEDURE DIVISION.
00153         0010-UPDATE-MASTER-FILE.
00154             OPEN INPUT TRANSACTION-FILE
00155                        PROMOTION-FILE
00156                        OLD-MASTER-FILE
00157                  OUTPUT NEW-MASTER-FILE
00158                         DELETED-RECORD-FILE.
00159             PERFORM 0015-READ-PROMOTION-FILE.
00160             PERFORM 0020-READ-TRANSACTION-FILE.
00161             PERFORM 0030-READ-OLD-MASTER-FILE.
00162             PERFORM 0040-CHOOSE-ACTIVE-KEY.
00163             PERFORM 0050-PROCESS-ACTIVE-KEY
00164                 UNTIL WS-ACTIVE-KEY = HIGH-VALUES.
00165             CLOSE TRANSACTION-FILE
00166                   PROMOTION-FILE
00167                   OLD-MASTER-FILE
00168                   NEW-MASTER-FILE
00169                   DELETED-RECORD-FILE.
00170             STOP RUN.
00171
00172         0015-READ-PROMOTION-FILE.
00173             READ PROMOTION-FILE INTO WS-PROMOTION-RECORD
00174                 AT END MOVE HIGH-VALUES TO PR-SOC-SEC-NUMBER.
00175
00176         0020-READ-TRANSACTION-FILE.
00177             READ TRANSACTION-FILE INTO WS-TRANS-RECORD
00178                 AT END MOVE HIGH-VALUES TO TR-SOC-SEC-NUMBER.
00179
00180         0030-READ-OLD-MASTER-FILE.
00181             READ OLD-MASTER-FILE INTO WS-OLD-MAST-RECORD
00182                 AT END MOVE HIGH-VALUE TO OLD-SOC-SEC-NUMBER.
00183
00184         0040-CHOOSE-ACTIVE-KEY.
00185             IF TR-SOC-SEC-NUMBER LESS THAN OLD-SOC-SEC-NUMBER
00186                 IF TR-SOC-SEC-NUMBER LESS THAN PR-SOC-SEC-NUMBER
00187                     MOVE TR-SOC-SEC-NUMBER TO WS-ACTIVE-KEY
00188                 ELSE
00189                     MOVE PR-SOC-SEC-NUMBER TO WS-ACTIVE-KEY
00190             ELSE
00191                 IF PR-SOC-SEC-NUMBER LESS THAN OLD-SOC-SEC-NUMBER
00192                     MOVE PR-SOC-SEC-NUMBER TO WS-ACTIVE-KEY
00193                 ELSE
00194                     MOVE OLD-SOC-SEC-NUMBER TO WS-ACTIVE-KEY.
00195
00196         0050-PROCESS-ACTIVE-KEY.
00197             IF OLD-SOC-SEC-NUMBER = WS-ACTIVE-KEY
00198                 MOVE 'YES' TO WS-RECORD-KEY-ALLOCATED-SWITCH
00199                 PERFORM 0060-BUILD-NEW-MASTER
00200             ELSE
00201                 MOVE 'NO' TO WS-RECORD-KEY-ALLOCATED-SWITCH.
```

FIGURE 9.8 *continued*

```
00202
00203                PERFORM 0070-APPLY-TRANS-TO-MASTER
00204                    UNTIL WS-ACTIVE-KEY NOT EQUAL TR-SOC-SEC-NUMBER.
00205
00206                PERFORM 0075-APPLY-PROMO-TO-MASTER
00207                    UNTIL WS-ACTIVE-KEY NOT EQUAL PR-SOC-SEC-NUMBER.
00208
00209                IF WS-RECORD-KEY-ALLOCATED-SWITCH = 'YES'
00210                    PERFORM 0080-WRITE-NEW-MASTER.
00211
00212                PERFORM 0040-CHOOSE-ACTIVE-KEY.
00213
00214            0060-BUILD-NEW-MASTER.
00215                MOVE WS-OLD-MAST-RECORD TO WS-NEW-MAST-RECORD.
00216                PERFORM 0030-READ-OLD-MASTER-FILE.
00217
00218            0070-APPLY-TRANS-TO-MASTER.
00219                IF ADDITION
00220                    PERFORM 0090-ADD-NEW-RECORD
00221                ELSE
00222                    IF CORRECTION
00223                        PERFORM 0100-CORRECT-OLD-RECORD
00224                    ELSE
00225                        IF DELETION
00226                            PERFORM 0110-DELETE-OLD-RECORD.
00227
00228                PERFORM 0020-READ-TRANSACTION-FILE.
00229
00230            0075-APPLY-PROMO-TO-MASTER.
00231                IF PROMOTION
00232                    PERFORM 0120-DO-TITLE-UPDATE
00233                ELSE
00234                    IF SALARY-RAISE
00235                        PERFORM 0130-DO-SALARY-RAISE.
00236
00237                PERFORM 0015-READ-PROMOTION-FILE.
00238
00239            0080-WRITE-NEW-MASTER.
00240                WRITE NEW-MAST-RECORD FROM WS-NEW-MAST-RECORD.
00241
00242            0090-ADD-NEW-RECORD.
00243                IF WS-RECORD-KEY-ALLOCATED-SWITCH = 'YES'
00244                    DISPLAY '    '
00245                    DISPLAY '   ERROR DUPLICATE ADDITION: '
00246                    DISPLAY '     TRANSACTION IN ERROR: ' WS-TRANS-RECORD
00247                ELSE
00248                    MOVE 'YES' TO WS-RECORD-KEY-ALLOCATED-SWITCH
00249                    MOVE SPACES TO WS-NEW-MAST-RECORD
00250                    MOVE TR-SOC-SEC-NUMBER TO NEW-SOC-SEC-NUMBER
00251                    MOVE TR-NAME TO NEW-NAME
00252                    MOVE TR-DATE-OF-BIRTH TO NEW-DATE-OF-BIRTH
00253                    MOVE TR-DATE-OF-HIRE TO NEW-DATE-OF-HIRE
00254                    MOVE TR-PERFORMANCE-CODE TO NEW-PERFORMANCE-CODE
00255                    MOVE TR-EDUCATION-CODE TO NEW-EDUCATION-CODE
00256                    MOVE TR-TITLE-DATA TO NEW-TITLE-DATA (1)
00257                    MOVE TR-SALARY-DATA TO NEW-SALARY-DATA (1).
00258
00259            0100-CORRECT-OLD-RECORD.
00260                IF WS-RECORD-KEY-ALLOCATED-SWITCH = 'YES'
00261                    PERFORM 0105-CORRECT-INDIVIDUAL-FIELDS
00262                ELSE
00263                    DISPLAY '    '
00264                    DISPLAY '   ERROR-NO MATCHING RECORD: '
00265                    DISPLAY '     TRANSACTION IN ERROR: ' WS-TRANS-RECORD.
00266
00267            0105-CORRECT-INDIVIDUAL-FIELDS.
00268                IF TR-NAME NOT EQUAL SPACES
```

FIGURE 9.8 *continued*

```
00269                         MOVE TR-NAME TO NEW-NAME.
00270                     IF TR-DATE-OF-BIRTH NOT EQUAL SPACES
00271                         MOVE TR-DATE-OF-BIRTH TO NEW-DATE-OF-BIRTH.
00272                     IF TR-DATE-OF-HIRE NOT EQUAL SPACES
00273                         MOVE TR-DATE-OF-HIRE TO NEW-DATE-OF-HIRE.
00274                     IF TR-LOCATION-CODE NOT EQUAL SPACES
00275                         MOVE TR-LOCATION-CODE TO NEW-LOCATION-CODE.
00276                     IF  TR-PERFORMANCE-CODE NOT EQUAL SPACES
00277                         MOVE TR-PERFORMANCE-CODE TO NEW-PERFORMANCE-CODE.
00278                     IF TR-EDUCATION-CODE NOT EQUAL SPACES
00279                         MOVE TR-EDUCATION-CODE TO NEW-EDUCATION-CODE
00280                     IF TR-TITLE-CODE IS NUMERIC
00281                         MOVE TR-TITLE-CODE TO NEW-TITLE-CODE (1).
00282                     IF TR-TITLE-DATE IS NUMERIC
00283                         MOVE TR-TITLE-DATE TO NEW-TITLE-DATE (1).
00284                     IF TR-SALARY IS NUMERIC
00285                         MOVE TR-SALARY TO NEW-SALARY (1).
00286                     IF TR-SALARY-DATE IS NUMERIC
00287                         MOVE TR-SALARY-DATE TO NEW-SALARY-DATE (1).
00288
00289                 0110-DELETE-OLD-RECORD.
00290                     IF WS-RECORD-KEY-ALLOCATED-SWITCH = 'YES'
00291                         WRITE DELETED-RECORD FROM WS-NEW-MAST-RECORD
00292                     ELSE
00293                         DISPLAY ' '
00294                         DISPLAY '   ERROR-NO MATCHING RECORD: '
00295                         DISPLAY '     TRANSACTION IN ERROR: ' WS-TRANS-RECORD.
00296
00297                 0120-DO-TITLE-UPDATE.
00298                     IF WS-RECORD-KEY-ALLOCATED-SWITCH = 'YES'
00299                         MOVE PR-TITLE-CODE TO NEW-TITLE-CODE (1)
00300                         MOVE PR-TITLE-DATE TO NEW-TITLE-DATE (1)
00301                         MOVE NEW-TITLE-CODE (1) TO NEW-TITLE-CODE (2)
00302                         MOVE NEW-TITLE-DATE (1) TO NEW-TITLE-DATE (2)
00303                     ELSE
00304                         DISPLAY '   '
00305                         DISPLAY '   ERROR-NO MATCHING RECORD: '
00306                         DISPLAY '     PROMOTION IN ERROR: ' WS-PROMOTION-RECORD.
00307
00308                 0130-DO-SALARY-RAISE.
00309                     IF WS-RECORD-KEY-ALLOCATED-SWITCH = 'YES'
00310                         MOVE NEW-SALARY (2) TO NEW-SALARY (3)
00311                         MOVE NEW-SALARY-DATE (2) TO NEW-SALARY-DATE (3)
00312                         MOVE NEW-SALARY (1) TO NEW-SALARY (2)
00313                         MOVE NEW-SALARY-DATE (1) TO NEW-SALARY-DATE (2)
00314                         MOVE PR-SALARY TO NEW-SALARY (1)
00315                         MOVE PR-SALARY-DATE TO NEW-SALARY-DATE (1)
00316                     ELSE
00317                         DISPLAY '   '
00318                         DISPLAY '   ERROR-NO MATCHING RECORD: '
00319                         DISPLAY '     PROMOTION IN ERROR: ' WS-PROMOTION-RECORD.
```

FIGURE 9.8 *continued*

Exercise 9.4—Report Writer

This exercise is based on the Report Writer listing of Figure 8.3. Input to the invalid program was shown in Figure 8.1, with the intent of producing output identical to Figure 8.2. Instead, the *erroneous* output of Figure 9.9 resulted. Note well the following errors:

1. Some, but not all, salesman totals are wrong; e.g., Tater is correct at $2,930, but Lavor should be $16,500 rather than the $6,500 shown.

2. Location totals are too high; e.g., Chicago's total should be $19,430 rather than the $25,360 shown.
3. The final total is also too high.
4. The transaction number prints only for the first transaction of every salesman; e.g., 888888 appears for Lee, but 905432 is missing.
5. The literal 'SALES ACTIVITY FOR' is missing in the location heading.

Find and correct all errors in the program of Figure 9.10.

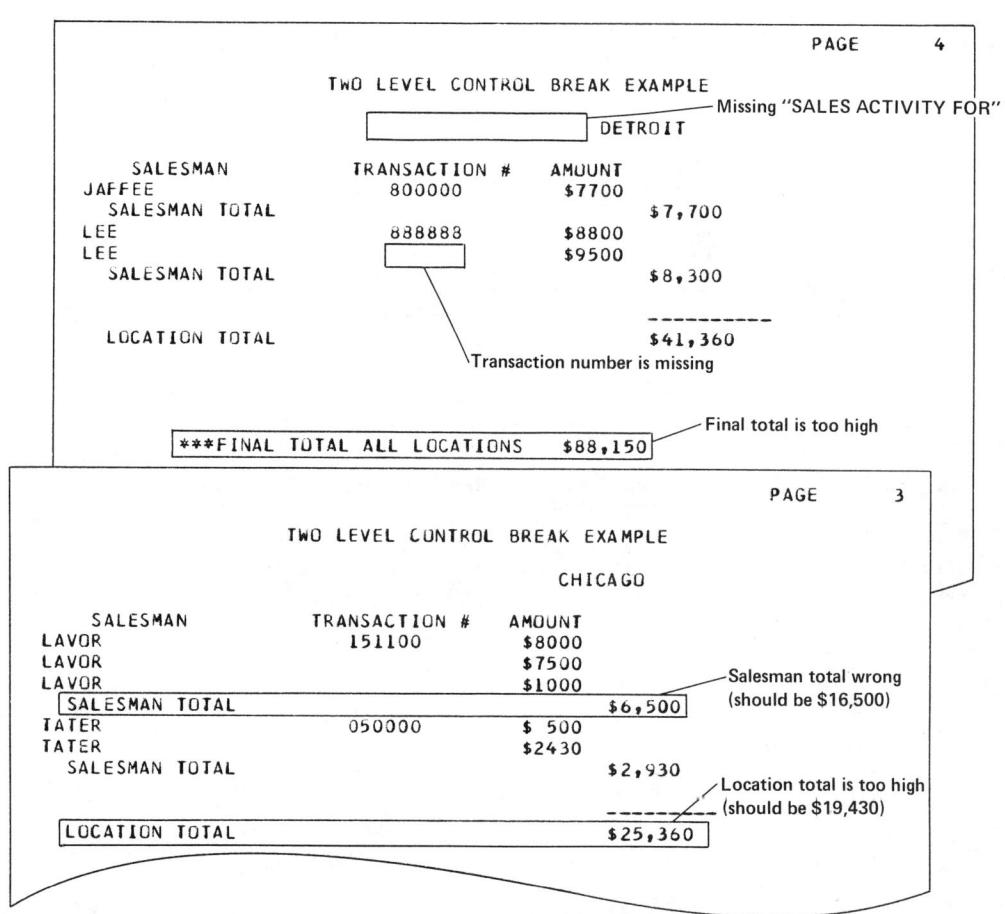

FIGURE 9.9 Erroneous output (produced by Figure 9.10).

```
00001              IDENTIFICATION DIVISION.
00002              PROGRAM-ID.  ERWONE.
00003              AUTHOR..     R. GRAUER.
00004
00005              ENVIRONMENT DIVISION.
00006              CONFIGURATION SECTION.
00007              SOURCE-COMPUTER.    IBM-4341.
00008              OBJECT-COMPUTER.    IBM-4341.
00009              INPUT-OUTPUT SECTION.
00010              FILE-CONTROL.
00011                  SELECT SALES-FILE
00012                      ASSIGN TO UT-S-SALES.
00013                  SELECT PRINT-FILE
00014                      ASSIGN TO UT-S-REPORT.
00015
00016              DATA DIVISION.
00017              FILE SECTION.
00018              FD  SALES-FILE
00019                  LABEL RECORDS ARE OMITTED
00020                  BLOCK CONTAINS 0 RECORDS
00021                  RECORD CONTAINS 80 CHARACTERS
00022                  DATA RECORD IS SALES-RECORD.
00023              01  SALES-RECORD                PIC X(80).
00024
00025              FD  PRINT-FILE
00026                  REPORT IS CONTROL-BREAK
00027                  LABEL RECORDS ARE OMITTED
00028                  RECORD CONTAINS 133 CHARACTERS.
00029
00030              WORKING-STORAGE SECTION.
00031              01  FILLER                      PIC X(14)
00032                  VALUE 'WS BEGINS HERE'.
00033              01  WS-DATA-FLAG                PIC X(3)       VALUE SPACES.
00034
00035              01  TRANSACTION-AREA.
00036                  05  TR-SALESMAN-NAME        PIC X(20).
00037                  05  TR-AMOUNT               PIC S9(4).
00038                  05  FILLER                  PIC XX.
00039                  05  TR-NUMBER               PIC X(6).
00040                  05  TR-TYPE                 PIC X.
00041                  05  TR-SALESMAN-REGION      PIC X(17).
00042                  05  TR-SALESMAN-LOCATION    PIC X(20).
00043                  05  FILLER                  PIC X(10).
00044
00045              01  FILLER                      PIC X(12)
00046                  VALUE 'WS ENDS HERE'.
00047
00048              REPORT SECTION.
00049              RD  CONTROL-BREAK
00050                  CONTROLS ARE FINAL TR-SALESMAN-LOCATION TR-SALESMAN-NAME
00051                  PAGE LIMIT 50 LINES
00052                  HEADING 1
00053                  FIRST DETAIL 5
00054                  LAST DETAIL 45
00055                  FOOTING 48.
00056
00057              01  TYPE IS PAGE HEADING.
00058                  05  LINE NUMBER 1.
00059                      10  COLUMN NUMBER 61    PIC X(4)
00060                          VALUE 'PAGE'.
00061                      10  COLUMN NUMBER 66    PIC ZZZZZ9
00062                          SOURCE PAGE-COUNTER.
00063                  05  LINE NUMBER PLUS 2.
00064                      10  COLUMN NUMBER 22    PIC X(31)
00065                          VALUE 'TWO LEVEL CONTROL BREAK EXAMPLE'.
00066
```

FIGURE 9.10 Erroneous Report Writer.

```
00067            01  TYPE IS CONTROL HEADING TR-SALESMAN-LOCATION.
00068                05  LINE NUMBER 5.
00069                    10  COLUMN NUMBER 44        PIC X(18)
00070                            VALUE 'SALES ACTIVITY FOR'.
00071                    10  COLUMN NUMBER 44        PIC X(20)
00072                            SOURCE TR-SALESMAN-LOCATION.
00073                05  LINE NUMBER 7.
00074                    10  COLUMN NUMBER 6         PIC X(8)
00075                            VALUE 'SALESMAN'.
00076                    10  COLUMN NUMBER 24        PIC X(13)
00077                            VALUE 'TRANSACTION #'.
00078                    10  COLUMN NUMBER 40        PIC X(7)
00079                            VALUE 'AMOUNT'.
00080
00081            01  TRANSACTION-LINE TYPE IS DETAIL.
00082                05  LINE NUMBER PLUS 1.
00083                    10  COLUMN NUMBER 2         PIC X(20)
00084                            SOURCE TR-SALESMAN-NAME.
00085                    10  COLUMN NUMBER 27        PIC X(6)
00086                            GROUP INDICATE
00087                            SOURCE TR-NUMBER.
00088                    10  COLUMN NUMBER 41        PIC $ZZZ9
00089                            SOURCE TR-AMOUNT.
00090
00091            01  TYPE IS CONTROL FOOTING TR-SALESMAN-NAME.
00092                05  LINE NUMBER PLUS 1.
00093                    10  COLUMN NUMBER 4         PIC X(15)
00094                            VALUE 'SALESMAN TOTAL'.
00095                    10  SALESMAN-TOTAL
00096                        COLUMN NUMBER 48        PIC   $$,$$9
00097                            SUM TR-AMOUNT.
00098
00099            01  TYPE IS CONTROL FOOTING TR-SALESMAN-LOCATION.
00100                05  LINE NUMBER PLUS 2.
00101                    10  COLUMN NUMBER 48        PIC X(10)
00102                            VALUE ALL '-'.
00103                05  LINE NUMBER PLUS 1.
00104                    10  COLUMN NUMBER 4         PIC X(14)
00105                            VALUE 'LOCATION TOTAL'.
00106                    10  LOCATION-TOTAL
00107                        COLUMN NUMBER 48        PIC $$$,$$9
00108                            SUM SALESMAN-TOTAL RESET ON FINAL.
00109
00110            01  TYPE IS CONTROL FOOTING FINAL.
00111                05  LINE NUMBER PLUS 5.
00112                    10  COLUMN NUMBER 10        PIC X(28)
00113                            VALUE '***FINAL TOTAL ALL LOCATIONS'.
00114                    10  COLUMN NUMBER 40        PIC $$$$,$$9
00115                            SUM LOCATION-TOTAL.
00116
00117         PROCEDURE DIVISION.
00118         0010-CREATE-REPORTS.
00119             OPEN INPUT SALES-FILE
00120                  OUTPUT PRINT-FILE.
00121             INITIATE CONTROL-BREAK.
00122             READ SALES-FILE INTO TRANSACTION-AREA
00123                 AT END MOVE 'NO' TO WS-DATA-FLAG.
00124             PERFORM 0020-PROCESS-ALL-TRANSACTIONS
00125                 UNTIL WS-DATA-FLAG = 'NO'.
00126             TERMINATE CONTROL-BREAK.
00127             CLOSE SALES-FILE
00128                   PRINT-FILE.
00129             STOP RUN.
00130
00131         0020-PROCESS-ALL-TRANSACTIONS.
00132             GENERATE TRANSACTION-LINE.
00133             READ SALES-FILE INTO TRANSACTION-AREA
00134                 AT END MOVE 'NO' TO WS-DATA-FLAG.
```

FIGURE 9.10 *continued*

Solutions

The author thought long and hard about including solutions directly in the text. In the end, he felt he had to, both in fairness to the reader, and for their pedagogical value. It is one thing merely to warn against a missing or extra period; it is quite another to observe the results first-hand in a non-functioning program. Accordingly, review the following solutions and explanations with your own findings.

Exercise 9.1

The first error, a $200 total for Baker rather than a $400 credit, illustrates the effect of omitting an "S" in the definition of a signed number. Simply stated, *if the S is omitted, then the result of any arithmetic operation will always be made positive.* The first transaction, number 444444, is a $100 return and is therefore subtracted from THIS-SALESMAN-TOTAL in line 147. However, because the latter field is *unsigned* (i.e., the "S" is missing in the picture clauses of lines 39, 40, and 41), THIS-SALESMAN-TOTAL assumes a value of *plus* 100. The second transaction, 555555, causes 300 to be subtracted from 100, temporarily producing a value of minus 200. Again, the omitted sign causes the result of the operation to become positive. THIS-SALESMAN-TOTAL is eventually moved to PRT-SALESMAN-TOTAL and the latter field contains CR in its edited picture. However, since THIS-SALESMAN-TOTAL is always positive (because of the omitted sign), CR will not appear in the printed report.

The error for Smith is more subtle and indicates a problem in the control break mechanism. Recall that there are two control breaks, on location and salesman, as the major and minor controls, respectively. In the test data of Figure 2.6a, the last salesman in Atlanta has the *same* name as the first salesman in Boston. A break on salesman should occur when *either name or location changes*, but the perform statement of lines 131–133 omits the test for a location break. The problem is corrected by inserting the clause OR TR-LOCATION NOT EQUAL WS-PREVIOUS-LOCATION after line 132.

The miniscule company total of $734.56 suggests that COMPANY-TOTAL is not being incremented. This in turn implies a missing ADD statement, but line 144 is in its proper place. It is *not*, however, an executable statement because it has been inadvertently asterisked out; i.e., *the asterisk in column 7 causes line 144 to be treated as a comment.* (The reader should be able to deduce how the total of $734.56 was arrived at. The subtract statement of line 149 functions properly; however, due to the omitted sign in its picture clause, COMPANY-TOTAL always assumes a positive value as per the previous discussion.)

The final error has to do with the *cumulative* nature of the location totals, suggesting that location total is not being reset to zero. A careful check of the program indicates that the statement MOVE ZEROS TO THIS-LOCATION-TOTAL is required after line 121.

Exercise 9.2

The calculated ages are *almost* correct, but in fact are wrong; e.g., Baker's calculated age is 25.0 when it should have been 24.9 (as in Figure 3.17). Attention is initially directed to lines 236–237 which compute age. After some careful checking, however, perhaps by plugging in numbers, the reader should conclude that the compute statement is *correct as written*.

What, then, is the problem? Simply this: *If there is nothing wrong with the statement to calculate age, then there may be something wrong with the data on which the compute statement operates.* Proceeding with this line of logic, we see that TODAYS-YEAR and TODAYS-MONTH are defined in Working-Storage (lines 104–107) as part of DATE-WORK-AREA. The latter is initialized by the ACCEPT statement of line 235, and therein lies the problem. The ACCEPT statement references DAY, a COBOL reserved word for the Julian date in the form yyddd, whereas DATE-WORK-AREA was formatted yymmdd. The problem is solved by substituting DATE for DAY in line 234. This error is one the author almost missed. He initially ran his programs on January 14, 1982, a date on which the ages were calculated *correctly*. This is because the first 4 digits of the Julian date, 82014, were *coincidentally* equal to the first four digits of the *calendar* date, 820114.

A similar line of reasoning also holds with the table lookups (school, major, and course). Examination of the Procedure Division code reveals that the logic for all three lookups is correct, leading one to believe that the problems lie with the tables themselves. Consider first lines 15–23 of the subroutine ESUB2 (Figure 9.6), which establishes the school table. *Four* codes are initialized in lines 17–20, but *six* values are implied by the OCCURS clause of line 23. (Note that the total number of bytes is 48 in lines 17–20 and again in line 23, otherwise a compilation error would result.) Each school value is assigned 8 bytes instead of the desired 12; SCHOOL (1) = 'BUSINESS' and is still correct; SCHOOL (2) = '   LIBE'; SCHOOL (3) = 'RAL ARTS' (the value shown for Baker in Figure 9.3), and so on. The problem is solved by changing the OCCURS clause in line 23.

The SEARCH and associated SET statement for MAJOR are correct (lines 59–63), as is the table definition in lines 25–44. Again, the problem resides in the data on which the SEARCH statement is operating, but this time in the incoming code and expanded value LS-MAJOR-CODE and LS-MAJOR-VALUE. These fields are defined in the Linkage Section with picture clauses of X(4) and X(14), respectively. These definitions are *inconsistent* with those in the calling program of X(3) and X(15) (lines 92 and 93 in Figure 9.4). The parameters are passed incorrectly and the SEARCH statement doesn't have a chance.

A secondary question is why 'N,' rather than 'unknown,' prints when the AT END condition is reached. This is attributed to line 61 in which UNKNOWN is moved to LS-MAJOR-CODE rather than LS-MAJOR-VALUE. The inconsistent picture clauses cause the *fourth* character of LS-MAJOR-CODE; i.e., the letter N, to correspond to the *first* character of WS-MAJOR-VALUE in the *main* program, causing N to appear in the printed report.

The error in the course expansion is also in the table itself, rather than the logic to do the course expansion. In Figure 9.5, the table of course codes is initialized dynamically by reading values from a file. (This technique was discussed in Chapter 3 as the most desirable way of establishing a table.) Recall that the purpose of WS-ALREADY-EXECUTED-SWITCH is to ensure that the initialization procedure is done only once; i.e., the first time the subprogram is called. The course table is *variable* length as per the OCCURS DEPENDING ON clause of line 33, but the value of WS-NUMBER-OF-COURSES is never incremented. The SEARCH ALL statement of lines 69-73 is dependent on a correct value for WS-NUMBER-OF-COURSES in order to execute a binary search. The solution is to insert the statement ADD 1 TO WS-NUMBER-OF-COURSES after line 88.

The problem of five courses printing, instead of six, is easily corrected by *changing the equal sign in line 256 to a greater than sign*. The perform statement increments, tests, and then branches; hence, to execute a procedure *n* times, one must specify *greater than n* in the condition portion of the perform.

The improper program termination resulted because STOP RUN appeared in the output procedure (line 203 of Figure 9.4). The SORT statement transfers control to the *section* specified in the input procedure, then to the sort utility, then to the *section* specified in the output procedure, and finally to the line immediately after the sort statement itself. The latter transfer takes place regardless of what happens in the output procedure; hence, the program is trying to continue execution after STOP RUN has been executed. The problem is corrected by placing STOP RUN after line 172.

Exercise 9.3

The first error attempts to force the reader to switch from one train of thought to another, and to sense when he or she has reached a dead end. All salary raises, both valid and invalid, are ignored. Initially, one considers the paragraph 0130-DO-SALARY-RAISE, but to no avail. Reversing directions, one may postulate that the paragraph is never called, causing one to go up a level on the hierarchy chart and examine 0075-APPLY-PROMO-TO-MASTER. The logic in that paragraph is also correct, so perhaps there is a difficulty in the *data* on which the paragraph operates. Sure enough, the *value* of the 88-level entry SALARY-RAISE is "S" (line 102), rather than "R," as in the actual transactions. Accordingly, the IF statement of line 234 is never satisfied, and 0130-DO-SALARY-RAISE is never performed.

The second error directs us immediately to the paragraph 0120-DO-

TITLE-UPDATE, where lines 299–300 are out of place; i.e., lines 299–300 should appear after line 302. The ease with which this error is corrected emphasizes the desirability of having strong *functional* paragraphs; i.e., an error in the title update procedure could only have occurred in one place, the title update paragraph.

The location of the third error is also readily apparent from the strong *functional* nature of the paragraph 0110-DELETE-OLD-RECORD. We see that the deleted record is written to the deleted record file. It is also written to the new master file because we neglected to set WS-RECORD-KEY-ALLOCATED-SWITCH to 'NO' in the delete paragraph.

The location code is missing from the new employee record because of a *missing* MOVE statement in the paragraph 0090-ADD-NEW-RECORD. One may think that the failure to correct an invalid title is also attributable to a missing statement in the module 0105-CORRECT-INDIVIDUAL-FIELDS, but lines 280 and 281 are correct as written. The latter problem is caused by a *missing period* in line 279 which has the effect of creating a nested IF in lines 278–281. In other words, TR-TITLE-CODE will be corrected only if TR-EDUCATION-CODE is also corrected.

Exercise 9.4

The errors in this exercise are straightforward, and should present little difficulty to anyone who understood the material in Chapter 8. The first problem should direct the reader immediately to the SUM clause of lines 96 and 97 in the control footing for TR-SALESMAN-NAME. The clue is that Lavor's total should be $16,500 rather than $6,500, which points to the picture clause as being too small. (In truth, this is one error which would not occur in conventional COBOL, because if one tried *explicitly* to move a field with PIC 9(5) to one with PIC $$,$$9, the compiler would produce a warning diagnostic. Unfortunately, no such warning is produced under Report Writer, and hence the error in execution.)

The second error is corrected by *eliminating* the RESET clause in line 108. Recall that totals are *automatically* reset to zero at the time of the current control break, and that the *RESET clause is used only if the total is to be reset at a higher level.* Inclusion of RESET ON FINAL has the effect of making location total cumulative from location to location; i.e., it is never reset to zero until after the final control break has occurred.

The total for the final control footing is computed by summing the individual location totals in line 115. Since location total is wrong as per the previous error, the final total will also be incorrect. No additional corrections are required.

One might attribute the missing literal in the location control heading to a simple omission, but lines 69 and 70 do contain the information. However lines 69 and 71 *both* specify column 44; hence the literal is *overlaid* before it is written; the correction is to change line 69 to specify column 25.

The fifth and final error is corrected by removing the GROUP INDI-

CATE clause of line 86. This clause was introduced in Figure 8.7 as a means of printing an elementary item in *only the first occurrence* after a control break. It was specifically requested in the output of Figure 8.6, but is erroneous in the present situation.

Summary

Debugging remains a fact of life, so much so that the average programmer probably spends as much time on debugging as on initial coding. Unlike the COBOL language, however, debugging cannot be taught explicitly. An individual learns from experience and by trial and error. The same problems continually occur, albeit in different forms. An important skill is knowing what to look for, and the reader may wish to review the common errors listed at the beginning of the chapter.

One should approach debugging with an open mind; suspect everything and eliminate nothing. The most difficult task is to maintain objectivity, and to know when you've hit a dead end. Avoid rehashing the same ideas, and try to let your mind "float" to different approaches. In Exercise 9.2, for example, we were stuck on the table lookups for school and course, then switched successfully from the table lookups to the tables themselves.

If all else fails, know when to stop. Everyone reaches a point where the coffee tastes bitter, the cigarettes are lousy, and no further productive thinking is possible. Stop! Put the problem away, go home, get a good night's sleep or whatever, and get a fresh start in the morning. You'll be surprised at what a difference a few hours can make. Moreover, the mind is funny in that the subconscious continues to work at a problem, and as often as not, the solution will come when you least expect it.

Debugging tends to be more art than science. There are no guaranteed debugging procedures, only debugging aids. A bug will not leap from the pages of a program, but must be coaxed out by logic, perseverance, and even luck. In short, debugging is an incomparable source of both frustration and satisfaction.

A The Next COBOL Standard

Overview

At its inception in 1959, COBOL was designed as "open ended and capable of accepting change and amendment." The revision process is the province of the COBOL committee of CODASYL (COnference on DAta SYstems Languages) which meets periodically to publish a JOD (Journal of Development). This document is submitted to the X3J4 Technical Committee of the American National Standards Institute (ANSI) which publishes the actual standard. To date, there have been two official standards; COBOL-68 and COBOL-74, the last version known officially as American National Standard COBOL X3.23-1974.

In 1977, the X3J4 committee began revising the 1974 standard based on the CODASYL JOD of 1976. Four intermediate publications, COBOL Information Bulletins 17, 18, 19, and 20, provided the public with its first glimpse of what to expect. (CODASYL subsequently published a JOD in 1978 which revised the 1976 publication.) Finally, in June 1981 the X3J4 committee completed its work and approved the content of a draft proposal to revise ANS COBOL X3.23-1974. The draft was made available in September 1981 for public review and comment. The review period ended in February 1982, and the comments received were overwhelmingly negative. Copies of the draft document may be obtained for $25.00 from:

> CBEMA/X3 Secretarial Staff
> 1828 L Street N.W.
> Washington, D.C. 20036

Different Versions of the Standard

The official ANSI document divides the COBOL language into 11 functional modules: Nucleus, Sequential I-O, Relative I-O, Indexed I-O, Inter-Program Communication, Segmentation, Sort-Merge, Source Text Manipulation, Debug, Report-Writer, and Communication. Some vendors do not include all 11 modules in their compilers; for example, Report-Writer is not implemented in many otherwise standard ANS-74 compilers. In addition, 8 of the 11 modules are divided into *level 1 and level 2* elements, with the former a subset of the latter. Hence, not every compiler has every feature. Finally, most vendors, IBM especially, include extensions to the standard to reflect special features of their hardware and/or operating system.

Highlights

The draft proposal consists of several hundred pages which can make for rather dry reading. Accordingly, the author highlights the more significant changes, particularly those relating directly to structured programming. We begin by listing changes which ought *not* to affect existing programs, followed by a second list which *will* impact existing code. It is the latter list which has sparked the controversy surrounding the new standard, *containing as it does significant incompatibility with existing programs.*

This discussion was written in March 1982 and refers to a *proposed* rather than an approved standard. Consequently, some of the discussion may not be applicable to the final version. Realize also that there is a significant delay, *often several years*, between approval of a new standard and the availability of a supporting compiler.

Changes Not Affecting Existing Programs

The proposed revision lists 89 changes which will *not* affect existing programs. Many of these pertain to seldom used features, while others appear to be change merely for the sake of change. Nevertheless, there are some significant improvements and the author has *arbitrarily* selected a list of 27, which he deems to be most interesting or useful. (The reader is referred to pages XVII-37-43 of the draft proposal for the complete list.)

1. *Nonnumeric literal.* A nonnumeric literal will have an upper limit of 160 characters as opposed to 120.
2. *Qualification.* 50 levels of qualification are supported as opposed to 5.
3. *Subscripting.* A table may have up to 48 dimensions; the old limit was 3. (See the concluding discussion in the section entitled Public Reaction.)
4. *Relative subscripting.* A subscript may be followed by the operators + or -, followed by an integer. (The current standard permits relative indexing, but *not* relative subscripting.)
5. *Reference modification.* Reference modification can address a string of characters *within* another string by specifying the leftmost character and length for the data item. For example the statements:

    ```
    05   DATA-NAME    PIC X(10)    VALUE 'ABCDEFGHIJ'.

    MOVE DATA-NAME (6:2) TO FIELD-A.
    ```

    will move "FG" to FIELD-A: i.e., reference modification of DATA-NAME begins at the 6th character for a length of 2.
6. *Sequence number.* The sequence number may contain any character in the computer's character set as opposed to only digits.
7. *INITIAL clause in PROGRAM-ID paragraph.* The INITIAL clause specifies that a program is to be initialized, whenever it is called.
8. *Environment Division.* The Environment Division is optional, and within the Environment Division, the Configuration Section is optional. The SOURCE-COMPUTER and OBJECT-COMPUTER paragraphs, the entries within the FILE-CONTROL paragraph, and the entries within the I-O-CONTROL paragraph are also optional.
9. *FILLER clause.* Use of the word FILLER is optional for data description entries. The word FILLER can appear in a data description entry containing a REDEFINES clause. The word FILLER may be used in a data description entry of a group item.
10. *OCCURS clause.* The data item in the DEPENDING ON phrase may have a zero value. Thus, the minimum number of occurrences may be zero.
11. *REDEFINES clause.* The size of the item associated with the REDEFINES clause may be less than or equal to the size of the redefined item.
12. *DAY-OF-WEEK phrase of ACCEPT statement.* The DAY-OF-

WEEK phrase of the ACCEPT statement provides access to an integer representing the day of week; for example, 1 represents Monday, 2 represents Tuesday, etc.

13. *ADD statement.* The word TO is an optional word in the format: ADD identifier/literal TO identifier/literal GIVING identifier.

14. *CALL statement.* The parameters passed in a CALL statement can be other than an 01 or 77-level data item.

15. *CONTINUE statement.* The CONTINUE statement causes an implicit transfer of control to the next executable statement.

16. *EVALUATE statement.* The EVALUATE statement describes a multibranch situation to implement the case construct of structured programming. It is discussed in detail later in the appendix.

17. *EXIT PROGRAM statement.* EXIT PROGRAM need not be the only statement in a paragraph.

18. *IF statement.* THEN has been added as an optional word. The IF statement also has an END-IF delimiter as described in a subsequent section.

19. *INITIALIZE statement.* The INITIALIZE statement provides the ability to set selected types of data fields to predetermined values.

20. *MERGE statement.* Multiple file-names are allowed in the GIVING phrase of the MERGE statement. A file named in either the USING or GIVING phrase of a MERGE statement can be a relative file or an indexed file.

21. *MOVE statement.* A numeric edited data item may be moved to a numeric data item; thus de-editing takes place.

22. *PERFORM statement.* Procedure-name may be omitted resulting in an in-line PERFORM of the imperative statements preceding the END-PERFORM phrase terminating the PERFORM statement. (See the section on Structured Programming Enhancements.)

23. *PERFORM statement.* The TEST AFTER phrase causes the condition to be tested *after* the specified set of statements have been executed. The TEST BEFORE phrase causes the condition to be tested before the specified set of statements are executed.

24. *PERFORM statement.* The number of AFTER phrases permitted in the VARYING phrase of the PERFORM statement is unlimited; a maximum of two AFTER phrases existed previously.

25. *READ statement.* Variable length records are allowed with the INTO phrase. The READ statement is allowed subsequent to an at end condition.

26. *RETURN statement.* Variable length records are allowed with the INTO phrase. The RETURN statement is allowed subsequent to an at end condition.

27. *SORT statement.* Multiple file-names are allowed in the GIVING phrase of the SORT statement. A file named in a SORT statement may contain variable length records. A file named in either the USING or GIVING phrase of a SORT statement can be a relative file or an indexed file. Records whose key values are identical remain in the same order as they were when they were input to the sort process after the sort process is completed.

Changes Potentially Affecting Existing Programs

This section is responsible for the controversy surrounding the proposed standard because of the *incompatibility* with its predecessor. The author has included *verbatim* 44 of the 45 proposals, omitting only the 25 new status codes listed in the 45th item. The numbers in parentheses indicate the module and level to which the change applies:

1. *Character substitution (1 NUC).* The rule that permits the substitution of double characters for a single COBOL character when the computer's character set has less than 51 characters has been deleted. However, substitution of a single character may be specified but is not required.
2. *Length of ALL literal (2 NUC).* When the figurative constant ALL literal is not associated with another data item, the length of the string is the length of the literal. The length was one in X3.23-1974.
3. *ALL literal and numeric or numeric edited data item (2 NUC).* The figurative constant ALL literal cannot be associated with a numeric or numeric edited data item.
4. *Special register DEBUG-ITEM (1 DEB).* The implicit description of the special register DEBUG-ITEM has been changed.
5. *MEMORY SIZE clause (1 NUC).* The MEMORY SIZE clause of the OBJECT-COMPUTER paragraph has been deleted.
6. *Alphabet-name clause (1 NUC).* The word ALPHABET is now required before alphabet-name within the alphabet-name clause of the SPECIAL-NAMES paragraph.
7. *Collating sequence (1 INX).* The collating sequence used to access an indexed file is the collating sequence associated with the native character set that was in effect for the file at the time the file was created.
8. *CURRENCY SIGN clause (1 NUC).* The literal specified within the CURRENCY SIGN clause may not be a figurative constant.
9. *RELATIVE KEY phrase (1 REL).* The relative key data item

specified in the RELATIVE KEY phrase must not contain the PICTURE symbol 'P'.

10. *MULTIPLE FILE TAPE clause (2 SEQ)*. Each file in a series of files sharing the same physical reel of tape must be created with a uniform labeling convention. A sort or merge file may not be specified in the MULTIPLE FILE TAPE clause.

11. *RERUN clause (1 SEQ, 1 REL, 1 INX)*. The RERUN clause of the I-O-CONTROL paragraph has been deleted.

12. *LINAGE clause (2 SEQ)*. Files for which the LINAGE clause has been specified must not be opened in the EXTEND mode.

13. *OCCURS clause (2 NUC)*. When a receiving item is a variable length data item and contains the object of the DEPENDING ON phrase, the maximum length of the item will be used. In X3.23-1974 the actual length was used.

14. *PICTURE symbol 'P' (1 NUC)*. When a data item described by a PICTURE containing the character 'P' is referenced, the digit positions specified by 'P' will be considered to contain zeros only when the reference requires a numeric item or when the data item is moved to a numeric or numeric edited item, or compared to a numeric item. In X3.23-1974 such digit positions were considered to contain zeros when used in an operation involving conversion of data from one form of internal representation to another.

15. *Order of execution for a conditional expression (2 NUC)*. The constituent connected conditions within a hierarchical level are evaluated in order from left to right, and evaluation of that hierarchical level terminates as soon as a truth value for it is determined regardless of whether all the constituent connected conditions within that hierarchical level have been evaluated.

16. *Class condition (1 NUC)*. The ALPHABETIC test is true for uppercase letters, lowercase letters, and space character. The ALPHABETIC-UPPER test is true for uppercase letters and space character. The ALPHABETIC-LOWER test is true for lowercase letters and space character. In X3.23-1974 the ALPHABETIC test was true for uppercase letters and space character.

17. *ALTER statement (1 NUC)*. The ALTER statement has been deleted. (See discussion in the section on Public Reaction.)

18. *CANCEL statement (2 IPC)*. The CANCEL statement closes all open files.

19. *CLOSE statement (2 SEQ)*. The NO REWIND phrase cannot be specified in a CLOSE statement having the REEL/UNIT phrase.

20. *DISABLE statement (2 COM)*. The KEY phrase of the DISABLE statement has been deleted.

21. *DIVIDE statement (2 NUC)*. Any subscripts for identifier-4 in the REMAINDER phrase are evaluated after the result of the DIVIDE operation is stored in identifier-3 of the GIVING phrase.
22. *ENABLE statement (2 COM)*. The KEY phrase of the ENABLE statement has been deleted.
23. *ENTER statement (1 NUC)*. The ENTER statement has been deleted.
24. *EXIT PROGRAM statement (1 IPC)*. When there is no next executable statement in a called program, an implicit EXIT PROGRAM statement is executed. This situation was undefined in X3.23-1974.
25. *EXIT PROGRAM statement (1 IPC)*. The following new rule appears for the EXIT PROGRAM statement: ". . . the ends of the ranges of all PERFORM statements executed by the called program are considered to have been reached." This situation was undefined in X3.23-1974.
26. *INSPECT statement (2 NUC)*. The order of execution for evaluating subscripts in the INSPECT statement is specified. This situation was undefined in X3.23-1974.
27. *MERGE statement (1 SRT)*. No two files in a MERGE statement may be specified in the SAME AREA or SAME SORT-MERGE AREA clause. The only files in a MERGE statement that can be specified in the SAME RECORD AREA clause are those associated with the GIVING phrase.
28. *OPEN I-O or EXTEND statement (1 SEQ, 1 REL, 1 INX)*. The I-O phrase and EXTEND phrase of the OPEN statement cause non-existing files to be created.
29. *REVERSED phrase of the OPEN statement (1 SEQ)*. The REVERSED phrase of the OPEN statement has been deleted.
30. *PERFORM statement (2 NUC)*. The order of initialization of multiple VARYING identifiers in the PERFORM statement is specified. This situation was undefined in X3.23-1974.
31. *PERFORM statement (2 NUC)*. Within the VARYING . . . AFTER phrase of the PERFORM statement, identifier-2 is augmented before identifier-5 is set. In X3.23-1974, identifier-5 was set before identifier-2 was augmented.
32. *READ statement (1 SEQ, 1 REL, 1 INX)*. The READ statement can be executed after the at end condition occurs. This situation was not permitted in X3.23-1974.
33. *READ statement (1 SEQ, 1 REL, 1 INX)*. The INTO phrase cannot be specified: (1) unless all records associated with the file and the data item specified in the INTO phrase are group items, or ele-

mentary alphanumeric items or (2) unless only one record description is subordinate to the file description entry.

34. *RECEIVE statement (1 COM)*. If a message size is greater than the area referenced, the message fills the area referenced left to right starting with the leftmost character of the message. Further RECEIVE statements which reference the same queue, subqueue, ..., must be executed to transfer the remainder of the message into the area referenced.

35. *RETURN statement (1 SRT)*. The INTO phrase cannot be specified if all records associated with the file and the data item specified in the INTO phrase are neither a group item nor an elementary alphanumeric item.

36. *STOP RUN statement (1 NUC)*. The STOP RUN statement closes all files.

37. *STRING statement (2 NUC)*. The order of execution for evaluating subscripts in the STRING statement is specified. This situation was undefined in X3.23-1974.

38. *UNSTRING statement (2 NUC)*. In the UNSTRING statement, any subscripting associated with the delimiter identifiers is evaluated once, immediately before the examination of the sending fields for the delimiters.

39. *WRITE statement (2 SEQ)*. The phrases ADVANCING PAGE and END-OF-PAGE must not both be specified in a single WRITE statement.

40. *Segmentation (1 SEG)*. Independent segments have been deleted. However, the segment limit is a value varying from 00 through 99.

41. *File position indicator (1 SEQ, 1 REL, 1 INX)*. The concept of a current record pointer is X3.23-1974 has been changed to a file position indicator.

42. *File position indicator (1 SEQ, 1 REL, 1 INX)*. Following an OPEN I-O statement, the file position indicator is set to the first record in the file. Execution of a WRITE statement of a record with a low key that is followed by a READ NEXT statement, causes the access of the low numbered record by the READ NEXT statement. In X3.23-1974, this situation of an OPEN I-O, WRITE, and READ NEXT execution sequence causes the access of the first record in the file by the READ NEXT statement.

43. *File position indicator (1 INX)*. If an alternate key is the key of reference and the alternate key is changed by a REWRITE statement to a value between the current value and the next value in the file, a subsequent READ NEXT statement will obtain the same record. In X3.23-1974, the subsequent READ statement would

obtain the record with the next value for that alternate key prior to the REWRITE statement.

44. *Reserved words (1 NUC)*. The following reserved words have been added:

ALPHABET	DEBUG-SUB-NUM	END-WRITE
ALPHABETIC-LOWER	END-ADD	EVALUATE
ALPHABETIC-UPPER	END-CALL	EXTERNAL
ALPHANUMERIC	END-COMPUTE	FALSE
ALPHANUMERIC-EDITED	END-DELETE	GLOBAL
ANY	END-DIVIDE	INITIALIZE
COMMON	END-EVALUATE	NUMERIC-EDITED
CONTENT	END-IF	ORDER
CONTINUE	END-MULTIPLY	OTHER
CONVERSION	END-PERFORM	PADDING
CONVERTING	END-READ	PURGE
DAY-OF-WEEK	END-RECEIVE	REFERENCE
DEBUG-LENGTH	END-RETURN	REFERENCE-MODIFIER
DEBUG-NUMERIC-CONTENTS	END-REWRITE	REPLACE
DEBUG-SIZE	END-SEARCH	STANDARD-2
DEBUG-START	END-START	TEST
DEBUG-SUB	END-STRING	THEN
DEBUG-SUB-N	END-SUBTRACT	TRUE
DEBUG-SUB-ITEM	END-UNSTRING	

Structured Programming Enhancements

The new standard is the first to be announced *after* the general acceptance of structured programming. Consequently, many of the enhancements deal specifically with making COBOL more conducive to the structured discipline. These include provision for the DO UNTIL construct by expanding the PERFORM statement, provision for the case structure through the new EVALUATE statement, and inclusion of an END-IF delimiter in the IF statement. A more detailed discussion follows.

PERFORM

The PERFORM statement has been expanded to provide for an *in-line* capability. Consider the simplest format of the PERFORM,

$$\underline{\text{PERFORM}} \left[\text{procedure-name-1} \left[\left\{ \begin{array}{c} \underline{\text{THROUGH}} \\ \underline{\text{THRU}} \end{array} \right\} \text{procedure-name-2} \right] \right]$$

[imperative-statement-1 END-PERFORM]

and note that procedure-name-1 is enclosed in brackets, indicating it is an *optional* entry. Hence, one can now code:

```
    PERFORM
        ADD 1 TO A.
        MOVE X TO Y.
        WRITE PRINT-LINE.
    END-PERFORM.
```

An in-line PERFORM functions according to the general rules of a regular PERFORM statement, except that the statements executed are those contained *within* the PERFORM statement itself; i.e., between PERFORM and END-PERFORM. (Accordingly, omission of procedure-name-1 requires that both imperative-statement-1 and END-PERFORM be coded.)

The UNTIL formats have been expanded to allow TEST AFTER and/or TEST BEFORE, with the latter as default; i.e.:

$$\underline{\text{PERFORM}} \left[\text{procedure-name-1} \left[\left\{ \begin{array}{c} \underline{\text{THROUGH}} \\ \underline{\text{THRU}} \end{array} \right\} \text{procedure-name-2} \right] \right]$$

$$\left[\text{WITH } \underline{\text{TEST}} \left\{ \begin{array}{c} \underline{\text{BEFORE}} \\ \underline{\text{AFTER}} \end{array} \right\} \right] \underline{\text{UNTIL}} \text{ condition-1}$$

[imperative-statement-1 END-PERFORM]

In other words, COBOL now accommodates both a DO WHILE and a DO UNTIL. The TEST BEFORE condition tests before performing the procedure and corresponds to a DO WHILE; i.e., *if the condition is satisfied initially the designated procedure is never executed.* TEST AFTER, on the other hand, corresponds to the DO UNTIL construct; consequently, *even if the condition is satisfied initially, the designated procedure will still be executed once.*

EVALUATE

In Chapter 1, we discussed COBOL implementation of the case (multi-branch) structure. Recall that Figure 1.11 required a GO TO DEPENDING statement, in addition to several *forward* GO TO statements pointing to an EXIT paragraph. Implementation of the identical logic is facilitated by the new EVALUATE statement. Consider:

```
            EVALUATE INCOMING-YEAR-CODE
                WHEN 1 PERFORM FRESHMAN
                WHEN 2 PERFORM SOPHOMORE
                WHEN 3 PERFORM JUNIOR
                WHEN 4 PERFORM SENIOR
                WHEN 5 PERFORM GRAD-SCHOOL
                WHEN OTHER PERFORM PROCESS-ERROR
            END-EVALUATE.
```

In this example, the value of the identifier INCOMING-YEAR-CODE is evaluated. If it is equal to 1, FRESHMAN is performed, if it is equal to 2, SOPHOMORE is performed, and so on. Observe use of the reserved word OTHER to accommodate an error processing routine, and the terminating entry, END-EVALUATE.

IF

The IF statement will be terminated by the END-IF phrase rather than a mere period. This is a *tremendous improvement* and should eliminate the "column 73" problem. Consider the COBOL code of Figure A.1 and its associated output.

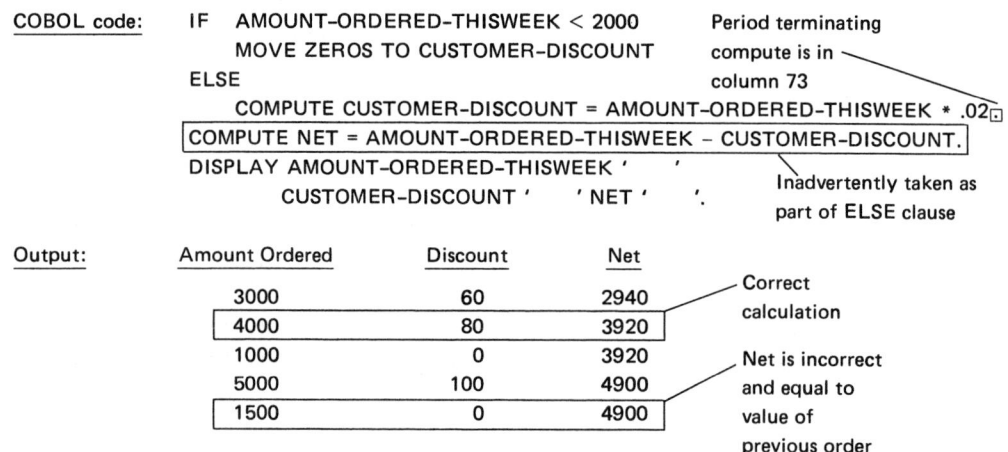

FIGURE A.1 The "missing" period.

The logic in Figure A.1 is straightforward, yet the output is unexpected. The specifications call for an order of $2000 or more to receive a discount of 2% on the entire order. The amount due (i.e., NET) is equal to the amount ordered minus the discount. The code seems correct, yet the *calculated net amounts are wrong for any order less than 2000*. The net amount printed for these orders equals the net for the previous order (i.e., the net for an order of 1000 is *incorrectly* printed as 3920, which was the correct net for the preceding order of 4000). The net amount for an order of 1500 was printed as 4900, and so on. Why?

The only possible explanation is that the COMPUTE NET statement is not executed for net amounts less than 2000. The only way that can happen is if the COMPUTE NET statement is taken as part of the ELSE clause, and that can happen only if the ELSE is not terminated by a period. The period is "present," however, so we are back at ground zero—or are we? The period is present, but in *column 73*, which is ignored by the compiler.

Hence, the visual code does not match the compiler interpretation, and the resulting output is incorrect.

Note well that a period in column 73 is *not* a contrived problem. True, it may not have happened to the reader, but chances are it did happen to *someone* in the shop. Inclusion of the ENDIF delimiter should eliminate future errors of this type. Syntactically, the new IF statement has the form:

$$\underline{\text{IF}}\ \text{condition-1 THEN} \left\{ \begin{array}{l} \{\text{statement-1}\} \ldots \\ \underline{\text{NEXT SENTENCE}} \end{array} \right\}$$

$$\left\{ \begin{array}{l} \underline{\text{ELSE}}\ \{\text{statement-2}\} \ldots [\text{END-IF}] \\ \underline{\text{ELSE}}\ \underline{\text{NEXT}}\ \underline{\text{SENTENCE}} \\ \text{END-IF} \end{array} \right\}$$

The "period in column 73 problem" is *not* limited to the IF statement, and delimiters have been added to several other verbs whose actions are terminated by the period. These include: ADD, MULTIPLY, SUBTRACT, DIVIDE, and COMPUTE (to terminate the SIZE ERROR clause); READ and RETURN (to terminate AT END); and WRITE and REWRITE (to terminate INVALID KEY). In the opinion of the author, this enhancement alone makes the new standard worthwhile.

Public Reaction

The proposed standard has been surrounded in controversy since its very inception. J. T. Brophy, of the Traveller's Insurance Company, has threatened a class action suit (*Computerworld*, January 26, 1981 and again, November 16, 1981). Other issues of *Computerworld* have detailed additional front page opposition (February 2, 1981, October 26, 1981, and March 15, 1982). The standard has also been the subject of numerous letters to the editor, both pro and con. Estimates on the cost of conversion have been put as high as *$500 million for the federal government alone.*

Objection to the standard stems from the 45 previously listed changes which are *incompatible* with existing programs rather than the proposed enhancements. Nevertheless this author believes that the overwhelming majority of incompatibilities can be resolved automatically by conversion aids (see Reader Commentary, *Computerworld*, July 20, 1981, pp. 33-36).

Consider, for example, the proposed elimination of the ALTER statement. Today, there is unanimous agreement that it should not be used, yet many existing programs have one or more ALTER statements. Arbitrary elimination of the verb would render such programs useless, while retaining the statement is undesirable from a structured viewpoint. Figure A.2 indicates how the establishment and setting of a switch can accomplish the identical logic as the defunct ALTER. The point of this example is that a well-written software package will do the conversion *automatically*.

A similar approach can be applied to almost all of the so-called "incom-

EXISTING PROGRAM (written according to ANS 74)

```
    ALTER BRANCH-PARAGRAPH TO PROCEED TO PARAGRAPH-2.
    .
    .
    ALTER BRANCH-PARAGRAPH TO PROCEED TO PARAGRAPH-3.
    .
    .
BRANCH-PARAGRAPH.
    GO TO PARAGRAPH-1.
```

REVISED PROGRAM (with ALTER eliminated)

```
WORKING-STORAGE SECTION.

77  BRANCH-PARAGRAPH-INDICATOR    PIC 9    VALUE 1.
    .
    .
    MOVE 2 TO BRANCH-PARAGRAPH-INDICATOR.
    .
    .
    MOVE 3 TO BRANCH-PARAGRAPH-INDICATOR.
    .
    .
BRANCH-PARAGRAPH.
    GO TO PARAGRAPH-1, PARAGRAPH-2, PARAGRAPH-3
        DEPENDING ON BRANCH-PARAGRAPH-INDICATOR.
```

FIGURE A.2 Elimination of ALTER statement.

patible" changes. Some enterprising programmers and/or software houses are going to get rich by providing such a product, and their work should greatly ease the cost and difficulty of a conversion.

Despite the author's cautious optimism about the availability of conversion aids, he is less than enthusiastic about the uncompromising attitude of the CODASYL committee. He does in fact wonder how serious CODASYL really is about getting the standard approved. Consider, for example, the absurdity of a proposed change to allow tables of up to 48 levels instead of the present limit of 3. This is not expected to impact existing programs, and hence is not a source of incompatability or objection. Nevertheless it is nonsensical and lessens the credibility of the entire effort.

Given that someone does create such a table and, further, that each OCCURS clause in the 48-level table has only 2 elements, one is confronted with the staggering number of 2^{48} (or approximately 10^{15}) elements.

Assuming a CPU speed of 1,000,000 operations per second, merely initializing the table would require one billion seconds or approximately *30 years of CPU time.* (This does not include the time necessary to page in and out from disk.)

Storing a table of 10^{15} elements presents additional difficulty. If each data element required only a single byte of storage, and if a disk device with a capacity of one billion bytes were available, then *one million disk packs* would be required to store the entire table.

The point is simply that the proposed extension to a 48-level table is utterly foolish. It is the author's fervent hope that the CODASYL committee become immediately responsive to public opinion in order that the many desirable changes can be incorporated into an approved standard. If this does not happen quickly, then the entire effort may be doomed to failure.

B Team Project

Acknowledgement

The author expresses his appreciation to Prentice-Hall for permission to use this appendix, and his admiration and respect for Ed Yourdon. The Mugwump Fertilizer Problem appeared originally in *Techniques of Program Structure and Design* by Edward Yourdon, published in 1975 by Prentice-Hall. The problem is beautifully constructed, and has worked extremely well in the author's classroom. This appendix contains a few minor revisions; but in the main, the problem appears as in the original Yourdon book. (The author has created his own extension which begins on page 291.)

Overview

Most of the chapters in this book have ended with one or more programming projects suitable for individual work. These projects were well structured, limited in scope, and emphasized material in the particular chapter. The

Mugwump Problem is different. It covers *everything*, and is well beyond the ability of any single individual in the time allotted.

The author uses the project in his school's equivalent of *the DPMA CIS-7 capstone course*. In so doing, he accomplishes two essential objectives:

1. Presentation of a unified example, encompassing most topics in the model curriculum; and
2. Providing students with an opportunity to work as a member of a project team, to learn first-hand the group dynamics existing in the real world, to experience the pressure of deadlines, and so on.

The overall plan is to supplement the normal lectures with periods of time devoted to working on the problem. The class is broken into groups, consisting of approximately five members, with each team choosing a *spokesman* and a *secretary*. Yourdon states that it is not imperative to choose a team leader, suggesting that the team members may prefer to consider themselves as equals. The author believes, however, that a team leader *must* be chosen, with the ultimate responsibility for the project and with the *authority to resolve disputes within a group*. If a problem with this individual should occur, the team leader can only be discharged by his or her boss, i.e., the instructor.

The teams should be judged on their ability (or inability) to *implement a working system*. The concepts of top down design and testing are critical; hence, the project should be implemented in a series of levels, beginning with the main program and progressing downward in a hierarchical sense until the most detailed modules are reached. Every module should be a complete functional entity, with a definite purpose, a definite beginning, and a definite end. Above all, each group should try to produce well-designed and easy-to-read code. Individuals should aim to achieve a project they will be proud to show to their friends and prospective employers.

The individual groups meet at their own discretion during the semester, with a significant number of classes devoted to walkthroughs of one type or another. Suggested walkthroughs include:

1. *Specification* walkthrough(s), consisting of test data and anticipated results. The author has found this session invaluable in clarifying ambiguities in the Yourdon problem statement.
2. *Design* walkthrough(s), covering the overall hierarchy chart. In all probability, it will be necessary to bring the group back a second time to include corrections and/or additions to their original hierarchy chart.
3. *Pseudocode* walkthroughs for the overall program, and perhaps for one or two of the more complex modules.
4. *Code* walkthroughs, toward the end of the semester, in which com-

pleted programs are reviewed with respect to coding practices and standards.

In addition to walkthroughs, the following activities are absolutely essential:

1. *Establishment of a test plan*, which is done once the overall hierarchy chart is accepted. Each group should be expected to produce at least three versions of the system in a top down manner. *Firm dates should be established and definite responsibility assigned to individuals for specific modules.*
2. *User signoffs*, in which one group functions as another group's user. The author assigns responsibility for accepting or rejecting the finished product to the user group. The user group should be in constant contact with the development team, and should test each of the intermediate versions.
3. *Preparation of documentation*, both technical and user oriented. The first package consists of hierarchy charts and pseudocode (or its equivalent). The latter packet should contain complete and unambiguous instructions to allow the user team to test each version of the system.

The author permits several groups to work from the same hierarchy chart and/or test data. Indeed, since much of the material is presented to the class via various walkthroughs, it is impossible to prevent this situation from occurring. It is imperative, however, that each group make its own vigorous attempt prior to the class sessions. The walkthroughs then become a true learning experience in which different approaches to the same problem can be discussed and compared.

It is completely reasonable to expect a working program from a team of five students at the end of a semester and grade accordingly. Not every group will complete the assignment, but then again, students as well as practitioners function at different levels of competence. It is also possible to assign different grades to members of the same team by requesting peer evaluations from the group. Students are usually quite honest and will readily admit who did the most and least within a team.

Given this overview, and the author's approach to managing the project, let's get to the specifics of the problem. Ed Yourdon has created a truly superb exercise.

The Mugwump Fertilizer Problem

MEMO TO: Our New Superprogrammer
FROM: President, the Mugwump Fertilizer Company

DATE: March 15, 1982
SUBJECT: Management Information System

Introduction

Congratulations! On the recommendation of an anonymous but internationally infamous American EDP consultant, I am pleased to welcome you into the EDP department of the Mugwump Fertilizer Company at the modest salary of $50,000. We have been assured that you are truly able to program faster than a speeding bullet, leap over tall reams of printout in a single bound, and generally bedazzle one and all with your programming virtuosity. As your first assignment, I would like you to develop a modest management information system that will help me, as president, to make better decisions about the current activities of the company.

Your system—actually, a single program—will be concerned with information that can be found on our Open-Order File. The file is a sequential file that contains information about the orders that have been placed by customers but not yet filled. Records are added to the file (as a result of a periodic update run) as soon as an order has been placed. Modifications may be necessary if it is later discovered that some of the information on the file is incorrect, or if the customer requests a change (e.g., if he cancels an order before it has been shipped). Records are deleted from the file when an order has been shipped to the customer. Details concerning the structure of the file follow.

The Open-Order File

The Open-Order File contains three different types of records: a Customer record, a Purchase-Order record, and an Item record. The Customer record may be considered a master record; there may be one or more Purchase-Order records subordinate to each Customer record; there may be one or more Item records subordinate to each Purchase-Order record. If a customer has one or more orders that have not yet been shipped, he will have exactly one Customer record on the file; this record indicates the customer's account number, account name, address, and other general information. For each distinct purchase order that the customer has placed, there will be a unique Purchase-Order record *following* the Customer record; the Purchase Order record indicates the date on which the order was placed, the salesman who placed it, the shipping address, and other information pertinent to that order. Each purchase order will have one or more Item records associated with it—for example, a Purchase-Order record may be immediately followed by three Item records to indicate that it consists of a certain quantity of item X, a certain quantity of item Y, and a certain quantity of item Z. The purpose of the Item record is to identify the type of product, the quantity of the product that has been sold, the unit price prevailing on the date of the sale, and other such information.

Note that each Customer record may be followed by a variable number of Purchase-Order records, though there must be at least *one* Purchase-Order record. Similarly, each Purchase-Order record is followed by at least one Item record. The structure of the file may thus be summarized by Figure B.1.

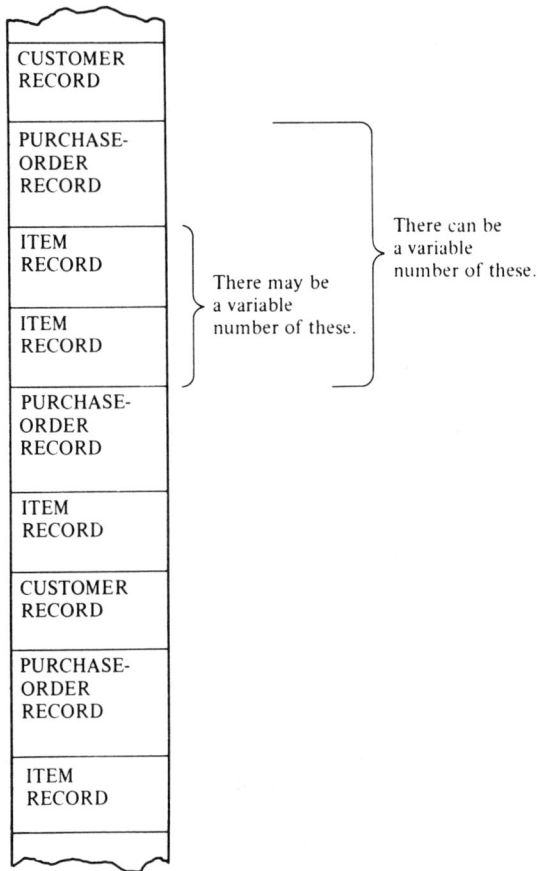

FIGURE B.1 The structure for the Open Order File.

The record structure for a Customer record is shown in Figure B.2; the record structure for a Purchase-Order record is shown in Figure B.3; the record structure for the Item record is shown in Figure B.4. Note also that each record is, in a sense, self-identifying: The first field in the record indicates whether it is a Customer record, a Purchase-Order record, or an Item record.

The basic purpose of your program is to print selected records from the Open-Order File, so that I may receive information about all pending orders for a particular product (e.g., decaffeinated guano), all pending orders placed by a specified salesman, etc. This information will be supplied to

RECORD TYPE CODE	1	CHARACTER
ACCOUNT NUMBER	6	
CUSTOMER NAME	30	
1ST LINE OF CUST. ADDRESS	20	
2ND LINE OF CUST. ADDRESS	20	
CITY	20	
STATE	2	
TELEPHONE NUMBER	10	
CUSTOMER CONTACT	20	
	129	CHARACTERS

FIGURE B.2 Format of the Customer Record. The RECORD TYPE CODE is 1 for this type of record.

RECORD TYPE CODE	1	CHARACTER
ACCOUNT NUMBER	6	
PURCHASE ORDER NUMBER	8	
SALESMAN ID CODE	3	
DATE OF ORDER—YYMMDD	6	
SHIPPING INFO: CUST. NAME	30	
1ST LINE OF SHIPPING ADDRESS	20	
2ND LINE OF SHIPPING ADDRESS	20	
CITY	20	
STATE	2	
REGION CODE WHERE ORDER WAS PLACED	1	
TOTAL $ AMOUNT OF ORDER	6	
	123	CHARACTERS

FIGURE B.3 Format of the Purchase-Order Record. The RECORD TYPE CODE is 2 for this type of record.

RECORD TYPE CODE	1	CHARACTER
ACCOUNT NUMBER	6	
PURCHASE ORDER NUMBER	8	
ITEM NUMBER	10	
PRODUCT NUMBER	4	
SALESMAN ID CODE	3	
DATE ORDER PLACED—YYMMDD	6	
DATE ORDER TO BE SHIPPED—YYMMDD	6	
DATE OF LAST PARTIAL SHIPMENT—YYMMDD	6	
QUANTITY	6	
UNIT PRICE, IN $	6	
TOTAL GROSS PRICE, IN $	6	
DISCOUNT PERCENTAGE	2	
NET PRICE	6	
	76	CHARACTERS

FIGURE B.4 Format of the Item Record. The RECORD TYPE CODE is 3 for this type of record.

your program in several discrete *sets* of control cards—e.g., in one execution of your program, I may wish you to print one report showing all pending orders for purple guano, followed by another report of all pending orders associated with customer 1234.

This may seem like an awkward approach to the problem, but it will allow us to select the records for several different reports with one pass through our incredibly large Open-Order File. The format of the input cards is described in more detail below.

I am not terribly concerned about the format of the output report. I assume that each report will contain a simple "header" that will indicate the criteria used to select records from the file (i.e., the criteria that were specified in the control cards). Other than that, I assume that for each selected record, you will essentially print the record onto the line printer—in some readable format. However, you should be warned that I am somewhat finicky about formats of reports, and I may eventually ask you to make some minor changes in your program in this area.

Format of Input to the Program

Your program will decide which records are to be selected from the Open-Order File based on information provided in control cards. For simplicity, let us assume that these control cards are, in fact, card images.

Each *set* of control cards (of which there may be a variable number for any execution of the program) will contain a variable number of cards, each of which will specify a condition that must be met before a record on the Open-Order File will be selected for printing. For example, it is possible that the first *set* of control cards will contain five individual cards of the general form.

```
                        A
                        B
                        C
                        D
                        E
```

This indicates that condition A *and* condition B *and* condition C *and* condition D *and* condition E must be met before a record will be selected for printing.

As indicated above, each execution of the program may involve several sets of control cards; each "packet" of cards will be separated by a single card with the word STOP occupying the first four character positions. Thus, it is possible that your program will read a set of control cards of the form

```
                        A1
                        B1
                        C1
                        STOP
```

```
             A2
             B2
             STOP
             A3
             B3
              .
              .
              .
```

Each record that is read from the file must then be matched against *each* set of control cards. For example, suppose the first record on the file satisfies conditions A1, B1, and C1; it would then be selected for printing in the first output report. Suppose the first record does not satisfy conditions A2 and B2; it would not be selected for output on the second report. Suppose it does satisfy conditions A3 and B3; the same first record would then be selected again for output on the third report—and so forth. Clearly, it is possible for one record to be printed on several different output reports.

Each control card consists of two fields: a transaction code and a parameter field. The transaction code will occupy the leftmost character positions of the control card and may take as many as ten characters. The parameter field will always begin in character position 11; it will usually consist of one or two integer numbers. For example, a typical control card format might be:

```
             CUSTOMER    123456
```

There is a total of eight types of control cards; each one is described in detail below. Any combination of control cards may exist in a control card packet, and they may occur in any order. However, each type of control card may appear once, at most, in a packet; thus a CUSTOMER control card may appear no more than once in a single packet of cards.

The CUSTOMER card requires a parameter field consisting of a single 6-digit integer. This specifies that all Customer records, all Purchase-Order records, and all Item records associated with the specified 6-digit customer account number should be included in the report that is associated with the current packet of control cards. Note that Customer records *and* Purchase-Order records *and* Item records on the file all carry the customer account number to simplify the processing of this control card. You should print an error message if this card is missing a parameter field, if it has more than one parameter field, or if the parameter field has an illegal format, i.e., anything other than a 6-digit integer beginning in column 11.

The PONUMBER card requires a parameter field consisting of a single 8-digit integer. This specifies that all Purchase-Order records and all Item records containing the specified purchase order number should be included in the output report. Note that this control card will *not* involve the printing of a Customer record. You should print an error message if this card is missing a parameter field, if there is more than one parameter field, or if the parameter field has an illegal format.

The Mugwump Fertilizer Problem

The ITEM control card requires a parameter field consisting of a single 10-digit integer. It specifies that the single Item record containing this number should be included in the output report. Note that each Item record on the Open-Order File has a unique number in this field—specifically so that each item that has been ordered by a customer can be individually referenced by a retrieval program such as the one being described here. You should print an error message if the card is missing a parameter field, if it has more than one parameter field, or if the parameter field has an illegal format.

The SOLDBY control card requires a parameter field consisting of a single 3-digit integer. It specifies that all Purchase-Order records and all Item records containing the specified salesman's identification number should be included in the output report. Note that when an order is initially placed by a customer, the Purchase-Order record and all subordinate Item records will contain the same salesman number. However, the subsequent updates of the file may cause certain Item records and/or Purchase-Order records to be modified, inserted, or deleted—at the direction of salesmen who receive such requests from customers whose orders have not yet been filled. Thus it is possible for the Purchase-Order records and their subordinate Item records to contain different salesman numbers; for simplicity, we can assume that the Purchase-Order record will contain the identification of the salesman who initially placed the order, and the Item records will contain the identification of the salesman who was last involved in some customer-related activity concerning that item. When processing the SOLDBY control card, we want to include *only* those Purchase-Order records and *only* those Item records that contain the specified salesman identification number. You should print an error message if this card is missing a parameter field, if it contains more than one parameter field, or if the parameter field has an illegal format.

The PRODUCT control card requires a parameter field consisting of a single 4-digit integer. It specifies that all Item records pertaining to the specified product (e.g., strawberry-flavored guano) should be included in the output report. You should print an error message if the card is missing a parameter field, if it has more than one parameter field, or if the parameter field has an illegal format.

The DATE control card requires a parameter field consisting of *two* 6-digit integers. Each integer is of the form YYMMDD, e.g., 811113 for November 13, 1981. The first such integer in the parameter field specifies a *beginning* date; it is followed immediately by a comma followed immediately by a second 6-digit integer that specifies an ending date. The purpose of the DATE control card is to select all Purchase-Order records *and* their subordinate Item records that were placed on a date greater than or equal to the beginning date, and less than or equal to the ending date. Thus, the control card

```
DATE    810104,811113
```

indicates that we should select all records pertaining to orders (and their associated items) placed between January 4 and November 13 (inclusive), 1981. You should print an error message if the DATE card is missing a parameter field, if it contains only one parameter field, if it contains more than two parameter fields, if the specified dates are in the wrong order, or if the parameter fields are in the wrong format.

The REGION control card requires a parameter field consisting of a variable number of one-digit integers. These one-digit integer codes specify different sales regions, e.g., it is possible that region 1 is New South Wales. Each region code will be followed immediately by a comma, and the last specified region code must be followed by the special code 0 as an end-of-field indicator. Thus, a typical REGION card might have the form

```
          REGION     1,3,2,4,0
```

The purpose of the REGION control card is to select Purchase-Orders records and their subordinate Item records that are being shipped to customers in *any one* of the specified regions. In the example above, we would include an Open-Order File record if it was being shipped to region 1 *or* region 3, *or* region 2 *or* region 4—*and* if the record satisfies all other control cards that may have been included in that packet. As many as nine region codes may be specified, and they may be specified in any order. You should print an error message if the card is missing a parameter field, if a region code is repeated more than once, if more than nine regions are specified, if the format of the parameter field is incorrect, or if the regions are not terminated by a 0.

The AMOUNT control card requires a parameter field consisting of a single 6-digit integer. The purpose of the AMOUNT card is to select all Purchase-Order records, and their subordinate Item records, whose total value (i.e., the amount on the purchase order), exceeds the specified 6-digit number. Note that the amount of the purchase order is included in the Purchase-Order record itself, and that it is the sum of the "amount" fields in the individual Item records that are subordinate to that Purchase-Order record. You should print an error message if the card is missing a parameter field, if it has too many parameter fields, or if the parameter field has an illegal format.

As noted before, each packet of control cards will be terminated with a single card that contains the characters STOP in character positions 1-4. The last packet of cards will be terminated with a STOP card, followed by a card with the characters END in character positions 1-3. Thus, the format of the input deck is

```
          A1
          B1
          C1
           :
          STOP
```

```
            A2
            B2
             ⋮
            STOP
             ⋮
            An
            Bn
            Cn
            STOP
            END
```

There will be no more than ten control packets in any execution of your program.

Other Editing Requirements

In addition to the local errors that might be associated with individual cards, there are a number of global errors that your program should be looking for. These are as follows:

1. No control cards at all—in other words, when your program calls for input, it immediately receives an end-of-file condition.
2. The END card is missing.
3. The last STOP card is missing, but the END card is present.
4. The END card is not the last card in the deck. If the input deck is arranged correctly, an attempt to read a card after the END card should result in an end-of-file condition.

In addition to the global errors mentioned above, it is possible to find a number of errors that are associated with an individual packet of cards. These errors are as follows:

1. A null packet, i.e., two STOP cards in a row.
2. More than one card of a type in a packet, e.g., more than one CUSTOMER card in a packet.
3. Illegal transaction code, i.e., the transaction code in columns 1–10 does not conform to one of the eight types described above. Note that this might be a mispunched END card or STOP card, which could lead to other error conditions.
4. Illegal parameter field for a specific type of input card—in fact, these are the local errors that were described earlier.

Output from the Program

From the information already given, it can be seen that the program will be called upon to print many different output reports. (It is suggested that all reports be written to the *same* output file, with additional fields appended to each print line to indicate the report and line numbers. The entire print file can then be sorted prior to output.)

The format of the output report has not been specified; you are free to print anything you consider reasonable. The report should contain a heading that indicates the criteria that were used to select the records that follow. It should then contain the Open-Order File records themselves, in essentially the same format as they exist on the Open-Order File.

In addition to the normal output reports, your program should have an error report consisting of all errors detected during the run. Your program should examine all of the control cards before beginning its processing; if any of the control cards are seen to be incorrect, an appropriate error message should be printed on the error report file, *and that control card packet should be eliminated* (however, to help the user, it would be a good idea to analyze the entire control card packet for possible errors, and print *all* appropriate error messages, before rejecting the packet). If nonrecoverable input/output errors occur during the processing of the program, an appropriate error message should be printed on the error report file and an intelligent recovery action should be made (*you* must determine what kind of intelligent recovery is appropriate).

Extension

Yourdon's statement in the original specification, that records are added, deleted, etc. from the Open-Order File in a periodic update run provides the opportunity for a *supplementary and/or alternate project*—namely, to develop specifications for a system to update the Open-Order File. This is a challenging problem which requires students to develop *clear and unambiguous specifications*, a task which is not as easy as it sounds. The project requires analysis of many different approaches, tradeoffs, and so on.

The author lists some considerations, but undoubtedly students will suggest many more. For openers:

1. The update mechanism must provide the capability for adding, deleting, and/or correcting each record type (Customer, Purchase Order, and Item).
2. Deletion of a Customer master record implicitly deletes all subordinate Purchase Orders while deletion of a Purchase Order deletes subordinate Items.

3. A correction to certain *Item* fields implicitly changes fields in a *Purchase-Order* record as well; e.g., changing an Item amount also changes the amount in the Purchase-Order record. Realize, however, that a Purchase-Order record appears (and is written to a new master) *before* the subordinate Item records. Consideration may be given to first creating three separate files (one for each record type) then subsequently merging them to form the Open-Order File.
4. The update mechanism is to incorporate "routine" editing checks. Additions, for example, are to have all fields completed; numeric fields should be numeric, and so on.
5. The update mechanism should prevent duplicate additions, and/or no matches (i.e., attempting to change or delete a record which doesn't exist).
6. The addition of a new customer record requires more than one card image in that the record exceeds 80 characters. One approach is to include a sequence field (1 or 2) in the incoming transaction and verify that both portions are there. A second approach is to prompt the user, in an on-line environment, for all necessary information, and then create the transaction records from the user supplied information. Students selecting this approach should design the necessary screens, and make the input portion "user friendly."
7. A problem analogous to item 6 is that the "fixed format" approach to corrections (i.e., specific fields entered in specific columns) may not be practical. An alternate approach is "free format," in which each field is given a number. Corrections will then contain the number of the field being changed followed by a blank and the corrected value, a second field number (if more than one is being changed), a second corrected value, and so on. (This information could alternately be collected on-line as well.)

All activities associated with the original Mugwump problem are applicable to the supplementary project. Structured walkthroughs of various phases will be of greatest value; e.g., specification, design, and test data sessions.

Answers to Selected Exercises

Chapter 1

True/False

1. False. It can contain logic errors, although hopefully less than with nonstructured code.
2. True.
3. False There is nothing in the compiler per se which relates to structured programming.
4. False. It's close, but not exact (see Problem 1 in this chapter).
5. True.
6. True.
7. False. It began in Europe with Bohm, Jacopini, Dykstra, et al.
8. False. Coding standards are still necessary.
9. False. There are definite exceptions; e.g., the INPUT PROCEDURE option of the SORT verb.
10. False. It's not ideal, but it is acceptable.

11. True.

12. False. It is an extension to sequence, selection, and iteration.

13. True.

14. False. The ELSE clause is optional, although there are those who would argue for making it mandatory, even if null (e.g., ELSE NEXT SENTENCE).

Problems

1. The DO WHILE construct executes block A as long as the condition is true. DO UNTIL, on the other hand, executes block A until the condition becomes true. Note well the different placement of block A with respect to the test; i.e., DO WHILE *need not* execute block A at all (if the condition is false initially), while DO UNTIL must execute it at least once.

   The PERFORM UNTIL is a cross between the two. It resembles a DO WHILE in that block A need not be executed at all. It follows the DO UNTIL with regard to the placement of true and false associated with the condition.

3. Insert the statement, ADD 1 TO WS-NUMBER-OF-ERRORS, after line 79 (and define WS-NUMBER-OF-ERRORS in Working-Storage). Modify the PERFORM UNTIL condition of lines 62 and 63 to include OR WS-NUMBER-OF-ERRORS > 9. (Insert parentheses around the original condition of lines 62 and 63.)

4. (a) 5 times
   (b) 4 times
   (c) 0 times

   In all cases, PERFORM VARYING *increments, tests, then branches*. Hence, if the condition is satisfied immediately, as in part (c), PARAGRAPH-A is never executed.

5. (a) The paragraphs FRESHMAN, SOPHOMORE, JUNIOR, SENIOR, and GRAD-SCHOOL would be executed sequentially, as control dropped from one to the next.
   (b) Error processing would occur, and then control would be passed to YEAR-IN-COLLEGE-EXIT.
   (c) Divide the incoming codes by 10 to obtain an integer from 1 to 5, then use a GO TO DEPENDING statement.
   (d) IF INCOMING-YEAR-CODE = 11
           PERFORM FRESHMAN
       ELSE
           IF INCOMING-YEAR-CODE = 17
               PERFORM SOPHOMORE
           ELSE . . .

6. (a) IF X > Y
           ADD 1 TO A
       ELSE
           IF W > Z
               IF Q > T
                   ADD 1 TO B
               ELSE
                   ADD 1 TO C
           ELSE
               ADD 1 TO D.

(b) i. False (it depends on the relationship between Q and T).
    ii. False (it depends on the relationship between W and Z).
   iii. False (it depends on the relationships between W and Z, and X and Y).
    iv. True.
     v. True.
    vi. False (it depends on the relationship between X and Y).

7. (a)

(b)

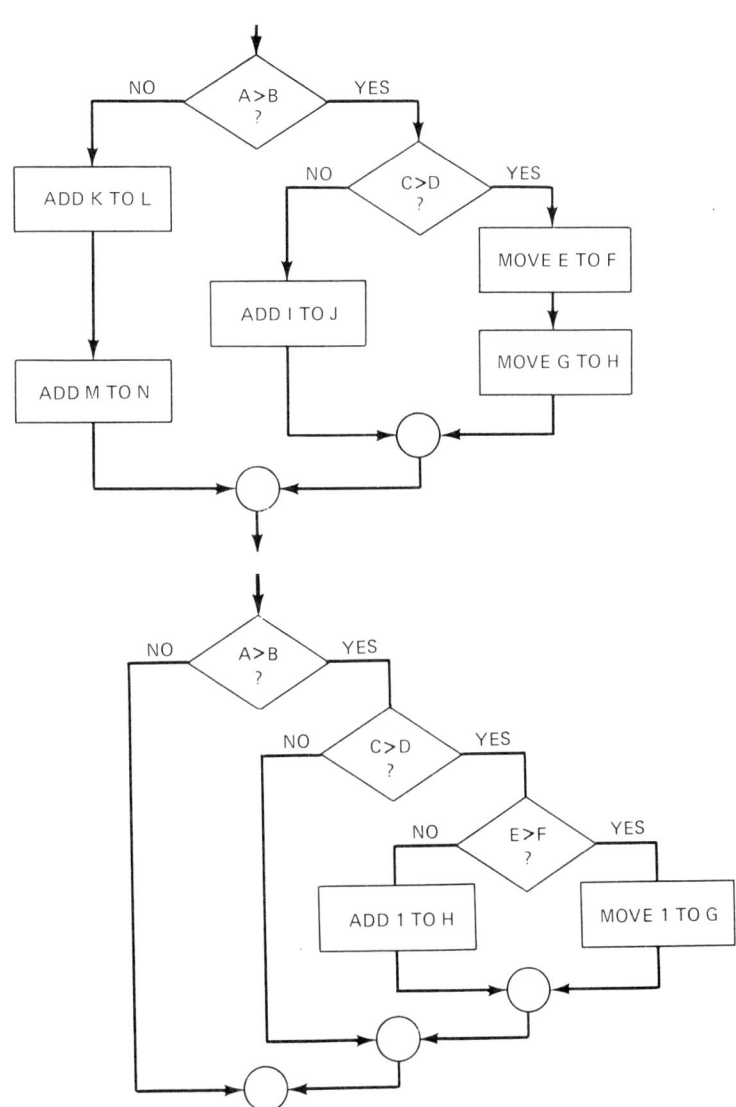

Chapter 2

True/False

1. False. *Top down design* refers to the order in which a system is tested or implemented, whereas *structured design* is concerned with the overall quality of a design.
2. False. Modules should be *loosely* coupled.
3. False. Functional cohesion is the highest level of cohesion.
4. False. Top down testing utilizes program stubs, and should begin as *soon* as possible.
5. False. All illustrations in the book pertain to individual programs.
6. False. It doesn't indicate what the module is doing.
7. False. It implies three functions.
8. False. A paragraph should do one, and *only one* function.
9. False. Perfectly horrible designs can be implemented in top down fashion.
10. False. It should be as uniform as possible, as depicted in Figure 2.4.
11. False. Span of control should be between 2 and 7 modules.
12. False. They are heuristic in nature.
13. False. Structured design implies the use of guidelines which determine how modules will be selected.
14. False. The relationship is generally nonlinear; i.e., a program of $2n$ statements is more than twice as complex as a program containing n statements.
15. False. It is anything but.
16. False. The higher level modules generally contain the more complex logic and should be developed first.
17. False. Beware of coincidental cohesion.
18. False. Data coupling is the lowest (and most desirable) form of coupling.
19. False. It provides a "pathological connection" in that it branches into the *middle* of a module.
20. False. It must be called from the module directly above it.
21. True.
22. True.
23. True.
24. False. A Yourdon structure chart contains additional information; e.g., loops and decisions.
25. True.

Problems

1. (a) See Figure C.1.
2. (a) A flowchart may not be worth the effort.
   (b) Pseudocode is shown in Figure C.2.

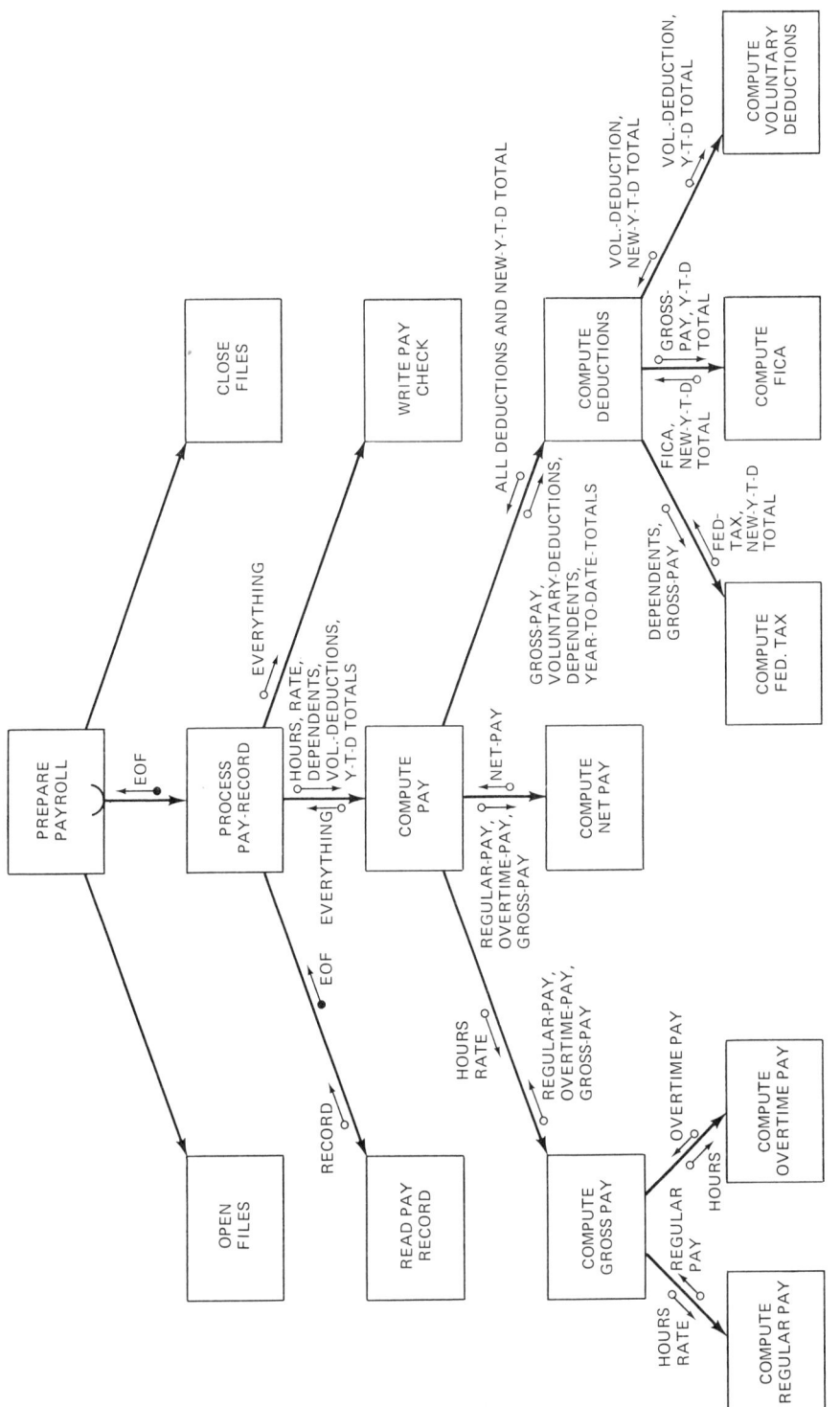

FIGURE C.1 Yourdon structure chart.

```
Initialize
Open files
Read SALES-FILE at end indicate no more data
┌ PERFORM until no more data
│     WRITE location heading
│     MOVE TR-SALESMAN-LOCATION to WS-PREVIOUS-LOCATION
│     Zero this location's totals
│   ┌ PERFORM until TR-SALESMAN-LOCATION ≠ WS-PREVIOUS-LOCATION or
│   │            no more data
│   │     Move TR-SALESMAN-NAME to WS-PREVIOUS-SALESMAN
│   │     Zero salesman totals
│   │     Write salesman heading line
│   │   ┌ PERFORM until TR-SALESMAN-NAME ≠ WS-PREVIOUS-SALESMAN or
│   │   │            TR-SALESMAN-LOCATION ≠ WS-PREVIOUS-LOCATION or
│   │   │            no more data
│   │   │     Determine transaction type
│   │   │     Increment salesman total
│   │   │     Increment location total
│   │   │     Increment company total
│   │   │     Write detail line
│   │   │     Read SALES-FILE at end indicate no more data
│   │   └ ENDPERFORM
│   │     Write salesman total line
│   └ ENDPERFORM
│     Write location total
└ ENDPERFORM
Write company total
Close files
Stop run
```

FIGURE C.2 Pseudocode for double control break

(c) The driving module CALCULATE-CONTROL-BREAKS calls a new module PROCESS-ALL-REGIONS. That in turn calls three other modules WRITE-REGION-HEADING (a new module), PROCESS-ALL-LOCATIONS (which was previously called from CALCULATE-CONTROL-BREAKS), and WRITE-REGION-TOTAL (a new module). The remainder of the original chart is unchanged.

(d) Modify PROCESS-ALL-TRANSACTIONS.

(e) Modify WRITE-LOCATION-TOTAL and eliminate WRITE-LOCATION-HEADING.

(f) Modification of the pseudocode is more time consuming and left to the reader.

Chapter 3

True/False

1. True.

2. False. Subscripts may be used in conjunction with indexes.

3. True.
4. False. An index must be defined with a table and is restricted to that particular table.
5. False. DAY is the Julian date (yyddd); DATE is the calendar date (yymmdd).
6. False. DAY is the reserved word for Julian date.
7. True.
8. False. It is permitted anywhere except within another COPY.
9. False. The OCCURS clause can appear at the elementary as well as group level.
10. False. It appears in the called program.
11. False. The order is *critical!*
12. False. One program may call several subprograms.
13. False. It is a complete program and contains all *four* divisions.
14. False. Indexing is more efficient than subscripting.
15. True.
16. True.
17. False. They denote a sequential and binary search respectively.
18. True.
19. True.
20. False. It is required only if SEARCH ALL is used.
21. True.
22. False. It could require as many as 500 guesses.
23. True.
24. False. It can if INPUT PROCEDURE is specified.
25. True.
26. True.
27. True.
28. False. It can contain up to 12, which is many more than a person can use effectively.
29. True.
30. False. It is the only place where a COPY *cannot* be used.
31. False. Its use is suggested to obtain more efficient object code.
32. False. EXIT PROGRAM returns control to the calling program.
33. False. It is preferable to initialize a table by reading values from a file, and thereby avoid the REDEFINES entry.
34. False. It must not appear in either as its presence would cause the program to terminate improperly. (See Exercise 9.2 in Chapter 9.)
35. False. It is invoked during compilation.

Problems

2. (a) SORT-LOCATION
   (b) SORT-NAME
   (c) SORT-WORK-FILE
   (d) EMPLOYEE-FILE

(e) SORT-WORK-FILE and EMPLOYEE-FILE
(f) EMPLOYEE-FILE
(g) SORT-WORK-FILE (The sort work file must contain the data names specified as keys.)
(h) *A section* (Both the input and output procedures must be sections.)

3. (a)

SALES-TOTALS									
REGION (1)						REGION (2)			
CITY (1)			CITY (2)			CITY (1)			
SL (1)	SL (2)	SL (3)	SL (1)	SL (2)	SL (3)	SL (1)	SL (2)	SL (3)	...

(b) i. Valid.
    ii. Valid.
    iii. Invalid. SALESMAN requires *three* subscripts.
    iv. Valid syntactically, but invalid logically as the second subscript *should not exceed 2;* i.e., CITY OCCURS 2 TIMES.
    v. Invalid—CITY requires two subscripts.
    vi. Valid.
    vii. Valid.

4. The input procedure processes an incoming file and passes records to a sort-work file. In Figure 3.18, the input procedure releases *every* record to the work file, even though most records are subsequently rejected in the output procedure (by the IF statement in line 207). It would be far more efficient, from an *algorithmic* point of view, to do the selection in the input procedure. In other words, do not create a work file which contains every input record, if the eventual report contains only a few of the sorted records.

A second improvement would be to move the ACCEPT statement of line 236 immediately after line 197, so that it is executed only once, rather than for every record.

Both of these changes are examples of algorithmic rather than machine efficiency. As will be pointed out in Chapter 4, efficiency is less important today than it was previously. Nevertheless, there is no excuse for "loose" code, and the suggested changes should definitely be made.

5. (a) LINEAR SEARCH OK FOR DENVER
    * ERROR IN LINEAR SEARCH FOR NEW YORK
  (b) SEARCH ALL LOCATION
        AT END DISPLAY '* ERROR IN LINEAR SEARCH FOR DENVER'
        WHEN LOCATION-CODE (LOCATION INDEX) = '045'
          DISPLAY 'BINARY SEARCH OK FOR DENVER'.

Denver will *never* be found using a binary search, as the table is not in ascending order; i.e., 045 Denver is out of sequence.

Chapter 4

True/False

1. False. Correctness is, maintainability is second.
2. False. A program can have *too* many comments as discussed in the chapter.
3. False. It is important in both divisions.
4. False. Such crowding only decreases readability.
5. False. Judicious insertion of blank lines significantly improves a program's readability.
6. False. Separate switches are better, especially for debugging.
7. False. Coding standards and/or guidelines are also necessary.
8. False. Algorithmic efficiency has more impact.
9. False. Current thought holds that 77-level entries should be eliminated entirely.
10. False. One may consider them, but should certainly not be preoccupied with them.
11. False. Report Writer should be used far more frequently (see Chapter 8).
12. False. There are exceptions, e.g., 1, 12 when converting inches to feet, 100 in percent calculations, etc.
13. False. Programming standards are a function of the individual shop.
14. False. The ANS standard does not require sequencing, although most shops impose it.
15. True. The question does not refer to indentation with respect to the A and B margins.
16. False. A comment is indicated by an asterisk in column 8. (A slash in column 7 causes the next line in a compiler listing to begin on a new page, i.e., eject.)
17. False. All code should be as simple and straightforward as possible.
18. False. It may be confused with a period, and hence should be avoided.
19. False. Performing sections can cause unexpected problems (remember the example in the chapter).
20. False. Meaningful data-names simplify debugging and maintenance.
21. False. PERFORM THRU makes the program dependent on the physical placement of paragraphs within it.
22. True.
23. False. *Think* first and code later.
24. False. Remember Murphy's law (and the corollary that Murphy was an optimist).
25. False. Unfortunately, they don't, which may result in subscript (index) errors of one kind or another.

Problems

3. Change CARD-FILE to STUDENT-FILE, and STUDENT-CARD to STUDENT-RECORD. (File-names should not reference a physical device.) Prefix all data-names within STUDENT-RECORD, e.g., SR-STUDENT-NAME. Change PICTURE IS to PIC (it's shorter and easier to code). Finally, change the alphabetic picture clauses to alphanumeric, as some names are not alphabetic, e.g., O'NEIL.

4.
```
PROCEDURE DIVISION.
INPUT-CODE-A.
        IF INPUT-CODE = 'A',
            MOVE INPUT-NAME TO HOLD-NAME
            IF INPUT-AMOUNT IS GREATER THAN 100
                PERFORM ADJUST-AMOUNT
                    VARYING WS-SUB
                    FROM 1 BY 1
                        UNTIL WS-SUB IS GREATER THAN 10
                    AFTER HOLD-SUB FROM 1 BY 1
                        UNTIL HOLD-SUB IS EQUAL TO 8
            ELSE,
                NEXT SENTENCE
        ELSE,
            DISPLAY INPUT-NAME.
```

- VARYING indented 2 columns under PERFORM
- UNTIL indented 4 columns under PERFORM
- IF/ELSE alignment

Chapter 5

True/False

1. True.
2. True.
3. True.
4. True.
5. False (at least in the opinion of the author).
6. False. It is restricted to the logic constructs of structured programming, but everything else is at the programmer's discretion.
7. False. They tend to be more difficult to modify.
8. True.
9. True.
10. False. It is written *before* code is developed.
11. False. Pseudocode is *procedural* in nature; hierarchy charts are *functional*.
12. True.
13. True.
14. False. Walkthroughs should be held for *everyone*.
15. True.
16. False. Two hours should be established as a maximum.
17. False. Walkthroughs are applicable during *any* phase of a project.

Problems

6. Initial decision table:

Conditions and Actions	Rules															
	1	2	3	4	5	6	7	8	9	10	11	12	13	14	15	16
1. Dollar amount of order exceeds credit limit.	F	F	F	F	F	F	F	F	T	T	T	T	T	T	T	T
2. Customer has special approval from credit dept.	F	F	F	F	T	T	T	T	F	F	F	F	T	T	T	T
3. Size of order is less than minimum allowed.	F	F	T	T	F	F	T	T	F	F	T	T	F	F	T	T
4. Customer has special approval from shipping dept.	F	T	F	T	F	T	F	T	F	T	F	T	F	T	F	T
1. REJECT ORDER, SEND TO CREDIT DEPT.									X	X	X	X				
2. REJECT ORDER, SEND TO SHIPPING DEPT.			X			X						X			X	
3. PROCESS ORDER, AND SHIP IT.	X	X		X	X	X		X					X	X		X

Note that this situation calls for two rejections. Is this practical, or even reasonable? For simplicity, we will proceed on the assumption that only action No. 1 is necessary.

Decision table rewritten to place similar actions together and to facilitate reduction.

Conditions and Actions	Rules															
	1	2	3	4	5	6	7	8	9	10	11	12	13	14	15	16
1. Dollar amount of order exceeds credit limit.	T	T	T	T	F	F	T	F	F	F	F	F	F	T	T	T
2. Customer has special approval from credit dept.	F	F	F	F	T	T	F	F	F	T	T	T	T	T	T	T
3. Size of order is less than minimum allowed.	F	F	T	T	T	T	F	F	T	F	F	T	F	F	F	T
4. Customer has special approval from shipping dept.	F	T	F	T	F	F	F	F	T	T	F	T	T	F	T	T
1. REJECT ORDER, SEND TO CREDIT DEPT.	X	X	X	X												
2. REJECT ORDER, SEND TO SHIPPING DEPT.					X	X	X									
3. PROCESS ORDER AND SHIP IT.								X	X	X	X	X	X	X	X	X

Note that we have arbitrarily decided to perform only action No. 1.

Chapter 6

True/False

1. True.
2. False. The beauty of the algorithm is that transactions may appear in *any* order.
3. True.
4. False. Top down testing implies that testing begin *before* coding is completed through the use of program stubs.
5. True.
6. False. One must assume the worst.
7. False. A "stand alone" edit verifies transactions in and of themselves. It cannot check for duplicate additions as it operates *without* the old master.
8. True.

9. False. Pseudocode is procedural in nature; hierarchy charts are functional.
10. True.
11. False. The programmer is biased toward his or her program, and is influenced accordingly. Test data should be designed by someone with no knowledge of the program.
12. True.
13. False. Variable-length records are common.
14. True.
15. False. A physical record contains one or more logical records.
16. False. A blocking factor of three means that each physical record contains three logical records. Buffers are used to speed sequential processing, and have nothing to do with blocking per se.
17. True.
18. True.
19. False. They are permitted and should be used.
20. True.

Problems

1. The author believes strongly that the pseudocode for a given module should be restricted to a single page. Insertion of additional logic directly into Figure 6.2 makes the result difficult to follow, and consequently it should be divided into distinct modules (on separate pages). See, for example, Figures 7.9, 7.10, and 7.11 in the next chapter.

2. With all due respect to Ed Yourdon, the author finds the additional information on a structure chart clutters rather than clarifies. The hierarchy chart of Figure 6.13 is eloquent in its simplicity and is best left alone. The reader may review the material on structure charts in Chapter 2, and come to his or her own conclusion.

3. Name and initials are *not* required on "C" type transactions. A distinct disadvantage of including this field is implied by lines 269-270 of Figure 6.14; namely, the transaction field replaces the existing old master field. Hence, if name and/or initials are entered *incorrectly* on a transaction, a new error will be introduced in the new master.

   On the other hand, inclusion of name and initials may simplify data entry, in that people are dealing with names rather than numbers. Further, requiring that name be entered enables a match on *both* name and social security number which may also reduce errors. As the saying goes, "Pay your money and take your choice."

4. The simplest approach is to put through a deletion and an addition; i.e., delete the old social security number of 100000000 and add a new record with social security number 100000001. The disadvantage of this technique is that one has to recopy the *entire* record in order to process the addition, an extremely error prone procedure.

   An alternative technique is to develop a new transaction type with its associated logic. It is far simpler from a data entry viewpoint, but far from trivial in terms of COBOL implementation as the programming project implies.

Chapter 7

True/False

1. False. ALTERNATE RECORD KEY substantially increases overhead, due to a second set of indexes. It should be used only when required by the program specifications.
2. False. It is permitted with any type of file organization.
3. False. Both clauses are enclosed in brackets, indicating they are optional. Omission implies that the equivalent processing will be done in Declaratives.
4. False. They appear at the beginning of the Procedure Division.
5. False. It is definitely recommended, together with WS BEGINS HERE, to simplify debugging (see Chapter 4).
6. False. One or more ALTERNATE AREAS, i.e., buffers, should always be used (unless memory is a major problem)
7. True.
8. True.
9. False. ALTERNATE RECORD KEY may be specified WITH DUPLICATES.
10. True.
11. False. It is optional in COBOL, but may be required by an installation's standards.
12. True.
13. False. The first byte of an ISAM (IBM implementation) record requires either LOW or HIGH-VALUES.
14. False. WRITE is used to add records to a file; REWRITE to change existing records.
15. False. HIGH-VALUES pertain only to an ISAM file.
16. True.
17. False. IBM's ISAM syntax is an entity unto itself.
18. True.
19. False. Unfortunately, no. (The equivalent may be generated through DECLARATIVES.)

Problems

1. Key 401 causes a *control interval split* which in turn causes a *control area split* as there are no free control intervals. Keys 723 and 724 are added in place in the last control area, but the addition of 725 causes a *control interval split* with appropriate adjustments in the sequence set.

    Deletion of 502 and 619 causes the space vacated to be immediately reusable; the latter requires an adjustment to the sequence set.

2. (a) ISAM.
   (b) VSAM.
   (c) Both.
   (d) ISAM (for random access only).
   (e) VSAM.

(f) VSAM.
(g) Both.
(h) VSAM.
(i) Both.
(j) Both.
(k) VSAM.
(l) ISAM.
(m) Both.
(n) VSAM.
(o) VSAM.

3. VSAM imposes a strict "less than" condition; i.e., in order to add a record to a control area and/or control interval, its key must be *less* than the existing entry in the index. Hence, 289 will become the *first* entry in the second interval and 620 will be added to the *third* control area. Note well that adding records in this fashion does not require any changes to existing indexes.

The addition of record key 900 mandates a new control area as per the "less than" condition. Since this record is added at the end of the existing VSAM data set, it does require additional entries in the highest level index.

Chapter 8

True/False

1. False. A program need not contain all seven report groups; e.g., the programs in the chapter did not contain page footings and/or report headings.
2. False. Very often one occurs without the other.
3. False. Report groups often contain multiple print lines.
4. True.
5. False. See Figure 8.5, for example.
6. True.
7. False. PROPAGATE is not a COBOL verb.
8. False. One must specify a sort explicitly.
9. False. (See Project 4.)
10. False. They represent absolute and relative spacing, respectively.
11. True.
12. True.
13. True.
14. False. Figure 8.7 illustrates how it can be used to compute averages.
15. True.
16. True.
17. False. Report Writer is one of 11 COBOL modules in the ANS 74 standard.
18. False. The GROUP INDICATE entry can suppress printing for subsequent records.
19. False. Try coding a program like Figure 8.5, without lines 96-103, and observe what happens.

Problems

1. Either or both clauses could be replaced, but with a loss of efficiency. As the program is now written, line 107 increments location total only on a salesman break. If line 107 were replaced by SUM TR-AMOUNT, then location total would be incremented for every transaction. In similar fashion, the final total is incremented only on a location break. Substitution of SUM TR-AMOUNT would increment the total on every transaction.

Bibliography

American National Standards Institute, *American National Standard Programming Language COBOL*, X3.23-1974, New York, N.Y., 1974.

———, *Draft Proposed Revised X3.23 American National Standard Programming Language COBOL*, New York, N.Y., September 1981.

Baker, F. T., "Chief Programming Team Management of Production Programming," *IBM Systems Journal*, January 1972, pp. 56–73.

Bohm, C., and G. Jacopini, "Flow Diagrams, Turing Machines, and Languages with Only Two Formation Rules," *Communications of the ACM*, May 1966, pp. 366–71.

Brooks, Frederick P., "The Flow Chart Curse," in *The Mythical Man Month*, Reading, Mass.: Addison-Wesley, 1975.

Demarco, Tom, *Structured Analysis and System Specification*, Englewood Cliffs, N.J.: Prentice-Hall, 1979.

Dijkstra, E. W., "GO TO Statement Considered Harmful," *Communications of the ACM*, March 1968.

Dwyer, Barry, "One More Time—How to Update a Master File," *Communications of the ACM*, vol. 24, no. 1 (January 1981).

Gildersleeve, Thomas R., *Decision Tables and Their Practical Application in Data Processing*, Englewood Cliffs, N.J.: Prentice-Hall, 1970.

Grauer, Robert T., *A COBOL Book of Practice and Reference*, Englewood Cliffs, N.J.: Prentice-Hall, 1981.

———, and Marshal A. Crawford, *Structured COBOL: A Pragmatic Approach*, Englewood Cliffs, N.J.: Prentice-Hall, 1981.

———, and Marshal A. Crawford, *The COBOL Environment*, Englewood Cliffs, N.J.: Prentice-Hall, 1979.

IBM Corporation, *HIPO—A Design Aid and Documentation Technique*, GC20-1851-1.

———, *IBM VS COBOL for OS/VS*, GC26-3857-1.

Johnson, L. F., and R. H. Cooper, *File Techniques for Data Base Organization in COBOL*, Englewood Cliffs, N.J.: Prentice-Hall, 1981.

Miller, G. A., "The Magical Number Seven, Plus or Minus Two: Some Limits on Our Capacity for Processing Information," *Psychological Review*, vol. 63 (March 1956), pp. 81–97.

Myers, Glenford J., *Composite Structured Design*, New York: Van Nostrand Reinhold, 1978.

Stevens, Wayne P., *Using Structured Design*, New York: John Wiley, 1981.

———, and G. J. Myers, and Larry L. Constantine, "Structured Design," *IBM Systems Journal*, vol. 13, no. 2, pp. 115–39.

Weinberg, Victor, *Structured Analysis*, Englewood Cliffs, N.J.: Prentice-Hall, 1980.

Wulf, William A., "A Case Against the GO TO," *25th ACM Conference Proceedings*, 1972.

Yourdon, Ed, *Managing the Structured Techniques*, Englewood Cliffs, N.J.: Prentice-Hall, 1979.

———, *Structured Walkthroughs*, New York: YOURDON, Inc., 1977.

———, *Techniques of Program Structure and Design*, Englewood Cliffs, N.J.: Prentice-Hall, 1975.

———, and Larry L. Constantine, *Structured Design*, 2nd ed., New York: YOURDON Press, 1978.

Index

A

ABEND, 235
ACCESS IS DYNAMIC, 181, 182, 183, 202
ACCESS IS RANDOM, 197
ACCESS IS SEQUENTIAL, 184, 188
ACCESS MODE, 168, 181
Action entry, 129
Action stub, 129
Active key, 140, 150, 159, 195
ADD, 95, 109, 269
AFTER ADVANCING, 95
Allocation status, 141
ALL PROCEDURES, 188-89
Alphabetic test, 117, 271
ALTER, 271, 277-78
ALTERNATE RECORD KEY, 182, 183, 202
American National Standards Institute
    (*see* ANSI)
ANS proposed standard, 266-79
ANSI, 266

Applied Data Research, 123
Arithmetic operator, 108
ASCENDING KEY:
    in OCCURS clause, 52, 57
    in SORT statement, 71, 72
ASCII, 71
ASSIGN (*see* SELECT)
AT END:
    in READ, 95
    in RETURN, 72, 79
    in SEARCH, 57, 95
AUTOFLOW, 123

B

Baker, F. T., 2
Balance line algorithm, 140-45, 159, 191
Batch environment, 191
BEFORE ADVANCING, 95
Binary search, 57, 58, 75, 116

Binding time, 42-43
Black box, 37, 47
Blank line, 98
BLOCK CONTAINS, 169
BLOCK CONTAINS 0 RECORDS, 8-9, 43, 169
Bohm, C., 2
Bottom-up approach, 146
Brooks, F. P., 28
Brophy, J., 277
Buffer, 168

C

Calculated field, 71
CALL, 41-42, 67-70, 81, 269
Called program (*see* Subprogram)
Calling program (*see* CALL)
Case structure, 13-14
Chapin chart (*see* N-S diagram)
CLOSE, 170-71
COBOL-68, 266
COBOL-74, 266
CODASYL, 266
Coding standards (*see* Standards)
Cohesion, 25, 37-39, 161
Coincidental cohesion, 38-39
COLLATING SEQUENCE, 71
COLUMN, 211
Comma, 98
Comments, 102-4, 238-39, 261
   in columns 73-80, 99
Common coupling, 40-41, 99
Completeness check, 118
Compound test (*see* IF, compound test)
COMPUTE, 81, 95, 108
Computerworld, 277
Condition entry, 129
Condition name (*see* IF, condition name)
Condition stub, 129
Consistency check, 117
Constantine, L., 22, 35, 39
Content coupling, 41-42
Continuation of non-numeric literal, 109
CONTINUE, 269
Control area, 176-80
Control break, 29-33, 206-7, 240-43
Control coupling, 40
Control element, 35
Control footing, 207-26
Control heading, 207-26
Control interval, 176-80
CONTROLS, 208
Cooper, R. H., 140
COPY, 84, 111, 113

CORRESPONDING (*see* MOVE CORRESPONDING)
Coupling, 25, 39-42, 161
Crawford, M., 51, 60, 112
CURRENT-DATE, 67

D

Data base, 182
Data coupling, 39
Data element, 35
Data exception, 235
Dataname, 96
Dataname qualification (*see* Qualification)
DATE, 66, 67, 262
Date check, 118
DAY, 67, 68, 262
DAY-OF-WEEK, 268
DDname, 181
DDstatement, 181
DEBUG-CONTENTS, 187, 189
Debugging, 234-65
DEBUGGING MODE, 187, 189
DEBUG-ITEM, 187
DEBUG-LINE, 187, 189
DEBUG-NAME, 187, 189
Decision table, 129-33
Decision tree, 133
DECLARATIVES, 185-91, 221, 222
De-editing, 269
Defensive programming, 116-18
DELETE, 184
Delete byte, 202
Demarco, T., 131
DEPENDING ON (*see* OCCURS DEPENDING ON)
DESCENDING KEY:
   in OCCURS clause, 52
   in SORT statement, 72
Design walkthrough, 134
Detail report group, 207
Dijkstra, E. W., 2
Direct access to table entries, 57, 58, 75
Displacement (*see* Index)
DISPLAY, 146, 150
DIVIDE, 95
Documentation, 28, 33
DO UNTIL structure, 15, 275
DO WHILE structure, 15, 275
DOWN BY (*see* SET)
DPMA model curriculum, 2, 281
Duplicate additions, 143
Duplicate datanames (*see* Qualification)
Dwyer, B., 140

E

EBCDIC, 71
Edit program, 143
Efficiency, 115, 168
Elementary item, 53
ELSE, 95, 237
END DECLARATIVES (*see* DECLARATIVES)
END-IF, 277
End-of-file condition (*see* HIGH-VALUES)
END-PERFORM, 275
ENTRY, 41-42
Entry sequenced data set, 176
Error messages, 110
Error processing, 141
EVALUATE, 13, 269, 275-76
EXIT, 14, 81
Exit paragraph (*see* PERFORM THRU)
EXIT PROGRAM, 68, 69, 269
EXTEND, 171

F

Factoring, 36
Fan-in, 36
Fan-out, 36
FD, 169-70, 237
File activity, 191
File maintenance:
    nonsequential, 191-202
    sequential, 139-66
Filename, 96-97
FILE STATUS, 168, 182, 185-86
FILLER, 268
FINAL, 208
FIRST DETAIL, 212, 227
Fixed length record, 169
Flowchart, 28, 123-24, 128
FOOTING, 212, 227
Free space, 178
Functional cohesion, 37-39, 47

G

GENERATE, 213, 217, 218, 223-24
Gildersleeve, T. R., 129
GIVING:
    with arithmetic verbs, 95
    with SORT verb, 74
GO TO, 2, 14, 76, 81, 237
GO TO DEPENDING, 13-14
Grauer, R., 51, 60, 112, 184, 235
GROUP INDICATE, 218, 221, 264
Group item, 53

H

Header label, 170
HEADING, 208, 227
Heuristics, 35
Hierarchy chart, 24-27, 33, 102, 122, 145, 159-60, 194, 263
HIGH-VALUES, 10, 152
    with ISAM, 202
HIPO, 33
Horizontal pointer, 177

I

IBM personal computer, 115
IF:
    changes in, 269, 277
    compound test, 107
    condition name, 107, 263
    implied conditions, 85
    indentation, 95-96
    nested, 95-96, 237
    period, 237, 276
Implied conditions (*see* IF, implied conditions)
IN (*see* Qualification)
Indentation, 94-96
Index:
    arithmetic on, 54-55
    versus subscript, 53-54
    with PERFORM verb, 59, 111
    with SEARCH verb, 57
    with SET verb, 54
INDEXED BY, 52, 54
Indexed file, 175-203
Indexed sequential access method (*see* ISAM)
Index set, 176-80
Inline perform (*see* PERFORM)
Initial read, 6-8, 236
INITIATE, 213
INPUT PROCEDURE, 14, 71-73, 81, 115
INSPECT, 89
Installation standards (*see* Standards)
INVALID KEY, 95
    with READ, 183, 201
    with START, 184
    with WRITE, 186
I-O CONTROL, 168-69
ISAM, 178
    versus VSAM, 202
Iteration structure, 3-5

J

Jacopini, G., 2
JCL, 9, 43, 169, 170, 181

JOD, 266
Johnson, L. F., 140
Journal of Development (see JOD)
Julian date (see DAY)

K

KEY, 72
Key sequenced data set, 176

L

LABEL, 169
LABEL RECORDS, 170
LAST DETAIL, 212, 227
Level numbers:
    suggestions for coding, 98
    01 entries, 98
    77 entries, 106-7
    88 entries, 107-8
Limit check, 117
LINE, 58
Linear search (see Sequential search)
LINKAGE SECTION, 67-70, 81, 262
Logic walkthrough, 134
Loop, 236
LOW-VALUES:
    with ISAM, 202

M

Maintenance, 158-67, 173-74
Microsoft, 229
Miller, G. A., 43
Module, 36
Morphology, 36
MOVE, 236
MOVE CORRESPONDING, 105-7
MULTIPLE FILE, 169
MULTIPLY, 95
Myers, G. J., 22, 35, 39

N

Nassi-Shneiderman chart (see N-S diagram)
Negative data (see Signed number)
Nested IF (see IF)
New York Times Project, 2
NEXT (see READ NEXT)
NEXT GROUP, 218, 221
NEXT SENTENCE, 57
NOMINAL KEY, 202

NO REWIND, 171
N-S diagram, 125-26, 128
NUMERIC, 117
Numeric test, 117

O

OCCURS, 52-54, 57, 238, 262
    changes in, 278-79
OCCURS DEPENDING ON, 52, 263, 268
OF (see Qualification)
OPEN, 170-71, 182
Operations walkthrough, 135
OPTIONAL, 168
ORGANIZATION IS INDEXED, 181
OS JCL (see JCL)
OUTPUT PROCEDURE, 71-73, 81, 115, 214
Overflow area, 178

P

Padding with blanks, 110
Page footing, 207, 226
Page heading in Report Writer, 207, 226
PAGE LIMIT, 208, 224, 227
Paragraph name, 39, 97
Pathological connection, 41
PDL (see Pseudocode)
PERFORM:
    changes in, 269, 272, 274-75
    in line, 153
    paragraphs vs. sections, 104-5
    TEST AFTER, 275
    TEST BEFORE, 275
    THRU, 14, 105, 237
    UNTIL, 16, 95
    VARYING, 16, 62, 63, 64, 65, 236
Period, 237
PICTURE clause, 98
Prefixing of dataname, 97
Priming read (see Initial read)
PROCEDURE DIVISION USING, 69, 70
Program Development Language (see
    Pseudocode)
PROGRAM-ID, 41
Programming style, 92-119
Program stub (see Stub)
Pseudocode, 124-25, 129, 141, 142, 195, 196

Q

Qualification, 68, 105, 268

R

Radio Shack, 229
Range check, 117
RD, 208, 226
READ:
   AT END, 183
   changes in, 269, 272
   INTO, 112
   INVALID KEY, 183
   NEXT, 183
READY TRACE, 188
Real time, 191
Reasonableness check, 117
RECORD CONTAINS, 169
RECORD KEY, 182-83, 197
REDEFINES, 57-58, 268
REEL, 171
Reference modification, 268
Relative indexing, 268
Relative subscripting, 268
RELEASE, 72, 73
Report footing, 207, 226
Report group, 207, 226-28
Report heading, 207, 226
REPORT IS, 208
REPORT SECTION, 208
Report Writer, 119, 205-30, 257-61
RERUN, 168, 269
RESERVE AREA clause, 168, 181
RESET (*see* SUM RESET)
RETURN, 72, 73, 269
REVERSED, 171
REWRITE, 184

S

S:
   in PICTURE (*see* Signed number)
SAME AREA, 168
Scope of control, 43-46
Scope of effect, 43-46
SD, 72
SEARCH, 55-58, 236, 262
SEARCH ALL, 57-58, 81, 236, 263
Section, 71
SELECT:
   indexed files, 181-82, 197
   sequential files, 167-68
Selection structure, 3-5
Sequence check, 12
Sequence set, 176-80
Sequence structure, 2-5, 176-80
Sequencing paragraph names, 97

Sequential file maintenance, 139-66, 251-57
Sequential search, 57, 58, 75, 84, 116
Sequential update (*see* Sequential file
   maintenance)
SET, 54-55, 57, 58, 84, 262
Signed number, 236-37, 261
SIZE ERROR, 95
Slash in column 7, 98
SORT, 70-75, 214, 263
SOURCE, 212
SOURCE-COMPUTER, 187, 189
Span of control, 22-23, 43
SPECIAL-NAMES, 71, 170
Specification walkthrough, 134
Stamp coupling, 40
Standards, 92-93
Standards walkthrough, 134
START, 184-85, 204
Stevens, W. P., 22, 35
STOP RUN, 73, 81
   changes in, 223
   in Output Procedure, 263
Structure chart, 35, 297
Structured design, 21-48
Structured English (*see* Pseudocode)
Structured programming, 1-15, 274-77
Structured walkthrough, 133-36, 174
Stub, 26, 146-53
Subprogram, 41, 42, 67-70, 82-84, 113,
   237, 244-51
Subscript (*see* OCCURS)
   in new standard, 268
   validity check, 84, 118, 238
   vs. index, 53-54
SUBTRACT, 95
SUM, 212
Summary reporting, 213, 217
SUM RESET, 221, 222, 264
SUM UPON, 221, 222

T

Tables, 52-66
   initialization, 58-60, 81, 111
   lookup (*see* SEARCH)
   two-dimension, 60-63
   three-dimension, 63-66
   variable-length (*see* OCCURS DEPENDING
     ON)
TERMINATE, 213
TEST AFTER, 275
TEST BEFORE, 275
Test data, 146
Testing (*see* Top down testing)

Test walkthrough, 134
Three-level table (*see* Table)
TIME, 67
Top down testing, 26-28, 146-53
Trailer label, 170
Two-level table (*see* Table)
TYPE, 212, 225-26

U

UNIT, 171
UNTIL (*see* PERFORM)
UP BY (*see* SET)
Update program (*see* File maintenance)
USAGE, 59, 60, 98, 116
USE statement (*see* DECLARATIVES)
USING:
    in CALL statement, 68-70
    in Procedure Division header, 68-70
    in SORT statement, 71, 73, 214

V

VALUE clause, 98, 110
    of FD, 170
    with Report Writer, 212
VALUES ARE, 107
Variable-length record, 169

Variable-length table (*see* Table)
VARYING:
    in PERFORM, 95
    in SEARCH, 57
Vertical Pointer, 177
Virtual sequential access method (*see* VSAM)
VSAM, 176-82, 186
    versus ISAM, 202
VTOC, 33

W

Walkthrough (*see* Structured walkthrough)
WHEN, 57, 58, 95
WITH DUPLICATES (*see* ALTERNATE
    RECORD KEY)
WRITE, 184, 237
WRITE FROM, 112
WS BEGINS HERE, 82, 83, 112, 229
Wulf, W. A., 115

X

X3J4 Technical Committee, 266

Y

Yourdon, E., 22, 36, 38, 103, 134, 280